DAVID F. LABAREE

How to Succeed in School Without Really Learning

THE CREDENTIALS RACE IN AMERICAN EDUCATION

Yale University Press
New Haven &
London

Set in Sabon type by Keystone Typesetting, Inc.
Printed in the United States of America.

Library of Congress Cataloging-in-Publication Data
Labaree, David F., 1947–
    How to succeed in school without really learning : the credentials race in
American education / David F. Labaree.
        p.   cm.
    Includes bibliographical references and index.
        ISBN 0-300-06993-6 (cloth: alk. paper)
            0-300-07867-6 (pbk.: alk. paper)
    1. Education — Aims and objectives — United States. 2. Education, Secondary —
United States. 3. School management and organization — United States.
4. Educational equalization — United States. 5. Teaching — Social aspects —
United States. 6. Teachers — Training of — Social aspects — United States. 7. Social
mobility — United States. 8. School credits — United States. I. Title.
LA210.L33   1997
370'.973 — dc21   97-7793

A catalogue record for this book is available from the British Library.

The paper in this book meets the guidelines for permanence and durability of the
Committee on Production Guidelines for Book Longevity of the Council on
Library Resources.

10 9 8 7 6 5 4 3

To Diane

Contents

Acknowledgments

I am indebted to a large number of colleagues for help in developing the ideas, arguments, and evidence that constitute this book. Those who were especially helpful in shaping a particular chapter are identified in the first note for that chapter. Here I would like to recognize a few people who had an impact on the book as a whole. First and foremost is David Hogan. He and I have had an ongoing conversation since the late 1970s — in person and in print — about the role that market processes have played in the history of education in the United States. We have traded ideas about this topic for so long that it is impossible to establish firm ownership over most of these ideas or to cite all the instances in which we have borrowed from each other. Suffice it to say that Hogan's thinking infuses this entire project.

In addition, I want to thank Michael Katz, for getting me started in this line of work and reminding me that the consequences of education are not always positive; Ivar Berg, for prodding me to think about the gap between job skills and job access; Randall Collins, whose work on credentialing theory underlies much of the argument in this book; Gladys Topkis, for her enthusiasm for this project and her staunch editorial support at Yale University Press, and Dan Heaton, for his thoughtful and graceful editing of the manuscript; Judy Lanier, for building a remarkable institution — the College of Education at Michigan State University — that has served as my home for the past dozen years, and for provoking me to think hard about educational issues; Carole Ames, dean, and Ruth Garner, department chair, for granting the sabbatical leave that allowed me to write this book; my colleagues in the College of Education, who have created and maintained a collegiate culture that is both intellectually stimulating and warmly supportive; and my students at MSU, on whom I have been trying out these ideas for years and from whom I have learned a great deal. I am also grateful to the following individuals for their help in a variety of capacities, both intellectual and personal: David Brown, Cleo Cherryholmes, David Cohen, Norton Grubb, Susan Melnick, David Pearson, Bill Reese, John Rury, Michael Sedlak, and David Tyack.

Finally, some acknowledgments that are closer to home. I am indebted to my parents, Benjamin Labaree and Jean Ridgley Labaree, who taught me at an early age that education should be a public trust and not a private possession. And most of all, I am deeply grateful to my wife, Diane Churchill, to whom this book is dedicated. She has shown me that there is a whole lot more to life than the paper chase of the scholarly existence, and through her example she has brought home to me the true value of pursuing substantive accomplishments rather than academic distinctions.

4 focus on issues arising from the sorting and selecting of students. Chapters 5 and 6 focus on the factors shaping the hierarchy of educational institutions. And Chapters 7, 8, and 9 focus on the mixed effects of expanded educational opportunity. The following overview is designed to give the reader an advance look at the way the argument builds from one chapter to the next and also a map of the book as a whole for the reader who wishes to read chapters more selectively.

In Chapter 1, I present the major themes and primary interpretive framework that weave through the remaining chapters. I argue that at the heart of the U.S. educational system is a fundamental ambivalence about whether education should be considered primarily a public good (one that is inclusive, providing shared societal benefits) or a private good (one that is exclusive, providing selective individual benefits). This ambivalence has manifested itself historically as a continuous conflict over the relative weight assigned to three competing goals for education: democratic equality (schools should focus on preparing citizens), social efficiency (they should focus on training workers), and social mobility (they should prepare individuals to compete for social positions). These goals represent the educational perspectives of, respectively, the citizen, the taxpayer or employer, and the consumer. Whereas the first two look on education as a public good, the third sees it as a private good. Historical conflict over these competing visions of education has resulted in a contradictory structure for the educational system that has sharply impaired both its effectiveness and its legitimacy. More important still has been the growing domination of the social mobility goal, which has reshaped education into a commodity for the purposes of individual status attainment and has elevated the pursuit of credentials over the acquisition of knowledge. The consequences are a matter of great loss to U.S. society — the growing dominance of a constricted and ungenerous vision of education and the threatened transformation of public education, once the most public of American institutions, into a private enterprise devoted to the production and protection of invidious distinctions.

In Chapters 2, 3, and 4, I focus on the sorting and selecting of students within schools, examining the historical roots of these processes, their consequences for both schools and society, and the implications of this analysis for an understanding of the schools today. My argument throughout these chapters is that the educational conditions that supported intense meritocratic competition, high academic standards, and social exclusivity in nineteenth-century schooling are no longer present. Secondary education was once a scarce commodity that could be doled out selectively and treasured as a form of social distinction, but this is no longer the case. Universal compulsory attendance has transformed the conditions under which schools can operate, and the result is a system that has become increasingly inclusive and egalitarian. Ironically, the success of efforts to extend educational opportunity to the whole population has undermined the elite status that education once conferred on the graduate and that served as a major impetus for the pursuit of educational opportunity in the first place. Under these irrevocably altered conditions, attempts to recapture the "glory days" of public education — when schools set high standards and only a few made the grade — are certain to be in vain. The consequences of this quixotic quest are predictably disastrous for both students and schools.

In Chapter 2, I explore the social meaning of the promotion and retention of students within the graded structure of American schooling over the past one hundred fifty years. During this period, promotion practices have ranged between two poles. At one pole is merit promotion; in this regime, nonpromotion is a distinct possibility and a frequent occurrence because students must earn advancement through individual demonstrations of academic competence at a given level. At the other pole is social promotion; in this mode of practice, nonpromotion is less common because students are advanced on social rather than meritocratic grounds, with priority given to keeping those of a given age moving through the grades together. In the nineteenth century, merit promotion was dominant; in the early twentieth century, social promotion grew more prominent, though retention of students never really disappeared; but in the past two decades, merit promotion has regained strength. My argument is that neither the persistence of retention practices nor the pendulum swings between high and low rates of retention can be explained by the impact of these practices on student learning. Rather, I argue that both are responses to ideological and social pressures on U.S. education that arise from the constitution of schooling as a market institution. Schooling in the United States is pressured to model itself after the meritocratic ideology that undergirds the market economy; simultaneously it is pressured to meet the demands of educational consumers for a form of cultural property that can provide them with an advantage in the competition for social positions. As a result, practices of promotion and retention arise from twin desires that are often at odds with each other — to act out the merit principle and to preserve educational distinctions.

In Chapter 3, I examine the social conditions that made it possible for American schools to organize themselves around principles of academic excellence and meritocratic process in the nineteenth century, and I show how none of these conditions exists in the present. Drawing on the historical case of the Central High School of Philadelphia, I explain why schools in the previous century were able to maintain a strictly academic curriculum and a mercilessly meritocratic pedagogy. The social conditions that supported this form of schooling included a strong cultural commitment to the merit principle; fully voluntary enrollment of students; competitive selection of students (along with freedom to eliminate those who didn't make the grade); competitive selection of faculty; and a sharply stratified structure of public education, with the high school occupying the top rung (making high school credentials quite valuable). These characteristics put the high school in a very strong position, requiring both students and teachers to adapt to its academic demands. In contrast, the contemporary high school cannot enforce the relentless focus on excellence and merit because all these conditions have changed dramatically. High schools in the United States today are characterized by a continuing rhetorical commitment to the merit principle but a set of educational practices (such as social promotion) that are antimeritocratic; compulsory attendance for students; legally mandated acceptance and retention of students by schools; noncompetitive selection and contractually regulated allocation of teachers; and a flattened pyramid of public education, in which the high school is only an intermediate stage and its credential is of only modest value. These changes in the conditions of schooling, I argue, make it unrealistic for us to ask contemporary high schools to reassert the academic standards that existed in "the good old days."

In Chapter 4, I analyze the historical interaction between curriculum and class. I argue that the high school curriculum evolved in the nineteenth century as a result of the complex relation between the U.S. high school and its middle-class constituency, a relation mediated by the changing market in educational credentials. Shaped by bourgeois ideological principles (merit, self-discipline, and utility), the curriculum of the mid-nineteenth century provided Central High School's middle-class constituents with credentials that constituted a valuable form of symbolic wealth. By the 1880s, however, the market in educational credentials had changed. Alternative suppliers appeared on the scene (as the number of high schools in the city began to grow), and the middle class began looking beyond a high school diploma to the acquisition of credentials from the university, which had the advantage of being scarcer and therefore more valuable and which also offered students access to the professions. This market pressure (both from other high schools and from the university) forced the high school to revamp its course of study. What had been an undifferentiated practical curriculum (in which all students followed the same program, oriented toward preparation for work) turned abruptly into a stratified array of academic courses of study (allowing students to pursue very different tracks and preparing them increasingly for advanced study at the university). One result was a tracked and academic secondary curriculum that became the model for the comprehensive high school in the twentieth century. Another was the expansion of high school enrollments with the simultaneous preservation of educational distinctions for the middle class.

In Chapters 5 and 6, I explore the role of reform in creating a hierarchy of educational institutions. In a review of two recent reports urging reform, I develop an analysis of the historical roots of these efforts, arguing that reform is frequently aimed at reshaping education around principles of social selection, social efficiency, and social control. The result is an educational system that is growing farther away from its democratic roots in the common school, where the emphasis was on preparing citizens and providing a common educational experience. Instead, such reforms as those proposed by the Carnegie Foundation and the Holmes Group lead to a structure of education that is increasingly stratified (organizing students and educational institutions into hierarchies of status, opportunity, and control) and also increasingly rationalized (developing technical processes for selecting and teaching students that diminish the political and moral dimensions of education).

In Chapter 5, I locate *Turning Points*, a 1989 Carnegie report on middle schools, within the historical tradition of Carnegie efforts to shape U.S. educational policy in the twentieth century. The Carnegie Corporation of New York and the Carnegie Foundation for the Advancement of Teaching have been issuing influential reports on education for the past eighty years. These have been instrumental in stimulating significant changes in education at all levels, such as the establishment of the Carnegie unit in high schools, the reorganization of medical education, and the creation of California's model three-tier system of higher education. Carnegie has often succeeded in institutionalizing its initiatives in the form of powerful nonprofit organizations that exert an ongoing impact on education in the United States — the Teachers Income Annuity Association (TIAA, the group that administers the pensions of college professors), for example. But it is perhaps best known for its long-standing and central role in promoting educational testing and its leadership in creating the Educational Testing Service, which administers the SAT, GRE, CLEP, and NAEP examinations, among many others. I argue that Carnegie commissions and their reports have long expressed an educational vision in which U.S. schools act as an efficient mechanism for sorting and socializing students for future positions in the existing social and economic structure. They have pursued this goal by promoting a system of education that is highly rationalized (that is, standardized, vertically integrated, and rationally planned), scientifically grounded, and meritocratic. *Turning Points* is an interesting exception to the rule, for it proposes a detracked and relatively egalitarian vision of the middle school. But I argue that this apparent shift in orientation is largely a result of the sizable gap separating middle school students from the work-force, which permits the report to focus less on socially efficient adaptation to the economy (Carnegie's traditional area of concern) than on the development of basic capacities.

In Chapter 6, I argue that the teacher professionalization movement — launched in 1986 with reports from the Carnegie Task Force on Teaching as a Profession and the Holmes Group — is likely to have a negative impact on American education and on the teachers, students, and citizens who have a stake in having this institution carry out its goals effectively. I suggest that the movement will inadvertently promote two effects that are not in the best interests of democratic education — augmenting the influence of the university over primary and secondary schooling (by reinforcing the authority of those who teach teachers), and accelerating the rationalization of classroom in-struction (by reinforcing a research-based model of teaching practice). This conclusion is based in part on the movement's appeal to the cultural ideal of professionalism, whose historical baggage weighs in on the side of expert authority and technical rationality. But in larger part it rests on an analysis of the historical roots of this particular professionalization movement. Accord-ing to this analysis, the movement derives its character and direction from the professional interests of the group of people leading the movement (research-oriented teacher educators) and the intellectual constructs that guide their thinking about schools (formal rationality and the scientific method). This combination of factors produces a university-centered and research-based movement likely to produce two undesirable outcomes: to promote the ratio-nalization of teaching and to reduce the influence of teachers and citizens on schools.

As suggested in Chapter 6, social stratification affects more than students. The analysis there shows how market pressures and the individual pursuit of status can create competitive educational hierarchies within higher education and between the university and the schools. In Chapters 7, 8, and 9, I con-tinue this analysis, exploring the ways in which market-based processes of sorting and selecting have affected the historical development of American high school teaching, the community college, and the education school. The argument running through these chapters is that the wide-open opportunity structure in U.S. education during its early days created an opening for am-bitious individuals, such as schoolteachers and college professors, and institu-tions, such as normal schools and land grant colleges, to climb the ladder of educational success. Yet the conclusion is that increased opportunity led to increased inequality. One problem was that the losers in this competition vastly outnumbered the winners. Teachers are a case in point: a lucky few rose from the one-room schoolhouse to the privileged precincts of the urban high school and even the university, but most pursued short careers under much less rewarding circumstances. Another problem was that the first groups up the ladder often blocked the way for those who tried to follow, as such late-arriving institutions as the normal school and the community college discovered when they sought collegiate status but achieved a position only on the second or third tier in the settled hierarchy of higher education. The result was that the competitive environment in fact produced sharp limitations on the prospects of most working-class students, who pinned their hopes for social mobility on institutions that were largely unable to deliver on their promises. Interestingly, one group — teachers — obtained the greatest benefit only after the bureaucratization of school systems leveled the old opportunity structure and created in its place a relatively egalitarian pattern of pay and working conditions for the teaching profession.

In the late nineteenth and early twentieth centuries, teaching was not yet a career for most of those who engaged in it. The most common pattern was for a woman to teach for a half dozen years or so during her late teens and early twenties, until she got married. But in Chapter 7, I explore the exceptional case of the woman or man who pursued teaching as a career across a lifetime, and the even more exceptional case of the lifelong teacher whose career was an unmitigated success. On the basis of biographies and autobiographies of these unusual teachers from around the turn of the century, I develop an argument about the nature of the educational opportunity structure through which they climbed and the conditions within school and society that made this climb possible. In part, the story that emerges is familiar: one key form of advancement for these teachers was positional, moving from teaching to administration, and one element that made this advance possible was education, especially the normal school. But there were other factors that facilitated their rise up the educational ladder, and these no longer exist today. One is that these teachers moved up through the educational levels, from one-room school to elementary school to high school to normal school and even to university. Another is that they moved geographically, from rural school to small town to larger town and finally to big city. Each step along the way represented a significant promotion, both in working conditions (from ungraded to graded schools, from teaching all subjects to specializing in one subject) and in social position (for city teaching offered much more money and prestige than country teaching, and higher grade levels much more than lower grades). In short, it was the radical inequality between country and city schooling and between the lower and upper levels of the educational system that gave this elite group of teachers the opportunity to move ahead so dramatically in their careers. The later growth of bureaucracy and unionism in education largely eliminated these forms of inequality, closing the gap between the elite and the average teacher and simultaneously removing the career ladder that the elite once climbed. While this change reduced opportunities for a few, it presented great benefits to most teachers, who had found little to cheer about in the old opportunity structure.

In Chapter 8, I pursue many of the same issues, but this time the focus is on the social mobility of an institution — the community college — rather than of individual teachers. One way of understanding the community college is to see it as a new version of the comprehensive high school, retracing the evolutionary path marked by the latter institution. The same contradictory mixture of democratic and market purposes (democratic equality, social efficiency, social mobility) that spurred the rapid growth of the high school helped to produce the expansion of the community college. But these contradictions also left it with an ambiguous identity (should it focus on terminal programs of vocational training or on academic programs aimed at transfer into the university?) and a questionable record of effectiveness (does it succeed in either of these roles?). Another way of understanding the community college is as the latest and lowest form of higher education. From this perspective, it is the last in a series of tertiary educational institutions created to serve both the vocational needs of a changing economy and the growing demand for advanced educational credentials. Although its predecessors (the land grant college and the normal school) quickly evolved into full-service universities, the community college has been compelled to retain its junior status and its vocational function. The result is a distinctively American educational institution that is broadly accessible and programmatically comprehensive while promoting starkly stratified social outcomes, for reasons inherent in the logic of a stratified and market-driven system of education: accessibility reduces the exchange value of an institution's educational credentials (and therefore the ability of these credentials to provide the graduate with a good chance at social mobility), while exclusivity enhances their value.

In Chapter 9, I argue that the issue of status is central to the problems facing education schools and teacher education in the United States. That is, in spite of what some critics have suggested, the lowly status of these institutions is not a simple reflection of the purportedly low quality of professional preparation it offers. Rather, I argue, this status is a primary cause of the kinds of failure that teacher education has experienced over the years. In particular, I explore the way in which the status of teacher education has been shaped by the workings of the market. It is my contention that market forces over the past one hundred fifty years have assigned teacher education to a position of meager prestige and influence and forced it to adopt frequently counterproductive practices. The bulk of the chapter presents a short history of market influences on the status of the education school. One theme in this history is the problem posed by the insatiable demand for teachers from a burgeoning public school system (the influence of the social efficiency goal). Another theme is the problem of how to meet the social aspirations and credentialing requirements of students who entered normal schools (the influence of the social mobility goal). A third is the impact of these problems on the evolution of teacher education, from its original setting in the normal school to the teachers college and eventually the university, and, in turn, the impact that this evolution had on people, programs, and status. Moving to the present, I show that market conditions have changed drastically but that market pressure remains on education schools today. I close by applying my analysis to two recent proposals for reforming teacher education in the United States. Both of these proposals recognize the status problems affecting teacher education and respond with remedies calling for professionalization, but they advocate contradictory strategies for achieving professionalization.

In Chapter 10, I conclude the discussion with a focus on the consumerism and credentialism that characterize contemporary education in the United States, considering the nature of this problem along with its roots and consequences. The chapter begins with an exploration of one of the primary problems confronting educators today — the growing disengagement of students from the learning process — and traces this problem to the increasing dominance of the view that education is primarily a mechanism for producing credentials, not knowledge. More than ever in the past, the publicness of public education is being called into question, so that it is increasingly acceptable, even canonical, to think of education as a commodity whose purpose is to meet the needs of individual educational consumers. I then examine the kinds of institutional factors (such as societal wealth, decentralized control, and competitive market conditions) that made possible the rise of a credential-oriented and consumer-driven system of education, and I analyze the educational and social consequences of such a system.

The book concludes with a discussion of the paradox that frames the whole argument of this book: how could the most admired, imitated, and (in many ways) progressive characteristic of U.S. education — its focus on providing a wide array of citizens with the chance to get ahead through educational attainment — produce so many negative consequences for both school and society? The answer, I suggest, is that the pursuit of educational advantage has inadvertently threatened to transform the public educational system into a mechanism for personal advancement. In the process, the generous public goals that have been so important in defining the larger societal interest in education — to produce politically capable and socially productive citizens — have lost significant ground to the narrow pursuit of private advantage at public expense. The result is that the common school has become increasingly uncommon, with a growing emphasis on producing selective symbolic distinctions rather than shared substantive accomplishments, and the community interest in education as a public good has increasingly lost ground to the individual interest in education as private property. The cost of this transformation is shared by all of us, for we cannot escape the collective consequences of our own self-interested uses of the public school. The relentless pursuit of educational credentials in the name of social mobility is gradually consuming our system of education, and we are already living with the unlovely consequences.

Public Schools for Private Advantage:
Conflicting Goals and the Impact on Education

Americans love to beat up on their schools. Particularly in the past couple of decades, we have taken schools to task for a multitude of sins. Among other things, we have complained that schools have abandoned academic standards, schools have undermined U.S. economic competitiveness, schools are disorderly places that breed social disorder, schools waste massive sums of money, schools no longer provide a reliable way for people to get ahead, and schools reinforce social inequality.

Many of these charges are unfair or even demonstrably false, but the result of these complaints has been a lot of hand wringing and an endless series of calls for fundamental reform.[1] Big problems call for big changes, and a wide range of such changes have been suggested: restructure the organization of schools; permit parents to choose which school their children attend; promote specialized magnet schools; establish autonomous charter schools; create black academies; require competency testing for teachers; open up alternative routes to teaching; upgrade the professional education of teachers; establish national achievement tests for students; require performance testing as a prerequisite for endorsed diplomas; equalize school funding; make funding dependent on school performance; extend the school year; reinforce basic skills; increase vocational education; beef up the academic curriculum; develop national curriculum standards; increase multiculturalism within the curriculum;

end bilingual education; stabilize the American family; provide economic opportunities for the poor; institute prayer in schools; attack the roots of racism; promote traditional values; and so on, ad infinitum.

This widely varied array of proposed reforms, in turn, is grounded in an equally varied array of analyses defining the root causes of problems with schools. Some argue that the root problem is pedagogical, arising from poor quality and preparation of teachers and from inadequate curriculum. Others argue the that the central problem is organizational, arising either from too much bureaucracy (the absence of market incentives) or from too little (the absence of effective administrative control). Still others charge that the primary cause of educational deficiencies is social, arising from chronic poverty, race discrimination, and the preservation of privilege. Yet another view is that the key problem is cultural, the result of a culture of poverty, disintegrating family values, and a growing gap between school culture and popular culture.

In contrast with these perspectives, I argue that the central problems with education in the United States are not pedagogical or organizational or social or cultural in nature but are fundamentally political. That is, the problem is not that we do not know how to make schools better but that we are fighting among ourselves about what goals schools should pursue. Goal setting is a political and not a technical problem. It is resolved through a process of making choices and not through a process of scientific investigation. The answer lies in values (what kind of schools we want) and interests (who supports which educational values) rather than apolitical logic. Before we launch yet another research center (to determine "what works" in the classroom) or propose another organizational change (such as school choice or a national curriculum), we need to engage in a public debate about the desirability of alternative social outcomes of schooling.[2]

Schools, it seems, occupy an awkward position at the intersection between what we hope society will become and what we think it really is, between political ideals and economic realities. This in turn leads to some crucial questions: Should schools present themselves as a model of our best hopes for our society and a mechanism for remaking that society in the image of those hopes? Should schools focus on adapting students to the needs of society as currently constructed? Or should they focus primarily on serving the individual hopes and ambitions of their students? The way you choose to answer these questions determines the kind of goals you seek to impose on schools.

The terms of this choice arise from a fundamental source of strain at the core of any liberal democratic society, the tension between democratic politics (public rights) and capitalist markets (private rights), between majority control and individual liberty, between political equality and social inequality. In the U.S. setting, the poles of this debate were defined during the country's formative years by the political idealism of Thomas Jefferson and the economic realism of Alexander Hamilton.[3] The essential problem posed by that tension is this: unfettered economic freedom leads to a highly unequal distribution of wealth and power, which in turn undercuts the possibility for democratic control; but at the same time, restricting such economic freedom in the name of equality infringes on individual liberty, without which democracy can turn into the dictatorship of the majority. Each generation of American reformers has tried to figure out a way to preserve the Jeffersonian ideal of political equality in the face of the Hamiltonian reality of economic inequality — and to do so without stifling the productivity of the market economy. Yet in spite of a wide variety of plausible and innovative attempts to find a remedy, this dilemma has outlasted all efforts at reform. Political equality and social inequality simply do not mix easily; and institutions that arise from efforts to pursue both of these goals reflect this continuing tension.[4]

Grounded in this contradictory social context, the history of U.S. education has been a tale of ambivalent goals and muddled outcomes. Like other major institutions in American society, education has come to be defined as an arena that simultaneously promotes equality and adapts to inequality. Within schools, these contradictory purposes have translated into three distinguishable educational goals, each of which has exerted considerable impact without succeeding in eliminating the others, and each of which has at times served to undermine the others. I call these goals democratic equality, social efficiency, and social mobility.[5] These goals differ across several dimensions: the extent to which they portray education as a public or private good; the extent to which they understand education as preparation for political or market roles; and the differing perspectives on education that arise depending on one's particular location in the social structure.[6]

From the *democratic equality* approach to schooling, one argues that a democratic society cannot persist unless it prepares all of its young with equal care to take on the full responsibilities of citizenship in a competent manner. We all depend on this political competence of our fellow citizens, for we put ourselves at the mercy of their collective judgment about the running of our society. A corollary is that, in the democratic political arena, we are all considered equal (according to the rule of one person, one vote), but this political equality can be undermined if the social inequality of citizens grows too great. Schools therefore must promote both effective citizenship and relative equality. Both of these outcomes are collective benefits of schooling, without which we cannot function as a polity. Democratic equality, then, is the perspective of the citizen, from which education is seen as a public good, designed to prepare people for political roles.

The *social efficiency* approach to schooling argues that our economic well-being depends on our ability to prepare the young to carry out useful economic roles with competence. The idea is that we all benefit from a healthy economy and from the contribution to such an economy made by the productivity of our fellow worker. As a consequence, we cannot allow this function to be supported only by voluntary means, because self-interest would encourage individuals to take a free ride on the human capital investment of their fellow citizens while investing personally in a form of education that would provide the highest individual return. Instead, society as a whole must see to it that we invest educationally in the productivity of the entire workforce. Social efficiency, then, is the perspective of the taxpayer and the employer, from which education is seen as a public good designed to prepare workers to fill structurally necessary market roles.

The *social mobility* approach to schooling argues that education is a commodity, whose only purpose is to provide individual students with a competitive advantage in the struggle for desirable social positions. The aim is to get more of this valuable commodity than one's competitors, which puts a premium on a form of education that is highly stratified and unequally distributed. This, then, is the perspective of the individual educational consumer, who sees education as a private good designed to prepare individuals for successful social competition for desirable market roles.

In an important way, all three of these goals are political, in that all are efforts to establish the purposes and functions of an essential social institution. But differences in social position give rise to different perspectives on the purposes of education. The democratic equality goal arises from the citizen, social efficiency from the taxpayer and employer, and social mobility from the educational consumer. The first goal expresses the politics of citizenship, the second expresses the politics of human capital, and the third expresses the politics of individual opportunity. Of the three approaches to schooling, the first is the most thoroughly political, in that it sets as its goal the preparation of students as actors in the political arena. The other two goals, in contrast, portray education as a mechanism for adapting students to the market. And this suggests another major differentiating factor, the way in which each goal locates education in the public-private dimension. For the democratic equality goal, education is a purely public good; for social efficiency, it is a public good in service to the private sector; and for social mobility, it is a private good for personal consumption.[7]

Three Defining Goals for American Education

These three goals of education in the United States have in some ways reinforced each other and in other ways undermined each other. This situation raises important questions. How can schools realistically be expected to promote all of these goals at the same time and remain coherent and effective? Yet at the same time how can they promote one at the expense of the others without eliminating important outcomes and abandoning important constituencies?

The incoherence and ineffectiveness that result from this standoff among conflicting goals help to explain many of the problems afflicting U.S. schools. But the most significant problems with education today arise from the growing dominance of one goal over the others. The social mobility goal has emerged as the most influential factor in American education. Increasingly it provides us with the language we use to talk about schools, the ideas we use to justify their existence, and the practices we mandate in promoting their reform. As a result, public education has increasingly come to be perceived as a private good that is harnessed to the pursuit of personal advantage; and on the whole, the consequences of this for both school and society have been profoundly negative.

DEMOCRATIC EQUALITY

There is a strong ideological tradition in U.S. history for viewing schools as an expression of democratic political ideals and as a mechanism for preparing children to play constructive roles in a democratic society.[8] For the Whig leaders who founded the common schools in the mid-nineteenth century, this political goal provided the most compelling justification for schooling.[9] Although its relative weight among the trio of American educational goals has gradually declined over the years, it has continued to play a prominent role in shaping educational rhetoric, school practice, and the structure of the credentials market. And at times, such as the 1960s and 1970s, it has reasserted itself with considerable vigor and effect. This, the most political of the major purposes of U.S. education, has taken three related but distinct operational forms within schools: the pursuit of citizenship training, of equal treatment, and of equal access.

The best single explanation for the founding and early diffusion of common schools in this country is that they were seen as essential to the process of nation building and the related process of training for citizenship.[10] "It may be an easy thing to make a Republic," wrote Horace Mann in 1848; "but it is a very laborious thing to make Republicans; and woe to the Republic that rests upon no better foundations than ignorance, selfishness, and passion."[11]

From the perspective of the common school founders, the American republic was still on shaky ground in the mid-nineteenth century, and its survival depended on a citizenry with a fully developed sense of civic virtue. They felt schools could help counteract the growth of selfishness (arising from a burgeoning capitalist economy) by instilling in their charges a personal dedication to the public good. They could make republicans who would be able to function in a market economy without losing their sense of citizenship in the commonwealth.[12]

Citizenship training has continued to play a significant role in the ideology and practice of U.S. education in both rhetoric and practice. No pronouncement about education or call for educational reform has been complete without a prominent reference to the critical consequences of schooling for the preservation of democracy. Even the authors of the influential national report *A Nation at Risk,* who focused primarily on economic consequences, felt compelled to stress that "A high level of shared education is essential to a free, democratic society and to the fostering of a common culture."[13] Curriculum in U.S. schools evinces this concern, both through specific courses (such as social studies, civics, government, and U.S. history) that are designed to instill in students a commitment to the American political system, and more broadly through a continuing strong emphasis on liberal arts over narrowly specialized education. The rationale for liberal arts is that all members of a free society need familiarity with the full range of that society's culture in order "to participate intelligently as adults in the political process that shapes their society."[14] As a result of this emphasis the United States promotes general education at even the highest levels of the system, in contrast to other countries, where specialized instruction begins much earlier.[15] The recent movement to raise educational standards has made it clear that the call for increased "competency over challenging subject matter" is intended in part to "ensure that all students learn to use their minds well, so they may be prepared for responsible citizenship."[16]

A second political goal for schools has been the pursuit of equal treatment, which also originated in the concern about preserving the republic. Fearful of the social differences and class conflict that arose from the growth of capitalism and immigration, the founders of the common school argued that this institution could help provide citizens of the republic with a common culture and a sense of shared membership in the community. Horace Mann stated the case for education's equalizing role with characteristic eloquence. Noting "that vast and overshadowing private fortunes are among the greatest dangers to which the happiness of the people in a republic can be subjected," he argued that "surely, nothing but Universal Education can counter-work this tendency to the domination of capital and the servility of labor," acting as "the balance-wheel of the social machinery."[17] The common school movement promoted these ends by establishing universal enrollment, uniform curriculum, and a shared educational experience for their students.[18] Over the years, this commonality has given way to an educational process that is increasingly stratified according to such characteristics as age, academic achievement, educational level, curriculum level, institutional prestige, and social class — largely in response to pressure to promote the social efficiency and social mobility goals.[19] But in the early twentieth century, reformers sought to mitigate this process of stratification and restore equal treatment through a variety of leveling mechanisms, including pressure for social promotion of students from grade to grade, the easing of academic standards, the sharp increase in non-academic curriculum options, grade inflation, and the institutionalization of the comprehensive high school.[20]

More recently, schools have sought to apply this egalitarian goal to groups whose ascribed status denied them equal educational standing in the nineteenth century. The recurring demand for equal treatment has removed the Protestant Bible, public prayer, and other divisive religious practices from the public schools. It has motivated a powerful movement to provide equal educational experiences for all people regardless of race, ethnicity, and sex — resulting in the formal desegregation of schools and in attempts to remove race and gender stereotypes from textbooks, to incorporate the experiences of nonwhites and females in the curriculum (through the movement for multiculturalism), and to reduce discriminatory practices in the classroom. It has led to attacks on tracking and ability grouping because of the potentially discriminatory effects of these practices, fostering in their place such alternatives as heterogeneous grouping and cooperative learning. It has brought about the nationwide effort to reintegrate special education students in the regular classroom, so that handicapping conditions will not consign students to an inferior education. It has spurred the movement by states to equalize financial support for school districts despite unequal tax bases. It has promoted programs of compensatory education and affirmative action in order to make certain that educational equality is not just a formal possibility but a realizable outcome. And it has helped support the recent demand by reformers that all students be held to the same high level of educational performance standards.

The pursuit of equal access is a third manifestation of the goal of democratic equality. It is in this form that the goal has perhaps exerted its most powerful impact on the development of schools in the United States.[21] Equal access has come to mean that every American should have an equal opportunity to acquire an education at any educational level. Initially this led to the effort that occupied school reformers for most of the nineteenth century, trying to provide enough schools so that every child could have a seat in an elementary classroom at public expense. After this end was largely accomplished late in the century, the focus of educational opportunity efforts expanded to include the high school, with dramatic effects. What had been a tiny sector of public education, enjoyed primarily by the elite, grew rapidly into a mass system of secondary schooling, with secondary enrollments doubling every decade between 1890 and 1940. Then after the Second World War, higher education became the object of the demand for equal access, leading to an extraordinary expansion of enrollments to the point where attendance at a postsecondary institution became the norm rather than the exception.[22]

This pressure to provide access to American schools on a continually widening scale has necessitated an enormous and ever-increasing outpouring of public funds. In addition, the requirement that education at all levels should be open to all segments of the population — and not just the most privileged or even the most able — has exerted a profound effect on all aspects of the institutional structure. It has led to the mass production of teachers, the proliferation of programs and courses, the search for ways to improve pedagogical efficiency, concern about enhancing administrative control, and a stress on fiscal parsimony — all in order to meet the educational problems raised by the sheer quantity and diversity of the pool of students.[23]

SOCIAL EFFICIENCY

On the one hand, Americans have sought to make schools an institutional expression of their democratic and egalitarian political ideals and a social mechanism for realizing these ideals. Yet on the other hand, they have also sought to make schools a mechanism for adapting students to the requirements of a hierarchical social structure and the demands of the occupational marketplace. This second educational goal, which I refer to as social efficiency, has exerted its influence on schools in the United States through structural pragmatism — operationalized within schools in the form of vocationalism and educational stratification.

The social efficiency goal has shaped U.S. schools by bending them to the practical constraints that are embedded in the market-based structuration of economic and social life.[24] One clear sign of this influence is the historical trend toward vocationalism. In the late nineteenth and early twentieth centuries, a heterogeneous alliance of leaders from business, labor, and education launched an effort to make the school curriculum more responsive to the needs of the occupational structure. Although these groups disagreed about the desired effect of this effort on social mobility, they united in the conviction that schools were in danger of becoming socially irrelevant and economically counterproductive unless they succeeded in better coordinating educational content with future job requirements.[25] Then as now, the simple reality was that students eventually leave school and enter the workforce, whether or not their schooling has prepared them to carry out this work effectively.

In its narrow form, the movement for vocationalism sought to shift the curriculum away from courses that trained students in traditional academic subjects and broadly defined liberal learning and toward programs that provided training in the skills and knowledge required to carry out particular job roles. The result was the creation of a series of strictly vocational programs — which quickly became an enduring part of the curriculum, particularly at the secondary and (later) community-college levels — preparing students for such future jobs as auto mechanic, lathe operator, beautician, secretary, and draftsperson. The value of these programs, from the perspective of social efficiency, is that they offer a thoroughly practical education, which provides a steady supply of employees who are adequately trained to fill particular jobs. Nothing could be more impractical, from this perspective, than the kind of general education promoted by democratic equality, in which graduates would emerge as an undifferentiated group with a common set of broad competencies that are not easily adapted to the sharply differentiated skill demands of a complex job structure. Following this logic, Michigan's governor in 1996 moved to shift funds from adult education into job training because, as the head of the state jobs commission put it, "It's more important to align adult education programs with the needs of employers rather than to educate people for education's sake."[26]

Yet the impact of vocationalism on schooling has been much broader than the emergence of an explicitly vocational curriculum, which has never accounted for more than a small minority of the courses taken by high school students. For example, only 16 percent of the Carnegie units accumulated by 1992 high school graduates were in vocational courses.[27] The true significance of vocationalism is visible in the philosophical shift that took place in the general aims of U.S. schooling in the period following 1890. The essence of this shift was captured by the president of the Muncie, Indiana, school board, who in the 1920s told Robert and Helen Lynd, "For a long time all boys were trained to be President. . . . Now we are training them to get jobs."[28] More important than the inclusion of typing classes alongside those in history was this fundamental change in the purposes of schooling — from a lofty political goal (training students to be citizens in a democratic society, perhaps to be president) to a practical economic goal (getting students ready to enter the workforce, preparing them to adapt to the social structure). This change affected students who were going to college as much as those in the auto shop.

The social efficiency argument for education is found at the heart of nearly every educational address delivered by a governor or president, every school board's campaign for a millage increase or bond issue, every educational reform document. Consider the florid but not atypical language found in the opening words of *A Nation at Risk,* the report that kicked off the movement in the 1980s and 1990s to raise educational standards: "Our Nation is at risk. Our once unchallenged preeminence in commerce, industry, science, and technological innovation is being overtaken by competitors throughout the world. . . . We report to the American people that . . . the educational foundations of our society are presently being eroded by a rising tide of mediocrity that threatens our very future as a nation and a people."[29] Other documents in the standards movement have also touted the economic benefits of raising academic requirements. The National Education Goals Panel, for example, asserts in its Goal 3 that "by the year 2000, all students will leave grades 4, 8, and 12 having demonstrated competency over challenging subject matter . . . so they may be prepared" not only for "responsible citizenship" and "further learning" but also for "productive employment in our Nation's modern economy."[30]

What makes this kind of appeal such an irresistible part of educational rhetoric is its immense practicality. The logic is compelling: schooling supplies future workers with skills that will enhance their productivity and therefore promote economic growth. This logic allows an educational leader to argue that support for education is not just a matter of moral or political correctness but a matter of good economic sense. Schooling from this perspective can be portrayed as a sensible mechanism for promoting our economic future, an investment in human capital that will pay bountiful dividends for the community as a whole and ultimately for each individual taxpayer. After all, the majority of taxpayers at any given time do not have children attending the public schools. These citizens are not deriving direct benefit from the education provided by these schools, and they may well feel that the indirect political benefits promised by the democratic equality rationale are remote and ephemeral compared with the immediate economic loss occasioned by an increase in school taxes. The social efficiency argument may well strike a chord with this group by pointedly asserting that their jobs, their pensions, and their family's economic well-being depend upon the ability of schools to turn out productive workers. At the same time, public officials who have to approve the annual budget for education — which swallows up fully one-third of all state and local revenues — also find the social efficiency rationale helpful because it reassures them that this expenditure is not a waste of public money but instead a sound investment.[31]

Over the years, the idea that schools should be making workers more than making republicans has undermined the ability of schools to act as a mechanism for promoting equality of access and equality of treatment. The notion of educational equality is at best irrelevant to the expansion of GNP, and it is counterproductive in a capitalist economy, where the pursuit of competitive advantage is the driving force behind economic behavior. Under the pressure to be economically productive, schools have adopted a structure that is highly stratified. Thus the hierarchy of educational levels emerges, leading from elementary school to high school to college and then graduate school. The upward expansion of enrollment in this hierarchy over time, while increasing the average years of schooling for the population as a whole, has also provided access to higher levels of education at which individuals can be distinguished from the herd, with the key division being between those who persist in education and those who drop out at an earlier level. From the perspective of democratic equality, this educational division represents a serious political and social problem. But from the perspective of social efficiency, the vertical distribution of educational attainment is quite desirable, for it reflects the vertical structure of the job market and therefore helps to allocate individuals efficiently to particular locations in the workforce: students move horizontally from a given level in the educational hierarchy to a corresponding level in the occupational hierarchy. And in the view of social efficiency, this allocation is seen to be both logical and fair, because those who have advanced farther up the educational ladder are seen as having learned more and therefore having acquired greater human capital — which promises to make them more skillful and productive employees.

These quantitative distinctions are further enhanced by the qualitative differences that have emerged between schools within each level of the educational system. For example, employers and students alike know that all colleges are not created equal. A degree from an Ivy League college is worth considerably more in the job market than one from a regional state university because employers assume that a graduate from the former is smarter and better educated — and thus, potentially at least, a more productive employee. As a consequence, college graduates are stratified in a way that reflects the stratification within the white-collar sector of the occupational structure. A similar logic is at work in stratifying high schools, with a diploma from a wealthy suburban high school granting the bearer greater access to advanced education and good jobs than a diploma from a high school in a poor inner-city neighborhood. Again, democracy and efficiency are exerting conflicting pressures on U.S. education to move toward greater equality on the one hand and greater inequality on the other.

Even within individual schools, the academic experience of students has become increasingly stratified.[32] Ability grouping and curriculum tracking guarantee that even those who have completed the same number of years in school will frequently have had educational experiences that are quite different in both academic content and economic value. The result is the same as with stratification between levels of schooling and between schools at the same level. With students sorted according to both putative ability and the requirements of different job roles (high reading group vs. low reading group, academic track vs. vocational track), schools create educational channels that efficiently carry groups of students toward different locations in the occupational structure. Thus although the goal of democratic equality promotes schools that prepare students for the full range of political and social roles in the community, the social efficiency goal promotes a structure of schooling that limits these possibilities in the name of economic necessity.

One thing to keep in mind, however, is that although social efficiency promotes the sorting of students, and although this sorting often limits opportunities for these students, at the same time this goal provides strong support for the social value of student learning at all levels of the system. From the social efficiency perspective, because society counts on schools to provide the human capital it needs to enhance productivity in all phases of economic life, they must assure that everyone engages in serious learning — whether they are in college or kindergarten, suburb or inner city, top track or bottom track. In this sense then, social efficiency treats education as a public good, whose collective benefits can be realized only if instruction is effective and learning is universal.

SOCIAL MOBILITY

Whereas social efficiency argues that schools should adapt students to the existing socioeconomic structure, the social mobility goal asserts that schools should provide students with the educational credentials they need in order to get ahead in this structure (or to maintain their current position). Both of these goals accept the inequality at the heart of a market society as given, and both are eager for schools to adapt themselves to the demands of such a society. Where they differ is in the vantage point they assume in looking at the role of schooling in a market society. The efficiency goal focuses on the needs of the social system as a whole (adopting the perspective of the providers of educational services — state, policymakers, and taxpayers — and of the employers who will put the graduates to work), but the mobility goal focuses on the needs of individual educational consumers. One sees the system from the top down, the other from the bottom up. One sees it as meeting a collective need, and the other as meeting an individual need. As a result, from the perspective of the efficiency goal, it does not matter who ends up filling which job.

As long as all jobs are filled with competent people, the individual outcomes of the allocation process are irrelevant to the efficient operation of the system. But from the perspective of the mobility goal, the outcome for the individual is precisely what matters most. The result is an emphasis on individual status attainment rather than the production of human capital.

One useful way of capturing these differences is to note that the social efficiency goal (like the democratic equality goal) conceives of education as a public good, whereas the social mobility goal conceives of it as a distinctly private good. A public good is one whose benefits are enjoyed by all the members of the community, whether or not they actually contributed to the production of this good. Police protection, street maintenance, public parks, open-air sculpture, and air pollution control are all examples of public goods that potentially benefit all members of a community, whether or not they paid the taxes that were necessary to provide these services. In the language of collective goods theory, public goods offer people a "free ride."[33] Schools that focus on giving everyone the skills required for effective citizenship (as proposed by the democratic equality goal) are public goods, for they offer a free ride to all children regardless of ability to pay and at the same time provide a benefit to all members of society (a sustainable political system, competent and informed fellow citizens) regardless of whether they or their children ever attended these schools. Schools are also public goods if they provide the human capital required by the economy and effectively fit students into slots in the occupational structure (as proposed by the social efficiency goal), because the community as a whole is seen as reaping the benefit from this institution in the form of a growing economy and a stable economic future. Once again, the benefits are collective in that they accrue to everyone, whether or not he or she contributed to the support of these schools or even attended them.[34] Childless adults and families with children in private schools all enjoy the political and economic benefits of public schools, according to the perspective of democratic equality and social efficiency. However, one reaches a very different conclusion when looking at schools as a private good.[35]

The consumer perspective on schools asks the question, "What can school do for me, regardless of what it does for others?" The benefits of education are understood to be selective and differential rather than collective and equal. The aim of pursuing education is for the individual student to accumulate forms of educational property that will allow that student to gain an advantage in the competition for social position. This means that what I gain from my educational experience is my own private property, and the more of this property that I can acquire the better chance I have to distinguish myself from the rest of the pack and win the social competition.[36]

The impact of this perspective on schools is profound. It promotes, for example, the stratification of education—which, as we have seen, is also promoted by the social efficiency goal. The last thing that a socially mobile educational consumer wants out of education is the kind of equal educational outcome produced in the name of democratic equality. Thomas Green and colleagues, in *Predicting the Behavior of the Educational System,* put it this way: "What parents want is not that their children have equal opportunity, but that they get the best that is possible, and that will always mean opportunities 'better than some others get.' "[37] This can take place only if education is structured in such a manner that its social benefits are allocated differentially, with some students receiving more than others.[38] In their role as self-interested educational consumers, therefore, parents want an educational system that is stratified, and this stratification takes the same three forms identified previously in the discussion of social efficiency.[39]

First, these consumers demand that schooling take the form of a graded hierarchy, which requires students to climb upward through a sequence of levels and institutions and to face an increasing risk of elimination as they approach the higher levels of the system. The result is a system shaped like a pyramid. As students ascend through high school, college, and graduate or professional school, they move into an atmosphere that is increasingly rarefied, as the numbers of fellow students begin to fall away and the chance for gaining competitive advantage grows correspondingly stronger. And from the social mobility perspective, the chance to gain advantage is the system's most salient feature. There is convincing evidence that consumer demand for this kind of educational distinction (rather than a societal demand for human capital) has been largely responsible for driving the extraordinary upward expansion of education in the United States during the past 150 years.[40] For as enrollments have moved toward universality at one level (first the grammar school, then the high school, and most recently the college), the demand for social distinction necessarily has shifted to the next higher level. Randall Collins describes the social consequences of this ongoing effort to establish and maintain relative educational advantage: "As education has become more available, the children of the higher social classes have increased their schooling in the same proportions as children of the lower social classes have increased theirs; hence the ratios of relative educational attainment by social classes [have] remained constant throughout the last 50 years and probably before."[41]

Second, because each level of the system constitutes a large category offering at best rather crude distinctions, consumer-minded parents or students also demand a structure of education that offers qualitative differences between institutions at each level. They want to attend the high school or college that has the best reputation and therefore can offer its graduates the greatest distinction in competition with graduates from the lesser institutions.[42] This kind of reputational difference can lead to preferential access to jobs and further education. Which is why the value of a house in any community depends in part on the marketability of the local school system; and why wealthy suburban communities aggressively defend the high status of their school systems by resisting any efforts to reduce the striking differences between systems — efforts to redistribute tax revenues in order to equalize per capita school spending, for example, or to bus students across district boundaries in order to reduce class and race discrepancies between schools.[43] At the college and graduate levels, the same kind of concern leads to an intense effort by consumers to gain admission to the best-regarded institutions.[44] Parents are willing to spend as much as $30,000 a year to send their child to an Ivy League school, where the reputational rewards are potentially the greatest.[45] As a result, universities must cultivate their reputational ranks to help maintain market position. "In the competition for resources," said a spokesman at Pennsylvania State University, "reputation becomes the great variable on which everything else depends. The quality of students, faculty and staff an institution attracts; the volume of research grants and contracts, as well as private gifts; the degree of political support — all these and more hinge on reputation."[46] Within this status-conscious world of higher education, high tuition may be not a deterrent but an attraction, because it advertises the exclusivity and high standing of the institution (which then offers discounts in the form of scholarships).[47]

Third, consumers demand a stratified structure of opportunities within each institution, which offers each child the chance to become clearly distinguished from his or her fellow students. This means that they want the elementary school to have reading groups (high, medium, and low) and pull-out programs for both high achievers (gifted and talented programs) and low achievers (special education); they demand high school tracks offering parallel courses in individual subjects at a variety of levels (advanced placement, college, general, vocational, remedial); they insist upon letter grades (rather than vague verbal descriptions of progress), comprehensive standardized testing (to establish differences in achievement), and differentiated diplomas (endorsed or not endorsed, regents or regular). Parents are well aware that the placement of their children in a high ability group or program or track can give them an advantage in the competition for admission to the right school and the right job and can forestall early elimination in education's process of "tournament mobility."[48] As a result, parents actively lobby to gain advantageous placement for their children; and they vigorously resist when educators (pursuing a more egalitarian vision) propose to eliminate some form of within-school distinction or another—by promoting multiability reading groups, for example, ending curriculum tracking, or dropping a program for the gifted.[49]

Because the consumer approach to education is so highly individualized, however, the kind of pressure that it exerts on schools in any given case depends on the particular social position of the individual consumer. For those at the middle and lower ends of the social structure, the aim is social mobility, a chance to move up; but for those toward the upper end, the aim is to hold onto an already attractive position and to transfer this advantage to their children through the medium of education. Bourdieu defines the latter strategy succinctly as the effort to transform economic capital and social capital into cultural capital.[50] In order to pull off this transformation, the advantaged call for an educational system that offers a variety of vertical options that allow them to get their own children into the upper levels of whatever options are available—the top curricular stratum within a given institution (the gifted program), the most exclusive institution at a given educational level (an Ivy League college), and the most advanced degrees (M.D., J.D., Ph.D.). But for disadvantaged families, these upper-level options are a long shot at best, and as a result they may well see such options as a refuge for the privileged that undermine the chances for their own children to gain access to more basic forms of educational property: a decent elementary school, a high school diploma, a vocational program at the community college.

The social mobility goal, therefore, by portraying education as a consumer commodity, produces different kinds of effects on education depending on the social class of the consumers in a given educational setting, because the social position of these consumers affects their perception of their own educational needs. One result is that pressures for intensive competition and radical stratification of education are likely to come more strongly from the those at the top of the social scale than from those at the bottom. It is elite parents that see the most to gain from the special distinctions offered by a stratified educational system, and they are therefore the ones who play the game of academic one-upmanship most aggressively. It is they who can afford to bid up the price of a house in the right school district and of a diploma from the right college. The social mobility perspective often puts groups in conflict with each other, such as when working-class parents press to get their children greater access to educational benefits (by being bused to a better school or being provided with stronger preparation in basic skills) and upper-middle-class parents press to hold onto the educational advantages they already have (by preserving their monocultural neighborhood school or establishing a gifted program).[51] This fractured and contradictory impact of the social mobility goal on schools, arising from its view of education as a private good, distinguishes it from both of the other goals, whose view of education as a public good leads to a more coherent and generalized form of pressure on education grounded in the perceived needs of the community as a whole.

Another major impact of the social mobility goal on education derives from the way it treats education as a form of exchange value. For the other two goals, education is a form of use value: the citizen and the taxpayer (or employer) place value on education because they consider the content of what is learned there to be intrinsically useful. Both look on education as providing students with a useful array of competencies that are required either for constructive citizenship in a democratic society (democratic equality) or for productive work in a market society (social efficiency). From the perspective of social mobility, however, the value of education is not intrinsic but extrinsic. The primary aim is to exchange one's education for something more substantial—namely a job, which will provide the holder with a comfortable standard of living, financial security, social power, and cultural prestige.

Jobs tend to be allocated to a significant extent based on the quantity and quality of education that the applicants have, characteristics that determine a person's location in what Thurow calls the "labor queue."[52] And the easiest and most common way for employers to measure these educational differences is by examining the level and institutional prestige of a candidate's educational credentials.[53] They assume that by selecting candidates with the best credentials (those at the head of the queue) they are obtaining employees who have acquired the highest level of productive skills; they rarely look beyond the credentials to test this assumption.[54] As a result, educational credentials come to take on a life of their own. Their value derives not from the useful knowledge they symbolize but from the kind of job for which they can be exchanged. And the latter exchange value is determined by the same forces as that of any other commodity, through the fluctuation of supply and demand in the marketplace—the scarcity of a particular credential relative to the demand for that credential among employers.[55]

From the perspective of social efficiency, the use value and exchange value of education are inextricably linked, and therefore this distinction does not pose any educational or social problems. Drawing on neoclassical economics, the proponents of this goal argue that the exchange value of a diploma is simply a reflection of the human capital that it embodies. Accordingly, a higher degree is seen as worth more on the market than a lower degree because it represents a greater amount of usable knowledge, of knowledge that is economically productive.[56] There is a wealth of evidence to the contrary, however, suggesting that from the moment educational credentials came to be a primary mechanism for allocating people to jobs, the exchange value of these credentials began to diverge from the learning that went into acquiring them. This emerging independence of educational exchange value from its connection to usable knowledge is the most persuasive explanation for many of the most highly visible characteristics of contemporary educational life — such as overcredentialing (the chronic overproduction of advanced degrees relative to the occupational need for advanced skills) and credential inflation (the rising level of educational attainment required for jobs whose skill requirements are largely unchanged).[57]

Consider the effects of all this on education. When students at all levels see education through the lens of social mobility, they quickly conclude that what matters most is not the knowledge they attain in school but the credentials they acquire there. Grades, credits, and degrees — these become the objects to be pursued. The end result is to reify the formal markers of education and displace the substantive content. Students learn to do what it takes to acquire the necessary credentials, a process that may involve learning some of the subject matter (at least whatever is likely to be on the next test) but also may not. After all, if exchange value is key, then it makes sense to work at acquiring the maximum number of markers for the minimum investment of time, money, and intellectual energy. The payoff for a particular credential is the same no matter how it was acquired, so it is rational behavior to try to strike a good bargain, to work at gaining a diploma, like a car, at a substantial discount. The effect on education is to emphasize form over content — to promote an educational system that is willing to reward students for formal compliance with modest performance requirements rather than for demonstrating operational mastery of skills deemed politically and socially useful.[58]

One final consequence of the social mobility goal is to pressure education to take on a meritocratic form. From the perspective of the consumer, education is an arena for zero-sum competition filled with self-interested actors seeking opportunities for gaining educational distinctions at the expense of each other. This is especially true for families from the upper middle class, whose experience demonstrates the enormity of the potential benefit that can accrue from education and whose privileged starting position means that they also have a long distance to fall if the educational outcomes do not turn out in their favor. In this Hobbesian setting, the competitors are equally worried about winning and losing, about taking advantage of others and having others take advantage of them. The resulting atmosphere of mutual wariness leads to a collective call for the educational system to organize the competition in a relatively fair and open manner, so that the competitors with the greatest individual merit will be most likely to emerge at the top.

This approach to establishing a fair structure for educational competition takes a meritocratic form in large part because of the dominant place that meritocratic ideology occupies in American life. That ideology captures in idealized form the entrepreneurial traits and values rewarded by a capitalist economy and projects them onto social life in general: the capacity and desire to struggle for advantage in a fiercely competitive social hierarchy, where success or failure is determined solely by individual merit. Whereas proponents of democratic equality have seen schools both as a hothouse setting for the practice of their political ideal (and as an institution that could produce the kinds of citizens required by a democratic society), proponents of meritocratic principles have seen schools as a proving ground for their market ideal (and as an institution for producing individuals who can function efficiently in a market society).[59]

Over the years the meritocratic principle has embedded itself within the structure and process of American schooling in a multitude of ways. The self-contained classroom, the graded curriculum, simultaneous instruction, and individual evaluation — the basic pedagogical pattern of modern schooling — emerged in short order after the introduction of the common school. This pattern was ideally suited to the construction of a model educational meritocracy.[60] It placed students into groups based on similarity of sociocognitive development and educational preparation, exposed them to the same course of instruction, and then rated them on the basis of their individual performance. The resulting structure, as Parsons and Dreeben have noted, has proven over the years to be an ideal environment for fostering interpersonal competition and individual achievement.[61] By partially buffering students from the effects of ascriptive social influences (such as age and social class), this form of school places students in the midst of a meritocratic game characterized by a degree of formal equality that is unrealizable in real life. It accomplishes this by means of physical isolation from society, a strong norm of achievement as the legitimate criterion of evaluation, an academic curriculum (which provides a formally neutral field of competition), and a set of abstract and distinctively academic rewards.

Of course, meritocracy is much more visible in the upper levels of the stratified structure of schooling than in the lower levels. It is in the gifted programs, the advanced placement tracks, the wealthy suburban high schools, and the elite universities that competitive achievement is most intense; but in the remedial classes, the vocational track, the poor inner-city high schools, and the open-admission colleges, the urge to compete is weaker, and the struggle for academic achievement is relaxed. Students from the lower and working classes see the possibility of social mobility through education more as a frail hope than a firm promise, for the experience of their families and friends is that the future is uncertain and the relevance of education to that future is doubtful. As a result, they are less likely to plunge into the meritocratic fray, often looking at educational achievement as a lost cause or a sucker's game.[62]

In spite of the weak hold of the meritocracy on the lower levels of the educational system, however, U.S. education defines itself in meritocratic terms and derives a considerable amount of cultural power from its position as the institution that tries hardest to achieve the meritocratic ideal.[63] The impact of this effort on the classroom is profound. We see it in the stress on evaluation — ranging from the informal question-response-evaluation triad that characterizes so much of classroom interaction to the formal standardized tests that play such a significant role. We see it in the stress on competition, over such things as who can give the right answer, who can finish first, or who can attain the highest grade. We can see it in the process of "normalizing judgment" — rating the performance of each student relative to the others on a bell-shaped curve of student scores — that is embodied in that characteristically American form of testing, the norm-referenced multiple-choice examination.[64] We can see it in the construction of merit-based hierarchies of learners — ability groups and curriculum tracks and the whole panoply of other forms of educational stratification. And we can see it in the emphasis on knowledge as private property, which is accumulated for one's personal benefit (under conditions in which sharing is cheating) and which has a value that is measured in the currency of grades, credits, and credentials.

HISTORICAL PATTERNS OF GOAL ASCENDANCY

At one level, the history of educational goals in the United States is a story of shifting priorities, as particular goals come into favor, then slide into the background, only to reemerge later with renewed vigor.[65] Such pendulum swings give the history of educational policy and reform its episodic quality, with old issues resurfacing regularly in policy talk and with old reforms continually recycling through the educational system.[66] In the common-school era (the mid-nineteenth century), democratic equality was the dominant goal of U.S. education; the primary outcomes education was asked to produce were political and moral, the preservation of the commonwealth in the face of the rise of capitalist social and economic relations. Issues of social efficiency and social mobility were present but muted.

But late in the century, both of the latter became prominent. The potential for getting ahead via education grew increasingly into a potent reality, and the growing enrollments in the upper elementary grades precipitated a consumer demand for distinctive credentials at the high school and college levels. At the same time, educational leaders were growing concerned about how to deal with an increasingly large and heterogeneous group of students at the high school level and how to prepare these students for entry into an increasingly differentiated workforce. As a result, the progressive era (at the start of the twentieth century) was dominated by concerns of social mobility and social efficiency, and school curriculum and educational opportunity became markedly more stratified, with the invention of tracking, vocationalism, ability testing, and the comprehensive high school. The democratic equality strain of progressivism was overwhelmed by the kind of administrative progressivism that pushed these changes.[67]

By the 1960s and 1970s, however, the tide turned toward democratic equality (in conjunction with social mobility), as the national movement for racial equality infused schooling and spilled over into efforts to provide an education that was socially inclusive and offered equal opportunity across lines of class, gender, and ability as well as race. Then in the 1980s and 1990s, the momentum shifted toward the movement for educational standards, which emphasized social efficiency (again in conjunction with social mobility). The standards effort reflected a growing concern about economic competitiveness and the need for education to supply the human capital required for increased economic productivity; it also reflected a growing worry about the exchange value of high school and college credentials in the face of their wide availability.

At another level, however, the history of U.S. educational change is a story less of pendulum swings than of steady evolution under the influence of one goal, social mobility — both in conjunction with and at the expense of the others.[68] Most striking from this perspective is the way that the consumer conception of education has gradually come to dominate the structure of American schooling as well as policy talk about schools. It seems increasingly that no reform is possible, and neither of the other two goals can be advanced effectively, without tapping into the concerns raised by social mobility: the need for education to maintain its value as a consumer good that can provide individuals with social advantage.

The role played by consumer-generated market pressures is one of the key distinctions between education in the United States and elsewhere in the world. As Ralph Turner has argued, U.S. education is uniquely influenced by a concern for promoting "contest mobility," with the result that the system emphasizes winning over learning and opportunity over efficiency.[69] A number of scholars have pointed out the ways that U.S. educational institutions act in a peculiarly entrepreneurial manner in an effort to cater to the demands of their consumers. This market sensitivity is the result of a number of factors, including: weak state and even weaker federal influence; radically decentralized control; vulnerability to local political and parental influence; a dependency on per capita funding (via state appropriations or tuition); the need to attract local support for millage and bond elections; the absence of general standards for curriculum and academic performance; the tradition of relatively free student choice in selecting classes, programs, and institutions; open access to higher education without effective standardized screening mechanisms; and a highly competitive buyers' market at the postsecondary level.[70] And as we have seen, the result is that U.S. education at all levels is infused with market structures and processes that emphasize consumer choice, competition, stratified curriculum, the preservation of local autonomy (for school districts and individual institutions), and a rapid response to consumer demand.[71]

The Peculiarities of Social Mobility: Interaction Effects

One source of the powerful influence of the social mobility goal in the United States is its remarkable flexibility. Over the years, people from a diverse array of political persuasions have incorporated this goal into their educational rhetoric. The reason for the heterogeneous uses of this goal can be found in the contradictory elements that lie at its core. At times it works to reinforce democratic equality in opposition to social efficiency, and at other times it works to reinforce social efficiency in opposition to democratic equality.

SOCIAL MOBILITY VS. SOCIAL EFFICIENCY

The social mobility goal for schooling, arising from the values and beliefs inherent in meritocratic ideology, embodies the liberal vision of free choice and limitless possibilities that has helped make capitalist democracy such an appealing model for the organization of political and socioeconomic life. This ideology promises students that through schooling they can achieve anything within the limits of their own desire and personal capabilities. The social efficiency goal, arising from the sobering reality of inequality within the socioeconomic structure, represents the collective limits that confine these possibilities. This structure provides schools and colleges with practical inducements to imitate society's hierarchical form and to adopt educational practices that will meet that society's basic structural needs — that is, to reproduce the current social structure by ensuring that children are competently prepared for and efficiently allocated to the society's full array of occupational roles and social positions. These two visions of schooling — one optimistic and expansive, the other pragmatic and restrictive — inevitably come into conflict over the course of development that schools should follow. In fact, much of the visible conflict about education in the United States has boiled down to this difference between mobility and efficiency. Politically this conflict has taken the familiar form of a dispute between liberals and conservatives. (A classic example is the long-standing fight over whether to increase the access to higher education beyond the minimum needed to meet employer demand.[72])

A key to the power of the social mobility goal to shape the course of U.S. educational history, however, lies in the educational concerns that it shares with the democratic equality goal.[73] One of these is a strong shared interest in expanding access to education, and another is a joint understanding that, at least for the near term, schools should be made more meritocratic. For those concerned with promoting democracy, the effort to provide ever-widening access to education is essential for the production of capable citizens who are able to participate politically on equal terms. For those concerned with promoting social mobility, such a trend toward greater access is necessary if everyone is going to have an equal chance to get ahead. Although meritocratic schooling can and does undermine democratic equality by promoting unequal educational and social outcomes, it nonetheless represents progress toward democratic equality to the extent that it introduces individual achievement as the basis for allocating educational rewards in place of allocation based on such ascribed characteristics as class, race, and gender.

Consider, for a moment, the basic political and ideological characteristics that define each of the three educational goals. The educational program for democratic equality has a democratic political identity and an egalitarian social ideology. The program for social mobility promotes classical liberal politics (based on personal liberty, free markets, and individual choice) and meritocratic ideology (promoting equal opportunity for individual advancement rather than equal outcomes for all). The political and social common ground between these two approaches is a territory that historians have generally referred to as progressive — a compromise between democratic and liberal politics and between egalitarian and meritocratic social ideologies. In contrast, the educational program for social efficiency projects conservative politics (grounded in preserving elite political control through the retention of differences in political competency and access) and a reproductive social vision (reinforcing the existing structure of social inequality by adapting newcomers to play needed rather than desired roles within this structure).

The two issues that constitute the area of overlap between the democratic equality and social mobility goals — educational opportunity and individual achievement — define the core of a consensus that has driven progressive educational politics in this country for the past century and a half. A disparate array of constituencies has rallied behind this program. Organizations representing the working class, ethnic minorities, and women have all seen this educational agenda as a means for becoming participants in the political process and for gaining access to the more attractive social positions. For the middle and upper classes, the progressive program offered the chance to move up the ladder another rung or two or to reinforce an already comfortable social position with the legitimacy that comes from being seen as having earned this position through educational achievement.

The successes scored by this coalition have been extraordinary, including the phenomenal expansion of educational enrollments over the years and the continual extension of educational opportunity upward into the secondary and tertiary levels; the sharp and largely effective attack on de jure racial segregation in schooling and similar efforts to reduce segregation and enhance educational opportunities for women and those with handicaps; the dramatic growth in the public subsidy for education at all levels; the explosion in the number of educational course, program, and institutional choices offered to students; the emphasis on general rather than specialized education at all levels in order to preserve student options; the openness with which the educational system welcomes back students who decide to reenter the system after dropping out; and the capacity of the system to consider both individual merit (grades, achievement tests, SATs) and community right (affirmative action, social promotion, open admissions) in determining access to higher levels of education. Most important of all these successes, however, is the strong trend in the United States toward a system of allocating status on the basis of a formal educational voucher of individual merit — that is, hiring persons because of their educational credentials rather than their ascribed characteristics. In this sense, the rise of the credentials market itself is perhaps the proudest achievement of this progressive coalition. As Hurn has noted, allocation by credentials, in spite of its limits and negative side effects, may still be the most progressive option available, because it keeps opportunity open by intervening in the process of simple status ascription.[74]

The primary opposition to this progressive strand of U.S. education politics has come from another complex coalition, the proponents of social efficiency. These include policymakers (politicians and educational bureaucrats) who are worried about the high cost of supporting many parts of the educational establishment when the economic utility of this investment is slight; employers and business leaders who fear that their immediate manpower needs are not being filled by persons with appropriate skills or that they will have to provide training for employees at their own expense; educational administrators who are concerned about how to justify the social investment in schools and how to carve out a stable share of the competitive educational market; middle- and upper-class parents who are less concerned about getting ahead (given their children's reasonably secure future) than about containing the cost of public subsidies for the less fortunate; and working-class and lower-middle-class educational consumers who are more worried about getting a job than about getting ahead and who therefore want an education with clear and immediate vocational prospects.

In addition, at the most general level, social efficiency in education is a concern for any and all adult members of U.S. society in their role as taxpayers. As citizens, they can understand the value of education in producing an informed and capable electorate; as consumers, they can understand its value in presenting themselves and their children with selective opportunities for competitive social advantage; but as taxpayers, they are compelled to look at education as a financial investment — not in their own children, which is the essence of the consumer perspective, but in other people's children. The result is that adults in their taxpayer role tend to apply more stringent criteria to the support of education as a public good than they do in their role as consumers thinking of education as a private good. Grubb and Lazerson put the problem this way: "In contrast to the deep love we feel and express in private, we lack any sense of 'public love' for children, and we are unwilling to make public commitments to them except when we believe the commitments will pay off. As a result, cost-benefit criteria have dictated the kinds of activities the state might support."[75]

Thus the taxpayer perspective applies a criterion to the support of education for other people's children that is both stingier than that arising from the consumer perspective and also loaded down with an array of contingencies that make support dependent on the demonstrated effectiveness of education in meeting strict economic criteria — to boost economic productivity, expand the tax base, attract local industry, and make the country more competitive internationally, all at a modest cost per student.

For taxpayers in general and for all the other constituencies of the social efficiency goal for education, the notion of education for social mobility is politically seductive but socially inefficient. Sure, it is nice to think that everyone has a right to all the education he or she wants, and of course everyone would like to get ahead via education; but (say those who hold the social efficiency perspective) the responsible deployment of societal resources calls for us to look beyond political platitudes and individual interests and to consider the human capital needs of the economy as a whole. From this pragmatic, fiscally conservative, and statist perspective, the primary goal of education is to produce the workforce that is required by the occupational structure in its current form and that will provide measurable economic benefits to society as a whole. As a result, efficiency advocates (in response to perceived necessity) work directly counter to many of the goals of mobility advocates — holding up the limited possibilities to be found among existing job openings as an antidote to the limitless optimism of the progressives, and promoting social reproduction rather than political empowerment or individual opportunity. While the progressives are actively raising students' hopes, the conservatives are arguing for the necessity of, in the words of Burton Clark, "cooling out" many of these same students.[76] Be realistic, say the conservatives; we need only a few doctors and lawyers compared with the required number of clerical workers and machine operators, so schools should be trying to direct students into practical studies that will prepare them efficiently for attainable positions.

The struggle between conservatives (representing the goal of social efficiency) and progressives (representing the common ground between the goals of democratic equality and social mobility) has often been fought in this country over the issues of tracking, guidance, and vocationalism.[77] Conservatives argue for guiding students into tracks (on the basis of individual abilities and preferences) where they will be taught the vocational skills required for a differentiated array of existing jobs and then channeled directly into these jobs. Progressives see this process as a mechanism that blocks individual chances for social mobility and political equality by means of a self-fulfilling prophecy — predicting a working-class job role for a working-class student and then preparing him or her in such a way that any other outcome is unlikely. The impetus for this form of social efficiency has generally come from the institutional leadership in U.S. education (as agent for the taxpayer, policymaker, and employer), and educational consumers have generally resisted this effort with vigor and considerable success.

The history of higher education in the United States makes this pattern particularly clear. The land grant college, teachers college, and community college were all invented in large part as a mechanism for providing practical vocational training that policymakers and educators felt was required in order to promote social efficiency. In each case, however, students successfully sought to convert these vocational schools into general-purpose institutions for promoting social mobility. They achieved this end by expressing a clear consumer preference for programs leading to the bachelor of arts degree over those that provided particular job skills. These students have understood the status attainment implications of the debate over vocationalism. Vocational training has meant preparation for the lesser positions in the occupational structure, while a B.A. has provided an entree to the higher levels of this structure. Both forms of education are vocational, in the sense of being oriented toward work; the difference is in whether a student's education blocks or facilitates access to the more attractive forms of work.[78]

The end result of this conflict between progressive and conservative visions of schooling has been a peculiarly American educational structure, characterized by a bold mixture of purposes. On the one hand, education reflects the conservative vision: its structure has a pyramidal shape similar to that of the occupational structure; tracking within this system is the norm; and the system has a large number of potential exit points and a variety of cooling out mechanisms that encourage students to use these exits and go to work. On the other hand, education also has a progressive cast to it: tracking and other school choices are formally voluntary; the barriers between tracks are low; the opportunities for achieving higher levels of education are realizable; and for every exit there is the possibility of reentry to the system.

As a result, high levels of educational and social attainment are a real possibility for students no matter what their social origins. The educational system never absolutely precludes this possibility; its defining characteristic is openness and a reluctance to make any form of educational selection final, Turner's "contest mobility."[79] Yet the probability of achieving significant social mobility through education is small, and this probability grows considerably smaller at every step down the class scale. Students from the lower classes tend to exit the system earlier than those from the upper classes, and the chances of succeeding grow more difficult with every attempt to reenter the system after exiting. In short, the surest way to succeed is to get it right the first time by staying in the fast track at each step along the way, as market-wise consumers from the upper middle class are so good at doing.[80]

This conflicted image of the U.S. educational system — as a mechanism for attaining social status that offers unlimited possibilities and restricted probabilities — is reflected in the central character of this system's social mobility goal. For this goal occupies a political and ideological middle ground between democratic equality and social efficiency. On the one hand, it shares some of the concerns of the former and, in combination with it, has helped to energize powerful movements of progressive educational reform. In important ways, social mobility has exerted an effect on education that is diametrically opposed to the effect of social efficiency. First, social mobility promotes expanded access to education, while social efficiency opposes that outcome in order to hold down costs. Second, the mobility goal supports the concentration of resources on the highest levels of education (which emphasizes access to the best jobs), while the efficiency goal supports education of high quality at all educational and occupational levels (to provide society with a full range of good human capital). Third, the mobility goal undercuts learning by promoting the acquisition of credentials with the minimum academic effort, while the efficiency goal reinforces learning by asserting the need to upgrade the skills of the workforce.[81]

But at the same time, other characteristics of the social mobility goal show a remarkable similarity to the social efficiency approach. The mobility and efficiency goals are both grounded in a pragmatic vision that sees the necessity for schools to adapt to the structure of inequality. Both subordinate schools to the needs of the market. And both lead to a highly stratified structure of education. The social mobility approach to education implies a pyramid of educational opportunity, analogous to the pyramid of available jobs, with the educational credentials market providing the link between the two. This model requires a high rate of educational attrition in order to be effective. Because the top of the occupational pyramid contains only a small number of the most desirable jobs, education can provide access to these jobs for only a small number of students. Allowing a large number of students to attain the highest levels of education would be counterproductive because it would put a crowd at the head of the labor queue, providing no one in that crowd with a selective advantage in the competition for the top jobs.

Education can promote social mobility (and simultaneously preserve the positional advantage of the privileged) only to the extent that it prevents most students from reaching the top of the educational pyramid. It carries out this mobility and maintenance function by encouraging students to exit at lower levels of the system and by stratifying the credentials earned by students at each educational level (via curriculum tracking within schools and prestige ranking between schools). The result is that, in the name of social mobility, Americans have sought to push their education system in a direction that is in many ways directly opposite the direction urged by the logic of democratic equality.

SOCIAL MOBILITY VS. DEMOCRATIC EQUALITY

The social mobility goal has a mixed relation with the three elements that define the goal of democratic equality. Whereas social mobility shares with its partner in the progressive agenda a concern for equal access, it stands in opposition to the notion of equal treatment and it works directly counter to the ideal of civic virtue.

Equal Treatment

As I have suggested, the effort to create a school system that promotes social mobility is antithetical to the ideal of equal educational treatment. The whole point of such a system is to provide some students with the chance to achieve a higher social position by acquiring an education that is somehow "better" than the education acquired by most other students. To meet this purpose, then, schooling must be highly stratified. In this sense, the social mobility goal is congruent with the social efficiency goal. As shown earlier, stratification has become thoroughly embedded in U.S. schools over the past century, in large part because this kind of structure answers to the demands of both goals. Although much of this stratification took place in response to the perceived human capital needs of the economy — for example, through the introduction of the vocational track — much of it occurred in response to consumer demand. Students who want to get ahead through schooling (and their parents, who want to create possibilities of success for them) have sought to transform common schooling into uncommon schooling. They have actively pursued educational advantage and spurred educators to meet this demand by developing such opportunities.

Civic Virtue

Schooling students for citizenship means implanting within them the seeds of civic virtue. Yet schooling for social mobility undercuts the ability of schools to nurture the growth of this character trait and the behaviors it fosters: devotion to the political community and a willingness to subordinate private interests to the public interest. Unlike the pursuit of democratic equality, the social mobility goal focuses on the needs of the market rather than those of the polity; and unlike the pursuit of social efficiency, it adopts a perspective on the market that is aggressively individualistic rather than collective. In combination, these mobility-oriented traits form a powerful value, characteristic of capitalist ideology; Macpherson calls this value "possessive individualism," asserting that it is desirable and legitimate for each person to pursue competitive success in the market.[82] This goal has proven to be a strong force in shaping U.S. schools. It has lured students away from the pursuit of civic virtue by offering them the chance to use schooling as a kind of "cultural currency" that can be exchanged for social position and worldly success.[83]

From the perspective of democratic equality, schools should make republicans; from the perspective of social efficiency, they should make workers; but from the perspective of social mobility, they should make winners. In the latter view, the individual sees schools as a mechanism for producing neither a democratic society nor a productive economy but a good job. The most salient outcome of attending school becomes the diploma, whose usefulness derives from its ability to provide the owner with cultural advantage in the competition for positions of privilege within the social structure. In this sense, then, social mobility is unique among the three goals in the way it has promoted the commodification of U.S. education. For while social efficiency has subordinated schooling to the human capital demands of the economy, giving educational primacy to the vocational use-value of school learning, the social mobility goal has turned schooling into a cultural commodity, whose value arises less from its intrinsic usefulness than from its exchangeability. From this point of view, school is worth pursuing because its credentials can buy success. And the negotiability of these credentials in buying success is determined by the forces of supply and demand in the credentials market that mediates between schooling and the economy.

In conjunction with social efficiency, the other market-centered educational goal, social mobility has had the effect over the years of radically narrowing the significance of citizenship training within U.S. schools. Once seen as the overarching goal of the educational effort, schooling for citizenship increasingly has been confined to one part of the curriculum (social studies) or even perhaps a single course (civics), while market-oriented practices have become more pervasive.[84] Citizenship training has become entombed in such denatured rituals as assemblies to commemorate Martin Luther King Day or Presidents Day, the study of sanitized stories in the history textbook, and learning about the three branches of government. As a practical matter, what schools identify and reward as good citizenship in their students today is often just organizationally acceptable conduct — behaving in accordance with school rules rather than showing a predisposition toward civic virtue. This shift away from the common school vision of schools as "republican machines" appeared as early as the third quarter of the nineteenth century, when schools began to downgrade the significance of shaping student behavior by construing it as a way to promote organizational efficiency rather than a way to promote the character traits required for a democracy. Under growing pressure from a meritocratic (social mobility based) vision of schooling, educators increasingly began to focus instead on fostering individual academic achievement.[85]

Classroom Learning

Although the social efficiency goal directs student attention away from civic virtue and toward the needs of the economy, it nonetheless reinforces the salience of learning, even as it reduces the range of useful learning to the limits defined by vocational skill requirements. As suggested earlier, however, the social mobility goal effectively undermines the intrinsic value of any learning acquired in school. For if the ultimate utility of schooling for the individual educational consumer is to provide him or her with the credentials that open doors to good jobs, then the content of school learning is irrelevant. What matters is not real learning but what Sedlak and his coauthors call "surrogate learning": "As long as the tests are passed, credits are accumulated, and credentials are awarded, what occurs in most classrooms is allowed to pass for education."[86] The essence of schooling then becomes the accumulation of exchange values (grades, credits, and credentials) that can be cashed in for social status, not the acquisition of use values (such as the knowledge of algebra or the ability to participate in democratic governance), which provide capacities and resources that an individual can put directly into practice.[87]

Neoclassical economics sees no tension between use value and exchange value because the latter is assumed to reflect the former. Marx, however, effectively challenged this assumption. In a capitalist society, he argued, the market abstracts social products from their original context and particular function, reifies this abstraction by converting it to a generic commodity, and makes it comparable to all other commodities by assigning it a monetary value.[88] This is as true of educational credentials as it is of any other social product, such as an agricultural crop, that is created in response to market demand. From this perspective, schooling for democracy or efficiency is like farming for subsistence.[89] The purpose of the latter is to feed one's family or community; therefore the farmer has an incentive to plant the full range of crops required to sustain life. Schooling for mobility is like farming for the market. The purpose here is not to grow food but to produce widgets, a generic commodity that can be exchanged for money. Under these conditions, the farmer has an incentive to grow whatever crop will yield the best price on the market. The fact that the farmer's family members cannot live on soybeans or feed corn does not matter, because they use the money generated by their cash crop to buy what they need to live. Similarly, in schools that operate under a social mobility mandate, students and educators alike have little incentive to see learning as much more than an arbitrary mechanism for accumulating merit points that eventually add up to a diploma.

A large number of recent reports and studies point to the relatively low level of academic achievement registered by contemporary students in the United States.[90] These writers explicitly or implicitly blame a wide variety of factors for this problem: undereducated and underskilled teachers; distracted, spoiled, and unmotivated students; an educational organization clogged with politics, bureaucracy, and unionism; and an unchallenging, watered-down curriculum. But it is more valid to point the finger at a powerful purpose for schooling that is at core antieducational. By structuring schooling around the goal of social mobility, Americans have succeeded in producing students who are well schooled and poorly educated. The system teaches them to master the forms and not the content.[91]

As Boudon has argued, the actors in this educational system are making rational choices.[92] If the goal of schooling is credentials and the process of acquiring these credentials is arbitrary, then it is only rational for students to try to acquire the greatest exchange value for the smallest investment of time and energy. The result is what Sedlak calls "bargaining" and Powell calls "treaties" — in which students seek to strike a good deal with the teacher (less work for a good grade) and the teacher has a weakened rationale for trying to hold them to high academic standards.[93] As Sedlak and colleagues suggest, the essence of this marketplace behavior in schools is captured by a question that echoes through American classrooms: "Will this be on the test?"[94] Under the bargain-basement educational conditions fostered by the pursuit of social mobility, whatever is not on the test is not worth learning, and whatever is on the test need be learned only in the superficial manner that is required to achieve a passing grade.

Equal Access

The mobility and efficiency goals for education have pushed the common school goal of democratic equality into a corner of the American schoolroom. Citizenship has largely given way to self-interest and economic necessity, and equal treatment has succumbed to the powerful pressure (from both consumers and employers) for educational stratification. The only component of the political purposes of schooling that still exerts an undiminished influence on the schools is the ideal of equal access. The expansive political hopes of the common schoolmen over the years have become lodged in this part of the original dream. Yet the influence of this remaining hope on the schools has proven to be substantial, and this influence is perhaps most visible in the way it has undermined the effectiveness of schools in promoting either mobility or efficiency.

From the perspective of the mobility and efficiency goals, democratic pressure for equal access to schools has simply gotten out of hand. The problem is that in a society that sees itself as devoted to political equality, it is politically impossible to contain the demand for schooling for very long. Equal access is compatible with either mobility or efficiency, as long as it is interpreted as providing an unlimited possibility for educational attainment combined with a limited probability of acquiring the highest levels of such attainment. Under these conditions, equal access education can still provide opportunity for mobility to a few individuals and can still fill the personnel needs of the pyramid-shaped occupational structure. But the continuing tradition of democratic equality interferes with this comfortable scheme of meritocratic achievement and human capital creation by making it appear hollow for society to offer people broad-based access only to those levels of education that are not associated with the better jobs.

In the late nineteenth century, when the experience of elementary schooling was shared by the many and high school was enjoyed by the few, a high school diploma was a ticket to a good position, and thus access to high school became a hot political issue. Keeping high school attendance at a low level was a

difficult policy to defend in democratic terms, because attendance at that level
was precisely what made the notion of equal access socially meaningful. In the
mid-twentieth century, the same political dilemma confronted policymakers,
only this time the venue was college. If high school was generic and college was
special, then college credentials were more valuable, and access to college
became the focus of political attention. In both cases the pressure for equal
access translated into a demand not just for some form of education but for the
level that was most salient for status attainment. And the most useful stratum
of schooling for social mobility was that relatively rarefied stratum whose
credentials had the highest exchange value.[95]

This pressure for access to the most valuable educational credentials has resulted in the paradox that bedevils modern societies with formally meritocratic
opportunity structures: levels of educational attainment keep rising while levels of social mobility remain the same. Raymond Boudon's simple arithmetic
model of educational opportunity and meritocratic status attainment demonstrates why this is so.[96] Politically induced opportunities for higher-level educational attainment have been growing faster than structurally induced opportunities for higher-level status attainment: there are more diplomas than good
jobs. The result is a stable rate of social mobility and a declining exchange
value for educational credentials.

Contradiction, Credentialism, and Possibility

Ultimately, these three dominant goals — democratic equality, social mobility, and social efficiency — have affected U.S. education in a variety of ways,
both negative and positive. On the negative side, they have led to internal
contradiction and rampant credentialism, but on the positive side they have
also provided workable mechanisms for combating these problems.

CONTRADICTION

One obvious effect of the three goals has been to create within U.S.
education a structure that is contradictory and frequently counterproductive.
In response to the various demands put upon them, educational institutions
are simultaneously moving in a variety of often contradictory directions. For
example, we systematically sort and select students according to individual
merit and then undermine this classification through such homogenizing practices as grade inflation, social promotion, and whole-class instruction. We
bring the entire array of social groups in a community together under one roof
in a comprehensive regional high school and then make sure that each group
has a distinctly different educational experience there. We offer everyone ac-

cess to higher education (at the expense of admissions standards, academic rigor, and curriculum prerequisites) while assuring that the social benefits of this access are sharply stratified (at the expense of equal opportunity and social advancement). We focus on using education to prepare people for work (thus undercutting other conceptions of what it means to learn) but then devote most of our effort to providing a thoroughly general education that leaves most graduates unprepared to carry out work responsibilities without extensive on-the-job training. And so on.

As a result of being forced to muddle its goals and continually work at cross-purposes, education inevitably turns out to be deficient in carrying out any of these goals very effectively. Pushing harder for one goal (for instance, seeking to promote advanced opportunities for high achievers through development of a "gifted" program) only undercuts another (for example, trying to promote equal learning opportunities for those with handicaps through inclusive education). What looks like an educational improvement from one perspective seems like a decline from another. All of this pushing and pulling leaves educational institutions in a no-win situation, for whatever way they move, they are goring someone's ox. And wherever they choose to stand, they are in a hopelessly compromised situation in which they are fulfilling none of the three goals effectively. Instead they must settle for a balancing act among competing pressures, an effort that aims only to create the minimum conflict, satisfying no one. So if schools do not seem to work very well, one key reason is that we continue to ask them to achieve ends that are mutually exclusive.

CREDENTIALISM

The primary medium through which Americans have expressed their peculiar mix of goals for schools — sometimes mutually reinforcing and sometimes contradictory — has been the market for educational credentials. This market, as Collins and Boudon suggest, is the mechanism that connects schooling and the economy, translating educational attainment into social attainment according to its own internal logic.[97] The centrality of the credentials market derives from the key role played by the social mobility goal in the ideological development of schooling in the United States. After all, in a school system that is determined primarily by the requirements of democratic equality, the problem of occupational placement is irrelevant, and thus the market valuation of educational credentials has little impact on the way schools work. Conversely, in a school system governed primarily by the demands of social efficiency, the problem of filling jobs is paramount, and thus the credentials market is wholly subordinate to the requirements of the occupational structure; under these restrictive conditions, schools produce the precise number of people with the appropriate skills for each of the existing job openings. In either case, the result is that the credentials market exerts no independent effect on schools, and therefore inefficiencies like credential inflation — which Boudon's model predicts and American consumers experience — are simply impossible.

In U.S. schools, however, where the standoff between democracy and the market economy prevents the hegemony of either, social mobility emerges as an intriguing alternative goal. Drawing from both poles of the ideological spectrum and blurring the differences between these poles, this goal establishes the credentials market as a zone of individual enterprise, located between school and economy, where a few students with "merit" can make their way. In this zone the dominion of social efficiency is relaxed, because here there is no one-to-one relation between school-acquired skills and jobs. Instead, this relation is mediated by market forces of supply and demand. The salience of the credentials market creates a realm of possibilities for status attainment and exalts schooling as an instrument for achieving the American dream. Portraying the social structure as a structure of opportunity that can be negotiated by those with the most valuable credentials, the social mobility goal puts a democratic face on the inequalities of capitalism. Yet at the same time, this market preserves the probability of social stasis and social reproduction, because the likelihood of getting ahead is limited by the social structure's pyramidal shape. Countering the pessimism inherent in the goal of social efficiency, the credentials market offers unlimited possibilities for status enhancement; and countering the optimism embodied in the goal of democratic equality, this market provides for only one certainty, the persistence of stratified outcomes.

If the social mobility goal holds the crucial middle ground between two opposing purposes for schools, then the credentials market holds the middle ground between two institutions (school and work) that reflect these cross-purposes. In spite of its involvement in the reproduction of inequality, education still represents the political hopes of Americans who see a higher purpose to social life than the achievement of social efficiency. As Carnoy and Levin have pointed out, schools continue to provide Americans with a social experience that is markedly more egalitarian and more open to free choice and possibilities of self-realization than anything that is available to them in the realm of work.[98] The credentials market, then, necessarily becomes the place where the aspirations raised by education meet the cold reality of socioeconomic limits, where high educational attainment confronts the modest possibilities for status attainment.

The credentials market exists in a state of partial autonomy. Constrained by the institutions that bracket it, this market also exerts an independent impact on both of these institutions. Understanding the nature of the latter impact is crucial to an understanding of the relation between school and society in the United States. As Collins and Boudon show, the inner logic of the credentials market is quite simple and rational: educational opportunities grow faster than social opportunities, the ability of a particular diploma to buy a good job declines, so the value of educational credentials becomes inflated. This outcome, the natural result of contradictory tendencies woven into the fabric of American life, shapes both schools and the economy.[99]

Credential inflation affects schools by undermining the incentive for students to learn. The social mobility purpose has already reduced this incentive by making credentials a more important acquisition for students than knowledge and skills. But the devaluation of these credentials then makes it seem like a waste to expend even the minimal effort required to pursue surrogate learning and the acquisition of grades, credits, and diplomas. Credential inflation also affects the larger society. It promotes a futile scramble for higher-level credentials, which is very costly in terms of time and money and which produces little economic benefit. Yet because the effect of putting a lid on this inflation would be to stifle opportunities for social mobility, the political will to implement this ultimate solution to the problem is unlikely to emerge. Instead, the credentials market continues to carry on in a manner that is individually rational and collectively irrational, faithfully reflecting the contradictory purposes that Americans have loaded onto schools and society alike.

POSSIBILITY

Conflicting goals for education can produce a contradictory and compromised structure for educational institutions that sharply impairs their effectiveness. These goals can also — through the medium of the consumer-driven mobility goal that plays such a key role in this compromised structure — lead to a kind of credentialism that is strikingly counterproductive for both education and society. The fact that educational goals are in conflict, however, is not in itself an unmanageable problem, but we cannot realistically escape it by simply choosing one goal and ditching the others. Any healthy society needs an educational system that helps to produce good citizens, good workers, and good social opportunities. Preparing young people to enter into full involvement in a complex society is itself a complex task that necessarily requires educators to balance a variety of competing concerns, and the educational institutions that result from this effort necessarily are going to embody these tensions.

But the biggest problem facing U.S. schools is not the conflict, contradiction, and compromise that arise from trying to keep a balance among educational goals. Instead, the main threat comes from the growing dominance of the social mobility goal over the others. Although this goal (in coalition with the democratic equality goal) has been a major factor in motivating a progressive politics of education over the years, the increasing hegemony of the mobility goal and its narrowly consumer-based approach to education has led to the reconceptualization of education as a purely private good.

We are in the late 1990s experiencing the sobering consequences of this ideological shift. We find credentialism triumphing over learning in our schools, with a commodified form of education winning an edge over useful substance. We find public schools under attack, not just because they are deemed ineffective but because they are public. After all, if education is indeed a private good, then the next step (according to the influential right wing in today's educational politics) is to withdraw public control entirely and move toward a fully privatized system of education. Charter schools and consumer choice are the current icons. The word *public* itself is being transformed, as public schools are renamed "government" schools (with all the stigma that is carried by this term in an antigovernment era), and private charter schools are being christened "public school academies" (the title accorded them by law in Michigan). Accordingly, the government is asked to abdicate its role in educational matters while the consumer is crowned king.

Fortunately, the long history of conflicting goals for education in the United States prepares us for such a situation by providing us with countervailing values. These arise from our belief in the publicness of the public schools, a belief that is reinforced by both of the other goals that have competed with social mobility within our politics of education. Both the democratic equality tradition and the social efficiency tradition are inherently hostile to the growing effort to reduce public education to a private good. Neither is able to tolerate the social inequality and social inefficiency that are the collective consequences of this shift toward private control. Neither is willing to allow this important public function be left up to the vagaries of the market in educational credentials. As a result, we can defend the public schools as a public good by drawing on the deeply rooted conceptions of education that arise from these traditions: the view that education should provide everyone with the capacities required for full political participation as informed citizens, and the view that education should provide everyone with the capacities required for full economic participation as productive workers. Both of these public visions have become integrated into the structure of U.S. education.

They are exemplified in a wide range of daily educational practices, and they are so firmly fixed in our conception of school that it is difficult for most of us to imagine a form of education that is not shaped by them.

All of this provides us with a potent array of experiences, practices, arguments, and values that we can use in asserting the importance of education as a decidedly public institution. It enables us to show how the erstwhile privatizers are only the latest example of a long-standing effort to transform education into a consumer commodity, and to demonstrate how this effort has already done considerable damage to both school and society — by undermining learning, reinforcing social stratification, and promoting a futile and wasteful race to attain devalued credentials. In short, the history of conflicting goals for U.S. education has brought contradiction and debilitation, but it has also provided us with an open structure of education that is vulnerable to change; and it has given educators and citizens alike an alternative set of principles and practices that support the indivisibility of education as a public good.

2

The Social Meaning of Student Promotion and Retention

Everyone hates to fail, children as much as adults. But the possibility of failure is a fact of life that is built into any graded system of schooling. At the end of the school year, a student is either promoted to the next level or retained in grade for another year; and at the end of high school, students either graduate or they don't. The choice is stark and the consequences are substantial. So it is not surprising that the issues surrounding promotion and retention are a matter of chronic concern for all of the parties involved in and affected by this decision—teachers, administrators, students, and parents, as well as the citizens and taxpayers who oversee and pay for the schools. In fact, these issues have been the object of great interest and considerable controversy in the United States since the invention of the graded school in the mid-nineteenth century.

The debate about promotion standards arises in part from issues of public concern. From this perspective, the central question is: to what extent is the practice of retaining students in grade functional or dysfunctional for society as a whole? But the debate also arises in part from issues of private concern. From this perspective, the central question is: to what extent is retention beneficial or harmful for my particular child? The contradictory answers to these questions have led to an array of promotion practices that range between two poles of a continuum. At one pole is merit promotion, which requires students to earn advancement through individual demonstrations of academic competence at a given level, and which therefore makes nonpromotion a distinct possibility that frequently occurs. At the other pole is social promotion, which determines student advancement based on criteria that are social rather than meritocratic (aimed at keeping students of a given age moving through the grades together), and which therefore makes nonpromotion a relatively rare event.[1]

My goal in this chapter is to explore the social meaning of this polarity, to examine the ideological and social significance of promotion within the graded structure of schooling in the United States. Policies for student promotion have been driven to a substantial degree by two factors, both of which arise from a conception of education as a private good. One is an ongoing effort to maintain the legitimacy of the graded structure of schooling by preserving the idea of advancement according to individual merit. The other is a continuing effort to maintain a distinction between winners and losers in the educational system, so that schooling can provide educational consumers with the kind of competitive social advantage they demand.

Trends and Issues

Over time, the balance between the poles of merit promotion and social promotion has shifted. Although there are no authoritative national statistics on historical patterns of grade-level promotions in U.S. schools, the overall trends are relatively clear.[2] In the nineteenth century, when the average student stayed in school for only five or six years, there was little expectation that most students would win promotion to the next grade every year; average rates of nonpromotion therefore were undoubtedly quite high. Merit promotion was the rule. By the start of the twentieth century, it is estimated that perhaps one student in every three failed to attain promotion in urban schools during any given year.[3]

Between this point and the middle of the century, however, the rate of nonpromotion steadily declined and school systems actively sought to reduce the number of overage students at each grade level. In the 1930s and 1940s, this pattern was reinforced by a growing conviction among educators that students would benefit most from the practice of automatic or "social" promotion, on the grounds that staying with their peers would best serve both the educational and developmental needs of most students. The numbers from individual school systems show a dramatic fall in rates of nonpromotion during this period. In Philadelphia, for example, the average annual rate of nonpromotion for students in any of the first eight grades fell from 18 percent in

1908 to a low of 2 percent in 1945, while the rate for high school students fell from 23 percent to 15 percent.[4] In New York City, the retention rate for elementary schools reached a low of 1 percent in 1948.[5]

The trend toward social promotion continued and spread to other districts during the next three decades, reaching a peak in the 1970s. By the late 1970s, however, rates of nonpromotion began to rise. For example, using census data, Shepard and Smith estimate that the proportion of 11-year-olds who were overage for their grade level rose nationally from 19.5 percent in 1976 to 26.1 percent in 1984.[6] By 1990, 32.4 percent of white male 11-year-olds were overage, and the rate for minorities was even higher.[7] Overall retention rates are difficult to estimate, but among fourteen states that kept retention data during 1986, the median rate was 7.2 percent — that is, an average of 7.2 percent of the students at all grade levels in those states were held back that year. These numbers are not high relative to the rates during the heyday of merit promotion at the start of the twentieth century, but they have continued to increase. In addition, the rate is high compared with other industrialized countries; UNESCO data from 1984 show that Japan and the United Kingdom retained no students at all during the years of primary schooling, and West Germany retained only 1.9 percent.[8]

A number of educational researchers have devoted their energies to the task of exploring the consequences of nonpromotion in U.S. schools. For the most part, they have concentrated on one particular aspect of this issue — the impact of retention versus social promotion on the achievement level and the emotional well-being of low-achieving students. The researchers ask, "Is it better for these students to be held back or to be promoted with their peers when they fail to meet a minimum level of achievement in a particular grade?" Social science inquiry often produces a muddle of contradictory or at best noncomparable findings, and there is some disagreement regarding this issue, too. But for the most part, the research findings add up to an unusually strong conclusion: at best, retention is no better than social promotion in encouraging student achievement, and at worst it actually slows student learning while at the same time impairing social adjustment.

During the past twenty-five years, eight reviewers have sought to evaluate the mass of studies on retention and social promotion. None of these review articles concluded that retention was an effective policy for raising the achievement levels of low-achieving students. Three determined that the evidence was not sufficiently conclusive to support either retention or social promotion.[9] The other five found in favor of social promotion.[10] The most comprehensive and rigorous of these reviews is a meta-analysis carried out by Thomas Holmes, which concludes as follows:

The meta-analysis of the sixty-three studies is consistent with previous reviews of research and an earlier meta-analysis finding largely negative effects for retention. On average, retained children are worse off than their promoted counterparts on both personal adjustment and academic outcomes.

Of the sixty-three empirical studies, fifty-four found negative results while only nine were positive.

When only well-matched studies were examined, a greater negative effect was found for retention than in the research literature as a whole. In studies where retained children and promoted controls were matched on IQ and prior achievement, repeating a grade had an average negative effect of -.30 standard deviations. The weight of empirical evidence argues against grade retention. As Holmes and Matthews concluded in 1984, "Those who continue to retain pupils at grade level do so despite cumulative research evidence showing that the potential for negative effects consistently outweighs positive outcomes" (p. 232).[11]

Researchers have become quite frustrated by the realization that the practice of retaining students in grade continues unabated in U.S. schools and now is even surging upward — in spite of the overwhelming research evidence that seems to confirm the negative consequences of this practice. No one likes to be ignored, and it certainly appears that everyone is ignoring what researchers have to say about this issue. This frustration bubbles up through a number of essays in an authoritative book on the subject, *Flunking Grades: Research and Policies on Retention*.[12] In a chapter near the end of the book focusing on "Policy Implications of Retention Research," Ernest House puts the problem this way:

> This book demonstrates that the practice of retaining students in grade is absolutely contrary to the best research evidence. Few practices in education have such overwhelmingly negative research findings arrayed against them. Yet educational professionals and the public are almost universally in favor. This is an unusual situation: much of the time the best educational practice is far in advance of educational research. That is, the finest teachers are capable of classroom judgments that are sounder and more effective than educational research can prescribe or even understand. Yet in this case I find the research evidence to be sounder than professional judgment. Why is there such an enormous discrepancy between the practice and the research?[13]

Why indeed?

One answer, of course, is that the consensus among researchers on the subject may be wrong. It wouldn't be the first time that scientific opinion has converged on an invalid conclusion. And some of the studies do find that retention works. The most recent and most persuasive of these is summarized in *On the Success of Failure: A Reassessment of the Effects of Retention in the Primary Grades*. The authors of this work criticize previous research on retention for its many methodological flaws and for the researchers' willingness to express "strong opinions" based on "weak evidence." Their own carefully constructed study leads them to the conclusion that overall in the early grades "retention has mainly positive consequences" for student achievement.[14]

It is not my aim, however, to focus on the validity of the various empirical claims about the effectiveness of retention in encouraging or deterring higher levels of academic achievement.[15] In fact, the debate about the educational effectiveness of retention is largely beside the point. No amount of empirical proof one way or the other is going to affect practices of promotion and retention in U.S. education, because neither the persistence of retention practices over the past 150 years nor the pendulum swings between high and low rates of retention during that time can be explained by the impact of these practices on student learning. Rather, we can best understand both the persistence and the changes in these promotion practices as a response to ideological and social pressures on U.S. education that arise from the constitution of schooling as a market institution. Schooling in the United States is pressured to model itself after the meritocratic ideology that undergirds the market economy; and simultaneously it is pressured to meet the demands of educational consumers for a form of cultural property (educational credentials) that can provide them an advantage in the competition for social positions.

Grading as Ritual Classification

John Meyer and Brian Rowan make an effective case for the proposition that U.S. schools as organizations are not under pressure to produce any particular set of educational outcomes but that they are under considerable pressure to adapt to cultural expectations about what form schooling should take.[16] School leaders lack a well-defined technology of instruction, exert little direct control over the content of instruction, and make little effort to measure the learning that results from instruction. In all these ways, schooling is notoriously "loosely coupled," as instructional "activity is disconnected from its effects."[17] But "in such matters as controlling who belongs to a particular ritual classification — for example, who is a certified mathematics teacher, a fifth-grader, an English major — educational organizations are very tightly, not loosely, organized." This state of affairs arises when a society increasingly calls upon education to allocate people to social positions, providing "a set of standardized public credentials to incorporate citizen personnel into society."[18]

Thus, as societies and nation-states use education to define their basic categories of personnel, a large-scale educational bureaucracy emerges to standardize and manage the production of these categories. . . .

Society thus becomes "schooled" (Illitch, 1971). Education comes to be understood by corporate actors according to the *schooling rule:* Education is a certified teacher teaching a standardized curricular topic to a registered student in an accredited school. The nature of schooling is thus socially defined by reference to a set of standardized categories, the legitimacy of which is publicly shared. As the categories and credentials of schooling gain importance in the allocation and membership processes, the public comes to expect that they will be controlled and standardized.[19]

A key corollary of the schooling rule is that an important set of rules arises to establish formal categories for the correct classification of students: "Students are sharply distinguished by level or grade, by programs or units completed, by subject area specialization, and even by special abilities (for instance, educationally handicapped). Student classifications are tightly controlled, and school can define exactly which students are fifth-graders, chemistry majors, or enrollees." But because these formal categories are disconnected from educational substance, there is little control over the kinds of skills and knowledge that a student can be expected to have at any given level: "Although there is a great clarity in formal assignment or transition, few formal organizational mechanisms ensure that these assignments are enacted substantively — for instance, that twelfth-graders are actually doing twelfth-grade work or that third-graders who are being promoted have actually met some standard."[20]

This analysis suggests a different interpretation of student promotion policies from the one that we find in the contemporary research literature on the subject. Nonpromotion may or may not do harm to a student's academic achievement and social development (as the two sides of this debate in the literature have argued), but identifying the substantive educational effect of nonpromotion does nothing to explain either the persistence of this practice over time or the changes over time in the rate of nonpromotion. A process of ritual classification, such as the allocation of students to grades in school, is not justified by the effectiveness of this process in enhancing the learning of students, because processes and outcomes are separated within educational institutions. Therefore, in order to understand the issue of nonpromotion more fully, we need to turn from examining its educational consequences and begin to analyze its institutional meaning.

In his discussion of nonpromotion as a policy problem, House provides us with a useful insight into the reason for the continuing social salience of this practice of ritual classification. He notes at one point that "parents did not want their own children retained, even though a majority of parents endorsed the practice in the abstract."[21] Why would parents adopt this paradoxical position? My interpretation (indirectly supported by House in his discussion of the subject) is that parents are responding rationally to two different sources of concern that are embedded in the practice of nonpromotion — one that arises from cultural belief and another that arises from self-interest.

On the one hand, most Americans share the belief that a fair and productive society must be grounded in the principle of meritocracy, which asserts that social rewards (power, money, jobs, prestige) should be distributed on the basis of individual merit — that is, people should get what they earn through individual effort and accomplishment. From this perspective, merit promotion is a necessary component of any fair and effective system of schooling, for only the demonstrably deserving should be allowed to advance to the higher levels of the system and attain the educational credentials that serve as the system's badges of merit. On the other hand, these same Americans are also consumers of educational services, who want the best for their children, including educational advantages that will help them capture comfortable social positions. For educational consumers, nonpromotion is a good thing when it happens to other people's children but a disaster when it strikes their own, for their children's future depends on winning the meritocratic competition within school, and this means gaining promotion while others are held back. Note that both of these perspectives are expressions of a society grounded in market processes, where meritocracy is the natural ideology of a market society and the competitive pursuit of individual advantage is the natural form of market-based social interaction.

The classification of students into grades and the process of promoting or not promoting them from one grade to another arose in response to these two forms of market pressure — as an embodiment of the merit principle and as a mechanism for acquiring social advantage. Let us now consider briefly the way these factors played out in the history of graded schooling in the United States.[22]

Inventing the Graded School: The Salience of Merit and Mobility

The graded school began to appear in the United States in the 1830s. Before that, students were organized in a loosely heterogeneous manner that had persisted for several hundred years in Western Europe and North America. Education then typically took place in a thoroughly mixed school, where students of all ages and all degrees of proficiency sat together in a large room overseen by a single teacher. The process of learning focused on individual work, as students studied texts and performed written exercises at their seats. At intervals, the teacher would call students (individually or in groups) to approach the teacher's desk, recite what they had learned, and receive correction and new assignments. Students advanced in their studies at their own pace. In this system, there was no formal grading of students, no process of group promotion, and no social entity known as a class, at least not in the modern understanding of these now-fundamental educational terms. This was a system that worked well under the conditions at the time, where schooling was voluntary, episodic, and small-scale.[23]

These conditions changed rapidly in the United States, however, with the rise of the common school in the 1830s. The common-school movement emerged in response to what its leaders perceived as a political and moral crisis. A young and fragile republic with a young and booming market economy seemed to need a mechanism for instilling civic virtue in its citizenry, so that individuals who were avidly pursuing their own self-interest in capitalist commerce would also be able to devote themselves to the common good and live a moral life. Fearing the rise of class divisions and moral decay, these largely Whig educational innovators saw the common school as a powerful way "to make Republicans" through the establishment of "republican equality."[24] This strategy required a system of schooling that would bring together all of the children in a community and provide them with a common educational experience, aimed at helping them to acquire both the useful skills and the republican values that would permit them to perform their citizenship roles with competence and dedication.[25]

At the same time that the common-school founders sought to produce citizens for the republic, they also wanted to create an institution that would express and model the social mobility through meritocratic achievement that is the ideal for social interaction in a market society. Just as entrepreneurs are expected to compete in a capitalist economy, with the prize going to the most efficient producer, students in the new common school were expected to compete for academic rewards that are granted to those with the highest merit.[26] A major sponsor of the common-school legislation in Pennsylvania in 1834 predicted that the new institution would promote precisely this combination of republicanism and meritocracy. The common school, he argued, would

> form an educational association between the rich, and the destitute. Let them all fare alike in the primary schools, receive the same elementary education, imbibe the republican spirit and be animated by a feeling of perfect equality. In after life, he who is diligent at school will take his station accordingly,

whether born to wealth or not. Common schools universally established will multiply the chances of success, perhaps brilliant success, among those who may otherwise forever continue ignorant. It is the duty of the State to promote and foster such establishments. That done, the career of each youth will depend upon himself. . . . Let them all start with equal advantage, leaving no discrimination, then or thereafter, but such as study shall produce.[27]

There was also a third concern that shaped the common school: social efficiency. Not only did the new mode of schooling have to take an institutional form that met the demand for civic virtue and merit-based attainment, but it also had to do so in a manner that was fiscally prudent and organizationally efficient. Bringing all students in the community into a single educational system under public funding was an enormously expensive undertaking for most municipalities, and it was made more so by the heavy political and ideological burden that this system was asked to bear.[28]

As a natural consequence of this complex array of purposes, the system of common-school education rapidly took on a graded form. In order to understand why this occurred, first consider the basic characteristics of a graded educational system. In such a system, students are classified according to their level of educational accomplishment, and those at a similar stage are gathered into the social unit known as a class. The curriculum is likewise graded, and students in a given class are exposed to the level of curriculum appropriate to their grade, usually through the mechanism of simultaneous instruction (by which the teacher provides instruction to the whole class in a particular subject at a particular level). Groups of contiguous grades are formed into schools, and these schools are themselves graded into a continuous hierarchy of schools across the system. A student's academic progress is measured by his or her promotion upward through these grades and schools.[29]

All of this appears quite natural, even trivial, to us at this point in the history of education, because these innovations long ago became embedded in what David Tyack and Larry Cuban call "the grammar of schooling."[30] This grammar, like the grammar of our spoken language, is easy to take for granted, but it nonetheless profoundly shapes our expectations for what is the right way to do school. Thus the graded school — one of the most successful educational reforms of all time — is now a key component of what we perceive as a *"real school."*[31] In fact, grading has come to be so much the norm that we require schools to defend vigorously the clarity and legitimacy of this classification system or risk losing our confidence and respect.[32] This mandate becomes a critical factor in helping us understand the recent resurgence of merit promotion.

In the mid-nineteenth century, however, the graded school was a startling innovation, which responded effectively to the three sorts of demands that the common-school founders placed on this new institution. From the perspective of republicanism, the graded school brought together a heterogeneous array of students under conditions of remarkable equality. Though different in social origins, students in a given class were equal in educational attainment, and together they underwent the same educational experience — studying the same curriculum and receiving simultaneous instruction. This process encouraged a convergence in student learning and provided a common preparation for the role of citizen.

From the perspective of social mobility, the graded school created a level playing field for academic competition. By equalizing students in each class according to level of educational accomplishment and by exposing them to common instruction in the same subjects, this system permitted clear comparisons of the academic performance of students and encouraged students to compete against each other (neither of which was possible under the old system of individual recitation). At the same time, the system as a whole neatly modeled itself "in the image of bourgeois social relations and mobility" by constructing within the school "a fluid class society based on continuous gradations and competitive individual achievement."[33] Promotion through the grades provided a clear scale for measuring comparative academic success.

Finally, from the perspective of social efficiency, the graded school permitted a shift from the old flexible but inefficient form of individualized instruction (craft production) to a much more efficient mode of group instruction (batch production).[34] This approach not only introduced efficiencies of scale by allowing group processing of students, but it also led to efficiencies in professional preparation by allowing school administrators to hire specialists to teach particular subjects at particular levels rather than having to look for teachers who had mastered the entire curriculum at all levels.

The process of grading the school system did not occur immediately with the advent of the common school but grew gradually during the period between the 1830s and the 1860s.[35] The process began in primitive form with the Lancasterian schools for the poor at the beginning of this period. In these schools, a large mass of students of all levels were gathered in a large room under the tutelage of a single master. Instruction, however, occurred in small groups led by student monitors, and students were encouraged to compete for prizes and seek promotion through a series of academic levels.[36] Within the emerging common schools, the first step in grading was to classify the curriculum into broadly defined levels by creating a hierarchy of schools — primary, secondary or middle, grammar, and high schools — although each level of school often remained internally undifferentiated at this point. By the 1860s, however, the pace of grading accelerated as reformers increasingly sought to divide individual schools into classes according to academic level. The graded school by this time had become "immensely popular," and as early as 1870 it had become accepted as the norm for educational organization.[37]

Reconstructing the Graded School: The Rise of Tracking and Social Promotion

The triumph of the graded system of schooling did not take place, however, without generating opposition or creating problems. One source of trouble was a conflict between those who put primary emphasis on the system's republican purposes and those who emphasized its meritocratic functions. This conflict took a particularly visible form in the public debate in the 1840s between Horace Mann and a group of Boston grammar school masters over the subject of pedagogy.[38] The masters supported a hard pedagogy, based on physical discipline and "emulation" — intense competition among students for extrinsic rewards in the classroom. Mann argued for a soft pedagogy — based on appeals to the interest of the student and efforts to have students internalize behavioral rules — while strongly attacking the pedagogy of emulation. As Hogan explains, the advocates of soft pedagogy won this debate (at least in educational theory if not necessarily in classroom practice): it was their formulation that became the pedagogical orthodoxy by the last quarter of the century. This is a significant development for the story of graded instruction because it represents an effort by educational leaders to tone down the meritocratic consequences of graded schooling. Hogan argues convincingly that the soft pedagogues saw emulation in the classroom as a dangerous example of the way market behavior and market morality had invaded schooling and social life more generally. In response to this threat, they sought to stress in the schools the importance of moral education, character building, and emotional warmth rather than the form of cold and self-interested meritocratic achievement that could so easily be fostered by the graded school.[39]

A good example of the kind of intense competition that could be spurred by the new graded system of schooling was the competitive struggle for admission to the high school in many communities. Philadelphia, for example, had only one high school for boys during most of the nineteenth century, and students vigorously vied for access to this scarce commodity by trying to pass a rigorous entrance examination.[40] It would be hard to find a purer and more intense locus of meritocratic achievement than this high school, sitting atop a sharply stratified structure of schooling. By the 1870s, however, parents who resented the exclusion of their children from the high school grew increasingly frustrated with the school's meritocratic admissions process, and this led to a strong political demand for wider access. The result was a strangely mixed mode of admissions that persisted for the next two decades, a combination of a competitive examination (meritocracy) and a quota system guaranteeing minimum access for students from all grammar schools in the city (political equality).

In short, two principles behind the graded school — on the one hand, competitive promotions through the graded system based on individual merit; on the other, the egalitarian tendency that emerges from the political-moral perspective on the graded school — collided, and the result was a compromise. At the same time, another challenge to the legitimacy of the graded school came from the social efficiency perspective. By the 1870s, educational leaders like William T. Harris were beginning to argue that the process of batch production in the graded school was inefficient, because of the way it held back some students in a class who were ready to move ahead before their peers and because of the way it discouraged others who failed to advance and thus dropped out.[41] When rolled together, these various attacks on the meritocratic character of the graded system of schooling during the nineteenth century provided the beginning of a rationale — grounded in political equality and social efficiency — for backing away from pure merit promotion and moving toward a form of social promotion.

The most direct challenges, however, arose at the end of the century, as a result of the enormous success of the graded school system and the effect of this success on the middle-class constituency that had most enjoyed its benefits over the years. Although the numbers varied widely from one community to another, promotion all the way through the graded structure of schooling was an exceedingly rare event in the nineteenth century. Gaining admission to the top level of the system, the high school, was in itself a major achievement, especially in the larger cities, and graduation was even more difficult. To consider the Philadelphia example again, in 1880 high school students accounted for only 1.4 percent of total enrollments in the public schools, and only a quarter of students admitted to the high school actually graduated. Under these conditions, a high school diploma was a scarce commodity indeed, and therefore its exchange value — its ability to buy access to a good job — was quite high. This credential provided a degree of distinction that is difficult to imagine today, when a high school diploma is thoroughly commonplace, and it granted the holder privileged access to the growing sector of white-collar work.[42]

Not surprisingly, the students who attended high school and won this degree were drawn disproportionately from the middle classes, especially those from the proprietary (upper) middle class. These, after all, were the families who could most afford the opportunity cost of sending their children to school during their teens instead of sending them directly into the workforce. And these were also the families who had the most to lose from the possibility of downward mobility. The sharp decline in the viability of small commercial and craft-production businesses in the late nineteenth century — businesses that had formed the main support for the self-employed middle class over the years — meant that these families faced the prospect of proletarianization if they were not able to find an alternative way to pass along social position to their children. The kind of cultural capital represented by the high school diploma offered an attractive, accessible, and valuable alternative to the transfer of economic capital that traditionally took place with the inheritance of the family business.[43]

By the 1890s, however, the exchange value of this credential began to drop as high school enrollments and graduations began to rise sharply. The lower grades were filling up, grammar schools were producing increasing numbers of graduates, and the pressure for admission to high school became intense. As a result, high school enrollments in the United States doubled in the 1890s and continued to double every decade for the next half century. The effects of this development on the credentials market were predictable: the growing numbers of high school diplomas meant a decline in their exchange value, which (as with any other commodity) depends on relative scarcity. So the upper middle class had to look to a higher level in the graded system of education for credentials that would serve their needs, and this meant reaching beyond the high school to the university. By the turn of the century, these families increasingly sought to send their children, particularly their sons, to the university and through this mechanism to gain access to the professions. A university diploma and a position in the professions became the new method for transforming economic capital into cultural capital and thereby preserving social position. As a result, university enrollments also increased sharply at this point.[44]

Under these conditions, the old undifferentiated high school diploma could no longer meet the social mobility aspirations of its clientele, and the old uniform high school curriculum had also become inadequate. In response to the growing number and social diversity of high school students, and to the new credentialing demands of the high school's most influential constituency, school systems in the 1890s began to restructure the graded structure of schooling. Until this point, this structure consisted of a single chain of promotions through a single hierarchy of twelve grades, according to a uniform set of academic criteria. But by the early twentieth century this system had been reconstructed around the organizational and curricular model we have come to call tracking. Instead of one curriculum there were now many, each serving a different constituency and preparing students for different future roles: academic (preparation for college and the professions), commercial (preparation for clerical roles), mechanical (preparation for engineering), industrial (preparation for skilled factory work), normal (preparation for teaching), home economics (preparation for roles as wives and mothers), and special education (for those who couldn't keep up with the rest). Instead of one path for promotion through the grades, there was now a different path through each curriculum track, and each path had its own promotion standards.[45]

This radical transformation of the graded system of schooling thus arose in large part because of changing conditions in the credentials market and the effort by educational leaders to adapt the structure of the school system to these new market conditions. But consumer-based market pressures — and the urge to preserve the benefits of social mobility and social preservation that had always been a part of the graded school system — were not the only factors pushing for this kind of change.

Another source of pressure arose from strong concerns about social efficiency. Echoing earlier complaints about the inflexibility of annual promotions in the graded school system, educational reformers after the turn of the century increasingly aimed their critical attention at the problem they called retardation — the large number of students who had been held back and now clogged the lower grades. In a city like Philadelphia, it took almost ten years for the average student to complete the first eight grades.[46] Critics argued, in part, that this high rate of nonpromotion imposed unnecessary costs on fiscally strapped school districts. Leonard Ayres, whose 1908 book *Laggards in Our Schools* played a leading role in the attack on retardation, pointed out that Philadelphia's school system paid almost $900,000 per year — more than 20 percent of the entire school budget — to teach students who had been retained in grade.[47]

But the attack on retardation extended beyond fiscal concerns. A bigger problem, according to the critics, was the impact that high rates of nonpromotion had on the social efficiency of the whole school system. In his book *The Elimination of Pupils from School*, Edward Thorndike pointed out that the existing structure of schooling seemed to be designed to meet the needs of only the most academically talented students, not the diverse array of students who were by that time filling desks at even the higher levels of the system.[48] By failing to offer curriculum that met the needs of the average student, the system was encouraging these students to abandon schooling altogether. As he put it, "One main cause of elimination is incapacity for and lack of interest in the sort of intellectual work demanded by present courses of study."[49] Ayres agreed with this analysis and argued that the whole system of grading and promotion should be restructured in order to produce the kind of school system that would efficiently meet the most fundamental societal goals for education: "What is the function of our common-schools? If it is to sort out the best of the pupils and prepare them for further education in higher schools, then the most rigorous system, with the severest course of study and the lowest percentage of promotions and the highest percentage of retardation is the best system. But if the function of the common school is, as the author believes, to furnish an elementary education to the maximum number of children, then other things being equal that school is best which regularly promotes and finally graduates the largest percentage of its pupils."[50]

Here we see a full-fledged rationale for both tracking and social promotion. We need tracking because schools are under obligation to supply appropriate courses of study for groups of students with different educational needs, rather than pushing one academic curriculum (designed for only the best students) on everyone. And we need social promotion because nonpromotion scares students away from school — an outcome that is unacceptable, for the purpose of schooling (according to the social efficiency rationale) is to provide a broad education to the entire population and not just advanced training for the academically and socially elite. This argument presents a frontal assault on the meritocratic assumptions underlying the graded structure of schooling as it developed during the nineteenth century. And this assault comes from two familiar sources — the call for greater social efficiency (lowering costs and increasing the effectiveness of schooling) and the call for greater political equality (furnishing a broad "elementary education to the maximum number of children").

As a result of all these pressures, educational leaders reconstructed the graded system of schooling into a form that has persisted to the present day. This new structure of grading has four main characteristics that set it off from its nineteenth-century predecessor. First, it reorganizes the course of study into a series of parallel curriculum tracks. In different tracks, groups of students pursue different courses of study leading to different kinds of future social roles; they move up a promotional ladder within each track, one that is parallel to but separate from the promotional ladders in other tracks.[51] Second, the full set of tracks in the system constitutes a graded hierarchy of its own, based on the future roles for which these tracks prepare students and on the degree of academic rigor that is understood to characterize the work demanded of students within each track. In this hierarchy, the academic or college-preparatory tracks occupy the top rungs and special education and vocational tracks occupy the lowest rungs. Third, schools at the same level but in different communities also occupy different strata in a hierarchy of schools within the complex structure of graded education. This occurs because some schools are understood to be better than others, primarily because they exhibit higher levels of academic achievement, and they are, in turn, generally found in communities with higher levels of income. Fourth, within each track and each school, the rate of student progress through the grades is defined by the norm of social promotion. That is, for the most part students are promoted from grade to grade along with their peers in a particular age cohort, with only a few exceptions.

This new differentiated structure of graded schooling that emerged in the early twentieth century offered valuable services to middle-class families who were looking for a mechanism that would mark their children off from the pack, a service that the earlier promotion system could no longer provide. First, it furnished a high school track that would usher students directly into the university and the world of middle-class jobs, giving them the academic preparation they would need to make this transition successfully. Second, it conferred a distinctive credential upon graduation from the upper track or from an upper-crust high school that helped label the recipient as worthy of access to a good college and a good job.[52]

Under these circumstances, the old way of gaining socially advantageous educational distinction—through the competitive pursuit of meritocratic achievement—was no longer either necessary or desirable. It was not necessary because the same benefit could be obtained by securing placement for one's child in the upper track or the upper-level school. It was not desirable because meritocratic competition was a risky proposition, one that prevented many middle-class children from winning the desired social rewards during the nineteenth century simply because they failed to make the grade academically. In contrast, it was a much safer proposition to place one's child in the right track or school and then watch the process of social promotion move that child predictably up the ladder to college and social position. In this sense, the loss of merit promotion under the new system was no loss at all for these middle-class parents, because track placement became a stand-in for achievement, and top-track students received credentials with the greatest meritocratic cachet without having to compete with everyone else to acquire them.[53]

Resurrecting Merit Promotion

After the groundwork was laid at the start of the twentieth century for the reconstruction of the graded system of schooling, tracking fell into place quickly, but the practice of social promotion emerged more gradually. The first stage, the definition of "overageness" as a problem, occurred in the 1910s, when the annual reports of school systems began to provide regular data on the age distribution of students in the various grades. The next step was the shift toward promotion "with conditions." Under this transitional system, administrators encouraged the promotion of students with their age group if possible; students who failed to pass particular subjects would be promoted subject to their expunging these deficiencies.[54] This procedure increased promotion rates and reduced overageness, but it created enormous administrative complexity, as schools tried to keep track of where students were in particular subjects, and it also created a considerable burden on students, who often reacted to the accumulation of deficiencies by dropping out of school. Partly for these reasons and partly as a result of the depression-induced increase in high school enrollments in the 1930s, full-scale social promotion came into its own in the 1940s, and rates of nonpromotion continued to fall nationally for the next thirty years.

Then, starting in the late 1970s, rates of nonpromotion started going up again nationally, and proponents of educational reform since then have strongly supported this trend. In 1983 the National Commission on Excellence in Education, in its report *A Nation at Risk,* advocated raised academic standards at all levels of the system, including increased requirements for promotion, high school graduation, and college admission. The report included a specific attack on social promotion: "Placement and grouping of students, as well as promotion and graduation policies, should be guided by the academic progress of students and their instructional needs, rather than by rigid adherence to age."[55] More recently Goals 2000, a joint effort of the federal and state governments to set national educational goals, pressed for higher academic standards and tougher performance requirements for promotion. According to the list of national goals, "By the year 2000, all students will leave grades 4, 8, and 12 having demonstrated competency over challenging subject matter including English, mathematics, science, foreign languages, civics and government, economics, arts, history, and geography."[56] Presumably, those who can't demonstrate such competency won't be promoted.

The national education summit in March 1996 inspired more talk about standards and promotion. Cohost Louis Gerstner, the chairman of IBM, asserted that "standards are the starting point, the sine qua non of school reform," and President Clinton asked for "meaningful standards" in the schools, in a speech in which he used the word *standards* forty times:

> I believe every state, if you're going to have meaningful standards, must require a test for children to move . . . from elementary to middle school, or

from middle school to high school, or to have a full-meaning high school diploma. And I don't think they should measure just minimum competency. You should measure what you expect these standards to measure. . . .

You will never know whether your standards are being met unless you have some sort of measurement and have some sort of accountability. And while I believe [standards] should be set by the states and the testing mechanism should be approved by the states, we shouldn't kid ourselves. Being promoted ought to mean more or less the same thing in Pasadena, California, that it does in Palisades, New York. In a global society, it ought to mean more or less the same thing.[57]

Meanwhile the Detroit Board of Education approved a new policy in April 1996 that required all students to meet specific exit-skill requirements in order to be promoted to the next grade.[58] And in the same month, the New York State Board of Regents announced its intention to require all students to pass the rigorous Regents examination in order to receive a high school diploma: "The new policy will be phased in starting this fall and will have the greatest impact on New York City schools, where only about 21 percent of the students successfully completed the battery of tests needed to earn a Regents diploma last year. Most of the rest earned local diplomas that are held in much lower regard. Eventually under the plan, the state's public schools will stop offering such local diplomas."[59]

With merit promotion now on the upswing, both in rhetoric and in practice, we need to consider why this change is happening and why it is happening now. Growing concern about the social efficiency of education is one obvious factor that helps explain the resurgence of interest in academic standards and merit promotion. Worries about American economic competitiveness internationally have focused attention on lagging measures of worker productivity, and this uneasiness in turn leads to questions about whether students are acquiring an adequate amount of economically useful knowledge in school. Proposing the elevation of academic standards for student promotions is a natural response to these kinds of concerns.[60]

Here, however, I will focus on two less visible factors that have helped bring about this change in the last two decades, both of which are long-standing themes in the saga of graded schooling and promotion policy in this country. One is social—the continuing demand among middle-class educational consumers for a system of schooling that can make and preserve social distinctions among students. The other is ideological—the continuing U.S. commitment to the ideal of meritocratic rewards in the schools.

From the perspective of the middle-class educational consumer, the key benefit that education has supplied over the years has been its ability to provide graduates with a credential that separates them from the herd. The distinction conveys an advantage for the credential holder in the competition for good jobs and comfortable social positions. But all this depends on a condition of relative scarcity in the credentials market. This condition evaporated for middle-class high school graduates at the turn of the century with the rapid increase of enrollments and graduates at this level. In response, the system shifted toward a differentiated structure of credentials, and these consumers for the next half century successfully rode the upper track into the university, where credentials remained sufficiently scarce that they could sustain a high exchange value and thus provide the desired degree of cultural advantage.

But by the 1960s, high school and college graduation rates reached saturation levels as a flood of baby boomers poured into a rapidly expanding college sector. As a result, the credentials market became glutted with degrees and exchange value began to decline. One sign of this was a decline in the economic returns on a college degree: "After increasing at an annual growth rate of 1.65 percent between 1963 and 1968, the returns to a college degree had a negative growth rate (-.42 [percent]) between 1969 and 1974 and an even worse growth rate (-.67 [percent]) between 1975 and 1980. At the time, the returns differential between a college degree and a high school diploma declined by almost a third between 1971 and 1979 for young graduates."[61] As a result, the system of graded schooling that was reconstructed at the start of the century was no longer able to produce the kinds of benefits that middle-class consumers sought. Increasingly, these families were forced to take a more defensive posture in an environment characterized by credential inflation and declining exchange values.[62] Lester Thurow analyzed the situation this way:

> As a supply of educated labor increases, individuals find that they must improve their educational level simply to defend their current income positions. If they don't others will and they will find current jobs no longer open to them. Education becomes a good investment not because it would raise people's incomes above what they would have been if no one had increased his education, but rather because it raises their income above what it will be if others acquire an education and they do not. In effect, education becomes a defensive expenditure necessary to protect one's "market share." The larger the class of educated labor and the more rapidly it grows, the more such defensive expenditures become imperative.[63]

More recently, the economic returns on education have started to increase again, along with the differential in earnings between high school and college graduates, but the status attainment problems of the middle class remain. There is a strong and persistent oversupply of college graduates relative to the number of openings in jobs that traditionally require such a degree as a minimum entry requirement, and this condition is projected to grow. A study by the Bureau of Labor Statistics shows that of the 29 million college graduates in the workforce in 1990, 5.8 million (or nearly 20 percent) were "educationally underutilized" — that is, they occupied jobs that did not require a college degree.[64] Between 1990 and 2005, the study projects that the number of college graduates will grow faster than the number of college-level jobs, with the result that 30 percent of these graduates will have to settle for a job below this level.[65]

Under these conditions of glut, credential inflation, and declining prospects for exchanging a college degree for a good job, middle-class consumers are justified in feeling that the educational system is not producing the kind of competitive advantage they want. At one level, this leads to a general perception that quality and standards in education are in a dangerous state of decline, because schooling is no longer able to provide the same automatic benefit that it did in the recent past. The obvious response to this problem is for these influential consumers to demand higher standards for curriculum, instruction, admission, and promotion in education at all levels — which is exactly what we are hearing in rhetoric of educational reform these days. At another level, the situation leads individual consumers to seek out solutions that will provide them with some kind of competitive advantage in an effort to get ahead in poor market conditions, a way to separate their children from other people's children. Here the obvious response is to call for a solution that is as old as the public school system itself: create more losers in order to make space for the winners. Most of the current strategies that fall under the heading of academic standards would in fact help achieve this end. Making promotion from grade to grade more difficult, raising the level of achievement required to obtain a high school diploma, and increasing standards for admission to college — all would increase the number of failures and thereby increase the relative benefit that educational credentials will be able to provide for those who succeed.[66]

The other factor behind the rise in merit promotion is ideological. One clue about the nature of this ideological factor can be taken from an observation early in this chapter. Nonpromotion never completely disappeared in this country, especially at key transition points between levels in the system — grades one, six or seven, and nine or ten. Nationally, nonpromotion bottomed out in the late 1970s at a rate of about 5 percent; that is, roughly 5 percent of all students in the K–12 system were held back during the course of a given year.[67] But this means that even at the low point for merit promotion, retention still affected a large number of students during their school careers: in 1976 almost 25 percent of sixteen-year-olds were overage for their grade.[68]

This suggests that U.S. educators have continued to hold onto the principle of merit promotion even when its practice was sharply reduced.

The simple fact is that meritocratic ideology is so central to American conceptions of fairness and due process that it cannot be eradicated from the practice of any institution that wants to call itself a school. No school is a "real school" without it.[69] Even after the dramatic changes at the turn of the century — when middle-class consumers and educational reformers succeeded in turning the coldly competitive structure of graded schooling and merit promotion into a multitrack structure with buffered competition and social promotion — the merit ideal remained integral to schooling. In part, that idea survived because the merit-based promotion ladder was transformed into a merit-defined hierarchy of curriculum tracks. In this hierarchy, each track was located in a continuum between high and low levels of merit, and the students in these tracks were automatically assigned the level of merit associated with their track location. With track as a proxy for merit, the real struggle was to get the right track placement; once that was accomplished, there was much less need for a competitive promotion process within each track.

Placement has not been sufficient, however, to provide full legitimacy to an educational system whose primary ideological grounding is in notions of meritocracy. In recent years, critics have mounted a withering attack on tracking on the grounds that it is both undemocratic and unmeritocratic. As studies consistently show, track placements are often more closely related to social class and race than to the academic performance of individual students.[70] The very property that has made the system of tracking and social promotion until recently so effective in meeting the status attainment needs of its middle-class constituents — its ability to protect students from free-for-all competition and to make success a self-fulfilling prophecy for those located in the top tracks — has also undermined the claim that track placement is an adequate proxy for merit.[71] From a meritocratic perspective, social promotion is acceptable only if the merit is embodied in the track placement, a situation that then permits everyone to relax the competitive process. (For example, once students are admitted to Harvard they very rarely flunk out; the understanding is that they earned the right to be there because of academic merit, and therefore subsequent failure is highly unlikely.) When the merit basis for this placement is less clearly established, however, the presence of social promotion poses a serious threat to the face validity of the entire educational system.

The consequence of this situation is that the educational system is compelled to defend the legitimacy of its ritual classification of students. As Meyer and Rowan suggest, the heart of educational organizations is their systems of classification, and therefore they must be vigilant in defining, defending, and controlling these systems.[72] One such system — the classification of students into grades based on individual academic merit — is fundamental to our cultural understanding of what constitutes a school in this country. The defense of this process took two forms during the middle portion of this century. First, merit promotion never disappeared entirely but persisted at a modest level. Enough students failed in order to provide at least anecdotal evidence that failure was possible and that the students who did gain promotion achieved this reward through their own efforts. Without failure, success is meritocratically meaningless; and without a merit criterion for success, schools fail to meet institutional expectations for what a school should be. Second, merit promotion began to make a comeback. The growing challenge to the benefits of tracking, combined with the growing failure of educational credentials to provide students with a boost in the job market, meant that educational leaders found it increasingly difficult to defend the practice of social promotion. Under these circumstances, the legitimacy of education as an institution was at risk unless educational leaders could succeed in reasserting the social salience and meritocratic power of its system of grading and promoting students. This, as we have seen, is exactly what they have been trying to do, by calling for (and to a lesser extent implementing) higher academic standards and tougher promotion rules.

Where does all this leave us? It seems that the ongoing effort in the United States to measure the effect of promotion policy on student achievement and emotional adjustment is an important pursuit for both pedagogical and ethical reasons; but the educational effectiveness of promotion practices is largely irrelevant to the story of why these practices came into existence, why they changed over time, and why they persist today. Instead, it turns out that many of the main forces shaping the history of these practices have little to do with the production of smart or well-adjusted children. One such force is the ideological demand for adherence to the principle of academic advancement according to individual merit, and the corollary requirement that real schools should publicly demonstrate their commitment to this principle. The other is the consumer demand for a form of schooling that consistently creates educational distinctions that can be translated into social advantages. Under these circumstances, then, the paradoxical position of the average parent toward nonpromotion makes very good sense: failing the low achiever is an excellent idea — as long as it happens to someone else's child.

3

Raising Standards in the American High School: Why the Good Old Days Are Not Much Help

In 1983 a series of high-level panels issued reports charging that education in the United States had lost sight of what had once been its dominant objective — the pursuit of academic excellence. The findings kicked off what turned into a national movement to raise academic standards. By far the most influential of these reports was titled *A Nation at Risk,* whose authors, the National Commission on Excellence in Education, issued a remarkably gloomy assessment of the situation facing U.S. schools.[1] The report's opening paragraph employed a language of disaster and decline that set the tone for the entire standards movement:

> Our nation is at risk. Our once unchallenged preeminence in commerce, industry, science, and technological innovation is being overtaken by competitors throughout the world. This report is concerned with only one of the many causes and dimensions of the problem, but it is the one that undergirds American prosperity, security, and civility. We report to the American people that while we can take justifiable pride in what our schools and colleges have historically accomplished and contributed to the United States and the well-being of its people, the educational foundations of our society are presently being eroded by a rising tide of mediocrity that threatens our very future as a Nation and a people. What was unimaginable a generation ago has begun to occur — others are matching and surpassing our educational attainments.[2]

This report and others issued in the years that followed placed blame for the decline in excellence on all levels of the educational system — from the elementary schools, which are accused of failing to ground students sufficiently in basic skills, to colleges, which are charged with failing to provide necessary advanced training. But the public high school has received the greatest critical attention, and for good reason. Students may experience a deficient academic education early in their educational careers, but these deficiencies are likely to accumulate over time and thus become more serious and more visible in high school. And because high school is the most advanced level of schooling at which enrollment is universal, these deficiencies affect a broader spectrum of the population than do the failings of colleges.

Perhaps the most frequently cited evidence of the decline in achievement at U.S. high schools is the drop in scores on the College Board's Scholastic Aptitude Test (SAT), a point that was emphasized in *A Nation at Risk*.[3] For example, between 1966–1967 and 1993–1994, the average combined score for the math and verbal portions of the test fell from 958 to 902.[4] This is not the most compelling proof that could be offered, however, for the decline in scores occurred during a period when the number of students enrolled in college increased by 142 percent and the number of high school graduates actually went down.[5] In fact, for high school students with a similar class rank, there has been no significant change.[6] The drop in test scores thus may be the result of an expansion of educational opportunity rather than a reduction in student achievement.

This same caveat applies to another favorite example of growing mediocrity in U.S. high schools. The Commission on Excellence noted that students in the United States scored low on achievement tests compared with students from other industrialized countries, but as Husen and others have pointed out, this difference is the result of differences in the selectivity of the various systems of secondary schooling.[7] "Such differences mean that American student-achievement scores may look bad simply because they are gathered from the full range of students in the country, whereas scores from other countries are gathered from biased samples."[8]

But if much of the evidence about low levels of achievement among U.S. high school students is unconvincing, the evidence is stronger that high schools in the United States have not succeeded in promoting a high level of academic learning. There is little doubt that the modern high school has a curriculum that is less academic and performance standards that are less demanding than was once the case. *A Nation at Risk* notes that the growth of electives in the high school curriculum has permitted students to avoid the more difficult academic courses, with the result that by 1979 only 31 percent of high school graduates took intermediate algebra, 13 percent took French, and 6 percent took calculus. At the same time, general-track students earned 25 percent of their credits in such subjects as physical and health education, remedial skills, and personal development.[9] This state of affairs seems to reflect a long-term decline in the academic portion of high school course work during the twentieth century. Between 1928 and 1961, for example, the proportion of total high school course enrollments that were devoted to academic subjects fell from 67 percent to 57 percent, continuing a trend that began in the late nineteenth century.[10]

At the same time that the academic content of the high school curriculum has grown thinner, the rigor of high school pedagogy has also declined. One expression of this phenomenon is a lowered level of required work. Over time, the language in textbooks has grown simpler, and demands for student performance have grown weaker. The 1983 report notes, for example, that two-thirds of high school seniors reported having less than one hour of homework per night. And while the amount of academic work has fallen, grades have been rising, which means that grades do not serve to measure a student's academic performance as they once did.[11] At the same time, a student's promotion from one grade to another is less likely to indicate mastery of the subject matter at the previous level. Instead of winning promotion on the basis of academic merit, students increasingly have been "socially" promoted as a matter of administrative routine in order to keep students together with others in their age group.[12]

In response to such complaints, a movement to raise academic standards arose during the 1980s and 1990s, and this movement has apparently borne some fruit. Since the early 1980s a variety of indicators of academic excellence have been on the increase. Students are once again taking more academic courses after a century of decline.[13] Between 1982 and 1992, the number of Carnegie units in academic subjects taken by the average high school graduate rose from 12.7 to 15.7.[14] During the same period, rates of nonpromotion have been rising, states have been raising curriculum requirements for high school graduation requirements, schools have been using tests of academic performance increasingly as a prerequisite for advancement, and a number of groups have been working vigorously to establish state and national standards for achievement in individual academic subjects.[15] And even before the College Board recalibrated the SAT, test scores had begun to rise.[16]

Both the academic critique of the public high school in the United States and the effort to raise academic standards within this institution are grounded in a vision of general educational decline. According to critics and reformers, the public high school is no longer dedicated to academic excellence as it once was. A tone of nostalgia suffuses the rhetoric of the standards movement, reflecting a desire to turn back the clock to the time when high schools taught the tough academic subjects and made students demonstrate mastery of these subjects. From this perspective, the grades, credits, and diplomas offered by the public high school really stood for something during its golden age (usually located in the nineteenth and early twentieth centuries) but have now become a debased form of educational currency, as once-proud badges of merit have turned into mere tokens of attendance.[17]

Although the ghost of the U.S. high school during this golden age hovers over the current debate, its inner workings are not very well understood. There is a vague perception of the early high school as a more austere and arduous place than its modern counterpart, but this perception has never been convincingly documented. Edward Krug's two-volume history of the high school in the United States, for example, picks up the story in the 1880s, sixty years after the first high schools were established, and it focuses primarily on national-level trends in curriculum policy.[18] In addition, there have been a number of studies of the early high school, but none of these has sought to establish how academically rigorous the early high school really was or what conditions might have made this rigor possible.[19]

This chapter draws from my earlier study of the first one hundred years of Central High School, Philadelphia's oldest and most prominent public high school.[20] This is a school with a strong commitment to academic excellence and one whose pedagogical practices were once rigorous to the point of harshness. Founded in 1838, it was one of the first public high schools in the United States. For the next fifty years it was the city's only public high school for boys, and today it is still considered the best. (A sister institution, Girls High School, was established in 1848.)

Central, like many early high schools, presented a curriculum that was heavily academic and held students to a performance standard that was intensely meritocratic. The conditions that supported this kind of academic rigor, however, were unique to a time when few people attended high school and when these schools could afford to be highly selective in their approach to teaching and learning at the secondary level. The conditions facing the high school today are much more demanding, for it must offer a curriculum that meets the needs of the entire teenage population rather than the select group of volunteers who populated its predecessor one hundred years ago. In short, the model of the U.S. high school during the good old days provides us with little help in meeting the challenges of high school education at the turn of the twenty-first century. We are better off dealing with the academic problems of the present with the tools that are appropriate for that task rather than trying to hold the contemporary high school to a standard from the past that, under current circumstances, is both unattainable and undesirable.

Central's Curriculum: Strictly Academic

During Central High School's first fifty years, its presidents liked to characterize the school's curriculum as "practical." This did not mean that the school was offering vocational training; in fact, vocational courses like stenography and bookkeeping never occupied more than 12 percent of a student's time during this period. Instead, the curriculum was practical in that it was intended to prepare students in a general way for direct entry into commercial life, by stressing sciences and modern languages, rather than for admission to college, which required a heavy dose of classics to the exclusion of modern subjects. To the modern eye, Central's practical curriculum appears heavily academic and restrictive. Indeed, from 1856 to 1889 there was no choice at all: everyone took the same classes. During the rest of the century students could choose from among several courses of study, but within these programs electives were few or nonexistent.

All students entering school in 1871, for example, had to take six yearlong units of science, four units each of mathematics, English, history, and drawing, three units of classical languages, two and a half units of a modern language, and three units of vocational courses over the course of four years.[21] Such nonacademic and nonvocational courses as health, physical education, and personal development were absent from Central's course of study. In contrast to the National Commission on Excellence in Education's complaint about the "cafeteria-style curriculum [of the modern high school] in which the appetizers and desserts can easily be mistaken for the main course," more than one hundred years ago Central High School was offering a fixed menu consisting entirely of main courses, emphasizing the subject areas now considered the most difficult in the liberal arts spectrum — science, mathematics, and foreign languages.[22]

In 1889 the uniform practical curriculum was replaced by two alternative courses of study — a college-preparatory course, with an intensified academic content, and a commercial course made up of approximately 80 percent academic subjects and 20 percent vocational material. In 1912 a mechanical (engineering) course was added, with roughly the same mix of academic and vocational subjects as the commercial course. Seven years later an industrial course was introduced, which committed 40 percent of the student's time to vocational pursuits. Thus by 1920 Central was edging in the direction of the modern high school, offering a variety of elective courses of study, most of which represented a dilution of the academic work demanded by the older curriculum.[23]

Central's Pedagogy: Mercilessly Meritocratic

Not only did the early Central High School subject its students to a relentlessly academic curriculum, but it also judged their performance according to a high standard of academic merit. By this standard, the school found few students who were worthy of admission and fewer still who were deserving of its diploma. Attrition was high at all levels of public education in the nineteenth century, and the biggest factor encouraging students to exit from the system was social class. Philadelphia's school system assumed the shape of a pyramid, its lowest grades populous, its upper grades increasingly exclusive. In 1880, for example, 52.3 percent of the students in the entire school system were in grades one and two, 24.6 percent were in grades three and four, 14.6 percent were in grades five through eight, and only 1.4 percent attended the two high schools. (The remaining 7.1 percent attended consolidated schools covering grades one through eight.)[24] Many students from working-class families were under pressure to quit school and go to work, and this pressure was most severe among high school–age boys, for whom the opportunity cost of attending school was prohibitively high. In a study of Hamilton, Ontario, during the 1860s and 1870s, for example, Katz and Davey found that the school attendance of working-class teenage boys was lower than that of middle-class boys and was inversely proportional to the availability of jobs.[25]

As a result, Central students were disproportionately middle class in origin. From 1840 to 1920 the middle classes consistently supplied two-thirds of the student population, although they accounted for only one-quarter to one-third of the city's household heads. At the same time the semiskilled and unskilled working classes were notably underrepresented at the school.[26]

Although the pool of candidates seeking admission to the high school was shaped by class considerations, the procedures employed by the school for selecting students from this pool were scrupulously meritocratic. Throughout the nineteenth century the competition for admission to Central was intense, and for most of this period the admission decision hinged entirely on a student's score on a written entrance examination. Grammar school masters from around the city sent only their best students to take this exam, after careful academic preparation. In spite of this preselection and preparation, between 20 percent and 50 percent of the students tested each year failed to achieve a score high enough for admission.[27] Central's student body, therefore, was composed of the most academically able sons of the city's middle classes.

Once admitted, Central students found themselves in a tough academic environment that provided no special privileges for the socioeconomically advantaged. The work was hard and the outcome was by no means guaranteed. During Central's first eighty-two years, only 26.9 percent of its students graduated. Most students left during their first two years. Out of all the students that entered between 1838 and 1920, 37.1 percent had dropped out by the end of the first year, 60.9 percent by the end of the second year, and 71.6 percent by the end of the third year. In addition, half of those who left prior to graduation were forced to repeat at least one term while at the school.[28]

Class helps explain the process of admission to Central High School, but it provides no help in explaining a student's chances for graduation. The graduation rate varied little from one social class to another. Overall, students from the proprietary middle class, employed middle class, skilled working class, and unskilled working class graduated at rates of 29, 26, 27, and 27 percent, respectively.[29] This means that Central had such a high rate of attrition not because so many students had to quit to go to work but because so many students of all classes failed to make the grade. During the school's first eighty-two years, students who attained academic honors at some point during their career at the high school (an average of 85 or higher) graduated at a rate of 72.5 percent, while those without any honors grades graduated at a rate of 19.8 percent. Even the best students had to struggle to meet the expectations of the Central faculty. One-third of the hardy and high-performing survivors in the 1910 and 1920 cohorts who succeeded in winning a Central diploma were compelled to repeat one or more terms during their high school careers.[30]

The addition of a variety of control variables does nothing to alter the conclusion that Central was thoroughly meritocratic in selecting its graduates. Multiple classification analyses of student chances for graduation revealed that such factors as nativity, birth order, family structure, siblings at work, prior school, and age had only modest impact. In conjunction with these variables, class exerted little or no influence on graduation, while student grades continued to be by far the most significant factor.[31]

In short, the early Central High School was thoroughly grounded in the principle of academic excellence. Although the socioeconomically able dominated the applicant pool (because they could afford to attend high school instead of going to work), only the most academically able of these actually won admission. Once admitted, students found themselves in an environment where their survival depended almost entirely on personal academic achievement. Uncompromising in its application of this single standard of evaluation, Central's faculty presided over a system of instruction that was both highly selective and scrupulously fair. The selectivity was dramatic: for example, in 1880 one boy in five from Philadelphia primary schools attended grammar school, one in fifty attended the high school, and only one in two hundred graduated.[32] But Central graduates earned their place at the apex of Philadelphia's elongated educational pyramid only through an intensive academic competition, especially during their high school years.

The Social Basis for Central's Meritocratic Character

The evidence is compelling that the early Central High School was a model academic meritocracy. The existence of this kind of institution in the early history of the American high school makes it understandable that contemporary reformers might wax nostalgic about the good old days and might want to want to return the high school of today to its earlier elevated position. But this response fails to take into account that Central's dedication to academic excellence developed from a peculiar and unreproducible set of social conditions within the school and the community. These conditions include the following:

1. *Cultural commitment to the merit principle.* Meritocratic ideology provided one of the primary influences over the founding and development of Central High School. This ideology seeks to accommodate democratic beliefs in political equality to the capitalist reality of economic inequality, and it does so through the concept of individual merit. From this perspective, the focus shifts from equality of outcomes to equality of opportunity: a level playing field is provided at the start of the competition regardless of social position, and unequal outcomes of this competition are explained as a result of the unequal merit of the individual competitors. Speaking to a group of alumni in 1851, one of Central High School's founders, Thomas Dunlap, defined the school's goals in just such terms:

> It is the School of the Republic — it is emphatically the School of the People . . . opening its portals alike to the son of a President or a ploughman, a Governor or his groom, a millionaire or a hewer of wood — treating with equal justice — rearing with equal fidelity, and crowning with all its honors alike the one and the other, and demanding no passport to its blessings, or to its laurels, save that which the people demand, and forever will demand from all its sons — INDIVIDUAL, PERSONAL MERIT.
>
> Such, fellow citizens, is your High School.[33]

This strong ideological charter for the school gave it an extraordinary degree of institutional autonomy, just the sort that it needed in order to impose and maintain its relentlessly meritocratic regime. As a result, throughout most of the nineteenth century Central managed to resist powerful political pressures to relax its standards in order to allow more students to attend and graduate from this very attractive institution, and it continued to fail just as many millionaires as hewers of wood.

2. *Voluntary enrollment of students.* Students attended Central because they wanted to and their families wanted them to. This voluntarism provided the faculty and students with a community of purpose which it would not otherwise have had. Central was a largely middle-class school, but it was even more homogeneous ideologically than it was in class terms. Its reputation for limited choice, focused academic curriculum, and meritocratic rigor was well established. Parents from any social class who disliked the things that the school stood for could and did keep their sons away, but those who chose to send their sons thereby announced their willingness to support the school's high academic standards. The result was a school with a tightly focused mission and a high degree of shared commitment in support of this mission.

3. *Competitive selection of students.* Until the entrance exam was abolished in 1900, the school also exercised a choice, based only on academic merit. By deliberately selecting only the most academically able students, the high school reinforced its own commitment to merit and shaped a student body that demonstrably thrived on competition. These winners in the struggle for academic achievement were unlikely to question the legitimacy of Central's own harsh system of merit selection. Even that large majority of students who dropped out or were eliminated before graduation were likely to have accepted the outcome as fair: they had performed well enough to enter the school but not well enough to graduate. At the same time, any students who were unhappy with the academic intensity of the school could simply be asked to leave if they did not do so voluntarily, which meant that the school did not have to contend with internal resistance to its way of doing things. Thus voluntarism and selectivity produced a relatively high degree of ideological homogeneity in the entering class, while selective attrition enhanced the homogeneity of the upperclassmen even further.

4. *Competitive selection of the faculty.* Central's faculty had even more reason to be committed to a regime of academic excellence than the students, particularly during the nineteenth century. Between 1860 and 1900 approximately half of the Central High School faculty was drawn from the rarefied ranks of Central graduates, which means that these men had already achieved a high degree of academic success, proving themselves against the school's

own exacting merit standard. By selecting alumni for the faculty, the school's oversight committee was picking men who could act as role models of academic merit for the next generation of students, men whose personal experience was living confirmation to themselves and their charges that meritocracy at Central was both a reality and a blessing. In addition, between 1860 and 1890 approximately half of these men had proved their merit pedagogically by rising through the ranks of public school teachers.[34] Typically, they won the promotion from grammar school master to high school professor on the basis of their success in preparing students to pass the high school entrance exam. In the mid-nineteenth century, therefore, Central's professors and students formed a closed and self-perpetuating system for rewarding academic achievement and transmitting meritocratic values.

5. *The pyramid of public education.* In the nineteenth century, the rate of attrition after the primary grades was quite high. The implications of this for Central High School were important. First, because attrition was high at all levels of the system, the high school's 75 percent dropout rate was seen not as a social problem but as part of a natural process of selecting the most worthy. That so few graduated from high school made the receipt of a diploma a rare honor. Because dropping out was the norm, it brought no connotation of shame. (After all, dropouts had succeeded in winning admission, itself quite an accomplishment.) Second, because Central was located at the very apex of the pyramid, it offered unique attractions. In the absence of competitors, Central could offer credentials bearing enormous prestige, and a large number of students were drawn to compete for admission to the school in the hope of earning these valued credentials. The scarcity of high schools and the rarity of graduation provided a powerful stimulus for student achievement. School officials were well aware of the social and educational consequences of the school's dominant position in public education. Alexander Dallas Bache, the man who served as the school's first head, put it this way in a speech to Central alumni:

> It seems to me that public education is like one of those great pyramids of eastern work, broad at the base, and gradually and gracefully tapering to its vertex, the number of its recipients, like the number of stones, decreasing from the base. That it is, in the accommodations needed, like a great ocean from which you pass to a wide and capacious bay, thence into a mighty river, thence, mounting towards the source, to a stream. That public education, to be thoroughly useful, should be general, the broad base of the pyramid; the ocean, vast, unlimited, with room and verge enough for all. Circumstances determine that the numbers who frequent the grammar school shall be less than those who pass through the primary, and so onward; the pyramid narrowing, the bay contracting.[35]

Comparisons with the Modern Public High School

The social conditions that provided the basis for Central High School's intense commitment to academic achievement during the nineteenth century are largely lacking in the modern public high school in the United States. Contrast the following characteristics of the modern high school with the traits discussed above:

1. *Continued commitment to the merit principle but a growing array of unmeritocratic educational practices.* Meritocracy is stronger in principle than it is in practice in the modern public high school. Merit is the key to the legitimacy of the entire educational system, which presents itself as a fair and open mechanism for allocating people to social positions based on educational achievement. This means that schools must be seen by the public as providing individual students with educational rewards — such as grades, credits, and degrees — in accordance with their academic performance. In the absence of this kind of meritocratic process, schooling appears merely arbitrary or, worse yet, appears to promote the transmission of social advantages from one generation to the next.

Under these circumstances, nonmeritocratic practices in schools become a source of outrage for parents and citizens and a source of severe embarrassment for teachers and administrators. Yet it is just such practices that have been growing increasingly common within the American high school during the twentieth century. All the things that the standards movement has been complaining about for the past two decades — grade inflation, social promotion, increased numbers of nonacademic courses, lowered demands for academic performance, little assigned homework, and so on — are part of the nonmeritocratic trend. Because the merit principle remains largely unquestioned by parents and educators alike, these nonmeritocratic practices are an easy target; and educational practitioners find themselves in the awkward position of defending policies that they may not believe in, or at least that they may not be able to justify in meritocratic terms. In sum, there has been a decline in meritocratic process in the modern public high school, but there has been no corresponding renunciation of the principle of merit. The resulting contradiction is quite awkward for everyone concerned.

2. *Compulsory attendance.* In all fifty states, students are required by law to attend school until at least the age of sixteen, and in seven states attendance is required until a student reaches eighteen.[36] As a result, high school enrollment is in effect mandatory. This loss of voluntarism is perhaps the most important difference between the modern high school and its predecessor. Voluntarism encouraged ideological homogeneity in the old Central High School, just as it does in contemporary private and Catholic schools.[37] Students who were not

interested in pursuing academic excellence simply did not enroll at Central; likewise, parents today do not enroll their children in a private or Catholic school unless they either share its values or are willing to abide by them.

The modern public high school, however, is filled with conscripts, not volunteers. In this situation there is no natural consensus among the students around the core values of the school and no reason to believe that students will necessarily be eager to devote themselves to intensive academic pursuits. Middle-class students may well buy what school is selling, because the experience of their families and friends tells them that schooling is a good investment in a comfortable future. But students from the lower class or working class, who see all around them evidence that the future is precarious and the relevance of education questionable, may calculate quite rationally that the ultimate payoff for academic excellence — getting a good job, securing a comfortable future — is not a realistic prospect for them and therefore does not justify a major investment of time and effort in schoolwork.[38] Compelling students to attend high school when they have reason to doubts its benefits and reject its academic work ethic, therefore, brings apathy and resistance into the institution, severely undermining its ability to promote a strong and single-minded atmosphere of academic achievement. In short, compulsory attendance has helped kill the consensus of purpose that supported the meritocratic practices of the old high school.

3. Automatic acceptance of students. Not only are students now required to attend high school, but the typical public high school is required to accept and retain all students from its geographical area. These regional comprehensive high schools have no entrance exams or admission requirements, except that the student must have completed the eighth or ninth grade, and they have no provisions for academic expulsion. Students do not need to believe in the value of rigorous studies or to demonstrate academic achievement in order to enter the high school or to remain there, so the modern high school contains students who are frequently both unwilling and unable to do serious academic work.

The result is that the modern high school is attempting to promote educational achievement in a context in which students may not value this goal and the school cannot offer them access to valuable educational commodities, such as a scarce and economically rewarding high school diploma. By contrast, the professors at Central High School in the nineteenth century had a relatively easy setting in which to create a model of meritocracy. They had a voluntary and selective student body whose members were predisposed toward the school's meritocratic ideology, had already demonstrated academic excellence in order to enter the school, and knew that they had to perform at a truly exceptional level to graduate.

A variety of private, Catholic, and special public high schools share the voluntarism and selectivity that helped make possible the dedication to academic excellence at the early Central High School. Private schools can choose whom to admit and whom to expel; Catholic schools and public magnet schools may not be as free to select incoming students, but they may expel or remove students, and they also enjoy the benefits of having only those students who want to be there. These special advantages that such schools enjoy are unaccountably ignored by researchers like James Coleman and Anthony Bryk, who argue that Catholic high schools in particular are more effective than public high schools in promoting academic achievement among students from all social classes.[39] They control for the effects of such family traits as class and race and such educational traits as prior academic achievement, but they fail to consider the extent to which parents and students are ideologically oriented toward the academic aims of the school before enrollment. Therefore, they attribute the superior academic performance of private and Catholic school students to the curriculum, instruction, and culture of these schools — rather than to the selection effect that arises from the school's ability to attract, choose, and retain only those students who buy into (or at least are willing to submit to) the school's climate of academic achievement.[40]

A special case is presented by a small but influential group of voluntary and selective modern public high schools. The present Central High School is such a place. After spending the first three decades of the twentieth century as an ordinary regional high school, it was restored to something of its former status in 1939. Since that time, Central has admitted boys from all over the city (and girls as well, starting in 1983), but only if they choose to apply and if they have high grades and test scores. These conditions have allowed Central to become rededicated to academic achievement: students who apply know that they are taking on a greater challenge than they would find in a regional high school, but they are motivated to respond to this challenge by the knowledge that a Central diploma carries greater value in the marketplace for educational credentials.

In a society that compels students to go to school until the age of sixteen and expects them to complete high school, however, few public high schools can operate on a voluntary and selective basis. School systems must provide secondary education for that large majority of the students in the community who either do not want, or do not qualify for, an intensively academic public high school (or do not want, do not qualify for, or cannot afford a private or Catholic high school).

As a result, the new Central High School has a very different impact on the school system than did the old Central. When the school was founded, it was one of a kind; students who did not go there could attend private school or go to work. The creation of the high school added another layer to the school system, which attracted middle-class support to the public schools and for-tified total enrollment. The modern voluntary and selective public high school, however — like the modern private and Catholic school — draws students who otherwise would have attended a regional high school. Instead of creating a new level of education, all of these schools drain students from one segment of secondary education into another as part of a zero-sum game. This is a sure way to create a meritocratic school. There is good reason to conclude, however, that such a rarefied creation will not promote higher levels of ag-gregate educational achievement across all schools but instead will undercut average achievement in the regional high schools by removing their most motivated students.

4. Less competitive selection of teachers. At the early Central High School, professors were chosen out of the exclusive and meritorious community of high school graduates. Today, however, as the National Commission on Excel-lence notes in a familiar complaint about the present reality, "Too many teach-ers are being drawn from the bottom quarter of graduating high school and college students."[41] Since the late nineteenth century, two important condi-tions have changed that help explain why the best students often turn their backs on teaching. First, modern teachers have no career mobility as teachers; their only upward route is out of teaching and into administration. In sharp contrast, the old Central High School acted as the top rung on a career ladder for male public school teachers, because Central's faculty was largely recruited from the ranks of the most successful grammar school masters.

Second, salaries for today's public school teachers are low compared with those of other college graduates. For example, in 1992 the average starting salary for teachers was $22,000, whereas the average for college graduates in other occupations ranged from $27,000 to $35,000.[42] To the extent that pay reflects job prestige, teaching does not seem to be held in very high esteem. In the nineteenth century, Philadelphia teachers were, on average, earning even less relative to other occupations than they do now, but this pay was dis-tributed much more unevenly. Men and teachers at higher-level schools re-ceived considerably more than others. For much of the century, a male high school professor (note the honorific title) could expect to be paid 20 percent more than a male grammar school principal, twice as much as a female gram-mar school principal, and more than four times as much as a female elemen-tary school teacher.[43]

The career incentives and pay differential in nineteenth-century Philadel-phia thus encouraged the most ambitious and the best male teachers to set sights on advancement. Yet this motivational tool was obtained at the expense of the vast majority of teachers, whose pay remained quite low and whose opportunities for advancement were negligible. In 1880 only 77 of the city's 2,075 public school teachers were men (3.7 percent), and only 16 of them taught at the high school (0.8 percent).[44] In the latter part of the century, the school board equalized pay between the sexes and across school levels while raising the average pay level of teachers as a whole, setting a pattern for compensation that has continued to the present.

The Commission on Excellence and other commentators have suggested at least a partial return to a more differentiated pattern of pay and position for teachers. The Commission argues for establishing master teacher posts and a structure of merit pay in schools as a means of reintroducing some of the kinds of incentives for the better teachers that existed in the early school systems. The potential danger of such a policy, as revealed by the Central case study, is that this increase in merit pay for a few may occur at the cost of continuing low pay for the many.[45]

5. The flattened pyramid of public education. Both the provision and the consumption of education have increased dramatically since the late nineteenth century. About three-quarters of those who enter primary school graduate from high school, and nearly two-thirds of those who drop out eventually obtain the equivalent of a high school diploma.[46] Educational expectations have risen to the point that many people consider a 25 percent dropout rate a major social problem. The rising level of education leaves the high school dropout in a state of educational and occupational disadvantage, and it leaves the school with the problem of trying to accomplish something that the faculty at the old Central would have seen as odd indeed — keeping underachieving students in school. In the nineteenth century, Central High School did its best to bar such students from entering in the first place, and it expelled those who later failed to meet its demanding standards. In contrast, the modern public high school takes everyone and tries to graduate everyone.[47]

One way to foster high graduation rates in such a situation is to set up intensive remedial instruction programs for students whose work is below par. Thus the modern high school expends considerable resources on raising the achievement of its low-achieving students to a minimally acceptable level. Whereas the early public high school devoted its energies to teaching the most advanced subjects to the highest performing students, the modern high school diffuses its energies to meet the needs of a wider range of students.

As a result, the inclusiveness of the modern U.S. high school makes it difficult for the school to concentrate resources on the promotion of academic excellence and to set standards for achieving this end. This undercuts the effectiveness of the academic incentives that the high school uses to motivate student achievement. The exclusiveness of the old Central High School meant that its diploma was a rare commodity in the educational credentials market; during most of the nineteenth century very few Central graduates went to college because the school's stature was the equal of many colleges.

Now that a majority of eighteen- to twenty-one-year-olds are attending a college or university, high school credentials have become less an endpoint than a stage in an elongated educational career. To find a contemporary level of education whose credentials are as exclusive today as Central's were in the nineteenth century, we have to look beyond college to the graduate professional schools of medicine, law, business, and engineering. Here, at the apex of the modern educational pyramid, the competition is intense, the numbers accepted are few, the level of academic rigor is high, and the marketability of the credentials received is extraordinary.

At this level the old meritocratic incentives that so spurred Central students to high levels of achievement are still very much in force. The problem for the modern comprehensive public high school is that these incentives are now so far removed that they are likely to influence only the most ambitious and future-oriented students, who perhaps are already planning to become doctors or lawyers. It is unrealistic to expect that the average tenth-grade student is going to strive for excellence in math class in the hope of attaining a medical degree, knowing full well that he or she is separated from this degree by a chasm of ten more years of schooling. Meanwhile, the more immediately attainable degree that the modern high school offers to its graduates has an exchange value that has been diluted by expanded enrollment. The high school's very success in attracting and retaining students over its 150-year history has therefore impaired its ability to promote high levels of academic achievement.[48]

The U.S. public high school in the twentieth century has gradually become dedicated to the principle of extending secondary education to the entire population. As a consequence, the problem that high schools face is how to promote educational excellence in a student body that is a true cross-section of the community. The Central High School case shows that the high standards of the early high school were achieved at the cost of radical exclusiveness. Modern private and Catholic high schools — along with selective public high schools in the United States and many public high schools abroad — continue to maintain an orientation toward excellence through exclusionary practices.

None of these old or new examples of meritocratic education therefore provides a useful model for the modern American public high school, for the inherited technology of educational achievement is simply inappropriate to the task of dealing with an inclusive population. What is needed is an approach that, in the words of *A Nation at Risk*, "sets high expectations for all learners, then tries in every way possible to help students reach them."[49] Continued reliance on exclusion and selection of students as the basis for high academic standards — such as by promoting school choice and by creating more schools that are special in some way or another — will only make the task of raising achievement in the residual comprehensive high school even more difficult. These approaches substitute sorting for schooling. The result is a system in which some high schools boast a concentration of high achievers, not because they teach students more effectively but because they attract students who are more capable in the first place. Such a system creates winners (those who get their children into the top schools) and losers (everyone else) but does little to enhance the learning capacities of the entire community. To fall back on the old meritocratic methodology in this manner — however attractive that might be ideologically — ignores the irretrievably altered character of the modern public high school.

4

The Middle Class and the High School

Everyone knows that school and social class are closely related, but there is considerable disagreement about the exact nature of that relation. You don't have to do a scientific study to determine that a person's future social position is in no small measure the result of the quantity and quality of education that person acquires; we can all see and understand the role education plays in allocating people to different levels in the occupational hierarchy. The disagreement arises over the question of how schooling accomplishes this allocation.

According to one perspective, schools exist primarily to provide society with the kinds of skill and knowledge that it needs in order to function effectively, and they sort students according to their individual level of achievement in these areas of competence, with the most competent attaining the most advanced levels of education and thus the best jobs. As a result, an individual ends up in the social class that corresponds to the level of merit that he or she has demonstrated in the educational system. According to a second perspective, schools exist primarily to provide the members of the upper classes with a mechanism for passing their social advantage along to their children, and schools accomplish this by sorting students according to their social origins rather than individual merit. The result, from this angle, is that students from higher social classes end up with a higher level of education, which in turn qualifies them for higher-level jobs. In the first view, then, schooling is socially functional (serving the human capital needs of the whole society) and meritocratic (distributing positions based on merit); in the second, schooling is functional only for the upper classes and therefore plays a role that is socially reproductive (by reproducing existing social inequalities).[1]

Each of these perspectives helps account for some of what we observe in the relation between school and social class, but the evidence for each tends to undercut the credibility of the other. The social outcomes of schooling match the social origins of students too closely to provide full support for the functional-meritocratic view, and yet at the same time schooling helps facilitate too much movement up and down the class scale to provide full support for the social reproduction view, either. In addition, both views tend to understate the autonomy of schools while simultaneously overstating their effectiveness. What we know about schooling suggests that it is a relatively powerful and independent institution, which compels families to organize their lives around its peculiarly academic priorities and practices. And what we know also suggests that schooling is more contradictory in its aims and more ineffective in accomplishing these aims than one might guess from the vision of schooling as a smooth-running engine of either meritocracy or reproduction.

In this chapter, I seek to unpack a few of the main components of this complex relation between schooling and social class. I focus on a particular historical case in point, that of Central High School of Philadelphia, to examine the relation that evolved over time between the high school and the middle class in one American city. And in order to keep the discussion within manageable bounds, I concentrate on one major aspect of the school, its curriculum.[2]

In the early nineteenth century, Central had a curriculum that was practical in orientation and undifferentiated in form; but by the end of the century, the school's faculty and administration had transformed this curriculum into one that was more academic (for its top students) and that took on a highly stratified form. This transformation can be understood only in light of the close relation between the high school and its primary constituency in the proprietary (that is, self-employed) middle class. I examine how this class helped to shape the school's curriculum and also how the curriculum influenced the formation of this class — both through the medium of the market in educational credentials.

The implications of this analysis are wide-ranging. The study suggests that schools are partially independent agents in the social arena, which can act as well as react; that curriculum is both an academic artifact that schools impose on the public and a social artifact that the public imposes on schools; that the more privileged social classes exert a significant impact on schools, but that this influence often comes at the cost of submitting to onerous courses of academic study and risky processes of academic selection; that market pressures play an essential part in shaping the way schools work and the way they interact with families; and that, as a result, the interaction between schools and social classes is not under the direct control of the parties involved but operates according to a market-based logic, under which education is treated as a cultural commodity whose value fluctuates according to the vagaries of supply and demand.[3]

The Early Curriculum: Practical and Meritocratic

Founded in 1838, Central High School was Philadelphia's first public high school, and it remained the only public high school for boys until 1885. Because of its unique position, the high school played a prominent and influential role in the school system and in the cultural and social life of the city.[4] During most of the nineteenth century, Central's curriculum was explicitly practical in orientation. The school sought to prepare students for direct entry into the city's commercial life rather than for college. Its purpose was, in the words of the school's second president, "not to educate boys above their business, but for it."[5]

This emphasis on practicality was manifested in three ways. First, the course of study reflected a deliberate shift in focus toward modern languages and science and away from the overwhelming emphasis on classical languages that characterized the traditional Latin grammar school curriculum at the time. Thus, students spent between zero and 15 percent of their time studying classics and more than 40 percent of their time studying French, German, and the various sciences.[6] Second, the science curriculum itself leaned heavily toward practical applications of scientific principles. This led the school to accumulate a considerable amount of scientific equipment for purposes of demonstration and to promote these acquisitions as symbols of the curriculum's practicality. The most expensive and highly publicized piece of equipment was an advanced telescope, which was enshrined in an astronomical observatory atop the original high school building. Third, the curriculum included several courses that were explicitly designed to provide vocational training for white-collar jobs, including classes in stenography, bookkeeping, mechanical drawing, and civil engineering.

These practical tendencies in the school's curriculum, however, need to be put in perspective. Central's aim was not to provide its students with a narrow apprenticeship for business. The vocational courses never constituted more than 12 percent of the students' schedule, and nearly all the remaining courses were academic.[7] Most of the courses were in such traditional liberal arts subjects as English, literature, composition, French, geometry, chemistry, and physics — none of which can be considered particularly practical, except in the broad sense of providing general cognitive skills. Even Central's much-vaunted astronomical observatory, which provided hands-on experience in scientific observation, was hardly relevant for future clerks, managers, and commercial agents. Therefore, the high school's practical curriculum was actually an academic curriculum with a practical orientation, and its usefulness was most striking when viewed in contrast to the traditional classical course.

Central's curriculum was by no means unique. Most nineteenth-century high schools offered a similar course of study, usually identified as the English course. Although probably less comprehensive and less rigorous than Central's practical curriculum, the generic English course was a close match, right down to the classes in bookkeeping and stenography. In most high schools, the English course was typically paired with a classical course intended for those who were college bound. Central also offered both options when it opened in 1838, but unlike many other high schools, it emphasized the practical course, which the catalogue referred to as the "principal" course. In 1856, the principal and classical courses were combined into a single program of academic subjects with a decidedly practical bent. For the next thirty-three years, public high school boys in Philadelphia were given no choice in their course of study. Central presented them with a single body of practical-academic knowledge.

Closely linked to the high school's practical curriculum was its meritocratic pedagogy. In both purpose and practice, this was a thoroughly meritocratic school. According to one of its founders, Central was "the School of the Republic . . . demanding no passport to its blessings, or to its laurels, save that which the people demands, and forever will demand from all its sons — INDIVIDUAL, PERSONAL MERIT."[8] Only those who obtained a high score on a competitive written examination won admission, and only those deemed most worthy succeeded in graduating. Between 1838 and 1920, only 27 percent of the students admitted to the school persisted long enough to earn a diploma. It might be tempting to attribute this low success rate to class pressures rather than high academic standards — because lower-income families presumably would be less able than wealthier families to forgo the income of their teenage sons, and therefore would have to withdraw these students from school at an early age. But graduation rates were almost entirely unrelated to social class: students from the middle classes were as unlikely to graduate as those from the working classes.[9]

In fact, by far the best predictor of a student's chances for graduation was his academic performance as measured by high school grades. Records show that 72.5 percent of students who achieved honor grades graduated, but only 19.8 percent of those without such grades graduated.[10] For the classes entering in 1910 and 1920 (when records permit the calculation of grade-point averages), the mean graduation rate was 77 percent for students with averages of A and B-plus, 54 percent for B-minus students, 28 percent for C-plus students, and only 5 percent for students with lower averages. When both class and grades are included in a multiple classification analysis (MCA) of graduation rates, grades still emerge as the most important predictor of success: The beta for grades (which measures the size of their impact on graduation independent of other variables) is .50 and the beta for class is only .03. A second MCA, using a smaller sample but a larger number of variables, yields a similar result. When separate MCAs are done for each entering class, grades are consistently the strongest predictor of graduation.[11]

Thus Central rewarded those students who displayed the greatest prowess in the individual competition for academic honors. The academic competition at Central, however, was undercut by an elaborate disciplinary policy that prevailed for the school's first twenty-one years. The explicit purpose of this policy was to instill self-control in the students, reflecting the ideals of the school's early leaders, who believed that the Central should not only transmit knowledge but also build character. What this meant in practice was that demerits were given to misbehaving students and then deducted from their grades before term averages were calculated. Grade-point averages, therefore, represented a combination of academic achievement and personal deportment. Thus both the original curriculum and the continuing pedagogy of Central High School reveal a less-than-full commitment to a strictly academic program of instruction. The academic purity of Central's program was muddied by the school's initial devotion to both practical content and personal conduct.

Middle-Class Ideology and the Early Curriculum

The emphasis on practicality, merit, and character in Central High School's early curriculum was an expression of the entrepreneurial form of bourgeois ideology that became dominant among the American middle and upper classes in the early nineteenth century. To explore the impact of this ideology on Central, we must first consider the class composition of the high school. More than two-thirds of the students who attended the school between 1838 and 1920 came from the middle classes, nearly half from the proprietary middle class; less than 7 percent came from the unskilled working class. The unrepresentativeness of Central's constituency becomes more apparent when we compare the class distribution of Central parents in a particular year with the class distribution of household heads in the city. In 1880 the middle classes were heavily overrepresented, and the working classes, particularly the unskilled working class, were heavily underrepresented.[12] This class distribution was remarkably stable over the eighty-two-year period covered by this study. In every year from 1838 to 1920, about half of the entering students were from the proprietary middle class.

For the most part, members of the proprietary middle class owned relatively small businesses. Although some wealthy and powerful families sent their sons to Central, they were more likely to opt for private schools. Central's constituency was dominated by shopkeepers and master craftsmen, the petty entrepreneurs who had been considered middle class long before the arrival of industrial capitalism and who continued to hold this position, albeit in declining numbers, throughout the mid-nineteenth century.

It was this class that jumped to the support of that vast array of institutional innovations and ideological initiatives that burst onto the American scene during the Jacksonian era. Petty proprietors rallied around the penitentiary, the mental asylum, the poorhouse, the privatized family, pietistic religion, the temperance movement, and, of course, the common schools.[13] There was considerable ideological consistency among these reforms. All reflected middle-class concern about the disruptive effects of the expansion of capitalist social relations on the existing social order, and all sought to establish a new order that was both compatible with capitalism and congenial with middle-class interests.

Let us consider, in turn, three principles promoted in Central's early curriculum — self-control, practicality, and merit — in light of the middle-class ideology reflected in these institutional reforms. From penitentiary to poorhouse and from pietism to prohibitionism, these reform efforts were all aimed at building character through the development of a rigorous self-discipline. Carl Kaestle, David Tyack and Elisabeth Hansot, and others have argued that the founding of the common schools, in particular, is attributable to bourgeois concerns about the development of self-control.[14] This obsession with self-control is a natural outgrowth of the experience of the petty entrepreneur in a competitive market. Central's second president believed that self-control learned at the high school would prepare the student for "the real accountabilities of life" — especially, one might add, for the rigidly self-sufficient existence of the proprietary middle class.[15]

Practical concerns — that is, work-related or work-enhancing concerns — permeated the institutions created during the Jacksonian period. Inmates in all the new institutions were expected to develop work skills or at least work habits during their tenure, so it is hardly surprising that high school students

faced similar expectations. One of Central's early leaders stated the core ideological principle succinctly: "It was very early a matter of anxiety with the
Controllers [of the school system] to avoid the error, not of over educating the
pupils, but of so educating them as to give them a distaste for business."[16] This
strong predilection for business over intellectualism and for practical education over classical education, like the emphasis on self-discipline, emanated
from the daily experience and developing thought patterns of the proprietary
middle class. The one-track practical curriculum put Central in a strong position to defend itself against the charge directed toward nineteenth-century
high schools generally — that they were designed to serve the needs of the
elite — while still allowing it to serve the privileged few. But this political consideration does not undercut the significance of the connection between practicality and middle-class ideology. The practical curriculum could hardly have
attracted so many middle-class students if they were ideologically committed
to a classical education.

Meritocracy is another concern that emerges from entrepreneurial activity.
In contrast to working-class culture, which is characterized by a pattern of
"cooperative coping," middle-class culture is characterized by what Connell
calls "competitive striving."[17] Significantly, of all the Jacksonian institutions
cited above, only the high school was capable of promoting the principle of
meritocratic competition. Penitentiary, asylum, poorhouse, family, church,
even the public elementary school — none of these provided a competitive
arena, an incentive for individual striving, or a legitimate, merit-based reward structure. Central High School, however, met all these requirements for
a truly meritocratic institution. This helps explain why nineteenth-century
high schools were so important, despite the small number of students they
enrolled. Only there could one of the most important elements of bourgeois
ideology be learned, practiced, and legitimized.

Of course, Central's meritocracy arose not only from middle-class ideology
but also from the school's admissions policy. Because admissions were highly
selective, Central's students were high achievers, and because of economic
pressures, most of them were middle class. Few working-class families could
afford to send a potential wage earner to high school, and those that did must
have been extremely committed to education and confident of its promise of
upward mobility. In short, Central's meritocracy consisted of those students
who were most likely to make it work — high achievers who were self-selected,
culturally homogeneous, and middle class.

As a matter of practice, therefore, Central's rewards were not distributed
purely on the basis of merit — but no pure meritocracy likely exists in any

class society. What is significant about this nineteenth-century high school, however, is that its formal procedures for admission and graduation were truly meritocratic. The school was in fact free and open to boys of all classes, and both admission and promotion were determined by written achievement tests. The forces of ascription, which intruded on the process, came indirectly from the class structure rather than directly from class-biased procedures within the school. Thus, Central's middle-class constituents had it both ways: they reveled in the school's class-blind meritocracy (perceived as a concrete expression of bourgeois ideology), while they enjoyed privileged access to its social rewards.

Middle-class beliefs exerted a strong impact on the high school's curriculum, but the curriculum also had a significant effect on its middle-class constituents. For this curriculum was not only practical, character-building, and meritocratic (traits that are easily identified as middle class); it was also quite academic. The core of the curriculum consisted of traditional subjects that were much more closely associated with schools than with the bourgeoisie. The primary middle-class contributions to the curriculum were a few clerical courses and a shift in emphasis from one type of academic knowledge to another. Central's curriculum, however, was not a pale reflection of middle-class ideology but an academic course of study shaped by this ideology. It offered experiences not freely available in daily middle-class life. It focused on providing the kind of knowledge that could be acquired only at the high school rather than on vocational training that could be obtained more efficiently in a business apprenticeship. Therefore, although Central High School was in many ways the creature of the city's middle classes, these same classes, by sending their sons to the school, submitted themselves to a regime of bookish academic knowledge that was an extension more of the school's values and concerns than of their own.

One indication that Central's academic autonomy not only was strong to begin with but grew stronger in its early years was its early abandonment of the focus on character building. In 1859, over bitter ideological opposition, the new principal abruptly ended the practice of grading students on both academic achievement and conduct.[18] "This practice," he argued, "was evidently unjust and injurious. It destroyed all incentive to study: it deprived the student of those honors which he had fairly won by diligence and industry."[19] The message was clear: that the school's prime function was to promote academic achievement. This represented an important narrowing of the high school's mission: instead of socializing students in the dominant ideology, it now focused on its academic mission, which was to promote the acquisition of the school's own body of knowledge.

Competing for High School Credentials

Almost from the moment Central High School opened its doors, a fierce competition began over the acquisition of its credentials. Starting with the first class admitted to the school, there were considerably more applicants than openings, and this state of affairs persisted even as the school grew. Why were the credentials provided by Central so highly valued in the local credentials market? There are three main reasons: the school's meritocratic admission and graduation procedures, the unique position of the high school in the local market, and, at the most basic level, the special structural needs of the high school's middle-class constituency. Note that the first two reasons involve supply considerations and that the third involves demand.

Central's meritocracy defined the high school diploma as a form of cultural property, for which many students could compete but which relatively few could acquire. The school bestowed its credentials upon only those students who demonstrated superior academic ability, and this selectivity, along with the legitimacy that these credentials conferred, made them a scarce and valuable cultural commodity. Only one out of every fifty male first-graders was eventually admitted to Central High School, and only one out of every two hundred ever graduated. Being a Central student was a source of some distinction, but being a Central graduate was a signal honor.

Another reason Central's credentials were so highly valued is the uniquely elevated position that the school occupied during the mid-nineteenth century. For fifty years it was the only public high school for boys in the nation's second-largest city; this fact alone gave it a kind of solitary prominence, which no high school has achieved since. In the loose, prebureaucratic structure of the Philadelphia school system, the high school became the dominant market presence around which the system coalesced: grammar school students, eager to gain admission to Central, and their teachers, equally eager to see their students admitted, reshaped the lower school curriculum to meet the high school's standard.[20] Few private schools could compete with the high school's prestige and meritocratic credibility, and none could match its free tuition.

Even colleges were threatened by the upstart competitor. In the mid-nineteenth century, colleges and high schools frequently competed for the same group of students.[21] Central's position relative to these colleges was strengthened by two factors. First, in 1849, the state assembly granted the school the right to award college degrees to its students, which it has done ever since (though recently only on an honorary basis). Thus, the term "people's college," which was popularly applied to high schools during this era, was uniquely appropriate to Central. Second, during the third quarter of the nineteenth century, the number of colleges in the United States grew considerably faster than the population, so that by 1880 there were 16.1 colleges per million people—a proportion that has not been exceeded since.[22] Under these market conditions, college credentials were devalued, while Central's unique market position helped it maintain its own credentials at a high value.

The supply of high-status educational credentials was strictly limited. But this alone cannot explain why such a high market value was placed on the credentials Central provided, which could have occurred only if there had also been a strong demand for these credentials. To examine the demand side of the market we need to explore the fit between high school credentials and the structural needs of the high school's primary constituency, the proprietary middle class. Before the nineteenth century, shopkeepers and master artisans in the United States enjoyed a relatively secure existence, protected by a traditional economy and stable prices and costs. Under these circumstances, a father transmitted his class position to his son by transferring economic capital—by passing on title to the business or by establishing his son in a business of his own.

As is shown in Paul Johnson's study of Rochester, New York, however, after the arrival of the Erie Canal, the rapid development of market capitalism and the resulting competition and price fluctuation created a sharp increase in economic and social instability.[23] Under these altered conditions, the transfer of economic capital became difficult. In a study of middle-class life in mid-nineteenth-century Oneida County, New York, Mary Ryan concludes that "small-business men who were struggling to keep their own firms solvent were particularly hard-pressed to put their progeny on a sound economic footing within the middling sort. Of all the wills processed in Utica after 1850 a mere five witnessed the transfer of a store or workshop to a second generation."[24]

In this era, the proprietary middle class was caught between two advancing dangers. On the one side, the encroachment of successful entrepreneurial competitors threatened bankruptcy. On the other, the rapid growth of wage labor threatened proletarianization. With the declining reliability of economic property as a guarantee of social reproduction, families in this class began to depend increasingly on cultural property, which can serve as a crucial means of preserving or attaining social status independent of economic property.

The proprietary middle class in the mid-nineteenth century was under such intense socioeconomic pressure from the advance of capitalist social relations that it jumped at the opportunity to acquire cultural property from Central High School. The school was ideally suited to fill this need: its curriculum was already partially shaped into the middle-class ideological mold, its credentials were scarce and prestigious, and its reward system was meritocratic. Thus demand for Central's credentials among the shopkeepers and master artisans at midcentury was strong indeed. By acquiring this unique form of cultural property, the proprietors' sons could ease into a very different kind of middle-class existence — one based on business employment rather than business ownership. The practical curriculum that Central offered was more relevant to such employment than was the purely academic classical course; it allowed students to learn a few useful skills, such as bookkeeping and drafting, and encouraged them to focus on acquiring a job rather than pursuing further education. But more important than the vocational training was the symbolic wealth that students accumulated at the high school. Such wealth had limited utility for those with substantial economic property, but for those with less money who pinned their hopes on the prospect of white-collar employment, this cultural property was what marked them off from the wage earners of the working class. A Central High School diploma, therefore, offered its constituents a cultural reinforcement of middle-class standing, an entree into business employment, and a hedge against downward mobility.

Market Forces Press for Curriculum Change

To understand the early curriculum of Central High School, we have to understand the school's relation to the city's middle classes. On the one hand, the curriculum was partly shaped by middle-class ideology, an influence that is apparent in the school's emphasis on merit, practicality, and character. On the other hand, the middle classes became dependent on the high school curriculum as a unique source of much-needed cultural property.

The key to the relation between Central High School and its middle-class constituency was the mediating role played by the market in educational credentials. And the relative strength of this relation at any point in time was both measured by and expressed through the exchange value of the high school's diploma in that market. During most of Central's first fifty years, the demand for the school's credentials was high, but the supply was scarce. This market condition led to a cycle of mutual reinforcement: heavy middle-class demand increased the value of Central's credentials; the increase in value raised the school's prestige and strengthened its independence; the enhancement of the school's position led to a further increase in credential value; and these increases in value further stimulated demand. Given the neat circularity of this process and the satisfactions it granted to both buyer and seller, it is hardly surprising that Central High School was reluctant to permit more than minor tinkering with its strikingly successful curriculum. Why change something that worked so well?

In the 1880s, however, the relation between the high school and the middle classes began to show signs of strain. Critics in the press and on the school board claimed that Central had lost its rigor and its direction, that its curriculum was elementary and outdated, and that it no longer served the needs of its students. The faculty was sharply divided over the issue of change, but in 1887 it voted for a new curriculum. Two years later, a new program was established. What had been uniform was now stratified, and what had been a careful mixture of academic and practical concerns now became separated into a purely academic track and a second practical-vocational track.

This curriculum shift was a response to dramatic changes in the market conditions that defined Central's relation with its middle-class clientele. A sudden increase in the number of high schools offering similar credentials, coupled with a shift in the demand for these credentials, caused the value of a Central High School diploma to decline sharply. Both the school's officials and its middle-class constituency believed that the curriculum should be changed in order to respond to this dramatically different market situation.

The pressures that made educational credentials attractive to the middle classes in the mid-nineteenth century intensified by the 1880s. In particular, the position of the proprietary middle class was even more threatened. From 1850 to 1880, while the proportion of middle-class employees in the male population of the city grew slowly, the proportion of proprietors remained the same. But between 1880 and 1900, the proportion of proprietors decreased and the proportion of business employees increased sharply, making the latter the dominant group within the middle class.[25] This reduction in the role of proprietors in the city's class structure, combined with the stability of Central's class distribution over the entire period, meant that the proprietary middle class was increasingly overrepresented at the high school after 1880. Faced with declining opportunities for independent businessmen and increasing opportunities for business employees, the proprietary middle class shifted its pattern of investment from economic property to cultural property. The question then became: what kind of cultural property would prove most valuable to this class in the midst of its accelerating structural change?

Several factors influenced the way this question was ultimately answered. First, the social meaning of business employment was undergoing change. At midcentury, a clerkship was an apprentice position leading either to management or proprietorship. In 1850, 56 percent of Central's students entered clerk-type positions upon leaving school. In this era, therefore, business employment — especially when combined with highly valued high school credentials — was an alternative route to the proprietary middle class. But by the 1880s, such employment was no longer a temporary stop on the way to proprietorship. For the first time, proprietors had to think seriously about the likelihood that their sons would be permanent salaried employees. Being a clerk was no longer a stage in the life cycle but rather a career, and such a career — separated from a working-class job by only a thin status differential and an even thinner pay differential — was not what middle-class families wanted for their sons. What kind of employment would be appropriate for the offspring of the proprietary middle class? What career would help preserve their social standing? The answer — which had always been available but which had not appeared so strikingly attractive until the last quarter of the nineteenth century — was offered by the professions.

The professions possessed a number of advantages over business employment, including higher prestige and higher income, but their most attractive feature (which enhanced both prestige and income) was autonomy. The professional was clearly no white-collar wage slave, subject to the authority of the boss. His expertise and his ideology buffered him from both management and the market, thus neatly shielding him from the twin threats facing the proprietors: workplace subordination and ruinous competition. Because of the attractiveness of the professions to the declining proprietors, middle-class culture in the late nineteenth century evolved into a "culture of professionalism."[26] On one level, this transformation reflected the change in the source of the class's social standing, from the autonomy of proprietorship to the autonomy of professionalism. But on another level, it represented an intensification of the class's dependence on academic credentials.

Most professionals in the nineteenth century achieved their positions by apprenticing themselves to an established member of the field. However, the most prominent members of each profession had generally received a degree from a professional school, and this pattern accelerated in the latter part of the century. The proprietors, who had already competed for the credentials offered by Central High School, had learned by experience that the accumulation of symbolic wealth was an important buttress for social position and that academic credentials were a significant addition to this wealth. If they were going to pursue the professions, they needed the appropriate academic certification, and this meant shifting their focus from the high school to the university. The result was an exponential increase in the middle-class demand for professional-school credentials. According to Joseph Kett, there was a substantial increase in the number of professional students between 1878 and 1899, but the most dramatic increase occurred between 1888 and 1899: the number of dental students increased by 988 percent, the number of medical students by 142 percent, the number of law students by 249 percent, and the number of theology students by 87 percent.[27] By 1889, when Central changed its curriculum, the school's clientele was no longer interested in a terminal program oriented toward business employment. Instead, these families wanted a strictly academic program that would prepare students for admission to the university. This is exactly what they got.

The supply side of the educational credentials market also underwent significant change in the 1880s, partly because of the shift in demand. By the end of the decade, Central faced stiff competition for the first time, both from newly created high schools and from newly invigorated universities. The success of the public high school (in Philadelphia and elsewhere) was at least partly responsible for both developments. The elements that made Central so attractive — uniqueness, selectivity, and scarcity of credentials — provoked a demand for more of the same. Before the 1890s, Central's enrollments were between five hundred and six hundred students. This represented more than 1 percent of the total enrollment in the city's school system during the 1850s but less than 0.5 percent by 1880. Under these circumstances, only a small fraction of the city's middle-class families could hope to educate their sons at the school.

Finally, in 1883, the school board yielded to middle-class demands and established a manual-training school as an alternative secondary institution. (Other such schools followed quickly on its heels, and by 1915 there were fifteen public high schools in the city.) Thus, after fifty years of monopoly, Central had its first public competitor. To make matters worse, the new school's curriculum was similar to Central's. It offered a terminal, practical education with a manual-training component that was a more systematic and more intensive form of Central's own hands-on approach. Therefore, to distinguish itself from its secondary competition and restore the value of its credentials, Central had to revise its curriculum.

Central had found that it could compete successfully with the midcentury college, which suffered from oversupply and underdistinction. But between 1865 and 1890, during the professionalization of the middle class, the university developed into the dominant force in American education.[28] The cultural property the university offered, which at the highest level was certification for admission to the professions, was much more attractive than anything the high school could offer. Central, like other high schools, had to make a choice: it could preserve its practical-terminal curriculum and become useless to those in quest of professional credentials, or it could adopt an academic college-preparatory curriculum and thus become subordinate to the university in the new hierarchy of U.S. education. Central chose the latter course.

Only purely academic courses were included in the new college-preparatory curriculum. All vocational courses were eliminated and the classics and science courses predominated.[29] These changes do not seem terribly dramatic, but as we have seen, the original curriculum was already largely academic. The practical curriculum was not created de novo by the middle class to reflect its worldview; instead, an existing body of school-bound knowledge was shaped into a program with a practical orientation. The change in the curriculum, therefore, occurred at the margins, not at the core, and the most significant change was in the orientation of the actors rather than in the content of classroom instruction. In these terms, then, the new curriculum represented a major turnabout in the perceived purpose of a high school education, from preparation for business to preparation for higher education and the professions.

In addition to the change in the content of the curriculum, there was also a significant change in its form. A uniform course of study with no electives was transformed into a menu of courses offering a variety of vertically organized clusters of knowledge. From the start, the academic course occupied the top stratum. After a few years of experimentation, the school settled on a format that further stratified the academic course into classical, Latin-scientific, and modern language courses. (The classical course was designed for preprofessionals.) Below the academic course was the commercial course (called the scientific course before 1898). Thus the old practical curriculum had been split in two, with its academic features embodied in the academic track and its practical features embodied in the commercial track. The latter, which prepared young men for entry into clerical work, included a mix of vocational courses and watered-down academic courses. (Science, for example, became "Raw Materials of Commerce.") A mechanical course (engineering) was added in 1912 and an industrial program (vocational preparation for skilled trades) was added in 1919. At the top level of the new stratified curriculum, the emphasis was on exchange value (that is, the amount of social benefit that an academic diploma could buy on the credentials market), but at the bottom levels the emphasis was on use value (the amount of practical usable knowledge that a vocational program of study could provide).

To understand the reasons for the stratification of Central's curriculum, we must look again at conditions in the credentials market. The opening of new high schools in the city was not sufficient to meet the demand for high school credentials, because it was Central's own distinctive credentials that were the most valuable and that had set off the demand in the first place. This posed a problem for Central's middle-class constituency, because if more people began to acquire the same piece of cultural property (a Central High School diploma), its exchange value would decline even further than it already had by the late 1880s — a simple case of market logic at work, with a growing supply leading to a falling price. In a democratic society, however, it is politically difficult to deny broad public access to a public good as attractive and valuable as Central High School. For a remarkably long period — most of the nineteenth century — Central managed to preserve its elitist policy of sharply restricting the number of students who were admitted and graduated, but finally, in the last decade of the century, political pressure forced it to open its doors to a larger and more representative group of students. After fifty years of stable enrollments, Central starting growing rapidly, from 561 students in 1890 to 1,235 in 1900 and 2,301 in 1910. The school managed to accommodate this sharp increase in public access and still enhance the exchange value of Central's credentials for the benefit of the middle-class families who had traditionally depended upon it. How? By stratifying the kinds of high school credentials that were available, and thereby leaving the middle class (especially the proprietary component) with an avenue for maintaining an educational leg up on the opposition. This process of stratification occurred both within Central itself and also between Central and the city's other high schools.

As soon as Central adopted an academic college-preparatory curriculum (which included the prestigious classical course), it reinforced its status advantage over the manual-training school (which offered only a practical and terminal course). These two schools were buffered from competition, because they operated on different planes and for different goals, and therefore the subsequent proliferation of new manual-training high schools did not threaten the value of a Central High School education. At the same time, Central also stratified its curriculum internally (with the advent of the scientific-commercial course), and it is no coincidence that it simultaneously began to expand its enrollment. This surge in the number of students did not swamp the local credentials market, because that market was separated into different tracks, which were ranked according to the strength of their association with the dominant culture of professionalism.

Predictably, the academic track at Central was the most popular; but just as predictably, this popularity was in part a function of the students' social class. In 1890, immediately after the installation of the academic and scientific tracks, 81 percent of the entering proprietary middle-class students opted for the academic course. Fewer than two-thirds of the other students who entered that year selected this course. By 1900, the new curriculum had settled into the format it would keep for the next twenty years: the academic (college-preparatory) course, which was itself divided into three levels, was on top, and the commercial course, which was more explicitly vocational than the earlier scientific course, fell below. The courses chosen by the students who entered in 1900 show a pattern of lessening interest in the academic course at each step down the class scale: this course was chosen by 72.2 percent of the students from the proprietary middle class, 66.7 percent from the employed middle class, 55.2 percent from the skilled working class, and by 14.3 percent from the unskilled working class. The top track of the high school's newly stratified curriculum was most popular among the most privileged students, for whom it served as a special school within a special school. The new academic diploma from Central High School therefore provided these students with a doubly exclusive and marketable piece of cultural property that served as leverage in their struggle for social position.[30]

There is, of course, a variety of alternative explanations for the changes instituted at Central High School — explanations that are not based on the actions of the educational credentials market. Consider what these changes might look like from the perspective of functional-meritocratic theory or social reproduction theory.

From the functional view, the development of stratification within and between high schools (which I have attributed to the changing supply of and demand for educational credentials) is best understood as part of a larger process of structural differentiation within societies. In this view, as societies (or organizational units within them) develop, they encounter increased population density and increased structural complexity. Thus the development of the stratified curriculum at Central would be seen as a result of this trend toward differentiation. But the order of events is all wrong for this to be true. Central's enrollment remained steady during the period in which the faculty debated and adopted curriculum change, which suggests that Central had not been pressed into instituting a multilevel curriculum by the force of numbers. Enrollments increased only after the change took place, which indicates that the newly stratified curriculum attracted the students and that this change was designed to enhance the school's attractiveness. The school was attractive to the proprietary middle class not because it provided a differentiated curriculum that was useful to the general population but because it provided an elite course of study and a highly marketable credential.

But according to social reproduction theory, the development of the new curriculum at Central is an example not of the power of the credentials market but of the power of the dominant classes to reproduce themselves through the schools. According to this perspective, Central's tracking system reflected the existing class structure and was installed to maintain that structure. This is certainly a more parsimonious explanation than the one I have presented, but it fails to take account of the evidence from this study. In regard to social outcomes, reproduction theory is correct: the school was highly responsive to the needs of the proprietary middle class, and the curriculum changes did indeed work to the benefit of this class. But this explanation overlooks important aspects of the way the school operated and the way change took place. The school's aggressively meritocratic pedagogy, for example, originally may have been an expression of middle-class ideology, but it also barred a large number of middle-class children from admission and caused most of those who were admitted to flunk out—hardly the picture of a school passively serving the interests of the privileged.

The proprietary middle class created Central High School, dominated its student body, and reaped most of its benefits, but the school was not simply manipulated like a marionette. Once the high school was established, its creators needed the cultural property it offered to preserve their class position. They had nowhere else to turn (in the public sector) to acquire it, so they had to compete for its honors, submit to its rules, accept its academic knowledge, and endure the fluctuations in the exchange value of its credentials on the open market. The credentials market, then, is a metaphor for the interdependency of the high school and the proprietary middle class. The transformation of the curriculum at Central in the 1880s was accordingly as much a sign of class weakness as it was of class power, a sign of just how much the members of the middle classes had come to depend on the high school and its credentials and of how quickly they and the school had to act in order to preserve the relation between them when it fell into jeopardy.

5

The Carnegie Cult of Social Efficiency:
An Exceptional Report That Proves the Rule

At first glance, the 1989 Carnegie report on middle schools — *Turning Points: Preparing American Youth for the 21st Century* — looks like just another in a long line of Carnegie reports on education in the United States.[1] The Carnegie Corporation of New York and the Carnegie Foundation for the Advancement of Teaching have been issuing reports on educational matters for ninety years, and recently these reports have had a distinctive look. Invariably encased in shiny blue and white covers, they are printed on heavy semi-gloss stock and boast generous margins broken by frequent headings and boxed inserts. It is a format designed to grab the attention of busy policy-makers and to provide them with the essence of the argument in one quick scan of the text.

This argument, the reports are careful to point out, is thoroughly authoritative. These publications are never cluttered with tedious data or fine points of theoretical analysis, which might slow down or confuse their distinguished readers, but the reports always refer to an impressive array of empirical studies commissioned for this purpose and prominently listed in the back. Moreover, these reports do not rely on science alone for their support. Right up front they display their first claim to credibility, which is the elite makeup of the task force or commission that provided oversight to the whole project. Governors, senators, superintendents, deans, and executives, the members are recorded with full honorific title and institutional location; and they are even given a page to sign their handiwork.

A Carnegie report is an impressive document. Produced in grand style and displaying the support of both Science and some Very Important People, it demands to be heard in the highest levels of the U.S. policymaking establishment. Perhaps nowhere else can one see so clearly the inseparable ties between power and knowledge in American public life. Under the circumstances, it is hardly surprising that writers who view schools as functionally subordinate to the demands of the ruling class are fond of pointing to the efforts of the Carnegie people.[2] Nowhere does an instrumentalist view of the impact of elites on schools appear more credible than in an analysis of the Carnegie role in the making of U.S. educational policy.

But for all the similarities between the 1989 report and its predecessors, some subtle differences emerge from a visual inspection. Consider a comparison between *Turning Points* and another highly visible Carnegie report that was published three years earlier, *A Nation Prepared: Teachers for the 21st Century*.[3] For one thing, we find that the cover of the latest report is tinted aquamarine, as opposed to the indigo hue of its predecessor. In addition, although both reports are 8½ by 11 inches in size, the newer report is bound on the long side of the page whereas the earlier report is bound on the short side. For a series of reports in which style of presentation is half the story, the reader can be pardoned for speculating that these superficial changes might suggest significant shifts in substance. Could it be that *Turning Points*—wrapped in a softer shade of blue—should be understood as a kinder and gentler Carnegie report? Is it even possible that this more recent entry in the field—with its rotated page format—should be understood as having taken the argument of *A Nation Prepared* and turned it on its side?

In this chapter, I explore the anomalous character of the 1989 report, not because this topic itself holds great intrinsic interest but because it offers a way of gaining insight into a more important problem: to define the impact that Carnegie has had on education in the United States over the years. Carnegie reports have long sought to make U.S. education a socially efficient mechanism for sorting and socializing students in order to fit them into the existing social and economic structure. They have pursued this goal of social efficiency by promoting a rational system of education that is integrated, standardized, differentiated, scientific, and meritocratic. *A Nation Prepared* fits this model beautifully, but in some key ways *Turning Points* does not. Instead, the latter report proposes a restructured form of middle school, one that is decentralized, varied in format and content, and focused on promoting cooperative process and convergent student outcomes. Yet in spite of these differences, the proposed reforms would still fit comfortably within the rationalized structure of U.S. education that has traditionally been promoted by Carnegie reports. The biggest change represented by the report is not a shift away from Carnegie's traditional concern with social efficiency — an institutional mission that remains alive and well — but a temporary shift in focus toward a lower grade level (the middle school), where entry to the workforce is more remote and therefore social efficiency concerns can be relaxed.

The Carnegie Approach to Educational Policymaking

In 1901, Andrew Carnegie sold the Carnegie Steel Company for nearly a half billion dollars to a syndicate organized by J. P. Morgan, a transaction that led to the creation of the trust known as United States Steel. In retirement, Carnegie devoted himself to full-time philanthropy, primarily through the creation of a remarkable series of foundations. Two of these took a particular interest in education: the Carnegie Foundation for the Advancement of Teaching, which was established with a modest endowment of $10 million in 1905, and the Carnegie Corporation of New York, created in 1911 with a gift of $125 million in U.S. Steel bonds. The latter was the first of the large general-purpose foundations, and it is still one of the best endowed. While the Corporation received the bulk of the money, it was the Foundation that took the early programmatic lead, focusing from the start on higher education. Over the years, the Corporation has cast its philanthropic net wider, but it too has supported a wide range of projects in education, either directly through grants or indirectly through subsidies to the Foundation.[4]

From the beginning, the primary aim of Carnegie educational endeavors has been to influence public policy. Alan Pifer, president of the Corporation between 1965 and 1982, discussed the importance of this goal in an essay on "Foundations and Public Policy," which was printed in the 1974 annual report. He argued that foundations should "be constantly sensitive to public policy issues in the field in which they operate and not be afraid to initiate or support activities that relate to these issues. Indeed, the greatest justification for foundations continuing to enjoy tax-exempt status lies in their making the maximum contribution they can . . . to the development of enlightened public policy for the nation."[5] In her history of the Foundation, Ellen Condliffe Lagemann notes that this policymaking effort left the foundation open to recurring charges that it was in fact manipulating public means for private ends.[6] But Pifer argues that no one should fear the policymaking power of the foundations, because their capabilities in this regard "are small indeed. Ultimately, whatever they do is subject to the harsh rule of the market place."[7]

The leaders of the Carnegie Foundation and Corporation were always eager to make a contribution to the formation of educational policy, however "small." But Lagemann suggests that these philanthropies had considerable impact by successfully shaping the politics of knowledge that is so critical for policy formation. She notes that the efforts of "large philanthropic foundations like the Carnegie Corporation . . . have not directly or exclusively determined the nature of policy-making or indeed the substance of public policy in the United States. But insofar as they have played a central role in shaping the politics of knowledge, their efforts have often been vital in determining which intellectual resources and which social groups would be brought to bear in defining the issues and questions that policymakers would address."[8] When we examine the educational initiatives of these foundations over the course of the twentieth century, a small number of related policy goals come repeatedly into view. In general, Carnegie projects have tended to promote four broad outcomes for U.S. education: social efficiency, rationalization of the educational system, professional expertise, and meritocratic process.[9]

SOCIAL EFFICIENCY

Henry S. Pritchett was the first president of the Foundation and remained in charge until 1930. During this time he managed to put an enduring stamp on the shape of its educational efforts. Lagemann defines his effect this way: "Pritchett . . . turned the Foundation into a forceful and effective proponent of systematization in American education, and through education, in American life. As an advocate for organization and efficiency, Pritchett was especially concerned with establishing the university as both a consolidated and a consolidating center of knowledge-related activities. His signal contribution . . . was to direct some of Carnegie's wealth and the power that came with it to the organization of American education along more modern, national, scientific, and bureaucratic lines."[10] Most of the key elements of the Carnegie vision for U.S. education are captured in this characterization of its first leader's personal vision, including a stress on social efficiency, systematic structure, and expert knowledge. (Significantly absent is any reference to equal opportunity, but this would come with time and changes in leadership.) The principle around which these concerns are organized is the idea of efficiency. As Pritchett himself put it in a 1907 speech, economic change since the end of the Civil War "has taken us out of the pioneer stage." In the more densely populated and complex society that developed, "it becomes more and more necessary that every human being should become an effective, economic unit."[11] To accomplish this goal, what is needed is an educational system that is carefully adapted to the needs of the economy. Such a system must seek to produce economically useful knowledge and to sort people efficiently into the various positions that need to be filled in the stratified occupational structure.

A RATIONALIZED SYSTEM OF EDUCATION

The primary way that the Carnegie Foundation and Corporation have sought to promote a socially efficient educational policy has been by working tirelessly to promote a rationalized system of education in the United States — that is, one that is standardized, vertically integrated, and rationally planned. Andrew Carnegie himself had something different in mind for his creations. An entrepreneur, not a bureaucratic manager, he had run his steel company as a simple partnership and had no desire to manage the kind of complex trust that it became after his retirement. His initial charge to his new Foundation was merely to provide pensions for college professors. However, Pritchett turned this mandate into a powerful mechanism for restructuring education in the United States.

The Foundation's head (a former president of MIT) and his fellow board members (all college presidents) were unhappy with the loose structure of education at the turn of the century, a situation that frequently compelled colleges to compete with high schools for the same students. They set up guidelines to limit eligibility for Foundation pensions to colleges; one requirement was that applicants must spend a certain amount of time studying college-preparatory subjects in a high school. In collaboration with the National Education Association and the College Entrance Examination Board, they settled on a measure of secondary instructional time which became immortalized as the "Carnegie unit" (defined as one quarter of the total time spent in instruction during an academic year). By requiring 14 units (3 ½ years of instruction) for admission to an approved college, the Foundation in effect mandated a four-year course of high school study for students applying to a college that sought to qualify for a Carnegie pension. Through the ostensibly innocuous offer of free pensions, therefore, the foundation established for the first time a clear and hierarchical relation between secondary and higher education and at the same time established a unit of educational progress defined by student seat time rather than a demonstration of content mastery.[12] Both of these innovations had a profound effect on education in the United States.[13]

Not only were the Carnegie philanthropies instrumental in differentiating secondary and higher education, they also played an important part in promoting differentiation within the latter sector. In 1932 a Carnegie panel known as the Commission of Seven issued a report on state higher education in California, which Steven Brint and Jerome Karabel call "a landmark in the rationalization of public higher education in the United States."[14] Motivated by concern about the role of education in providing for the socially efficient allocation of people to jobs, the commission established the outline of what was to become the enormously influential "California model" for the structure of higher education. Under the terms of this model, "the state university had an effective monopoly on research and training for the higher professions; the state colleges concentrated in preparation for such middle-level professions as teaching and social work; and the junior colleges focused on training for the semiprofessions, general education for the masses, and vocational education. The Commission of Seven thus provided a philosophical rationale for the tracking structure that was then emerging in higher education and also a set of concrete proposals designed to sharpen the lines of demarcation between the tracks."[15]

The Foundation maintained a continuing concern for the stratification of higher education. In 1967 it established a Commission on Higher Education under the leadership of Clark Kerr, the former president of the California university system. One of the key conclusions of the Commission was, in the words of one chapter title in its final report, the need for the "Preservation and Enhancement of Quality and Diversity."[16] In practice this goal could be attained by keeping community colleges in their assigned position as two-year institutions focusing on vocational training and by preserving " 'elite' institutions of all types — colleges and universities — [which] should be protected and encouraged as a source of scholarship and leadership training at the highest levels."[17] Pleading that higher education "should not be homogenized in the name of egalitarianism," the final report drew its rationale for stratification from a Commission-sponsored study by Eric Ashby, who asserted that "all civilized countries . . . depend upon a thin clear stream of excellence to provide new ideas, new techniques, and statesmanlike treatment of complex social and political problems."[18]

PROFESSIONAL EXPERTISE

In order to achieve a socially efficient mechanism for training and allocating people to play diverse social roles, the Carnegie Foundation and Corporation have promoted a rationalized system of education. And, as the Ashby quotation suggests, "all civilized countries" can operate efficiently only if they have the benefit of well-informed and highly skilled leaders. Within the Carnegie vision of the ideal society, therefore, it follows that the natural role of the university in the hierarchical structure of schooling is to produce this socially necessary expertise.

One sign of the Carnegie stress on professional knowledge is the series of studies that it commissioned on the subject of restructuring and upgrading professional education. The most famous early report that the Foundation issued was Abraham Flexner's 1910 study of medical education. After examining all 155 medical schools in the United States, he issued a scathing attack on them for producing too many doctors with too little professional skill and then proposed a remedial plan. Most of the basic elements of his plan were eventually adopted, and the result was a system of professional education that became a model for other professions. According to this model, professional education should be solidly grounded in scientific knowledge, in which a candidate should receive substantial undergraduate preparation; it should be strongly linked to the university in the form of a graduate-level degree program; and it should have a curriculum that combines concentrated instruction in theory with supervised practice in a clinical setting. Following upon its success with the Flexner report, the Foundation commissioned a series of other studies of professional education in such fields as dentistry, law, engineering, and teaching.

The Carnegie devotion to professional knowledge also manifested itself in the structure of the work it commissioned. First, the Foundation tended to use professionals to carry out its studies. Flexner himself was a layman (an ex-schoolmaster), but the growing tendency was to have university professors perform the research. Second, there was gradual movement toward the model of forming elite commissions to sponsor Carnegie work in particular areas. This pattern led to such groups as the Commission on Higher Education, the Task Force on Teaching as a Profession (which produced *A Nation Prepared*), and the Task Force on Education of Young Adolescents (which produced *Turning Points*) — each consisting of a star-studded cast of highly credentialed and institutionally sponsored experts.

Third, every Carnegie foray into a new area was fortified with a bewildering array of scientific data, usually constituted as a series of surveys of different parts of the terrain. The ultimate effort in these terms was the work of the Commission on Higher Education, which produced twenty-three commission reports, sixty sponsored research reports, and twenty-three technical reports in addition to hosting twenty-four conferences.[19] As one critic put it, "Kerr and the commission decided to do a strictly science job on higher education — they climbed all over it, counting, measuring, describing, gauging, and projecting enrollment trends, demographic patterns, financing practices, student and alumni attitudes, governance procedures, and community relations."[20]

Fourth, the recommendations that emerged from each of these forays into policy analysis tended to embody a vision of reform by means of rational planning. The image has always been of social and educational problems that are amenable to the prudent intervention of scientifically informed leaders. Problems, the Carnegie philosophy implies, are the result not of political differences or contradictory interests but of a lack of solid information and professional competence. Carnegie studies have consistently aimed to enhance both.[21]

MERITOCRACY

With its long-standing interest in social efficiency, rationalization of the educational system, and professional expertise, the Carnegie Foundation (with the backing of the Corporation) inevitably became an enthusiastic supporter of objective testing in U.S. education. Such tests offered a method of educational evaluation and selection that promised to be both efficient and fair, promoting the rationalization of student advancement within and between schools while grounding such advancement in an objective measure of each student's academic merit.

In 1928, with Foundation support, William Learned and Ben Wood began a massive study of high school and college students in Pennsylvania; the results were published ten years later in the bulletin *The Student and His Knowledge.* At the core of the study was a series of norm-referenced objective tests of aptitude and achievement given to high school seniors, college sophomores, and college seniors between 1928 and 1932. One key outcome was the demonstration that objective testing on a massive scale was feasible at all levels of the educational system. (With the assistance of IBM, the researchers pioneered a method for machine grading test answers.) The study also appeared to demonstrate that such tests were an effective mechanism for identifying the educational capabilities and accomplishments of individual students and thus promised to provide schools and colleges with the scientific information they needed as a basis for differentiating instruction. The result would be a vertically integrated system of schooling, which could provide an efficient and effective mechanism for creating tracks within high schools. This system would help meet the individual needs of the hordes who were invading this level, purportedly providing equal opportunity for these students to gain access to higher education and selecting those for college admission who were most capable of doing the work.[22]

With Foundation support, Learned followed up on the Pennsylvania study by creating the Graduate Record Examination (GRE), a standardized test that was designed to rationalize the transition from college to graduate and professional school in the same way that the College Board's Scholastic Aptitude Test mediated between high school and college. A third testing organization, the Cooperative Testing Service, which had been founded by Ben Wood (Learned's partner in the Pennsylvania study) under the sponsorship of the American Council on Education, was mass-producing objective tests for elementary and secondary schools. After a great deal of negotiation, and with a sizable grant from the Carnegie Corporation funneled through the Foundation, the College Board, American Council on Education, and Carnegie Foundation for the Advancement of Teaching agreed to merge their testing functions in 1947 within a single monolithic testing organization, the Educational Testing Service (ETS).

After ETS was established, Carnegie money continued to pour into testing projects. In the mid-1960s the Corporation initiated an effort to raise educational standards by establishing a national census of student achievement. It put $2.5 million into the planning and test design for what came to be known at the National Assessment of Educational Progress (NAEP), whose funding was then taken over by the federal government. In another testing effort, the Corporation funded the College Board in its development of the College-Level Examination Program (CLEP), which allowed nontraditional students to test out of college course requirements.[23]

Other Carnegie projects helped to promote the kind of stratified structure of education within schools that seemed to follow naturally from the work of Learned and Wood and from the possibilities posed by the new testing technology. In his famous Carnegie Corporation report *The American High School Today,* James B. Conant argued vigorously that "in the required subjects and those elected by students with a wide range of ability, the students should be grouped according to ability, subject by subject . . . one [track] for the more able in the subject, another for the large group whose ability is above average, and another for the very slow readers who should be handled by special teachers. The middle group might be divided into two or three sections according to the students' abilities in the subject in question."[24] The continuing Carnegie concern for testing and tracking, therefore, promised to lead to a system of schooling that was sensitive to both individual merit and social efficiency.

The Ultimate Carnegie Report

In 1986, the Carnegie Corporation's Task Force on Teaching as a Profession issued a report called *A Nation Prepared: Teachers for the 21st Century,* which stands as an ideal representation of the Carnegie tradition in educational policy formation. All of the elements of the classic Carnegie report are there.

As one might expect for a report published under the authority of a Corporation entity known as the Carnegie Forum on Education and the Economy, this report sounds the social efficiency theme loud and clear. The opening paragraphs of the report's executive summary leave no doubt that the primary goal of the educational reforms proposed by the task force is economic:

> America's ability to compete in world markets is eroding. The productivity growth of our competitors outdistances our own. The capacity of our economy to provide a high standard of living for all our people is increasingly in doubt. As jobs requiring little skill are automated or go offshore, and demand increases for the highly skilled, the pool of education and skilled people grows smaller and the backwater of the unemployable rises. Large numbers of American children are in limbo — ignorant of the past and unprepared for the future. Many are dropping out — not just out of school but out of productive society.
>
> As in past economic and social crises, Americans turn to education. They rightly demand an improved supply of young people with the knowledge, the spirit, the stamina and the skills to make the nation once again fully competitive.[25]

Another prominent theme of the report is the important role of expert knowledge, which appears in several different forms. First, there is the membership of the task force itself, which consisted of a formidable array of experts on education and the economy. Out of the fourteen members, there were two business executives (including the chairperson), two governors, two state school superintendents, two heads of teachers unions, an education writer and foundation head, a former HEW secretary, the speaker of a state assembly, a professional association official, the dean of a college of education, and the head of a policy center. (Characteristically, the membership did not include any practicing teachers, to say nothing of students.) In addition, there is a list of commissioned papers and workshop participants in the back, which reinforces the image of expertise that surrounds the report.

But expert knowledge is not simply embodied in the names and credentials of the report's sponsors; it rests at the heart of the task force's proposals. The central theme of *A Nation Prepared* is the need to professionalize the teaching force — a theme it shares with another prominent report *(Tomorrow's Teachers)* issued the same year by an organization of education school deans known as the Holmes Group. (The latter group also received the support of the Carnegie Corporation.) According to both of these reports, education will not improve until it can attract the most qualified people into teaching and give them the kind of training that will allow them to carry out their jobs with the highest level of professional skill. The model for professional education found in both documents is, not surprisingly, drawn directly from Flexner's report on medical education (as noted in the preface of the Carnegie report). Just as Flexner recommended, the two teacher reports call for a system of teacher education that would begin only after students had completed a bachelor's degree focused on the acquisition of subject-matter knowledge; continue at the graduate level in a college of education, where they would focus on what the Holmes Group calls the "science of education"; and culminate in a supervised clinical internship.[26]

Also running through *A Nation Prepared* (and *Tomorrow's Teachers* as well) are the classic Carnegie aims of creating a rationalized, stratified, and meritocratic structure of schooling. Both of these reports are openly hostile to the present bureaucratic control of schools, and both seek to establish a stronger role for the newly professionalized teacher.[27] But in their haste to avoid bureaucracy, both of them run headlong into the embrace of rationalization. In quick succession they endorse sharp increases in standardized testing, occupational stratification, university credential requirements, and (in the case of *A Nation Prepared*) the creation of a system of national certification.

Both reports seem to recommend that prospective teachers be tested before being allowed to enter or exit from a teacher education program, although the Holmes Group is more explicit on this subject: one critic noted that words like *examination, standards,* and *certification* appear fifty-seven times in the first twenty pages of the Holmes report.[28] They both propose to transform the presently undifferentiated status of teaching into a hierarchy leading from regular teacher to the new position of "lead teacher" (in the terminology of *A Nation Prepared*), which would involve broader responsibilities and higher pay. (The Holmes Group adds a third stratum, labeled "instructor," below the other two.) This occupational hierarchy is intended to provide a meritocratic mechanism for upward mobility, as the most able and deserving teachers would be able to get ahead without having to leave the classroom. Guarding the door to this top level of the teaching profession, according to the Carnegie Task Force, would be a newly established National Board for Professional Teaching Standards. The latter group, with Carnegie support, is currently in the process of designing and administering tests through which a select group of teachers will attain national certification in their respective fields. With the first groups of board-certified teachers beginning to emerge only recently, it is unclear whether the board will be pushing certification primarily as a mode of professional development for teachers (which is the way participating teachers tend to see it) or as a mode of meritocratic credentialing (which is the way *A Nation Prepared* and the Carnegie tradition define it).[29]

A Different Sort of Carnegie Report

David Hamburg, the president of the Carnegie Corporation, begins his foreword to *Turning Points* with a display of social efficiency rhetoric that sounds all too familiar to a follower of the Carnegie tradition, echoing the language of the 1986 report on teachers:

> The world is being rapidly transformed by science and technology in ways that have profound significance for our economic well-being and for a democratic society. One upshot is that work will require much technical competence and a great deal of flexibility. . . . Successful participation in a technically based and interdependent world economy will require that we have a more skillful and adaptable workforce than ever before — at every level from the factory floor to top management. . . .
>
> We need to develop the talent of all our people if this nation is to be economically competitive and socially cohesive in the different world of the next century.
>
> To do so, we must take advantage of the neglected opportunity provided by the fascinating period of early adolescence, ages 10 to 15 years.[30]

But the Task Force on Education of Young Adolescents, which issued the report, takes a somewhat different tack from that of the Corporation president. The social efficiency themes are present but in a rather muted form within the main body of the report, largely limited to a small subsection titled "Unprepared Millions Cost Society."[31] And the executive summary, which in *A Nation Prepared* was dominated by economic concerns, touches on these issues in only three scattered sentences. Instead of promoting the relentless pursuit of economic productivity through more efficient schools, as in *A Nation Prepared,* the more recent report focuses on promoting the personal development and the mental and physical health of middle school students.

Consider the image of the kind of fifteen-year-old whom the task force would like to see emerging from middle schools in the United States. This student would be:

> An intellectually reflective person;
> A person en route to a lifetime of meaningful work;
> A good citizen;
> A caring and ethical individual; and
> A healthy person.[32]

As this list suggests, when job roles are mentioned in the report, they are frequently viewed from the perspective of the needs of the individual student for "meaningful work" rather than the economy's need for human capital. This represents a significant shift in the Carnegie approach to education. Instead of looking on schools as efficient mechanisms for sorting and training students for future slots in the occupational structure, the task force focuses on trying to create a middle school environment that will allow early adolescents to develop in ways that will be healthy and personally fulfilling.

The makeup of the task force demonstrates the elements of both continuity and change that are reflected in the new report. In many ways the members of this group look like the standard array of policymaking elites that observers of the Carnegie scene are used to seeing. The chair (David Hornbeck) was also the chair of the Carnegie Foundation trustees; the remaining seventeen members included a governor, a U.S. senator, a retired admiral, a current and an ex-superintendent of schools, a school principal, two executives of other foundations, two education school professors, and an education school dean. But what is new here is the addition of such people as the dean of a college of health, an official of the Girls Clubs, and no fewer than four professors of psychiatry or psychology — additions that suggest a shift toward a concentration on personal growth rather than economic function.

The most striking differences between *Turning Points* and its predecessors in the Carnegie tradition, however, are not the marginal shifts in rhetoric and task-force composition but rather the main thrust of its proposed educational reforms. *A Nation Prepared* reinforced its social efficiency stance with a series of reform proposals that would promote this end through standardization, stratification, meritocratic competition, certification, and the enhancement of professional knowledge. But while the new report takes a position that supports the last two goals, it strongly opposes the others.

As in previous reports, certified professional knowledge is held in high esteem in *Turning Points*. The task force — itself constituted on the basis of its members' expertise — commissioned fifteen papers, brought in seven consultants, held five workshops around the country with a distinguished cast of participants, and relied heavily on the evidence of academic studies to support its conclusions in the report. In addition, it argues that one part of the middle school problem, albeit a small part, is the absence of special training for the teachers in these institutions. They propose that "teachers in middle grade schools should be selected and specially educated to teach young adolescents."[33] The specialized training would include an internship in a middle school, graduate course work on the particular problems of teaching students at this level, and the eventual award of a specialized middle school endorsement on a candidate's teaching certificate. This is familiar-sounding stuff.

The report, however, actively rejects the rest of the reform agenda laid out in *A Nation Prepared* and a long line of previous Carnegie reports. It goes a considerable distance beyond the antibureaucratic stance of the earlier report by proposing that middle schools be broken up into semiautonomous "houses," which would in turn be subdivided into teams of teachers and students. Within these teams, teachers would be able to develop their own interdisciplinary curriculum and would take charge of allocating the use of instructional time during the school day. Even the community would be given a say in educational matters, through such mechanisms as a building-governance committee. The result would be a radically restructured middle school, in which the control over curriculum and instruction is lodged in the hands of teachers operating in groups. Under this approach, the form and content of classroom learning would vary considerably between schools in the same district, between houses in the same school, and even between teams in the same house.

Such a change would not only free classrooms from the clutches of bureaucrats (as *A Nation Prepared* also thought necessary) but would also attack the element of standardization in schooling, which has always been so central to the Carnegie vision. The Carnegie unit (the granddaddy of standardization measures) and that alphabet soup of Carnegie-sponsored testing efforts — GRE, ETS, NAEP, CLEP — have all been top-down attempts to set nationwide standards for U.S. education, the assumption being that schools and teachers at the bottom of the system would have little choice but to go along. To encourage local variation and bottom-up reform goes very much against the grain of the long-standing Carnegie tradition.

Just as dramatic a change is the rejection by the task force of the stratified and meritocratic model of school organization that has also been so much a part of the Carnegie approach. The authors of *Turning Points* turn away from a differentiated curriculum and embrace a strong emphasis on a core academic program for all students. More striking is their strong opposition to the use of tracking and ability grouping, which earlier Carnegie studies had so fervently promoted. "In practice, this kind of tracking has proven to be one of the most divisive and damaging school practices in existence. Time and again, young people placed in lower academic tracks or classes, often during the middle grades, are locked into dull, repetitive instructional programs leading at best to minimum competencies. The psychic numbing these youth experience from a 'dumbed-down' curriculum contrasts sharply with the exciting opportunities for learning and critical thinking that students in the higher tracks or classes may experience."[34]

The report goes even further in turning its back on the long-standing Carnegie devotion to meritocratic competition by urging that merit-based groups should be replaced by heterogeneous groups organized around the goal of cooperative learning. "In cooperative learning situations, all students contribute to the group effort because students receive group rewards as well as individual grades."[35] In addition, the report calls for schools to rely on cross-age tutoring, "which casts older students in the role of teaching younger students and is a proved method of providing additional support for students who need it"; the task force notes that "students at every level of achievement can be effective tutors."[36] Thus instead of focusing on individual differences and organizing school into a competitive hierarchy based on these differences, the report calls for a pedagogy that will promote cooperation among students and attempt to reduce differences between them.

Explaining the Changes

The 1989 report on education represents several apparent "turning points" in the Carnegie approach to educational policy. Trying to explain the reasons for these changes is not a simple matter, and trying to interpret their significance is equally difficult. But three factors have clearly helped to bring about these changes: the shift in the priorities of the Carnegie Foundation and Corporation in the direction of equal opportunity; the fact that the focus for the analysis in *Turning Points* is the problems of adolescents rather than the problems of schools; and most important, the decision in this report, unlike most previous Carnegie studies, to concentrate on a level of schooling that is far removed from the job market.

The Carnegie philanthropic effort has undergone a significant shift in its orientation during the past thirty years. Internal and external sources agree that, in the mid-1960s, the Foundation and the Corporation adopted a growing commitment to the issue of equal opportunity in a belated but nonetheless significant response to the civil rights and antipoverty movements. John Gardner, who headed the Foundation and Corporation from 1955 to 1965, was primarily concerned with the effort to preserve academic standards from the "galloping mediocrity" that threatened to overtake educational institutions as their enrollments expanded in the postwar boom.[37] But according to Alan Pifer, Gardner's successor at both posts, "During the years 1961–1981, the Corporation developed a major commitment to the furtherance of social justice in our national life — to the right of every human being to enjoy equal opportunity and equal treatment before the law."[38]

This shift was signaled by James B. Conant's 1961 book *Slums and Suburbs* (sponsored by the Corporation), in which he moved from his earlier emphasis on excellence to a new focus on educational inequality. A concern over social inequality runs through many of the Carnegie-sponsored reports on education that emerged in the next two decades. It was a central focus of the massive work carried out by the Commission on Higher Education, as suggested by the title of its agenda-setting initial report, *Quality and Equality* (1968), and also of such influential books as *Crisis in the Classroom* (by Charles Silberman) and *Inequality* (by Christopher Jencks).[39]

Ellen Lagemann notes that during the Pifer era — in line with the theme of equal opportunity — there was also "an effort to introduce 'wider representation' into the Foundation's board of trustees. Not only minority group members and women were appointed, but also representatives from a more varied, less elite and homogeneous cross section of American higher education."[40] This effort spilled over into the construction of particular task forces, as the Task Force on Education of Young Adolescents demonstrates. For example, the school principal on this panel, Deborah Meier, heads New York's Central Park East Secondary School, an alternative public school that has an identity quite distinct from that of the traditional American high school and an ethos far removed from Carnegie's stress on social efficiency.[41]

In all, these changes represent a shift in direction toward a goal that had long been near the top of the Carnegie agenda, the development of a more meritocratic system of schooling. Such a shift, however, fails to explain the full significance of the middle school report, which deliberately tries to move beyond this long-standing Carnegie goal. As we have seen, the new report launches a direct attack on the notion that middle schools need to adopt the meritocratic model in order to be fair and effective — arguing, in fact, that tracking and competitive achievement actually undermine both fairness and effectiveness within these schools.

In addition, in contrast to the middle school report, the Carnegie approach in the 1980s generally sought to maintain a focus on social efficiency while simultaneously promoting equal opportunity. When Ernest Boyer (who took over from Pifer as president of the Foundation in 1979) wrote his Carnegie reports on high school (in 1983) and college (in 1987), he was careful to strike this kind of balance. As Pifer put it in his final thoughts upon leaving the presidency of the Corporation in 1982,

> Despite the great variety that has characterized my daily existence at the Corporation, . . . virtually everything I have done as its president . . . has been guided by a single motivating force — a lifelong belief in social justice and the equality of all people under the law. . . .
>
> As time went by this outlook was supplemented by a second perspective that gradually became as strong and as clear as the first. The new outlook grew from an interest I began to take during the 1960s in human resource development or, as it is sometimes called, "human capital formation," which over time has led me to the view that the very future of our society depends absolutely on the broad development of all our people. . . . Investment in such things as nutrition, health, decent housing, education . . . is, therefore, not only a matter of social justice but of practical necessity.[42]

Unlike *A Nation Prepared* and other reports in the Carnegie tradition, however, *Turning Points* seeks to subordinate concern for social efficiency to a concern for social justice and individual opportunity. And in order to facilitate the pursuit of the latter goals, it argues for a change from the present hierarchical structure for the middle school to a decentralized and flexible structure that is more compatible with these goals.

A second factor that has helped to distinguish *Turning Points* from earlier Carnegie reports on education is that it was commissioned by a group whose primary focus was on youth rather than schooling—the Carnegie Council on Adolescent Development. It appears that Carnegie projects tend to present a less confining and more flexible view of the world—one that is less intent on standardization, stratification, and social efficiency—when they focus on the problems of people rather than the problems of educational institutions. Consider Gunnar Myrdal's pathbreaking study of race relations in the United States, *An American Dilemma,* or the array of books on children and youth, such as Kenneth Keniston's *All Our Children* and Richard de Lone's *Small Futures.*[43] In contrast, there seems to be something about the institutional structure of schooling that brings out the most rigid and hierarchical side of the Carnegie tradition, and that something is the connection between schools and jobs.

In a society where the occupational structure is highly stratified, it is difficult for schools to resist the pressure to adapt themselves to this structure. There is a tradition in U.S. schools, however, that does resist this pressure, a tradition that puts forward a vision of schooling as an arena for promoting democratic citizenship and social justice. *Turning Points* successfully taps into this tradition as the ground for its discourse on middle schools. But the forces on the other side of the issue are powerful indeed. With a hierarchical economy as a structural fact of life, any effort to make economy and society operate effectively leads to pressure on schools to sort and train people for differentiated work roles. Also, from an individual's perspective, any effort to get ahead in such a society leads to pressure on schools to provide access to the more attractive job roles. The end result is that the demand for social efficiency and social mobility both act as a spur for organizations like the Carnegie Corporation to promote the rationalization of the relation between school and work.

The pressure on schools for such rationalization is most intense at that the point in the educational structure where students are most likely to leave school and go to work. During most of the twentieth century, high school was that point for working-class youths and for many middle-class youths as well. In the past two decades, however, college enrollments have grown so quickly that most high school graduates now continue with their education rather than heading off to work right away. As a result, college has become the primary point within the educational system at which most students make the transition to the workforce. Under these circumstances, the early decision by Carnegie leaders to focus on higher education naturally led them to work at creating a system that was socially efficient, one that was effective in producing human capital and sorting people for future work roles. Thus when they confronted a demand for social justice and democratic equality (as they did in the 1960s), they tended to translate it into the language of equal opportunity. Operationally this simply meant more of what they had been doing all along — redoubling their efforts to promote a stratified and standardized system of education (with a strong emphasis on objective testing), all under the banner of meritocracy.

David Cohen and Barbara Neufeld point out, however, that as the school-leaving age rises, the pressures on lower levels of schooling to adapt to the workforce decline: "If high school is no longer the last stop before adulthood and work, then secondary students can be treated in a more informal and playful fashion. Deferring the immediacy of work defers the pressures of preparing for it, and permits a reinterpretation of the curriculum to suit students' intellectual or cultural interests."[44]

But because high school still remains "the last stop before adulthood and work" for most working-class youths, this analysis of the declining economic pressures on schooling in fact applies most directly to the middle school. For the middle school is the highest level of schooling that has universal attendance but that is still buffered from immediate concern about preparation for work. In this sense, then, the most significant factor shaping the novel preferences expressed in *Turning Points* compared with earlier Carnegie reports may be the grade level involved. The distance from the workforce at this level may best explain why this report, against all precedent, argues for community over stratification, cooperation over competition, decentralized control over hierarchical control, and local flexibility over standardization. In a middle school — even from the perspective of that great engine of educational rationalization, the Carnegie Corporation — educators may have the luxury of approaching education from the perspective of the personal development of students rather than the socially efficient production of human capital.

Therefore, while *Turning Points* may in fact promote a kinder and gentler form of schooling than *A Nation Prepared* and its predecessors, this may have occurred primarily because of the hothouse setting of the middle school, whose economic irrelevance means that educational innovations there pose no threat to the social efficiency of schooling (Carnegie's traditional focus of concern). Perhaps it is acceptable, even desirable, to create an undifferentiated and nonstandardized learning community in these grades simply because there is still plenty of time in high school and college to select and socialize students for their future roles in a stratified society. After all, the Carnegie Foundation and Corporation have always focused on higher education — and rightly so, because it is at this level that the concern for social efficiency is most salient, which in turn makes the rationalization of education at this level most essential. Opening up education a bit for middle-schoolers still leaves intact the system of education that Carnegie initiatives helped construct during the course of the twentieth century.

One last clue about the contradictory character of this report is the manner in which it is introduced. The report proposes a bottom-up reform of American middle schools, but it does so in the classic top-down Carnegie fashion — with an elite panel, a glitzy report, and a big press conference, all designed explicitly to influence high-ranking policymakers rather than to mobilize reform efforts within individual schools. Perhaps, then, the form of the report really does give some insight into its function — and both form and function suggest substantial compatibility with the Carnegie legacy. *Turning Points,* therefore, may indeed be just what it appears to be, a Carnegie report of a slightly different hue. It proposes a radical restructuring of the middle school, but one that fits neatly within the existing Carnegie-endorsed structure of education. The Carnegie tradition, it seems, will survive this recent turning point in its long history.

6

Rethinking the Movement to Professionalize Teaching

Critical reports about U.S. education proliferated in the 1980s. These reports took a wide range of approaches to the subject; they diagnosed a variety of ailments that appeared to afflict schools and prescribed a variety of reform measures that promised to effect a cure. Some of the less complex reform proposals, which permitted easy implementation within the existing structure of schooling, were quickly put in place. A large number of states and school districts, for example, raised the number of academic credits required for high school graduation. Other more radical proposals, which called for a restructuring of the educational process, have met more resistance. But one of the more radical proposals has managed to gather institutional support and forward momentum: the movement to professionalize teaching.

In 1986, major reports from two groups proposed this solution to some of the dilemmas confronting U.S. schooling. *A Nation Prepared: Teachers for the 21st Century* was issued by the Carnegie Task Force on Teaching as a Profession, an elite assortment of public officials, executives, leading educators, and teachers union officials under the sponsorship of the Carnegie Corporation of New York. *Tomorrow's Teachers* was issued by the Holmes Group, a consortium of the deans of colleges of education at about one hundred leading research universities.[1] Both reports argue that the quality of public education can improve only if schoolteaching is transformed into a full-fledged profession. In "the pursuit of excellence" through education, according to the Carnegie report, "the key to success lies in creating a profession equal to the task — a profession of well-educated teachers prepared to assume new powers and responsibilities to redesign schools for the future."[2] One key element of these reform efforts is the proposal to enhance the professional education of teachers, a step that would mean eliminating undergraduate teacher certification programs and raising professional training to the graduate level. Teacher education, the reformers argue, should include undergraduate preparation in a particular subject matter; graduate training in what the Holmes Group calls the "science of teaching," which would lead to a master's degree (the new entry-level credential for teachers); and an extended clinical internship in a "professional development school," analogous to a teaching hospital. The explicit model for these reforms comes from medical education, because medicine provides the best available example of a successful effort at professionalization.[3]

The second major element of these reforms is the proposal to transform the structure of teaching. The reports argue for the abandonment of the present undifferentiated structure — in which teachers all occupy the same stratum and rewards are distributed according to seniority and educational credentials — in favor of a stratified system that would create a second tier of teachers known as "lead teachers" (Carnegie) or "career professionals" (Holmes). This new group, as the elite of the profession, would assume higher-level duties and earn higher pay than regular teachers. These duties, undertaken in addition to a continuing role in classroom teaching, would include instructional consulting with teachers in the lower tier, supervision of teacher interns, curriculum development, and involvement in teacher education at the university. In order to attain such a position, a teacher would have to demonstrate instructional excellence, pursue advanced graduate training in a college of education (perhaps including a clinical doctorate or an educational specialist degree), and attain board certification by passing an examination offered by a National Board for Professional Teaching Standards, again modeled on medical education.[4]

In the ten years since these reforms were first proposed, many of them have moved substantially along the path toward implementation. A number of colleges of education have committed themselves to the creation of graduate programs in teacher education, extended internships for student-teachers, and the collaborative construction of professional development schools; the National Board, meanwhile, has begun the process of examining candidates and granting advanced professional certification.

In this chapter, I argue that the teacher professionalization movement has the potential for doing more harm than good in its impact on U.S. education, and on the teachers, students, and citizens who have a stake in seeing this institution carry out its goals effectively. My fear is that the movement will inadvertently have two effects that are not in the best interests of democratic education: augmenting the influence of the university over primary and secondary schooling by reinforcing the authority of those who teach teachers, and accelerating the rationalization of classroom instruction by reinforcing a research-based model of teaching practice.

The Meaning of Professionalization

Before examining the historical roots and political implications of the movement to professionalize teaching, we consider some questions about the professionalization process: what it means to professionalize an occupation; why the achievement of such a goal can be difficult (especially in the case of teaching); why past efforts by occupational groups to pursue this goal have received mixed reviews; and how a professionalization movement can be analyzed.

DEFINITION

The current effort to professionalize teaching is grounded in an analysis of how other U.S. occupational groups historically established their professional claims.[5] The two prongs of the teacher-professionalization effort proposed by the reports — restructuring both the professional education and the work roles of teachers — point to two key elements that are demonstrably part of any successful claim of professional status: formal knowledge and workplace autonomy. These characteristics lie at the core of what we generally mean by the term *profession*. Consider, for example, Andrew Abbott's definition: "Professions are exclusive occupational groups applying somewhat abstract knowledge to particular cases."[6] From this perspective, the claim to professional status rests on a simple bargain: technical competence is exchanged for technical autonomy, practical knowledge for control over practice. The upwardly mobile occupational group must establish that it has mastery of a formal body of knowledge that is not accessible to the layperson and that gives it special competence in carrying out a particular form of work. In return, the group asks for a monopoly over its area of work on the grounds that only those who are certifiably capable should be authorized to do such work and to define appropriate forms of practice in the area.

The Carnegie and Holmes reports argue that teachers must advance on both of these fronts if they hope to attain professional status. This would mean increasing the level of professional knowledge held by practitioners through extending university training in subject matter and pedagogical skills and strengthening professional control of the process of teaching through a transformation of the authority structure within schools. The reports assert that both teachers and society would benefit from this professionalization effort. Teachers would win greater prestige, greater opportunity for career advancement, more varied and stimulating working conditions, and, presumably, higher pay. Society, on its side of the professional bargain, would gain a more competent and dedicated teaching force, which in turn would enhance student achievement and, ultimately, create a more skilled and productive workforce. This comfortable scenario is supported by the arguments put forward by functionalist sociologists, who portray professionalization as a natural accompaniment to modernization that benefits both practitioners and the public.[7] Other voices suggest that this process can be more problematic, however, both because the effort to achieve professional status is fraught with difficulty and because the public benefits of such an achievement are questionable.

FEASIBILITY

Early accounts, using physicians as the primary model, have portrayed professionalization as a process that follows a well-worn path forward to a seemingly inevitable conclusion. Recent writers, however, have come to adopt a more complex vision, whose most comprehensive expression is found in Abbott's book *The System of Professions*.[8] Abbott portrays professionalization as an open-ended struggle that must operate without the benefit of a single path to success, a secure mechanism for preserving success, or even a stable set of criteria for establishing what constitutes success. His analysis of the sociological and historical literature suggests that professionalization is always tentative: a rhetorical claim that is perennially subject to counterclaims and changing fortunes as conditions in the "system of professions" change over time. The best evidence for this characterization is the way in which the seemingly invulnerable position of U.S. physicians has come under heavy attack in recent years.

There are a number of reasons for thinking that the path to professionalism for teachers in particular is filled with craters and quicksand: the problems inherent in trying to promote professional standards in a mass occupation; the likelihood of credential devaluation as a consequence of raised educational requirements; the leveling legacy of teacher unionism; fiscal and political limits on raising teacher salaries; the historical position of teaching as a form of women's work; political resistance from parents, citizens, and politicians to the assertion of professional control over schools; the late entry of teaching into an already crowded field of professionalizing occupations; the prior professionalization of school administrators and the entrenched power of the administrative bureaucracy; the long tradition of carrying out educational reform by bureaucratic means; the problem of trying to convince the public that knowledge about apparently nonesoteric school subjects is a form of exclusive professional expertise; the difficulty of constituting pedagogy as a formal system of professional knowledge; the extensive role of nonprofessionals (parents and other laypersons) in the instruction of children; the low status of education schools and teacher educators; university reluctance to relax its monopoly over high-status knowledge; and the diversity of sites in which teacher education takes place.[9]

Given these potential roadblocks, the archetypal case of an occupation group that has faced a crisis of status similar to that of teachers — as Gary Sykes points out — is not the success story told by physicians but rather the story of failure and frustration told by nurses.[10] Yet Sykes argues that partial success would be better than nothing, and therefore that professionalization for teachers is worth pursuing in spite of all the factors likely to impede the process.[11] After all, as Abbott and others suggest, professionalization is more a process than an outcome. Thus the most important issue is not whether the current effort to professionalize teachers will win them a position among the high professions but whether it will yield any results at all. There are good reasons to believe that the pursuit of professional status for teachers will produce some observable consequences for U.S. schools, even if these consequences may not necessarily include those proposed by the professionalization movement. For one thing, this movement developed institutional backing within colleges of education, teacher unions, and the foundations; for another, it became embedded in organizations (such as the Holmes Group and the National Board) that worked systematically to achieve professionalization.[12] Factors such as these suggest that this educational reform effort will not simply evaporate, as have less substantial reform efforts in the past, but that it will leave its mark on the educational and social environment.

DESIRABILITY

If the teacher professionalization movement does have an impact, how will the public benefit? Characteristically, the Carnegie report makes the most sweeping positive claims for this reform proposal: "Our argument, then, is simple. If our standard of living is to be maintained, if the growth of a permanent underclass is to be averted, if democracy is to function effectively into the next century, our schools must graduate the vast majority of their students with achievement levels long thought possible for only the privileged few. The American mass education system, designed in the early part of the century for a mass-production economy, will not succeed unless it not only raises but redefines the essential standards of excellence and strives to make quality and equality of opportunity compatible with each other."[13] According to this view, the creation of a professional teaching force will enable us to pursue more effectively all of the major social goals that Americans have traditionally assigned to public schools: social efficiency (raising the standard of living via enhanced skill training), social mobility (increasing social opportunity for the underclass), and political equality (enhancing students' ability to function in a democracy).

Functionalist sociology tends to support this rosy picture of the consequences of professionalization, but other approaches see a variety of negative consequences.[14] For example, Marxists consider professionalization to be an extension of class control under the guise of expertise or an ideological cover for proletarianization.[15] Foucaultians see it as a symptom and agency of the rise of disciplinary power.[16] Weberians see it as a mechanism for legitimizing the raw self-interest of socially mobile occupational groups.[17] Even some supporters of teacher professionalization find it fraught with potentially negative side effects, such as inequity and elitism.[18] As a result, there is good reason to be suspicious of any movement that calls for professionalization, on the grounds that it may benefit only the interest group leading the way, or reinforce structural tendencies toward social and political inequality, or both. Yet, however justified these suspicions might be in general, to dismiss a particular reform movement solely on the basis of its concern for professionalization would be to attribute guilt by association and to reject the possibility that this process could be harnessed to socially progressive ends.

Under these circumstances, where the meaning of professionalization remains contested and diffuse, any effort to understand the current movement to professionalize teaching must approach it as something more than an example of a general process. Instead, we need to consider the particular case at hand, as presented by the two 1986 reports, and securely locate this analysis in time and place.

METHODOLOGY

Let us approach the problem of determining the likely outcomes of the current teacher professionalization movement by asking why the movement emerged at this time and in this form. That is, why did it develop in the late 1980s and take on the character defined by the Carnegie and Holmes proposals? To explore teacher professionalization in this context is to attempt to establish its genealogy.[19] This approach to the analysis of teacher professionalization offers several important advantages. It focuses attention on the analytical task of examining the roots of the movement rather than on the more speculative project of divining its ultimate purpose. It also frees us from the confining assumption that the movement is a result of a process of rational planning, deliberately invented as a rational mechanism for accomplishing a particular educational goal. Instead, genealogy opens up the possibility of finding a heterogeneous mixture of elements embedded within the movement, elements that may be rationally incompatible with the stated purposes of the movement. Finally, by focusing on the lineages of teacher professionalization, we can develop a useful perspective for deciding where it fits in relation to the broader goals of education (as spelled out in Chapter 1) and therefore which particular tendencies it would foster. The relative balance of historical components that make up the movement help to establish its central thrust and thus provide us with information about the political baggage that this reform effort carries with it.[20]

Roots of Teacher Professionalization

Why is it, then, that the Carnegie-Holmes version of teacher professionalization emerged as a significant movement in the late 1980s? Let us consider some of the more important antecedent elements that contributed to it.

THE SHIFT FROM EQUITY TO EXCELLENCE IN THE GOALS FOR PUBLIC EDUCATION

Throughout their history, U.S. public schools have been subject to periodic waves of reform. One reason for this wavelike pattern is the contradictory purposes pursued by educational reformers. Over the years, reformers have swung back and forth between political goals (equity, equality, citizenship training) and market goals (excellence, vocational training, individual status attainment).[21] Whereas the 1960s and 1970s were marked by a push for more equity in schools, with attacks on racial segregation and class-based tracking, the early 1980s brought a shift in the direction of excellence. In one report after another, critics charged that schools were failing to provide adequate levels of academic achievement and that this would undermine worker productivity and threaten the United States' competitive position in the world economy.[22]

Teacher professionalization emerged as one reaction to the problems posed in these critiques. The Carnegie report stresses the need to raise standards for teachers and the importance of the link between effective instruction and social efficiency — goals that are directly descended from the emphasis on excellence that shaped educational discourse in the early 1980s. But in addition, the professionalization movement emerged as part of a second wave of reform that sought to restore the balance between equity and excellence that was lost in reports that came out earlier in the decade.[23] Thus the Carnegie report argues that restructured schools should seek "to make quality and equality of opportunity compatible with each other," and the second Holmes Group report devotes considerable space to concerns about equity in detailing its vision of "tomorrow's schools."[24]

DISENCHANTMENT WITH BUREAUCRATIC REFORM EFFORTS

Educational reform over the years has been "steady work," in part because it has not been successful in solving the most important educational problems: "Reforms that deal with the fundamental stuff of education — teaching and learning — seem to have weak, transitory, and ephemeral effects; while those that expand, solidify, and entrench school bureaucracy seem to have strong, enduring, and concrete effects."[25]

For the past 150 years, educational reform efforts have tended to originate at the top of the system (in the statehouse and the superintendent's office) and then work their way down through the hierarchy, usually petering out by the time they get to the classroom door. As a result, the primary effect of these reforms has been to increase the size and complexity of the educational bureaucracy, but this bureaucratic approach has been remarkably ineffective in shaping the instructional process.[26] The chronic failure of bureaucratic reform to deal effectively with educational problems has not led to its abandonment. In fact, the calls for reform that emerged in the early 1980s generally responded to past bureaucratic failures by intensifying bureaucratic administration through such mechanisms as raising graduation requirements and introducing state- and districtwide testing programs.

At the same time, however, a rising number of educators and educational researchers have been proposing a mechanism for reform that is intended to be more effective and less hierarchical than the traditional bureaucratic approach. These voices have argued for restructuring schools in a way that reduces centralized administrative control and increases the role of individual schools, smaller organizational units within schools, communities, and teachers.[27] The teacher professionalization movement is one natural outgrowth of these decentralization efforts, because it seeks to increase the autonomy of teachers and institutionalize their impact on classroom instruction. Both of the reports that initiated this movement express the view that bureaucracy must recede if professionalization is going to become a reality. One of the five main goals of the Holmes Group, for example, is "to make schools better places for teachers to work, and to learn." The report adds, "This will require less bureaucracy, more professional autonomy, and more leadership for teachers."[28]

THE SHIFT FROM STATE TO MARKET SOLUTIONS

The Reagan presidency brought a significant shift in the discourse on social engineering, as state remedies for social problems lost ground to market-based remedies. This increased preference for the market over the state helped reinforce the parallel preference for decentralization over bureaucracy. According to the administration's ideology, bureaucratic government's intervention in social life was ineffective, inefficient, and even counterproductive, and the private sector (capitalism and "volunteerism") was capable of handling many of these areas better than the state. This was the decade when state-run schools came under attack for being both bureaucratic and monopolistic, and when a market-based alternative model for school governance made serious headway. Under the latter "choice" model, schools would have to compete with each other for the patronage of parents, who would have the freedom to choose where they would enroll their children.[29]

The teacher professionalization movement has explicitly chosen to pursue a market-based strategy of implementation. The Carnegie report, for example, makes it clear with reference to board certification that "the certification process is envisioned by the Task Force as completely voluntary. There would be no requirement imposed on new teachers or teachers currently in the workforce to participate. But the Task Force expects that many teachers will wish to do so, because the certificate will be an unambiguous statement that its holder is a highly qualified teacher. Certificate holders can expect to be eagerly sought by states and districts that pride themselves on the quality of their schools."[30]

In a paper commissioned by the task force, Shulman and Sykes argue strongly for adopting this market strategy over a political strategy.[31] The advantage of the market approach, from their perspective, is that it provides an incentive for individual teachers to strive for excellence in the practice of their profession, whereas the political approach (for example, state-mandated certification requirements) can only establish minimum criteria for entry into practice. In the best tradition of market-oriented initiatives, then, board certification of teachers promises to promote higher standards for public education by means of individual initiative and unfettered competition.

The Holmes Group's proposals for reforming teacher education also point to a market approach. Instead of lobbying for an increase in the state mandate for preservice teacher training, the group is establishing model programs for graduate professional education at the country's most prestigious colleges of education. The idea is that once these colleges set a higher standard for teacher education, school districts will seek the graduates from these programs because of their superior qualifications, and students will compete to get into these programs. Consequently, the less prestigious teacher-training institutions (which prepare the majority of the new teachers every year) will eventually feel compelled by market pressure to adopt the new standard.

THE RISE OF FEMINISM

The 1970s and 1980s also brought the rise of feminism and a growing, if still limited, acceptance of feminist views by the public at large. Polls began to show that traditional conceptions of gendered work were increasingly being called into question — particularly the notion that women should naturally seek jobs that call for them to nurture children and serve men. Teaching has long been the prototypical form of such women's work. Not only are most of its practitioners female, but it puts women in a situation that mimics both the nurturing role of a mother (in relation to students) and the subordinate role of a wife (in relation to male administrators).[32] Not only has teaching been ideologically congruent with notions of female domesticity, but, given the traditionally restricted options for women in the workforce, it has also been one of the most socially and financially rewarding jobs accessible to educated women.[33]

In the increasingly feminist environment of the 1980s, however, teaching began to look less attractive to women seeking a professional career. A declining proportion of female college graduates were eager to pursue such a stereotypically female occupation. And as prestigious and traditionally male professions such as medicine, law, and business began to open up to women, fewer women were forced to fall back on teaching as the most attractive alternative.[34]

The teacher professionalization movement, therefore, can be understood in part as a natural outgrowth of these changing social and ideological patterns in U.S. gender relations. Professionalization offers the teacher a way to escape identification with the unpaid and uncredentialed status of mother. The new professional teacher — especially a board-certified "lead" or "career professional" teacher — would be well paid and formally credentialed, with an education and a status within hailing distance of the high professions. In addition, the movement offers female teachers an opportunity to get out from under the thumb of male administrators (thereby shrugging off the long-standing association with the status of wife) by asserting their right to autonomy in the classroom and to a significant influence in the operation of the school. These professionalized teachers would be empowered, independent, and well rewarded—skillful decision makers who could apply the special knowledge base of their profession to the particular learning requirements of the students.

This analysis suggests that the Carnegie-Holmes vision of teacher professionalization grew out of what Kathleen Weiler identifies as the liberal version of feminism, which dominated feminist discourse in the 1980s.[35] Stressing the need to liberate women from the constraints of gender-differentiated socialization and selection, liberal feminists argue that women should be encouraged to escape from traditionally female forms of work in order to compete with men in traditionally male occupations. From this perspective, female teachers should not be content with their current situation but should remain in the classroom only if teaching adopts the model set by the male professions.

Radical feminists reject this strategy. They argue that the differences between men and women should not be "resolved" by having women play out male roles in the traditional male manner.[36] From this alternative perspective, the teacher professionalization movement runs the risk of abandoning the distinctive and desirable characteristics of the female teacher (nurturing, emotionally supportive, person-centered, and context-focused) in order to take on the frequently undesirable characteristics of the dominant male professional (competitive, rationalistic, task-centered, and abstracted from context). The Holmes and Carnegie reports make virtually no reference to the former traits in their description of teaching as a profession; instead, they argue that this profession should be grounded in a scientific knowledge base, arranged competitively into a meritocratic hierarchy, and focused on the task of increasing subject-matter learning. Apparently thinking of teaching's femaleness as unprofessional, the professionalizers seem to be trying to reshape the female schoolteacher in the image of the male physician.[37]

THE LOWLY STATUS OF TEACHERS IN A PROFESSIONALIZING ENVIRONMENT

At one level, the teacher professionalization movement is an extension of the broader movement that seeks to raise the status of women workers by eradicating the category of "women's work." At another level, it arises from the narrower effort to raise the status of teachers. There is nothing new about this effort. In the mid-nineteenth century, during the early days of the U.S. common school system, teachers occupied a pitifully low position in the social hierarchy. This was the era when "teachers were paid in pumpkins and firewood" and, if they were lucky, a small amount of cash; when job security was nonexistent because school boards handed out positions as a form of political patronage and as a dole for widows; when girls taught for a few years between the end of school and the start of marriage, and men taught only until they could find a real job; and when the rapid growth of school enrollment put a premium on finding anyone at low cost to act as a "schoolkeeper," leaving the question of instructional competence as a secondary issue.[38]

After these unpromising beginnings, teaching had nowhere to go but up. By the turn of the century, bureaucratizing school systems were beginning to increase teacher pay and job security and raise educational requirements for job entry.[39] The upward trend continued for fifty years or more, signaled by the elevation of teacher-training requirements from a couple of years of a high school–level normal school to a four-year college degree and by the increasing number of teachers who were making a career in the classroom. At midcentury, however, teacher status peaked and started to slide downward. One supporter of teacher professionalization explains the problem this way: "In recent years, the college-educated segment of the population has increased in our society, with two consequences. Teachers are no longer among the best educated members of many communities. The minimal status they once enjoyed is slowly eroding. And, for many college graduates today, teaching represents downward, not upward, mobility."[40]

From this angle, teacher status was the victim of creeping inflation in educational credentials. As more people acquired college degrees, teachers lost their educational distinctiveness and slid back into the pack.[41] This relative slippage in social position received reinforcement from another long-term trend in status competition. Entire occupation groups were trying to attain what Magali Larson calls "collective social mobility" by advancing claims for professional status, which they supported by raising standards for professional education, instituting entry-level testing and peer certification, establishing national organizations, and asserting commitment to the public interest.[42] Under these circumstances, teachers found themselves — individually and collectively — dropping toward the bottom of the white-collar hierarchy. Perhaps the last straw came in the 1980s, when registered nurses moved toward adoption of the bachelor's degree as their new entry-level educational requirement (replacing the old requirement of a nursing school certificate or an associate's degree). Teaching and nursing had long been the main competitors for the loyalty of young women seeking semiprofessional careers, and now teaching was about to lose its educational advantage. A natural way to respond to this threat was for teachers to pursue professionalization themselves.

THE RISE OF THE SCIENCE OF TEACHING

The literature on professions suggests that teacher professionalization cannot take place until there is a well-developed body of knowledge on teaching that is able to guide teaching practice. As the Holmes Group report states, "The established professions have, over time, developed a body of specialized knowledge, codified and transmitted through professional education and clinical practice. Their claim to professional status rests on this." The report argues that this situation is already close at hand for teaching: "Scholarship and empirical research on education has matured, providing a solid base for an intellectually vital program of professional studies." The authors continue:

> Until the last two decades, scholarship in education and the content of the hundreds of university courses in the subject had to rely heavily upon the findings in other disciplines, particularly the behavioral sciences. . . . Within the last twenty years, however, the science of education promised by Dewey, Thorndike, and others at the turn of the century, has become more tangible: The behavioral sciences have been turned on the schools themselves and not just in laboratory simulations. Studies of life in classrooms now make possible some convincing counter-intuitive conclusions about schooling and pupil achievement. Ironically, now that the promise of science of education is about to be fulfilled, many current reform recommendations recall an older literature that demands a decrease in the time given to the study of this scholarship.[43]

Arguing against initiatives in states such as Texas, New Jersey, and Michigan that have sought to limit or sidestep formal instruction in the science of teaching, the Holmes report proposes to extend this area of study. After all, its authors assert now that we have accumulated such a substantial amount of research evidence about teaching, we can for the first time provide prospective teachers with solid training in a form of knowledge about teaching practice that is specialized (no longer dependent on the disciplines), authoritative (scientific), and inaccessible to the layperson ("counterintuitive") — the crucial prerequisites for any occupational group claiming to be a profession.

THE PROFESSIONALIZATION OF TEACHER EDUCATORS

At the heart of the Holmes Group report is a harsh critique of the current state of teacher education as well as teaching: "Unhappily, teaching and teacher education have a long history of mutual impairment. Teacher education long has been intellectually weak; this further eroded the prestige of an already poorly esteemed profession, and it encouraged many inadequately prepared people to enter teaching. But teaching long has been an underpaid and overworked occupation, making it difficult for universities to recruit good students to teacher education or to take it as seriously as they have taken education for more prestigious professions."[44] The teacher professionalization movement has chosen to move toward reform on both fronts at the same time, seeking to transform both the structure of teaching and the process of teacher education.

The critique of teacher education implies that a key obstacle to professionalization is the weakness of the teacher educators themselves. Judith Lanier, president of the Holmes Group and member of the Carnegie Task Force on Teaching as a Profession, also was the lead author of a devastating portrait of the faculty who carry out teacher education.[45] This review appeared as a chapter in the third edition of *The Handbook of Research on Teaching*, which came out the same year as the Carnegie and Holmes reports. Lanier and Little argue that teacher educators have generally received less rigorous training than other academics, because "the doctorate in education can often be completed more quickly than the doctorate in other fields" and because such training is often carried out while the student is holding down a full-time job. In addition, they note that teacher educators show "an extremely low record of scholarly accomplishment." One study showed that "less than 20 per cent of the 1,367 education units in higher education had faculty involved in education research and development."[46] In short, teacher educators generally do not meet the primary professional standard that exists for other college professors, research productivity.

It is not surprising, therefore, that the Holmes report calls for upgrading the teacher-education faculty to bring it in line with the norms of the academic profession as a whole. At the back of the report are a set of proposed "Holmes Group Standards," one of which demands that "the academic faculty responsible for teacher education contribute regularly to better knowledge and understanding of teaching and schooling." The report goes on to explain this goal as a necessary component of the larger goal of teacher professionalization: "The scholarly productivity of the academic faculty in teacher education contributes to the codification of effective practice and to better understanding of aspects of education that have promise for improving teaching and learning in schools."[47]

In effect, the report argues that one cannot professionalize teachers without first professionalizing teacher educators. It is unreasonable to think that teachers can be successfully elevated to the status of high professionals by an unprofessional group of education school faculty. And it is equally unreasonable to expect that teachers can become professionals without a specialized, authoritative, and counterintuitive professional knowledge base. The professionalization of teacher educators helps solve both problems. It raises the status of the status raisers, and it does so by promoting a science of teaching, which both affirms the academic professionalism of teacher educators and legitimizes the professional authority of teachers.

The Holmes Group, therefore, portrays the effort to professionalize teaching as an exercise in rational planning. The professionalization of teacher education is seen as a means to the movement's greater ends, a first-stage goal that colleges of education can accomplish on their own. However, a different interpretation seems more credible: the professionalization of teacher education is more than a component in the strategy for teacher professionalization; it is a process that was already in motion long before the two reports emerged in 1986 and that served as a crucially necessary precondition for these reports. In short, in a significant way, the teacher professionalization movement of the 1980s is descended from the prior movement to professionalize teacher educators and from the scientific knowledge base that was developed during that process.

Tomorrow's Teachers provides evidence for this interpretation. It shows that at least some teacher educators were generating a sizable amount of respectable research on schools and teaching during the two decades before the report was published. This finding suggests strongly that these teacher educators were already establishing an increasingly effective claim of professional status for their field within the academic community. And these professionalizing teacher educators were and are located almost exclusively within the very institutions — colleges of education at research-oriented universities — that constituted the membership, and especially the leadership, of the Holmes Group.

This genealogy of the teacher professionalization movement that emerged in the 1980s shows that the movement traces its lineage back to a wide range of preexisting social events and ideological orientations. Before considering the likely outcomes of teacher professionalization, we must examine the last two roots of this movement more closely. These two elements are particularly important for a sound understanding of how the movement came about and why it took the form that it did. First, teachers cannot establish an effective claim to professional power without a credible base of professional knowledge; and, second, a socially powerful mechanism is required for carrying out professional education in this knowledge. These two components, in turn, are thoroughly interconnected. Teacher educators cannot professionalize unless they produce a solid body of research on teaching, and there cannot be a science of teaching unless there is an authoritative (that is, university-based) interest group with an incentive to generate it.

The Rise of Teacher Educators

Why did the professionalization of teacher educators and the rise of the science of teaching develop interactively during the two decades prior to the Holmes and Carnegie reports, and why did this joint development take the form that it did? By analyzing some of the key elements that contributed to this process, we will be able to explore the ways in which these elements are embedded in the particular proposals made in the reports.

THE WEAK POSITION OF TEACHER EDUCATORS WITHIN
THE UNIVERSITY

The first U.S. institutions devoted specifically to teacher education were the state normal schools, which developed in Massachusetts in the 1830s under the sponsorship of Horace Mann and then spread around the country.[48] Originally designed as secondary schools for the training of elementary teachers, neither their status nor their function remained stable for very long. They began to move up the ladder of institutional mobility, propelled by a combination of individual and professional ambition. For many educational consumers, these normal schools increasingly served as places to acquire a high school education and a chance to achieve a position that was not necessarily limited to teaching. The rapid proliferation of high schools at the end of the nineteenth century posed a competitive threat to normal schools but also gave normal-school faculties the opportunity to raise admission standards and pursue college status. By the 1920s, normal schools were being converted wholesale into state teachers colleges, which in turn transformed the faculty members into college professors. Students still tended to treat these institutions as mechanisms for acquiring the educational credentials needed to get ahead as much as for acquiring a teaching certificate. After the Second World War, state teachers colleges continued to adapt to this demand and to the professional aspirations of their faculties by rapidly converting themselves into full-service state colleges and finally, in the 1970s and 1980s, into state universities.

These historical developments have brought enormous benefits to most teacher educators. Riding on the backs of their upwardly mobile institutions, they have experienced an elevation over the past one hundred years from the status of high school teacher to that of university professor. In this sense, the professionalization of teacher educators has been going on for a long time. However, this rapid rise in status has caused problems, especially in the past twenty years, as a growing proportion of these teacher educators found themselves in a university environment. In this new setting, teacher education is no longer the centerpiece but must compete with a wide range of other occupational and liberal arts programs with greater prestige. Not only that, but teacher educators increasingly have been held accountable according to university norms of professional conduct rather than the norms that originated in the normal school. Thus they have been under growing pressure to carry out research and publish in academic journals, activities, as Lanier and Little point out, they have little training for or interest in.[49]

As a result of these recent developments, most teacher educators have come to enjoy the formal status of a university professor but with a weak substantive claim to professional standing in the university community. In this competitive arena, the only route for making such a claim was through research productivity.[50] Pressure to do so was particularly strong for teacher educators at the older and more prestigious universities, in which the research norm was most firmly established (and from which the Holmes Group eventually emerged). Fortunately, a model of how to assert a claim to professional status successfully in an educational setting was close at hand. Since the turn of the century, educational psychology has been one area within education schools that has been able to establish itself as a credible producer of academic knowledge and thus establish its faculty as legitimate members of the university professoriate. Consequently, it is not surprising that the push for professionalization of teacher educators began with applying the methods of educational psychology to the problems of teaching.

THE WEAK POSITION OF TEACHER EDUCATORS WITHIN COLLEGES OF EDUCATION

The comparison with educational psychology points up another problem facing teacher educators in the two decades preceding the publication of the Holmes and Carnegie reports. They have occupied a weak position not only within universities but also within colleges of education. Following the scientific approach to the study of learning pioneered by Edward L. Thorndike at the turn of the century, educational psychologists seized the academic high ground in education schools from the very beginning and have held on to this position throughout the twentieth century. While these researchers were carrying out experiments, publishing results, and developing theories of child development and student learning, the teacher educators were left with the less prestigious task of training teachers.[51]

While the educational psychology faculty dominated colleges of education academically, the educational administration faculty dominated them organizationally. This situation was a legacy in part of the social efficiency movement of the early decades of this century, which stressed scientific administration as the answer to the problems in U.S. schools, and in part of the long-term tendency for educational reformers to view bureaucracy as the primary mechanism for carrying out any form of school improvement.[52] But it also arose because school administrators were able to achieve professionalization long before either teachers or teacher educators. As Arthur Powell has shown, universities began establishing their own schools of education at the turn of the century, several decades before normal schools became teachers colleges and more than half a century before they evolved into universities.[53] The initial force behind the development of these university education schools came from male high school teachers, who saw university training as a way to protect themselves from the rising feminization and falling prestige of their calling. When this effort to preserve the exclusivity of high school teaching failed, the schools quickly adapted themselves to preparing these same male high school teachers for positions as educational administrators.

As a result, the earliest colleges of education that developed in the most prestigious universities were focused primarily on the professional preparation of school administrators and other educators working outside the classroom. This early history of administrative professionalization put the field of educational administration in a strong position within education schools more generally, especially when combined with the male dominance of the field and the functional centrality of administrative reform. Therefore, control of education schools traditionally has rested in the hands of the faculty from the administration department. This left teacher educators in a subordinate status that parallels the position of their graduates within schools, where nonprofessional teachers have had to answer to professional administrators.

From this perspective, one of the most significant things about the Holmes Group is that it consisted of deans from colleges of education who were arguing for the centrality of teacher education within their own schools. This strongly suggests that the traditional power relations within these colleges have been changing in recent years. Another clue along these lines comes from the school-restructuring proposals that, like the teacher-education proposals, have emerged from the teacher professionalization movement. Given the way in which the relative status of fields within colleges of education parallels the status of their respective groups within schools, the central thrust of these proposals — elevating the role of teachers while diminishing that of administrators — again suggests a move toward collegial ascendancy by teacher educators.

THE WEAK IMPACT OF TEACHER EDUCATORS ON TEACHING PRACTICE

The movement to professionalize teacher educators — and, by extension, teachers — can therefore be understood in part as an effort by these faculty members to respond to the relative weakness of teacher education within the university and within colleges of education. But it can also be seen as a way to remedy the surprising inability of the faculties in this field to put their stamp on the classroom practice of their own graduates. Larry Cuban's study *How Teachers Taught* examines evidence about the pedagogical practice of U.S. elementary and secondary school teachers during the twentieth century and finds that it was remarkably impervious to the kind of pedagogy urged as part of teacher education.[54] Although the dominant ideology of teacher education during most of this period has been to promote child-centered pedagogy in classrooms, these teachers (especially at the secondary level) persisted to a remarkable degree in conducting their classes in the traditional teacher-centered manner.

The problem seems to be that teacher educators feel they know more about how to teach than they knew a few years ago, but teachers seem to be unwilling or unable to put this knowledge into practice. As we have seen, the rise of a research base for knowledge about teaching is one of the fundamental axioms of the movement for teacher professionalization. And for empirical verification of the existence of this base, one need only leaf through the three editions of the *Handbook of Research on Teaching,* which require a total of 3,481 pages of text just to summarize this literature.[55] *Tomorrow's Teachers* argues that "competent professional teachers" should be familiar with the key insights in this literature and be able to use them in class. It notes, however, that such is not the case in today's schools: "Such professionals are deeply concerned by mounting evidence that many of this country's teachers act as educational functionaries, faithfully but mindlessly following prescriptions about what and how to teach. Conducting classes in routine, undemanding ways, far too many teachers give out directions, busywork, and fact-fact-fact lectures in ways that keep students intellectually passive, if not actually deepening their disregard for learning and schooling."[56]

This evidence shows that teacher education is not exerting a very substantial impact on the way teachers teach. In his classic sociological study of teachers, Dan Lortie captures this inefficacy in the title of his chapter on teacher training, "The Limits of Socialization."[57] As he and a number of other writers on the subject argue, teachers learn more about teaching from the thousands of hours they have spent as students in K–12 classrooms than they do from their relatively brief time under the tutelage of teacher educators.[58] And what they do learn from teacher educators often has little connection to the growing body of scientific knowledge about teaching, because the bulk of the instruction of preservice teachers is done not at research-oriented colleges of education but at institutions where the teacher-education faculty have little incentive to produce or even keep up with educational research.[59] Thus pedagogical tradition carries more weight than research-based evidence on effective teaching techniques. This tendency is reinforced by the sudden immersion of students in the classroom during the brief experience of student-teaching and their abrupt separation from professional mentoring after graduation. The school is the reality to which new teachers must adapt, and the learning they acquire about teaching in colleges of education is easily shrugged off once they close the classroom door.[60]

The movement for teacher professionalization advocates a number of measures designed to increase the impact of teacher education on teaching practice. It proposes to do this indirectly by strengthening the influence of formal educational knowledge (generated or codified by teacher educators) on the way teachers think about teaching, and directly, by increasing the influence of teacher educators over the educational process in schools. As spelled out in the Holmes and Carnegie reports, the movement will try to accomplish these goals by redesigning the content of teacher education around the developing scientific knowledge base about professional practice; by extending the length of teacher education and introducing an extended and intensively supervised clinical internship (steps that would deepen the degree of professional socialization experienced by the student); by creating professional development schools in which teacher educators would continue in an advisory role concerning school structure and classroom practice; and by establishing new intermediary positions for teachers, in which, after undergoing advanced training in an education school, they could serve as both lead teachers in their schools and clinical faculty at the university.

Formal Rationality and the Science of Teaching

I have argued that the teacher professionalization movement can, in part, be traced back to the professionalization of teacher educators and the rise of a science of teaching, and that the latter developments can, in part, be traced to the occupational concerns of teacher educators who have been seeking a remedy for their low status and weak influence within universities, colleges of education, and schools. At this point I would like to step back and examine the broader intellectual context that helped to shape these developments.

The changes in colleges of education during the past several decades bear the distinctive stamp of a pattern of thought that first emerged at the start of the modern era and that is best characterized as formal rationalism. Stephen Toulmin argues that this modernist approach arose during the seventeenth century, through the efforts of natural philosophers like Descartes and Newton, and has dominated our way of thinking about the world ever since.[61] He argues that this rationalist worldview has several essential characteristics: it emphasizes formal logic over rhetoric and proof over argumentation; it focuses on the development of abstract principles rather than the study of diverse, concrete individual cases; and it concentrates on constructing timeless theories grounded in the permanent structures of life rather than exploring the shifting and context-bound problems of daily practice.[62] For better or worse, formal rationality has shaped modern life. It constitutes the core of what we think of as the scientific method, and in this form it has exerted a profound effect on technological development, economic growth, and the vast expansion of our knowledge about the world. It also defines the modern principle for the organization of social life — what Max Weber called "rationalization" — by which relations among human beings are structured according to the same formal logic and timeless abstractions that we see as the basis for planetary motion.[63]

Starting in the 1960s, teacher educators began to adopt this formal, rationalist worldview and to apply it to the task of constructing a science of teaching. First, they naturally turned toward an intellectual approach that over the centuries had proven effective for understanding social life and guiding social practice, and that had accumulated an enormous reservoir of cultural legitimacy. Given the weak position from which teacher educators were starting, they needed to draw on the most powerful form of intellectual technology that was available, which led them naturally to the edifice of law-seeking science. In addition, as university professors they were already under increasing pressure to develop a research agenda in accordance with academic professional norms, and the most prestigious form of academic research traditionally has been structured around the canons of the scientific method. And finally, educational psychology had already established a model for carrying out academically credible and scientific research in education.

The pursuit of a scientific basis for classroom instruction probably began in 1906 with Thorndike's *Principles of Teaching* and continued during the 1920s and 1930s with a series of pedestrian quantitative studies that sought to connect teacher attributes with student achievement.[64] Even Dewey took up the issue in his 1929 lectures on *The Sources of a Science of Education,* but unlike Thorndike and company, he argued that this science should play a supportive rather than an authoritative role for teachers, giving them "intellectual tools" rather than "rules for overt action," for "no conclusion of scientific research can be converted into an immediate rule of educational art."[65] It was not until the 1960s that a systematic and sustained effort to apply formal rationality to the study of teaching finally developed. This movement was kicked off officially in 1963, when the American Educational Research Association (AERA) published the first *Handbook of Research on Teaching.*[66] In his preface, editor N. L. Gage noted that "in the half-century since research on teaching began, thousands of studies have been made," and that one purpose of the handbook was to summarize this work; he argued, however, that another purpose of the book was to criticize the existing work for being insufficiently scientific: "In recent decades, such research has lost touch with the behavioral sciences. It has not drawn enough nourishment from theoretical and methodological developments in psychology, sociology, and anthropology. . . . To remedy this condition — to bring research on teaching into more fruitful contact with the behavioral sciences — is a purpose of this Handbook."[67]

In the 1960s, Gage and other educational psychologists succeeded in establishing such contact by applying their field's well-developed experimental methodology and quantitative analytical techniques to the study of teaching. The resulting body of research measured what happened to student achievement as a result of variations in the pedagogical behavior of teachers. The burgeoning literature on teaching effects (or "process-product") provided an ideal expression of the modernist perspective, because it allowed researchers to develop formal principles for effective teaching that could serve as a prescriptive guide for both public policy and classroom practice. Out of this work emerged a scientifically grounded and lawlike field of research that gave teacher educators the opportunity to establish professional credibility within the university community and gave teachers a growing body of formal knowledge from which to base a future claim for professional status.

Since those early days, the field of research on teaching has grown enormously. A second *Handbook* appeared only ten years after the first.[68] Teaching and teacher education research expanded rapidly within AERA until it grew into a whole division in 1985.[69] A series of federally funded centers helped to lead the charge, the most prominent of which was the Institute for Research on Teaching (IRT) at Michigan State University. Perhaps the peak moment in the joint elevation of teacher educators and their science of teaching occurred in 1986, when the Holmes and Carnegie reports and the third *Handbook of Research on Teaching* were published and the new National Center for Research on Teacher Education at Michigan State University was funded.

In recent years, several leading scholars have argued that the research on teaching has developed well beyond its recent roots in process-product research. While vigorously defending this tradition of research, Gage suggests that the field is now legitimately open to alternative approaches, even some that are quite different from his own scientific and law-seeking perspective — because, in fact, teaching is both a science and an art.[70] Lee Shulman, in his review of research paradigms for the third *Handbook of Research on Teaching,* takes a more critical stance toward the process-product opus but comes to a similarly heterodox conclusion.[71] Yes, he argues, the model of measuring the effects of teacher behavior did constitute the dominant paradigm in the field for a significant period, but then research began to branch out into the study of the cognition of teachers and students. More recently, methodological trends have emerged that seem to signal a more radical divergence from this paradigm. One trend is the rise of various forms of interpretive research (often lumped together under the label *ethnography*) that involve the qualitative analysis of classroom interaction based on observation and interview. Another is the emergence of the case study, which represents a shift in emphasis from a positivist concern about generalizability to a focus on texture and context. A third trend is the effort to examine the ways in which teachers understand and guide their own practice, as an example of reflexive and contextualized knowledge that is practical rather than theoretical. As a result, the field appears to have outgrown its early stress on law seeking, abstraction from context, and prescriptions for practice, and has, in short, moved away from the model of Cartesian formal rationality.

But the original scientific paradigm drawn from educational psychology still seems solidly entrenched.[72] The vision of methodological diversity presented by Gage and Shulman is a bit misleading. Gage continues to see scientifically grounded knowledge on teaching as the core of the field, as illustrated by the title of his book, *The Scientific Basis of the Art of Teaching*.[73] And the shift from behavioral measures to cognitive measures, which Shulman portrays as a change in paradigms, simply represents an expanded number of variables employed within what is still a psychologistic and formal nationalist model. Although alternative approaches to this model have emerged, they are currently operating only at the margins of the central structure of research on teaching. Although Shulman gamely tries to bring these approaches into the center of his review of research paradigms, he is forced to concede that "this [interpretive] perspective is somewhat alien to the majority of researchers on teaching who have, like the author, been raised as psychologists (or at least with the unquestioned assumptions of positivist and reductionist social science)."[74]

The central problem here is one that Foucault would appreciate, because it revolves around the complex connections between power and knowledge for the research-oriented teacher educators who have led the movement to professionalize teachers. The quotation from Shulman is revealing about one such connection. It supports my contention that these educators and the scientific model of teaching arose together in a symbiotic fashion that has made it difficult for the educators simply to shrug off the latter model as an outmoded paradigm. This model was enormously empowering for these researchers. It helped to make them successful, prominent, and influential within colleges of education, the university, and the schools; it was the paradigm around which they established their competence, shaped their careers, and developed their basic understanding of teaching and learning. In such a situation, a paradigm shift, if it occurs, is likely to be instigated by a new generation of researchers who lack the personal and professional investment in the old intellectual structure.[75]

There are some signs that such a new generation may be emerging in the field. Postpositivist philosophers have been waging war on the scientistic paradigm in the pages of *Educational Researcher* for the past decade, and they seem to be winning.[76] As suggested earlier, education schools and journals are showing signs of opening up to interpretive and contextualized accounts of teaching. However, this trend runs up against a second power-knowledge problem — the power of the scientistic research on teaching to authorize and legitimize efforts by teacher educators to change classroom behavior. While Shulman expresses doubts about the "appropriateness" of "natural science models" in educational research, he argues that we still need to fall back on these models when we have to make decisions about teaching practice: "It is . . . apparent why the results of positivist research are more typically employed to guide policy while those of interpretive researchers most frequently are employed to criticize and question, to vex with precision."[77] The context-bound and particularistic accounts of instruction that emerge from postmodern research simply do not provide an authoritative, foundational, and technical justification for policy interventions in the same way as those scientistic accounts that philosophers love to deconstruct.[78] This conflict poses an intellectual and professional dilemma for teacher educators. Although the science of teaching is increasingly difficult to defend empirically and theoretically, to abandon it in favor of the postmodern approach is to give up the very thing that gives the teacher educators' words a privileged status within educational discourse. If they are not speaking authoritatively from the platform of positive science, then why should their ideas on education be accorded any greater weight than those of laypersons — of teachers, parents, and citizens?

The desire to improve teaching and schooling therefore leads teacher educators to draw on and express the "disciplinary power" of the science of teaching, even as their rhetoric begins to turn away from process-product research and its overtly prescriptive approach to pedagogy.[79] The second Holmes Group report abandons the emphasis on scientific knowledge that characterized the first report in favor of a rhetoric of equality and collaboration as the basis for the proposed professional development schools.[80] What makes this a credible reform effort by a group of education school deans, however, is the authority it derives from the scientific research that these schools produce. The influential role of formal rationality within the movement to professionalize teachers therefore derives in part from the recent occupational experience of teacher educators, who have relied on this intellectual structure for their own professional advancement, and in part from their continuing need to hold on to a privileged form of knowledge that adds weight to their efforts at educational reform.[81]

Implications: Rationalizing the Classroom

Based on this genealogy of the movement for teacher professionalization, we can consider some of the effects that the movement might have on the major actors in the educational arena. The effort to enhance the workplace autonomy, professional education, and social status of teachers could, in the abstract, serve a wide variety of possible goals. But my analysis suggests that this particular effort — given the time, place, and agents that define the circumstances of its emergence — has embedded within it a distinctive mix of preexisting elements. These elements give this effort a character and momentum that significantly narrow the range of probable outcomes and make some effects more likely than others. Because these elements do not present a picture of a coherent and rationally planned effort, the movement contains the potential for moving in several different and even contradictory directions. From one perspective — the stress on raising academic standards and on using market incentives as a mechanism for reform — the roots of teacher professionalization show it to be an extension of the neoconservative ideology of the late twentieth century. From a second perspective — the concerns for promoting equity, attacking bureaucratic control, supporting liberal feminism, and raising the status of teachers — its roots suggest that the movement is part of an effort to promote the interests of teachers and students as oppressed groups within the educational system. From a third perspective — the rise of a science of teaching and the professionalization of teacher educators — these roots depict the movement as an outgrowth of a process of scientific rationalization and collective status mobility.

The first tendency is an expression of the ideological context during the movement's formation, showing that it was constructed in part out of the most potent cultural materials available in the 1980s. This conservatism has left its mark on the form of the movement through the structure of the National Board for Teacher Certification (which promotes a multitiered structure for teaching to replace the profession's present egalitarian structure) and through the emphasis on academic excellence for teachers (which promotes increased levels of academic rigor, credentialing, and performance screening). Both of these characteristics reflect a strong current of social efficiency concerns that have dominated conservative discourse about education. The second tendency has provided a sense of mission that promises to carry the movement in a more progressive direction than that promoted by the first. The 1990 Holmes Group report in particular resonates with concern about promoting greater social opportunity and personal empowerment for students and teachers alike. A number of teacher educators and others have chosen to support the teacher professionalization effort because they see it as a movement through which they can help education advance toward such progressive goals, promoting democratic equality and social mobility for oppressed groups in society — both beleaguered teachers and disadvantaged students. They may be right: these concerns are embedded within the movement and are prominently championed by many of its supporters.

But I see several problems that may channel the movement in a different direction. One arises from the movement's orientation toward market influences and excellence; this tendency enhances social inequality and educational hierarchy and thereby undermines efforts to achieve progressive ends. Another problem arises from the choice of professionalism as a mechanism for pursuing these ends in the face of the professions' long-standing identification with the politics of expert rule and with male-oriented work roles. And yet another difficulty arises from the tendency toward rationalization of the classroom that is driven by the professional concerns and orientations of university faculty. In short, given the contradictory elements built into it, the teacher professionalization movement is contested terrain, and its outcomes are still very much up for grabs.

I have emphasized one particular lineage — with its roots in the professional mobility of teacher educators and the science of teaching — and its potentially harmful effects on the way in which the movement approaches educational reform. Such emphasis focuses attention on the two elements likely to exert the most fundamental constraints on the shape and direction of the movement: the social position of the leading actors in this movement and the worldview that shapes their actions.[82] This is professionalization shaped primarily by social mobility concerns, but the beneficiaries from this angle are not teachers and students but education school faculty members; and the consequences are greater social efficiency in teaching and learning rather than greater social opportunity for those at the bottom of the educational system. The teacher professionalization movement has been molded by the particular structure of power and knowledge that developed during the course of events that brought it to life. Teacher educators and the science of teaching arose together in the two decades preceding 1986 under conditions that bonded one to the other. It was a marriage between an upwardly mobile occupational group and an authoritative intellectual construct. As a result, teacher educators at research universities have tended to look at schools through the lens of scientific rationality and to propose solutions for school problems that draw on their own technical skills. This approach tends to work to their benefit not because they are manipulative but because they are caught in a genealogical web of power and knowledge that limits the way they customarily think and act about schooling. The scientistic logic of their own professionalization effort leads them to envision a rationalized structure of reform for teachers and students that plays out familiar themes of professionalism and technical skill. This type of structure has profoundly conservative implications for U.S. education.

ENHANCING THE PROFESSIONAL POSITION OF TEACHER EDUCATORS

One outcome of the movement for teacher professionalization may already be in the works, and that is the elevation of teacher educators within colleges of education. By moving the issue of teacher education closer to the center of the national debate about schools, the movement has helped to raise the status of the faculty in these programs. This process has been measurably helped by the efforts of the Holmes Group, in which deans at the most prestigious colleges of education asserted the focal importance of teacher education within their own colleges. As a result, teacher educators may have less need to bow to the organizational leadership of the administration faculty and to the professional stature of the educational psychology faculty than has been true in the past. Likewise, the status of teacher educators within the university community may be rising marginally in conjunction with their increased research productivity.

But this description of collective mobility needs to be qualified in two ways. First, although this strategy may be helping the teacher education faculty at elite universities, where the research on teaching and the leadership of the teacher professionalization movement have originated, it is less likely to help teacher educators at the second-tier state universities (former teachers colleges) and less still for those in four-year institutions, where teaching loads are heavy and research productivity is low or nonexistent. The movement may, in fact, serve to emphasize the gap in status between the upper and lower levels of teacher education if many institutions in the latter category do not adopt a graduate-level program of teacher certification.

Second, even for teacher educators at research-oriented universities, the timing of the movement poses a problem. Teacher educators have come to the professionalization process rather late in the game, when the field is glutted and many predecessors have staked out the prime positions. Within the university, the humanities have a strong hold on high culture, the natural sciences have a claim to technology and the scientific method, and the social sciences have a lead in the application of research to problems of social policy. Education is left to play catch-up, with borrowed equipment and a rookie's track record. In addition, teacher educators are coming late to the adoption of the scientific-rationalist model of research, which is now under attack and in partial retreat in the waning years of the twentieth century.[83] Philosophy has abandoned this model, architecture and literary criticism have developed strong challenges to it, and it now occupies a reduced position within social science. Even physics, which has long been the model for modernist formalism, has turned away from its Newtonian roots and recognized the diversity of the universe and the difficulty of reducing it to timeless formulas. Therefore, teacher educators may well be hitching their hopes to a research structure that is in the process of imploding, and in danger of falling into a theoretical black hole.

ENHANCING THE INFLUENCE OF TEACHER EDUCATORS WITHIN SCHOOLS

As we have seen, teacher professionalization promises to increase the impact of teacher educators on schools. By emphasizing the importance of a formal knowledge base for the teaching profession, the movement reinforces the position of teacher educators relative to teachers, for it is the job of the former to produce, codify, and transmit this knowledge. Further reinforcement comes from the requirement that prospective teachers undergo an augmented period of professional education and clinical internship, both of which will be administered by the education school faculty. This process is likely to lead future teachers to a closer identification with the teaching profession and, presumably, to a greater respect for the teacher educators who play such a prominent role in this profession. A particularly strong professional identification is likely in the case of lead or career-professional teachers, whose advanced professional education and close ties to the university should make them significant voices for the college of education within the schools. In addition, the emergence of professional development schools will provide the teacher educator with a direct role in the school that may be similar in influence to that of the attending physician in a teaching hospital.

INCREASING THE RATIONALIZATION OF CLASSROOM INSTRUCTION

The literature on educational organization shows that bureaucratic control has strongly shaped the administration of schools but has never been very successful at managing instruction.[84] Behind the classroom door, teachers have been able to carry out the business of teaching and learning with a surprising degree of autonomy. Many reform efforts in the 1980s sought to promote bureaucratic control over instruction (through testing, rigid curriculum guidelines, and so forth), but the teacher professionalization movement opposes such measures, both in its antibureaucratic rhetoric and in its programmatic emphasis on enhancing teacher autonomy. However, while opposing bureaucratization, the movement promises to enhance the rationalization of classroom instruction. The difference is that bureaucratization focuses on organization in the narrow sense of the word, locating power in a hierarchy of offices and thus producing outcomes by command from supervisor to subordinate, whereas rationalization focuses on organization in the broader sense — as process — embedding power in the principles of formal rationality that shape the discourse and procedures by which people guide their actions. Historically, rationalization has promoted the growth of bureaucracy by providing the latter's ideological and procedural prerequisites; but, as an extension of the modernist worldview, rationalization has exerted an influence far beyond the limits of organization charts.

The teacher professionalization movement promotes a vision of scientifically generated professional knowledge that draws heavily on the movement's roots in formal rationality. It portrays teaching as having an objective empirical basis and a rational structure. It argues that a professional teacher should have substantial mastery of the empirical literature on teaching methods and should be able to demonstrate the ability to conduct a rationally structured class that reflects the insights of this literature. To the extent that this effort is successful, the result would be to enhance the rationalization of classroom instruction. Teaching would become more standardized — that is, more technically proficient according to scientifically established criteria for accepted professional practice. In this sense, then, professionalization could achieve a degree of procedural control over classroom instruction that bureaucratic managers have long sought but chronically failed to attain. Instead of deriving from administrative edict or state law, this control would arise in part from a more extended and effective system of professional socialization (imbuing prospective teachers with the principles of acceptable professional practice) and in part from the market forces set in motion by new career ladders and the system of board certification (providing existing teachers with career incentives to adapt their practice to the professional standard).

REINFORCING THE VISION OF TEACHING AS A TECHNICAL ACTIVITY

It follows that the current proposal for professionalizing teaching will tend to focus attention on the technical aspects of this activity. After all, in the eyes of the public, if there is one characteristic a professionalizing occupation seeks to attach to its members, it is technical competence. This cuts to the essence of the exchange that a profession offers to the rest of society — a guarantee of collective competence in return for workplace autonomy. Therefore, above all else, the reports assure us that the professional teacher will be a competent teacher: in one three-page stretch *Tomorrow's Teachers* uses the words *competent* or *competence* thirteen times.[85] And the way the profession seeks to establish its competence is through a complex array of mechanisms for testing and certifying its membership, which the reports promise to carry out with a vengeance. One critic notes that words such as *examination, standards,* and *certification* appear fifty-seven times in the first section of the Holmes report.[86]

The professionalizers promote this technical view of teaching in part to offset an older view of teaching as a philanthropic activity, in which "caring about kids" is seen as a sufficient justification for allowing someone to take on the task of classroom instruction. From the professionalizing perspective, portraying teachers as people who have to be able to "do" science as well as to "do" good elevates the discussion about teaching above a simple consideration of naive intentions and focuses attention on the need to have teachers who can deliver desirable educational outcomes.[87] As a number of critics from the left have argued, however, this technical vision tends to divert attention from a view that training programs should take into account: that teaching is also a political activity.[88] From this perspective, the problem with promoting the rationalization of teaching is that it tends to hide the political content of instruction under the mask of a technical decision about the most effective means to promote unexamined educational ends. Yet a good teacher should in fact examine these ends with a critical eye and should be open with students about the fundamentally political way in which these ends are chosen in and for schools. One potential danger of professionalization, therefore, is the way in which it pushes technical questions into the foreground and political questions into the background as either unscientific or unproblematic.

INCREASING THE POLITICAL DISTANCE BETWEEN TEACHERS AND PARENTS

One last political implication of the professionalization movement is the danger that, by emphasizing the specialized expertise of teachers, it will undermine democratic control of schools. Sykes confronts this issue and, drawing on the work of Amy Gutmann, argues that professional autonomy for teachers will actually enhance democratic politics by creating a buffer against the domination of education by the whim of the majority.[89] The problem with this argument, however, is that the source of teachers' professional authority is a technical rationality that denies that education is a legitimate matter for political debate. The roots of the professionalization movement suggest that education will be considered a technical matter that must be left in the hands of certified experts, and that efforts by the laity to set the direction or shape the content of education will not be seen as an appropriate democratic action but as an unacceptable form of interference.

The frequent use of medical analogies becomes particularly problematic at this stage of the discussion. The implication is that laypersons should have no more say about how a teacher conducts a class than about how a surgeon conducts an operation; both cases are seen as technical matters of professional competence that are best dealt with by peer review. But it is not clear that shaping minds, instilling values, and preparing citizens are the same sorts of technical problems as removing an appendix or reducing a fever. The former tasks have an irreducibly political character to them — because they involve the teacher in making choices about which ideas, values, and social ends are worth promoting, and because they exert an impact on the way students will make their own choices about these things. Every parent — and, more broadly, every citizen — is constantly making these kinds of decisions and exerting these sorts of influences on their own children and on the adults around them. Therefore, this political component of teaching is not a closely held form of professional expertise but a capacity that is universally accessible to the lay public, and this makes the construction of professional barriers to public influence over classroom instruction nothing less than a threat to an essential component of democracy.

7

Career Ladders and the Early Schoolteacher

In American society, where the right to get ahead is as fundamental as the right to breathe, teachers are an anomaly. Unlike almost everyone else in the white-collar job sector, they pursue a career that does not offer a career ladder. They assume the position of teacher when they first enter the classroom, and they hold the same position until they retire thirty years later. True, their pay rises over the course of this career, but in response to their accumulating graduate credits and years of service rather than a process of merit evaluation. Throughout a lifetime of teaching, the title, job description, and duties remain the same. Teachers face a remarkably flat career path.

In contrast, students must ascend a daunting hierarchy during their careers in school. Year after year they have to win promotion from one level to the next in the graded structure of schooling, submitting themselves to a process of continual evaluation designed to determine their worthiness for advancement. And they have to face this kind of sorting and ranking in other ways as well—through their placement in particular tracks, programs, and ability groups within a particular institution, and through their placement in an institution (a high school or college) that occupies a particular rank in the institutional status order.

Increasingly, commentators have argued that the "careerless" nature of teaching constitutes an educational problem.[1] In the absence of a promotional ladder and any other form of occupational differentiation, critics contend, teaching offers its practitioners none of the usual meritocratic spurs to ambition and achievement. The result is that teachers have little incentive to excel at or remain in their profession, and potential prospects for teaching may seek other careers that offer chances to get ahead. One particularly prominent reform proposal focuses on altering the arrangement of work incentives for the teacher through the introduction of career ladders. Both the Holmes Group and the Carnegie Forum on Education and the Economy suggest a form of career ladder that would eliminate the present undifferentiated structure of teaching and erect in its place a new structure with distinct tiers.

The Holmes Group calls for three different positions — instructor, professional teacher, and career professional; the Carnegie Forum calls for two — teacher and lead teacher. These different levels of occupational attainment would carry with them corresponding sets of differential rewards and responsibilities for a teacher who remained in the classroom.[2] How would these proposed career ladders help resolve any of the problems facing contemporary schools? The aim is to give good teachers the incentive to stay in the profession instead of moving on to "more rewarding" jobs, and to provide all teachers with the impetus to work hard at improving their craft. The Holmes Group report puts it this way: "Differentiating the teaching career . . . would make it possible for districts to go beyond limited financial incentives and to challenge and reward commitment. This is essential to encourage teachers to reinvest in their work, and earn rewards while remaining in their classrooms; it will also counterbalance the defection of talented, committed teachers into administration."[3]

Though unmentioned by current reformers, there was a time in the history of U.S. education when teaching did have a system of career ladders — which offered teachers an extended hierarchy of career opportunities that were sharply differentiated by pay, prestige, and work expectations. My aim in this chapter is to explore the possibilities for career advancement that confronted teachers during this earlier period and to relate these career ladders to the present flat structure of the profession.

High school teachers in the United States during the late nineteenth and early twentieth centuries were faced with a complex set of market incentives that encouraged them either to move out of teaching altogether (which is what most of them did) or move up to a higher occupational level within the profession. These incentives presented no fewer than three different routes to advancement, three distinct career ladders, and the most successful practitioners tended to combine all of these routes. Only one such route, however — moving from teaching to administration — is still available to teachers today. The other routes to advancement — moving from country to city and moving from lower to higher levels of the system — have largely disappeared as possibilities for getting ahead of the pack.[4]

The fact that most teachers did not attain upward mobility suggests that the career-ladder metaphor is a bit misleading, because it projects an image of accessibility that simply did not exist. A career pyramid is a more appropriate (if awkward) image for a process in which most teachers stayed at the lowest level and the numbers dropped off sharply at each succeeding level above. This pyramid model of career mobility is the same pattern found in large bureaucratic organizations, where only a small number of management employees ever reach the executive suite. By examining the careers of those teachers who succeeded under such selective conditions, we can gain insight into the workings of this occupational mobility structure, the incentives and disincentives it offered to teachers in general, and the feasibility of reinstituting a form of such a mobility structure in contemporary schools.

What this analysis suggests is that the secret to the extended career opportunities open to teachers at the turn of the century was the vast inequality that characterized the structure of teaching. A few highly motivated teachers pursued extraordinary careers during this period, but the career rewards that they enjoyed were made possible by the extraordinarily deprived conditions facing most teachers. Career ladders existed because, for the large majority, teaching was not a career at all but a transitional phase, providing a useful occupation for women until they got married and for men until they got a real job. This situation provided no incentive for school systems to elevate the condition of the average teacher, but there was enormous incentive for the few career-minded teachers to climb up from the dank and crowded lower levels of the profession as quickly as possible. The inequalities in the system offered opportunities for betterment to these individuals, as they pursued a path that took them toward larger communities (which could afford a more expensive form of schooling) and higher levels in the system (where small numbers made it possible to sustain more generous salaries and comfortable working conditions).

It follows that the "loss" of these routes to advancement within teaching came as a result of a substantial improvement in pay and working conditions for teachers in general during the course of the twentieth century. The much maligned flatness of the current career path in teaching is therefore the result of a leveling upward of conditions within the occupation, a change that benefited the large majority of teachers and made it possible for most teachers today to pursue a lifelong career in their chosen field instead of having to move on to something else. From this angle, therefore, the absence of the old career ladders looks like a very good thing.

High School Teachers in the 1890s

In 1894, at the same time that high school enrollments began to soar throughout the country, U.S. Commissioner of Education William T. Harris published the results of the first relatively comprehensive survey of the nation's high schools. The survey uncovered a total of 3,964 public high schools at that point, each with an average of seventy-three secondary students. But these schools contained twice as many elementary students as they had high school students; many appear to have been little more than extended elementary schools. A total of 12,120 teachers worked in the public high schools, an average of 3.1 teachers per school, and these teachers were highly concentrated geographically: 48.2 percent taught in the north central states and 32.2 percent in the Northeast, leaving only 14.8 percent in the South and 4.8 percent in the West. Overall, 52.7 percent of public high school teachers were women, but the sex ratio was relatively even in all areas of the country except the Northeast, where women accounted for 59.3 percent of the total.[5]

Four Career Histories

By looking at the career histories of four high school teachers, we can see many of the central elements in the structure of occupational mobility that existed in the nineteenth and early twentieth centuries.[6]

MARY DAVISON BRADFORD

Born in Kenosha County, Wisconsin, in 1859, Mary Davison entered Kenosha High School in 1870. In the spring of 1872 and 1873 she taught in a one-room country school at a pay of $25 a month, returning to her high school studies each fall. She never graduated, however, because a smallpox quarantine imposed on her family prevented her from finishing her senior year. Instead, she taught in another rural school in the spring of 1874, and then picked up a yearlong job teaching third grade in Kenosha. She spent the following year studying at Oshkosh Normal School, then went back in 1876 to teach at Kenosha High. The job was second assistant (at $400 a year) in a school where the rest of the faculty consisted of a female first assistant and a male principal.

After two years at this position she quit to get married and bear a son. Her husband died in 1881 after an extended illness. The following year she had no choice but to return to the classroom, spending two years teaching third grade and then regaining her second-assistant position in the high school at a salary of $500. In 1886 she moved up to the first-assistant spot, and in the next year won a raise to $600. At this point in her career she began to pursue a life teaching certificate, which required her to study in Madison every summer for the next half-dozen years. Her pay jumped to $1,000 in 1890, and in 1894 she finally received her life certificate.

That same year, Mary Bradford left the high school and took a teaching position at the Normal School in Stevens Point, where she remained until 1906. Then from 1906 to 1909 she taught in the kindergarten training school at the Stout Institute in Menomonie and spent the following year in the Normal School at Whitewater. Finally, in 1910 she returned to Kenosha as the superintendent of schools, a position she held until retirement.

PAUL H. HANUS

Paul Hanus was born in Prussia in 1855. Four years later, his family moved to Wisconsin. In 1871 he entered the preparatory department of the State Normal School at Platteville, and after a year was admitted into the school proper. In 1873, however, he left without graduating and took a job as a clerk for a New York City drug company. A year later he came back to Platteville and taught a fifth-grade class for a term before entering the University of Michigan in the scientific course. He received a bachelor of science degree in 1878 and took a job teaching science and mathematics at Denver High School, at a salary of $950, turning down an offer of a job teaching German at a rural Iowa high school for $780. A year later he became an instructor of mathematics (salary: $1,200) at the University of Colorado, then only a small college with a large preparatory department, both of which were housed in a single building. At the end of that year he quit when he was denied a promotion and a raise and, with the help of a partner, bought a drugstore in Denver. After only one year, Hanus sold his share in the store and returned to the University of Colorado in 1881, as a full professor of mathematics and with an increase in salary.

He remained at the university until 1886, when he accepted a position as principal of a new high school in Denver. When he arrived, this school (located on the upper floor of an elementary school) consisted of 35 students, two teachers, and the principal. By the time he left in 1890 it had grown to 150 students and four teachers and had a full four-year course of study. In that year he became a professor of pedagogy at the brand new Colorado State Normal School in Greeley; he was the only college graduate on the faculty. Then in

1891, Charles W. Eliot recruited him to go to Harvard and head that school's new department of education at a salary of $2,000. He remained in this position long enough to preside over the founding of the Harvard Graduate School of Education in 1920, then retired one year later.

MARGARET FOGELSONG INGRAM

Margaret Fogelsong was born around 1885 in a small town in Missouri.[7] After graduating from high school, she taught in a series of one-room rural schools (starting at $7 a week) on one-term contracts, while attending teachers institutes during the summer. In pursuit of a life certificate, she enrolled in the State Normal School at Kirksville while continuing to teach part of the year in a one-room school and a graded elementary school. After graduation, she took a position as principal and solo teacher of a high school in a small town in Montana, at $80 a month — doubling the salary of her previous job. The school had fifty-four students enrolled in a three-year program. After one year, the board decided to replace her with a man and offered her a combined second- and third-grade class instead, at $75. She accepted; but when the students revolted against the new principal and the board asked her to take over her old job again, she angrily refused.

As a result of this experience, she resolved to seek a university education in order to ensure her access to high school teaching positions, and she began attending the University of Chicago during the summer. While continuing with her studies, she obtained a better job in a bigger town, teaching seventh and eighth grade in Bozeman, Montana. But there she found a superintendent who failed to support her efforts at establishing discipline. So she moved on: "Once again I packed my zinc-bound trunk and headed for Chicago, this time with no hint of a job for the next season. And I had expected such success once I had my life diploma from Kirksville. I was a hobo teacher! Anyway, I still had close connection with that resolution to get an education. The trouble seemed to be that education had a queer way of seeming to rise higher and move farther out of my reach, the more I struggled to attain to its lofty eminence."[8]

In desperation, she for a time considered a career in journalism, even taking a correspondence course in the subject. But she kept teaching. The next job was as supervisor of the fifth and sixth grade at the model school attached to a state normal school in Kentucky. Here she was dropped summarily in an economy move, and she trundled once again back to Chicago, mulling over a decade of penury and gender discrimination in her chosen profession. In ten years of teaching she had earned an average of only $430 a year — which, with careful budgeting, was just enough to tide her over every summer.[9] Money aside, though, "What rankled within my soul was the discrimination against me because of sex, upon the very threshold of my career." She summed up the situation this way: "Too many good men left the profession. Too many weak superintendents leaned heavily upon their strong teachers, usually women, while they drew the lion's share of the pay, took the credit, and bossed, merely because they were men. Meantime, localities engaged in the expensive pastime of wrangling, the petty larceny of Nepotism, and the exacting of missionary devotion from their women teachers."[10]

Graduating from the University of Chicago about 1912, she resolved to resist any situation that left her dependent on men and to hold out for a minimum of $100 a month. Finding no such jobs available, she became a traveling agent for a textbook publisher for a time before finally landing a position as head of the English department at a high school in another far-flung locale, Marshall, Texas. During her summers, she continued to study at Chicago, receiving a master's in education in 1914. In 1920 she left Marshall for Spearfish, South Dakota, to become head of the English department at the State Normal School. Four years later she enrolled at Columbia's Teachers College and earned a Ph.D., moving on to a position where she taught English to teacher candidates at the Jamaica Training School in the New York City public school system. Her account breaks off in the 1930s while she was still in this position.

SADIE SMITH TRAIL

Sadie Smith was born in 1873 in a sod house near the town of Western, Nebraska. Her mother died fourteen months later, and she was raised by foster parents. When she reached the appropriate age, her father sent her to high school in Crete, where she boarded with a family. She intended to become a teacher, but friends warned her that graduation from high school would make her overqualified for a teaching job in rural schools. She still completed high school, but hedged her bet by apprenticing herself to a local dressmaker.

In her senior year, she taught as a substitute in a one-room school, and then, after graduation, attended a county teachers institute and obtained a certificate. Subsequently, she taught for a two-month term (at $25 a month) at one rural school, and another term at a second school (at $30); she was not rehired at the latter because a local girl underbid her by $5. After this disappointment she worked in a Crete dressmaking shop for a while, then moved to Colorado Springs to join her father and stepmother. There, while she continued sewing, she studied for a third-grade teaching certificate. Upon earning that credential, she taught in yet another one-room school (now at $45 a month). Finding living conditions unpleasant, she passed another teaching examination and took over a village school.

After two years in Colorado, Sadie Smith went back to Nebraska and attended Peru State Normal School, graduating a year later. She taught for a year in Dunbar and attended the normal school in Lincoln that summer. In the fall of 1896 she took a job as assistant teacher in a high school in North Bend, Nebraska. Her letters to her fiancé, Rollin Trail, provide a vivid picture of that experience.

Teaching duties were divided between the male principal and his new assistant, which meant that she was responsible for teaching no fewer than eight subjects during her first term alone: "Caesar, Latin Lessons, Algebra, General History, Literature, Botany, Physical Geography and Grammar." As she commented to Trail, "Perhaps I shall have plenty of spare time, but I can't see it now."[11] During her first year she was paid in scrip, not receiving the first cash payment until the following spring. But she was cheerful about attaining re-election for the next year at a raise of $5 per month. Meanwhile, she continued shuttling back to Lincoln every summer to pursue her studies, in the hope of finding a better-paying job.

During her third year at North Bend, the principal assumed the title of superintendent and announced that Smith was now the principal. This elevation in title had little effect on either his or her work, however, and she was unimpressed, telling Trail, "If it amounted to anything I should feel elated, but it doesn't so I am no larger than before."[12] She still did the lion's share of the teaching. As her fiancé put it, "Your principal or superintendent Sherman must have learned how to draw pay with little work. Don't you grow weary of doing all the work? Does he get a good salary?" "Yes," she responded, "his salary is a thousand a year. Somewhat larger than mine, you see," which at that point was $495 per year.[13]

Sadie Smith left North Bend in 1900 to become principal of the high school in Holdredge, Nebraska, where she stayed until her marriage to Trail in 1906. She then kept house for her civil-engineer husband in a variety of locations around the western United States, raising three children. When she became ill, they returned to Nebraska, where they lived until her husband died in 1916.

Widowhood propelled Sadie Trail back into teaching. Her daughter records that "she was principal of the high school in Waco, [Texas,] 1917–1919; superintendent of school at Carleton, [Texas,] 1919–1920; and high school principal at Castana, Iowa, 1920–1922."[14] At this point she returned to Lincoln, with family in tow, and taught in nearby Malcolm for a year, ending her career by teaching as a substitute in the Lincoln schools.

Alternative Routes to Advancement

All four of these high school teachers reveal at least one trait in common, and that is ambition. Each in her or his own way was perpetually in pursuit of a better position. Unwilling to leave education for very long (although each of them did so for at least a short period), they aggressively sought to improve on their situation within the profession. They were generally aiming to attain two goals: better pay and better working conditions.

Not surprisingly, the discussion of money runs through all of the personal accounts of early high school teachers. These teachers complain bitterly about the pay they received early in their careers, and they make clear that the pursuit of higher salary was the most prominent reason motivating them to move from one job to another. And move they did. They shuttled from one position to another and from one place to another, in a zigzag pattern which made sense mostly in monetary terms.

But money was not the only factor. In addition, these teachers were seeking better conditions for living and working. These included a variety of factors: having a home of one's own instead of continuing to board out; living in a town that offered social and cultural amenities; working in a school that permitted the teacher to focus on a specialized subject area, instead of having diffuse responsibility for the whole curriculum; and finding a position that permitted a degree of autonomy and personal respect, free from arbitrary interference and sexist dependency.

Read as a group, these career histories suggest that there were at least three different routes to upward mobility for high school teachers in the late nine-teenth and early twentieth centuries. First, all four teachers sought to advance their careers by means of geographical mobility, particularly the movement from country to city. Second, they all climbed the school-level hierarchy from primary to secondary teaching, with three of them ending up in higher educa-tion. Third, all of them also moved up the positional ladder from teacher to such positions as department head, principal, and superintendent. In addition, these histories suggest that education was a key factor that helped teach-ers climb these career ladders; all of these teachers pursued advancement by means of acquiring additional education and certification. But these histories also point out factors that restricted this climb — most notably gender and (as we will see in later examples) race. Let us consider each of these issues in more detail.

GEOGRAPHICAL MOBILITY

The most striking characteristic of common schools in the United States in their first century was the gross inequality of conditions that marked off the country from the city, and nowhere was this inequality more evident than in the high school. Large cities had both the population and the wealth to sup-port large freestanding high schools with a graded four-year course taught by a well-educated and well-paid array of instructors responsible for only their area of specialization. By contrast, rural areas could at best support small ungraded schools located in a corner of the elementary school building and taught by one or two poorly paid instructors whose limited education and experience were matched against a breathtaking range of subject-area responsibilities. The obvious result of this disparity was to induce career-minded high school teachers continually to seek positions in progressively larger communities in order to improve both their pay and their working conditions.[15]

To a degree, this disparity still exists. Pay levels in large urban and suburban school districts today often are higher than those in rural areas, a condition that provides continuing incentive for teacher migration. There are several factors that help undercut this incentive, however: state equalization formulas reduce the differences in local tax revenues and thus differences in teacher pay; tenure and pension concerns make teachers less willing to pursue opportunities in other districts and states; and the perception that urban districts offer poorer working conditions helps offset the attraction of higher salaries. As a result, compared with their contemporary counterparts, early elementary and high school teachers were faced with an occupational structure characterized by much more geographical diversity and fewer constraints against capitalizing on it.

Lotus D. Coffman's 1910 national survey of U.S. primary and secondary teachers suggests that teachers in general had a strong incentive to move from country to town to city.[16] The median education level, age, and experience of city teachers was markedly higher than that of rural teachers, presumably in part because the former were paid two or three times as much as the latter.[17] Urban districts could afford to spend four times as much per student and even keep school open twice as long as rural districts.[18]

Data on high school teachers, however, are sketchy. Thorndike's 1907 study of this population did not distinguish between urban and rural settings, but it does show a wide range in pay. He found that 5 percent of male high school teachers earned less than $500, 51 percent earned between $500 and $1,000, 27 percent earned from $1,000 to $1,500, and 17 percent earned more than $1,500. For women, he found that 22 percent earned less than $500, 59 percent earned from $500 to $1,000, and 19 percent earned more than $1,000.[19]

Other evidence suggests that a prime explanation for this highly differentiated pay structure is the gap between country and city. A national survey of teachers' salaries in 1905 by the National Education Association showed that the pay of high school teachers increased steadily with the size of the community supporting them. The average pay for men ranged from $674 in communities of less than eight thousand to $1,886 in cities of more than a million, while women's pay ranged from $575 to $1,387.[20]

Data from Indiana, compiled in 1903 by the state superintendent of public instruction, provide additional insight into the degree of differentiation among high school work settings according to location.[21] The key differentiating factor in Indiana at the turn of the century was whether or not a high school was "commissioned." A commissioned high school had to meet a variety of minimum state standards for curriculum and faculty — for example, at least two full-time teachers, one of whom had to be college-educated — which were closely related to the size of the community supporting the school. In 1903 there were approximately 1,003 high schools in the state; of these, 763 had two or more teachers, but only 185 of these were commissioned.[22]

The average commissioned high school had nearly eight times as many students and five times as many teachers as the average noncommissioned school, and these teachers were paid 68 percent more.[23] There was therefore a powerful financial incentive for a teacher in a small rural high school to move on to one of the larger schools. The same superintendent's report provides data on conditions at each of the commissioned high schools. Even within this relatively elite group, the larger schools paid their teachers 33 percent more than did the smaller schools.[24] But in addition, the teachers in the larger schools were expected to teach only one subject area, while the teachers in the smaller schools had to teach three.[25]

The incentive to move was not entirely financial. In their personal accounts, high school teachers complained frequently about being required to teach subjects in which they did not feel competent, and of thus being forced into the demeaning position of having to rely heavily on the text. Recall Sadie Trail's comment about being stuck with eight subjects in her first term. When Henry Johnson took a job in 1890 at Lutheran High School in Albert Lea, Minnesota, he had to teach thirteen classes covering seven subjects.[26] There was a serious difference in the workload facing teachers in rural and urban settings, and it provided a stimulus to seek positions in larger towns that was nearly as great as the desire for higher pay.

The Indiana data contain another interesting fact: most schools were closer to the smallest high schools in terms of pay and specialization than they were to the largest schools, and this was within the category of commissioned high schools that constituted the most advanced 20 percent of the high schools in the state.[27] Thus the proportion of high school teachers in Indiana who were receiving more than $800 to teach only one subject was very small indeed. To the rest, the kinds of rewards and working conditions that existed in places like Laporte, Millersville, and Indianapolis (three places in the large-school sample) were both remote from their own teaching experience and thoroughly enticing.

If teaching in an urban high school was as attractive as I suggest, then teachers would have been likely to stay longer there than at a rural school, and they also would have been likely to stay in the profession longer after landing a position in a city than if they were trapped in a rural school. The geographical mobility pattern, therefore, would have produced a situation in which urban high schools would collect teachers who had lengthy tenures in the school and extended professional experience.

Consider the experience factor first. Thorndike argues that years of experience provide the strongest explanation for the differences in pay among high school teachers: for the first twenty-two years of teaching, women received $27 in additional pay for each year of experience; men received $28 for each of the first twelve years and $8 for the years between thirteen and twenty-two.[28] The median number of years of experience was six for women and eight for men, so most high school teachers never climbed high enough on the experience ladder to cash in on it.[29] Thorndike does not include a variable measuring the urban-rural dimension, however, and as a result he overlooks the distinct possibility that the city was the crucial link between pay and experience, as high urban salaries attracted the most experienced high school teachers.

School-level data on length of tenure at a given school provide more direct, if still fragmentary, support for the greater attractiveness of urban high schools. Princeton Township High School was founded in 1867 through the formation of a special high school district around a county seat in a rural northwestern Illinois. In 1892, its supporters celebrated the school's twenty-fifth anniversary and published a memorial volume that contains the names of its faculty for each year.[30] This record shows that, on average, these teachers remained at the school less than three years. In fact, 43 percent left after one year, and 66 percent were gone after two; only 16 percent stayed as long as five years.[31] This was a substantial rural high school, with an enrollment of about two hundred students, a faculty of six or seven, and enough backing to produce a memorial volume; it would have ranked among the largest of the commissioned high schools in neighboring Indiana a quarter-century later. Even so, it experienced a very high faculty turnover. Its teachers either left teaching altogether or moved on to better opportunities in larger towns.

One step up the geographical mobility ladder from the township high school was a school such as the English High School in Worcester, Massachusetts. Founded in 1845, this was an older and larger school in a middle-sized eastern city; according to our assumptions, teachers would find it a more attractive place to seek a job and would be more likely to stay there. Data on the tenure of the women and men who taught there between 1845 and 1892 provide some support for this view. In one way, the experience in Worcester was identical to the experience in Princeton, for in both schools about 45 percent of the teachers left after the first year. But those teachers who remained at Worcester beyond this point, especially the women, showed a stronger tendency to stay for the longer term. The average tenure for women there was about a year longer than at Princeton, and 24 percent of the female teachers at Worcester taught there for six or more years, compared with only 6 percent of those in Princeton.[32]

At the top end of the opportunity structure for high school teachers were a small number of schools like Central High in Philadelphia. Founded in 1838 in the second-largest city in the country, Central offered an extraordinarily attractive maximum salary ($1,925 in 1880, for example), considerable prestige (its teachers, known as professors, were among the leading educators in the city), subject specialization, and urban amenities; as a result, its faculty stuck with it for the long haul. The 16 men who taught there in 1880 ultimately stayed at the school for an average of no fewer than 30.3 years — more than ten times as long as teachers stayed in Princeton. In fact, the average tenure of all 120 men who taught at Central from 1838 to 1900 was 23.0 years.[33] The evidence suggests, then, that teachers were drawn to the larger urban high school by means of relatively high pay and good working conditions; and once there, they stayed.

Survey data show that the relatively low position of the rural high school teacher continued into the 1930s. In 1921, Emery N. Ferriss did a survey of rural high schools in New York State and found that the median teacher in these schools had 3.4 years of experience and that 49 percent were in their first year at their particular location.[34] In a national survey of rural high schools published in 1925, Ferriss reported that 72.6 percent of the teachers in schools with faculties smaller than four were teaching three or more subjects every day. The median school in this sample had 3.5 teachers, so most rural high schools fit into this category.[35]

John Rufi's 1924 study of five small high schools in Pennsylvania showed that the average teacher was expected to cover between six and eight subjects.[36] Small-school working conditions and pay were even worse in the South. A 1929 study of Alabama high school teachers shows that the median rural teacher had 2.1 years of experience and 0.9 years at a particular job, compared with 4.8 and 2.5 respectively for the city teacher, and that the median rural salary was $1,066, compared with $1,411 in the city.[37] Combined, these studies show that the rural high school continued to act as a turnstile for teachers, and that one reason for this was that these schools still offered difficult working conditions.

Given the heavy subject loads and low pay that characterized rural high school teaching during the late nineteenth and early twentieth centuries, it is little wonder that the more ambitious and career-oriented minority of the high school teaching population moved on as soon as it got the chance. Indeed, in his 1924 interviews with teachers at five small rural high schools, Rufi found that all of them wanted to leave for better jobs. The reasons they gave were understandable: unreasonable teaching schedule, lack of facilities, absence of social life, meager salaries, and poor living conditions.[38] Because the high schools in the larger towns and cities offered teachers a significant improvement in all of these conditions, it is hardly surprising that ambitious teachers migrated in that direction; nor is it surprising that, once lodged in these schools, they tended to remain.

SCHOOL-LEVEL MOBILITY

In the late nineteenth and early twentieth centuries, public-school teachers sought to gain career advancement by several methods in addition to geographical mobility. Prominent among these was to climb the ladder leading from one level of school to another. The main rungs of this ascent led from the primary to the secondary level and from there, for a number of individuals (especially in a success-biased sample drawn from memoir writers), into some form of higher education.

Yet in an era when the grading of schools in the United States was far from perfectly realized, there was a second form of school-level mobility, interstitial in character, which led from the ungraded to the graded form of schooling at each level. That is, ambitious teachers not only sought to rise to the next higher level of schooling, they also tried to find positions within a given level at schools that practiced the sharpest form of differentiation—both internally (by grading and subject specialization) and externally (by distinguishing itself clearly from the level of schooling below it).

At the elementary level, teachers sought to move as quickly as possible from the ungraded one-room school in the country to the graded multiteacher school found in towns and cities. Shifting then into an ungraded one- or two-teacher high school (often located in the elementary school building) was an important form of career advancement, but the next step was to try for a position in a fully differentiated high school (with its own building and a specialized faculty).[39] Following this, the next logical move might be into a normal school, which (depending on time and place) had some of the characteristics of both a high school and a college. Finally, at that point a more clearly collegiate form of school, such as a teachers college or university, offered the best promise of career enhancement.

We saw evidence of this kind of upward mobility through the graded structure of schooling in the four career histories presented earlier. Mary Bradford started in a one-room country school, shifted to a graded elementary school, moved up to a high school, and then leveled off in a normal school. Paul Hanus taught briefly at a graded elementary school, then at a high school, a university preparatory department, high school again, a state normal school, and finally a university department of education. Margaret Ingram started in a one-room school, moved to a graded elementary, an ungraded high school, several graded elementaries, a graded high school, a state normal school, and then a university. Finally, Sadie Trail went from a series of country schools to several graded elementaries, then to an ungraded high school and several other high schools that may or may not have been graded.

Let us examine some of the routes that ten teachers followed through the hierarchy of schools by considering evidence from their career histories. Then we can explore how the incentives offered by this mobility structure spurred the pursuit of advancement. The summaries that follow (presented chronologically by birth date) focus exclusively on the schools at which these teachers worked, leaving out other aspects of each person's career. School positions are as teachers unless otherwise noted.[40]

Edward Hicks Magill

1825	born in Solebury, Pa.
1841	one-room school
1844	graded elementary
1852	Providence High School (ungraded)
1859	Boston Latin School (partially graded)
1869	Swarthmore College (president)

John Swett

1830	born in New Hampshire
1847	one-room schools in New England
1853	ungraded grammar school in San Francisco
1862	superintendent of public instruction for California
1867	graded grammar school for girls (principal) in San Francisco
1869	deputy superintendent of schools
1873	graded grammar school for girls
1876	Girls High School (principal)
1890	superintendent of schools
1894	retired

Samuel Thurber

1837	born in Providence, R.I.
1858	ungraded grammar school
1859	Providence High School (ungraded)
1867	Bangor High School (principal)
1869	high school in St. Louis (headmaster)
1870	high school in Hyde Park, Mass. (principal)
1872	Syracuse High School (principal)
1878	Worcester English High School (principal)
1880	Boston Girls High School
1883	Milton (Mass.) Academy (principal)
1887	Boston Girls High School
1909	retired

Julia Anne King

1838	born in Milan, Mich.
1858	ungraded high school in St. Clair
n.d.	Lansing High School (principal)
n.d.	Kalamazoo College (head of ladies' dept.)
n.d.	high school in Flint (nine years)
1876	high school in Charlotte (principal)
1881	State Normal School at Ypsilanti (preceptress, head of history department)
1915	retired

Lizette Woodworth Reese

n.d.	born in Baltimore
1873	one-room elementary parish school
1876	public elementary grammar school
1897	Colored High School
1901	Western High School
1921	retired

Henry Johnson

1860	born in Sweden
1885	one-room school in Minnesota
1890	ungraded high school, Albert Lea
1891	superintendent of schools, Rushford
1894	ungraded high school, Northfield

1895	superintendent, Rushford
1895	State Normal School, Moorhead
1899	State Normal School, Charleston, Ill.
1906	Teachers College, Columbia University
1936	retired

Emma Lott

1867	born in Lansing, Mich.
1887	ninth grade in Portland High School
1891	second grade in Lansing
1893	Lansing High School (teacher, dean of girls, assistant principal)
1933	retired

Grace Annie Hill

1874	born in Dedham, Mass.
1896	private schools in Michigan
1900	Detroit Central High School
1917	Detroit Junior College (grew out of Central HS)
1923	College of the City of Detroit (grew out of Detroit JC)

Inez Taylor

1877	born in Ohio
1894	one-room country school
1895	third and fourth grade in Hillsdale, Mich.
1903	left teaching to raise children
1917	Hillsdale High School (graded)
1933	retired

Marie J. Rasey

1891	born
1907	ungraded high school
1910	another ungraded high school
1913	graded high school in Illinois
1917	graded high school in Detroit
1919	Detroit Junior College

Overall, the careers of all ten of these teachers show signs of significant upward mobility — from lower- to higher-level schools, from ungraded to graded schools, most often both. Only two of these ten teachers, Emma Lott and Marie Rasey, started their teaching careers in a high school; all the rest began at the elementary level. And, depending on how one counts state normal schools, either four or five of those teaching in them ended up in some form of higher education. One teacher (Grace Hill) actually rode up the school-level ladder as her school, Detroit's Central High School, transformed itself into a junior college (later becoming Wayne State University). Note also how frequently mobility across school levels overlapped with mobility from country to city. The strategy for getting ahead involved seeking a graded higher-level school, and these were most likely found in the more populous areas.

The incentives for pursuing a position at such a school were, once again, the superior pay and working conditions one could find there. After teaching several years in various ungraded high schools and simultaneously acquiring two degrees, for example, Marie Rasey found a job in the Detroit suburbs in 1917. But "the stay here was short and unprofitable, largely because the great city beckoned to something more in keeping with her ambitions." When she suddenly attained a job in Detroit, she was exultant: "Marie [Rasey] Garn was at last a high school teacher in Detroit, at a salary of $120 a month, and she did not question for a moment that with that princely salary she would soon be able to buy Cadillac Square."[41]

But let us look at the effect of school level on teacher pay, apart from the effects of the rural-urban factor. Coffman estimates that the median pay for all male teachers in 1910 (the large majority of whom taught at the elementary level) was $489, while Thorndike fixes the pay of male high school teachers (in 1907) at $900, 84 percent more. For all female teachers the median pay was $450, while female high school teachers earned $650, 44 percent more.[42] The 1905 NEA salary survey showed that the average elementary teacher earned $661 while the average high school teacher earned $1,046, a 58 percent advantage, and this advantage held for every size of community, ranging from those of less than one thousand to those of more than one million in population.[43] Thus high school teaching in general was substantially more lucrative than elementary school teaching, and this fact alone was sufficient to explain why teachers aspired to gain what in effect was a promotion to the high school.

Because high school teachers were more highly concentrated in the better-paying urban districts, however, we need to examine pay differences within districts in order to isolate the effect of school level. Consider the distribution of teacher pay in Lansing and Philadelphia for two different years, 1894 and 1918. In 1894, Lansing male and female high school teachers made between 41 percent and 79 percent more than the city's all-female elementary teachers; and in 1918, male high school teachers enjoyed a 60–220 percent advantage over the elementary teachers, while the female high school teachers earned between 13 percent less and 150 percent more than women at the elementary level.[44]

Philadelphia had a much more highly differentiated system of schools than Lansing, and thus a more complex structure of rewards. Yet high schools there offered teachers the same sort of powerful financial incentive to seek a position at the secondary level. In the hierarchy of pay, there were three levels of high school teaching in 1894, with men earning more than women, and teachers at Central earning more than those at other schools. In 1918, male high school teachers there earned 93 percent more than men teaching grammar school, and female high school teachers earned 59 percent more than their grammar school counterparts.

The 1894 data for both cities reveal something else about the opportunity structure for teachers: they received a bigger reward from being promoted to the high school than they did for being made principal. That is, school level provided a bigger incentive to teachers than did position in school. In Lansing, male and female high school teachers earned from 20 percent to 56 percent more than did female elementary school principals. In Philadelphia, male high school teachers earned between 7 percent and 34 percent more than male grammar school principals, while female high school teachers earned 8 percent less than female lower-school principals. Thus, at least for men, the salary gap between high school and elementary school was wider than the gap between principal and teacher within a given level. As a result, ambitious teachers were forced to pursue a path of career advancement that took them into higher academic levels.

POSITIONAL MOBILITY

Not only did high school teachers pursue career mobility by moving to the city and by aiming for higher-level schools, they also sought advancement by aspiring to administrative positions at each school level. In particular this meant seeking to become principal or superintendent. For the contemporary American teacher, administration has become the primary remaining route for attaining occupational advancement — a route that the Holmes Group and others have complained about because it draws some of the most ambitious and (perhaps) most accomplished practitioners out of teaching and into full-time administration. However, two characteristics distinguish the form of positional mobility that was open to the early high school teacher from the contemporary form: a blurring of the boundary between administration and teaching, and an extreme pattern of gender-differentiated access to administrative opportunities.

In the previous section we saw that an elementary school principal frequently was paid less than a high school teacher, which suggests that school-level mobility was a better way to get ahead than was promotion into administration within a given level. One reason for this was that, in a system marked by staggering attrition, high schools and high school teachers were scarcer and more valuable commodities than elementary schools and their principals. Another reason was that being a principal or superintendent in most school systems around the turn of the century did not mean much. Most high schools were very small. As Harris reported in 1894, the average public high school had 3.1 teachers, and this estimate left out a large number of the smallest schools. In Indiana, the average in 1903 was only 1.8, and by 1925, the median rural high school in the country still had a total faculty of only 3.5 teachers.[45]

All of these figures include the principal as part of the teaching force, for the simple practical reason that in schools this small there was no room for a full-time administrator. These principals were in fact principal teachers. Sometimes they were the only teachers. More often they were the lead teachers, who taught advanced students and did administration part-time. Ferriss found that among the rural high schools, the principal spent about two hundred minutes a day teaching, fifty-five minutes doing clerical work, and forty minutes supervising instruction.[46] Not a very glamorous or distinctive position for a teacher to aspire to.

In addition, about half of the time spent on instructional supervision was devoted to overseeing the workings of the elementary schools. For small districts, the high school principal often was seen as the instructional leader of the system as a whole, acting as a quasi-superintendent. Some districts had no superintendent, and others had someone filling a clerical role under this title; in both cases, the high school principal had to take charge. In a number of districts, however, it was the superintendent who acted as the instructional leader, frequently occupying an office in the high school and teaching classes there. The possibilities were rife for widespread confusion about the boundaries separating these positions. Often it was difficult to tell the difference between a high school teacher and a principal, or between a principal and a superintendent, for frequently their functions were interchangeable.

One need only recall the situation that faced Sadie Trail in the high school at North Bend, Nebraska, in 1896. She was hired to teach in a school where the only other teacher was the principal, who, in the absence of a superintendent, also supervised the lower schools. Yet in her third year, the principal suddenly took the title of superintendent, and she became principal — although there was no discernible change in the duties of either. Did this constitute positional mobility for either of them? She thought not. Later in her career, she was a principal in three towns and a superintendent in one, but each time she left the position within two years. It is unclear whether any of these administrative posts consisted of much more than a teaching job with an impressive title. And this question leads us to the problem of gender.

The mobility of high school teachers into administration was eased by the muddle over what distinguished an administrator from a teacher, but this led to a two-track system based on gender. Normally, women were offered jobs as high school principals and superintendents only when no man wanted those positions. This generally meant that women ended up as administrators in the smallest districts, where the pay was too low to attract a man and where the job was basically a teaching job anyway.[47] Even under these circumstances, the appointment often was considered temporary until such time as a male candidate appeared. Remember how Margaret Ingram took a job as a small-town high school principal, only to be summarily replaced after one year by a man who quickly turned out to be incompetent. Even when women succeeded in making it to the college level, they tended to do so as regular faculty instead of as chair, dean, or president.

For men, however, the picture was quite different. Blessed with the right of first refusal for administrative jobs in general, they could choose to pursue the most attractive possibilities, which meant the larger schools in the larger communities. Paul Hanus rose from high school teacher in Denver to college professor, high school principal, and finally university dean. John Swett found his way to San Francisco, where he went from grammar school principal to state superintendent of public instruction to high school principal to city superintendent.[48] For these men, the promotional ladder seemed to reflect an opportunity structure that was more meritocratic than the one confronting the women. For example, Jesse Stuart started out in Kentucky in the 1920s teaching in a one-room rural elementary school, then moved to a one-room high school. But when his students won a statewide academic achievement contest, he became principal of a city high school and later the city and county superintendent — another story of male merit rewarded that would have set Margaret Ingram to gnashing her teeth in frustration.[49]

The Role of Education in Promoting Mobility

A key method by which high school teachers moved up any or all of the three career ladders open to them was to pursue further education and acquire additional levels of certification. This is a familiar story, and a couple of examples will serve to flesh it out. Recall that Margaret Ingram graduated from high school, then taught while attending teachers institutes in the summer. Later she chose to seek a life certificate, attending the state normal school while continuing to teach during the year. After some unpleasant experiences in small-town jobs, she began spending her summers attending classes at the University of Chicago, earning her B.A. about 1912. She continued studying during the summer, gaining a master's in 1914 and attaining a Ph.D. from Teachers College in the 1920s. All of her education after high school, with the possible exception of her doctorate, was obtained part-time while teaching. Each stage in her educational process in turn led to a higher-level position, and when each new position failed to satisfy her professional ambition, she went back to school.

Fern Persons graduated from Olivet (Michigan) High School in 1913 and spent the following year at Eaton County Normal School.[50] For the next ten years she taught at three elementary schools, gradually working toward a life certificate, which she received in 1922 from Western Michigan College. She immediately began working on a bachelor's degree at Olivet College. In 1926 she moved up to teaching math at Olivet High School, and a year later received her B.A. and won the position of dean of women at the school. Continuing her education, she did graduate work at Northwestern and the University of Michigan. She became principal at Olivet in 1931, the first woman to hold such a position in that part of the state. In 1939 she was awarded a master's from Michigan, then became acting superintendent while the male incumbent was absent during the war. Meanwhile, she continued piling up credits toward a doctorate.

This pattern runs through most of these teachers' personal accounts in one form or another. Educational enhancement provided a crucial catalyst for the ambitious high school teacher seeking to get ahead. The education itself took on a variety of shapes — from teachers institutes to city or county normal schools, state normal schools, teachers colleges, liberal arts colleges, and universities. It ranged from an informal study program in preparation for a certifying examination to a formal graduate degree. Education in all these various forms was then combined with one or all of the other mechanisms for occupational mobility, as degrees and certificates helped to support a teacher's upward progress toward a city school system, a higher-level school, and a higher position.

The most successful careerists among the early high school teachers were the ones like Margaret Ingram, Fern Persons, Paul Hanus, and Mary Bradford, who used education to pursue all three routes to upward mobility at the same time. Here is where the analogy of the career ladder simply deconstructs, for it is awkward to picture them climbing all of these ladders simultaneously.[51]

The Role of Gender and Race in Restricting Mobility

There are two additional elements that, unlike education, have served to limit the possibilities for teacher mobility: gender and race. The impact of these factors on the process of teacher advancement was to create largely separate mobility tracks leading up each of the three career ladders already identified. The routes to career success for men and whites were in this way parallel with those for women and blacks, yet the mechanisms for getting ahead worked more effectively for the former pair than for the latter.

We have seen a variety of statistics that show a significant difference in pay between men and women high school teachers. Let us consider the evidence about whether or not these differences were the result of sexist pay practices or other factors. One plausible explanation might be that women were paid less because they left the profession earlier than men.[52] In apparent confirmation of this point, Thorndike, it should be recalled, found in 1907 that male and female high school teachers earned a nearly identical pay increment ($28 and $27, respectively) for each additional year of experience during their first twelve years of teaching. Yet the median salary was $900 for men and $650 for women, while the median years of experience were eight and six, respectively. Thus the extra two years of experience enjoyed by the men would account for less than $60 of their $250 pay advantage. This suggests that the gender difference in pay arose not through differential pay increases or longer tenure but from the pay levels set when men and women were first hired to teach high school.

This interpretation receives some support from the data on pay differences between country and city. Thorndike's study drew on data from high school teachers nationally, and, because the number of urban high school teachers constituted a small fraction of this population, his median figures primarily reflect the condition of country and small-town teachers. Another source from a decade earlier provides some insight into urban pay levels. In 1895, A. F. Nightingale, superintendent of the Chicago high schools, sent a questionnaire to superintendents in most of the largest school systems around the country, asking them how much they paid their male and female high school teachers.[53] He received salary data from fifty-two schools. The average male high school teacher in the larger districts earned about $1,470, while his female counterpart earned $900.[54] Thus in urban high schools, male teachers earned 63 percent more than female teachers, while in small-town high schools (a decade later) the male advantage was 38 percent.[55] The respondents to Nightingale's survey explain this differential in terms of market pressures. One speaks for most of them when he says: "Why do we pay men more than women? The market demands it. . . . The woman will stay at her work for years — the man, as soon as he becomes of value to the school, must be promoted, or he will leave to go where higher salaries are paid. It is a simple question of supply and demand, governing the price of work for the two sexes."[56]

Under these conditions, the city schools were in a better situation to compete for male teachers simply because they could afford to pay more than the country districts. Thus the gap between male and female teachers was greater in the city because the upper pay limit was less restrictive, allowing the high schools to attract and hold male teachers, while the absence of market alternatives prevented the female high school teacher from capitalizing on these possibilities to the same extent. In the country high school, however, the limited local tax base put a lower ceiling on male salaries (even at the expense of driving men out of these jobs altogether), while the floor on female salaries could not be held at a level that was proportionately as far below the male level as was true in the city. After all, there was a certain annual pay below which even a country woman could not eke out a living.

This argument implies that city high schools had a higher proportion of male teachers than did country high schools, even though the evidence shows that cities had a smaller proportion of males in the teaching population as a whole. In fact, the NEA's 1905 survey shows that in cities with a population of more than one hundred thousand, the males made up 41.0 percent of the high school teaching force, while in towns of less than fifteen thousand the male proportion dropped to 25.1 percent.[57]

Two factors can explain this discrepancy. First, as noted, cities could afford to pay what men demanded. Second, urban high school teaching offered a degree of prestige and influence that made it attractive even in light of the other opportunities open to men. Given the small number of high schools that existed before this century and the prominence of these institutions within their respective cities, high school teachers — accorded the honorific title of professor — constituted leading figures in the local educational community and played a respected role in the public life of the noneducational community. In Philadelphia during the nineteenth century, for example, the professors (all men) from the only boys' high school were listed in back of the city directory along with judges and elected officials.

Two other elements contributed to the gender differences in pay among high school teachers. The first was positional. Men were much more likely to hold the position of principal, and principals were paid more than other teachers. A prime reason for this situation was an ideological preference for having men in charge. One of Nightingale's superintendents put the case simply: "Why do we pay men more than women? The most important and responsible positions are filled by men. It is of quite rare occurrence for a woman to be considered successful either as a city superintendent or a high school principal."[58] The second contributing force was educational. Men at the turn of the century were more likely to be college graduates than women, especially at the start of their careers, and this gave them an advantage in competing for a high school job, in demanding higher pay for such a job, and in making a claim for the principalship. By contrast, the career histories of even the most successful women high school teachers show that they tended to acquire their education gradually over a lifetime, and that university training came (if at all) years after they entered the teaching profession.

Myra Strober and Laura Best did a remarkable study of male-female pay differentials among San Francisco public-school teachers that pulls together many of these elements. They found that in 1879 position and school level had a larger impact on these gender-based pay differentials than did experience and education. But when the effect of the other three variables was controlled, the most powerful factor influencing gender differences in pay was school level. The male high school teacher enjoyed an advantage over his female counterpart that extended beyond education, experience, and position, and that simply came from being in a high school.[59] When the expansion of high school enrollment in the 1890s undercut the exclusiveness of high school teaching, male teachers scrambled to hold on to the special position they had once occupied. For many, this meant returning to the university and seeking credentials that would take them into educational administration.[60] But the change propelled others into unionism, wherein male high school teachers have continued to play a leadership role since the turn of century.[61]

If gender created a partially divergent and shortened career ladder for women in high school teaching, race constructed a radically separated and truncated track for blacks. Whites could teach in black high schools (Lizette Reese, whose career, as we have seen, included an assignment at the "Colored High School" in Baltimore, was white), but blacks could not teach in white schools. And the situation facing black teachers in black high schools was grim. One study found that as late as 1933 about half of the southern black high schools in rural areas offered only one- or two-year programs, and about half had fewer than forty students. Overall, 60 percent of all southern black high schools had less than a four-year program, and these schools had on average less than one full-time teacher.[62]

In effect, being a high school teacher under these conditions was a part-time addition to one's grammar school duties. And pay levels for these teachers were commensurate with their abysmal working conditions. Average monthly pay levels for southern public school teachers in 1909–1910 were $60 for whites and $33 for blacks; in 1928–1929 the percentage gap had narrowed only slightly, to $118 and $73.[63]

The career ladders available to high school teachers in the late nineteenth and early twentieth centuries offered three different routes to career advancement — moving from country to city, from lower- to higher-level schools, and from teaching into administration. A small number of the most ambitious early high school teachers took advantage of all of these routes to achieve a substantial degree of career mobility.

The evidence for this mobility process that I have presented is not of the sort that leads to strong and confident conclusions about the nature of early schoolteaching as a form of work. One reason is that I have focused almost exclusively on the most successful cases, while in fact most teachers never moved beyond the first rung or two on any of the three career ladders. Another is that my sources have largely consisted of rather idiosyncratic personal accounts, which are difficult to organize into a systematic understanding of the condition of high school teachers more generally. But then the function of this discussion is not to analyze the typical teacher but to examine the structure of incentives that shaped the possibilities for advancement by the exceptional teacher who stayed in the profession long enough to consider it a career.

With this limited goal in mind, I can venture two comments about general tendencies that appear in the preceding discussion. First, the opportunity structure within the profession was molded by forces arising from the social context of schooling: a meritocratic ideology and a structure of occupational opportunity stratified by gender and race. Second, the substantial changes that affected high school teaching in the twentieth century had the effect of undercutting the importance of the first two routes to advancement (geographical and school-level mobility) and of ritualizing the positional route.

The career ladders of early schoolteachers modeled meritocratic ideology in two related ways.[64] First, the career histories of those teachers I found in print are framed in the style of the classic American success story. The full title of one of these accounts captures the spirit of this tradition: *Memoirs of Mary D. Bradford: Autobiography and Historical Reminiscence of Education in Wisconsin, Through Progressive Service from Rural School to City Superintendent.* The genre is familiar, but instead of plotting the path from the log cabin to the White House, these authors display the triumphant steps leading from the rude one-room schoolhouse to the comfortable administrative offices of a major urban school system or university. It was a tough world, they grimly tell us, but true merit still ultimately gained its just reward.

Yet these stories do provide evidence that career advancement for the early high school teacher was in fact partly structured along meritocratic lines. Given a form of school organization at the turn of the century that was, for the most part, prebureaucratic or only partially bureaucratic, career advancement was highly unstructured, and thus rewards tended to go to those teachers who were the most entrepreneurial.[65] These were ambitious women and men who carefully managed their careers, seeking out opportunities and promoting their interests. The open structure of U.S. schooling during this period, in combination with the radical inequalities that existed within this structure, provided them with a set of rewarding ladders to climb. It is worth remembering that what made advancement possible was the abject poverty (financially and educationally) of education at the bottom of these ladders. The poor conditions and low pay that existed in rural districts and in elementary schools —unpleasant facts about the early teaching experience for most teachers— were themselves the source of great opportunity for the ambitious few. What made the incentives effective was that so few could take advantage of them. What made the career pyramid worth climbing was the extreme narrowing that occurred between bottom and top.

As we have seen, however, the meritocratic character of career mobility for schoolteachers was sharply undercut by the extreme differentiation of career opportunities by gender and race. Women and men, blacks and whites, had their own separate structures of inequality to climb, and these structures did not have the same shape. The pyramid of opportunity for women and blacks narrowed much more quickly as one moved upward. Women like Mary Bradford could move "from rural school to city superintendent," but the chances of succeeding were much smaller than for a man. During the course of this century, there has been a gradual but significant reduction in the differences in opportunity open to women and blacks in U.S. secondary education. But one result of this change is that the range and flexibility of meritocratic career opportunities has at the same time declined for teachers of both sexes and both races.

During the course of the twentieth century, the opportunity structure for schoolteachers has undergone significant change. Two factors that helped bring about this change were the growing equalization of previous educational differences and the relentless bureaucratization of school organization.

One important characteristic of U.S. educational development in this century has been a gradual reduction in the extreme differences that marked off rural areas and small towns from cities. The migration of a large portion of the rural population to the city, the growth in the relative vitality of rural economies, and radical consolidation of rural school districts have helped reduce some of the old advantage enjoyed by urban schooling. And states have pushed the process even farther through their recent efforts to promote greater equality in per capita support for schooling by means of redistributive funding formulas. As we have seen, these changes by no means ended differences in pay between urban and rural high schools; teachers still move to urban and suburban districts in pursuit of a better salary. But the financial incentive is less now than it was, and it is even smaller if one takes into account cost of living. In addition, teachers frequently choose the less urbanized district, even at lower pay, because the teaching conditions there are seen as preferable. Finally, tenure and pension rules make mobility generally less attractive.

There has also been a reduction in the incentive once offered by moving from one level of schooling to the next higher level. Bureaucratization has brought elementary and secondary schooling together under a common set of rules, and unionization has equalized the pay differences attributable to school level alone. Through its subject-matter specialization and departmental structure, the high school retains a different set of teaching conditions from the elementary school, but the old pay differential is gone. Also gone is the financial incentive to seek "promotion" from high school to university teaching. Now that unions have succeeded in raising pay scales for public-school teachers, experienced teachers find that taking a college teaching position generally requires a substantial cut in pay. When teachers do make this change, therefore, it tends to be in pursuit of different working conditions rather than more money. The pay incentive to change school levels — so powerful fifty years ago — simply has evaporated.

The ascendancy of bureaucratic organization has brought with it the emergence of position as the key incentive for upward mobility among ambitious high school teachers. One reason for this is that bureaucratization led to a sharp differentiation of function between teachers and administrators, in place of the blurred boundaries and ill-defined responsibilities that characterized these positions in early school systems. Another reason is that, as the chances for advancement within teaching — by means of moving to the city or climbing to a higher school level — diminished over the course of the twentieth century, the prospects offered by the newly differentiated administrative positions looked increasingly attractive. "Getting ahead," which used to have multiple meanings, came to mean one thing: leaving the classroom and entering administration. A variety of routes to career advancement finally converged on a single preferred path, which led to the principal's office and the superintendent's staff.

Even the way that education leads to advancement has changed in character. Teacher contracts and district policies have formalized the previously more entrepreneurial role of education in career enhancement by establishing a rigid connection between the accumulation of graduate credits and degrees and the awarding of pay increases. But at the same time, education leads to less differentiation among contemporary teachers than it did fifty or one hundred years ago. The higher minimum for entering the profession (a bachelor's degree) and the prevalence of state rules requiring graduate credits to maintain certification have made it difficult for teachers to differentiate themselves from the pack by means of any sort of educational distinction short of a doctorate.

The gradual equalization of what was once a radically differentiated opportunity structure for high school teachers and the bureaucratization of what was once an open and improvised organization of schooling produced momentous changes for those trying to make a career within public education. The privileged teachers at the older high schools in large U.S. cities experienced this change as a form of proletarianization through which they lost their former advantages of pay, prestige, and professional autonomy.[66] But for the more typical teacher — working at a lower level in a smaller school and a less populous area — these changes looked more like a thoroughly benevolent and desirable process of professionalization, one that was raising their status, improving their working conditions, and enhancing the quality of education for students. This general elevation of the entire occupational group led to the erosion of the old routes by which a select group of early schoolteachers once pursued career mobility. Yet for most teachers, the loss of career ladders from which they were unlikely to benefit anyway was hardly cause for alarm. They lost a long shot at fulfilling the American dream of individual success, but they gained the ability to make a comfortable living in public school classrooms.

Contemporary proposals for a multitiered teaching profession (such as those offered by Holmes and Carnegie) are an attempt to create a new form of career ladder to replace the one that was lost earlier in the century. The aim is to set up a structure of opportunity that will spur ambition and achievement among teachers in the United States, thereby making a teaching career more attractive and promoting an improvement in the quality of instruction. But a glance at the history of teacher career ladders suggests that contemporary teachers have good reason to be wary of such a plan.

In the past, such opportunities for advancement have been based on a structure of inequality that allowed a few to get ahead at the expense of the many. Against this backdrop, a key outcome of the plan to create a small upper tier in the teaching profession — reserved for the new lead teacher, career professional teacher, or board-certified teacher — would be to place the ordinary teacher in what would then become the lower tier, occupying a diminished position and playing a more limited role. Such a change would effectively roll back the equalization in the condition of teachers that took place during the twentieth century, and it is thoroughly understandable that teachers might be unwilling to abandon this hard-won collective equality in return for selective opportunity.

8

The Rise of the Community College: Markets and the Limits of Educational Opportunity

> The public junior college will become the characteristic educational institution of the United States, just as the public high school has been up to now.
> — Robert M. Hutchins, 1936

When the president of the University of Chicago made this prediction in 1936, the public junior college was a growing but still minor presence on the U.S. educational scene. By the 1970s, however, it had indeed become the characteristic educational institution in the United States. The public high school had held this position for a half century by reason of both its rapid ascent and its distinctive form. Between 1890 and 1940, enrollments at American public high schools doubled every ten years, rising from 203,000 to 4,399,000, and the proportion of fourteen- to seventeen-year-olds enrolled in schools rose from 3.6 percent to 62.4 percent.[1] During this same period, the high school developed a comprehensive structure in which a widely differentiated array of programs was offered to a heterogeneous mix of students under one roof. Both its inclusiveness and its comprehensiveness made this educational institution distinctively American.

The public junior college has followed the high school model closely, and it attained a similar institutional status in a much shorter time than its prototype. After an uncertain beginning at the turn of the century, it gradually adopted the same consumer-oriented comprehensive form as the high school, an identity that was confirmed fifty years later by the new label *community college*.[2] After midcentury the pace quickened, as degree-credit enrollment quadrupled in fifteen years, rising from 1.0 million to 4.3 million between

1965 and 1980.[3] During this same period, the community college share of higher education enrollment rose from 17.5 percent to 35.8 percent, expanding the overall college enrollment to the point where the proportion of recent high school graduates who attended college exceeded 50 percent.[4]

The similarities between the community college and the high school extend beyond their parallel histories to their parallel current status. Both institutions suffer from the twin maladies of a confused identity and an uncertain future. Both have been imbued with contradictory purposes, as powerful constituencies have pressed each institution to pursue sharply differentiated and mutually incompatible goals. In particular, both have been subjected to intensive market pressures that have shaped these institutions around competing concerns of employers (seeking productive workers) and consumers (seeking advantage in the struggle for social position). The result is that each has followed an erratic path of compromise that serves none of the goals effectively, leaving each school open to charges of failure and demands for radical reform.

The high school came under heavy attack in the 1980s and 1990s, and the community college, while not yet the subject of such a volume of abuse, is showing the early signs of concern generated by a leveling off of enrollments. The confused condition of these two characteristically American educational institutions reflects in many ways the larger problems of U.S. education in the late twentieth century. To understand the relation between the two is to understand something important about how the current educational situation in the United States developed and where it might be headed.

Surprisingly for such a significant institution, the community college until quite recently has attracted very little serious historical attention.[5] I shall not attempt to fill this gap with this chapter, which is based largely on secondary sources. Instead my aim is to try to provide a general sketch of key issues in the historical sociology of the community college, which I seek to accomplish by comparing it with two other educational institutions. My argument, in essence, is that the community college — when viewed in light of the history and sociology of U.S. education — is best understood as both the new high school and the last college.

On the one hand, the community college is in effect the new comprehensive high school for the late twentieth century. As already suggested, it embodies both the successes and the failures that characterized the historical development of the high school. The same contradictory mixture of public and private purposes that spurred the rapid growth of the high school has helped to produce the extraordinary expansion of the community college. Yet these same contradictory purposes have led the latter to reproduce the former's ambiguous image and potential for failure. For better and worse, the community college seems to be replaying the history of the high school, though this time events seem to be rushing by in fast forward mode.

On the other hand, the community college also shows every indication of playing a rather different role, that of the last of the colleges. It is the last in two senses of the word — the latest and the lowest. It is the latest in the series of new collegiate forms that have been created to promote the social goals of political and economic development and then transformed to serve the private goal of individual status attainment. The land grant college edged away from its practical social mission and climbed the educational status ladder toward the more prestigious academic curriculum and university organizational form, largely in response to pressure from students seeking access to upward mobility. This left room at the bottom for the teachers college, which then succumbed to the same pressure and turned itself into a pale version of the university. This in turn left room for the last in the series, the community college, to provide opportunity for a new wave of status seekers. Yet unlike its predecessors, the community college was confined to the lowest rung on the ladder by strong forces that wanted to see it remain a two-year institution and continue to play its practical vocational role, preventing it from following the same trajectory of institutional mobility that had served its predecessors. This barrier to institutional mobility has brought serious social consequences by reducing the chances for community college students to achieve individual social mobility. In this sense, then, the community college is best understood as replaying the history of U.S. higher education, but with mobility prospects deferred indefinitely.

One way of combining these alternative visions of the community college is to think about it as the old comprehensive high school in a new collegiate form, afflicted with both the traditional contradictions that emerged in the history of the former and the novel restrictions that emerged in the history of the latter. What links these histories are the contradictory concerns for democratic equality, social efficiency, and social mobility that helped shape the path followed by all three levels of educational institution — high school, community college, and university.

The New High School

In one sense, the public junior college originated quite literally as a simple extension of the public high school. As late as the 1930s, 85 percent of these new institutions of higher education were physically located in high school buildings.[6] In California and other states where the public junior college developed earliest, it was most often founded and controlled by the local school district, and thus housing it initially in the high school made good sense. In this way, as in so many others, the history of the junior college paralleled that of its predecessor. For during the nineteenth century, most high schools occupied space in the local grammar school, and as a result there was no clear organizational distinction between a high school and an enhanced grammar school.[7]

Like the high school, the public junior college developed as an extension of the level of schooling below it. And like its predecessor, it also followed a course of development marked by contradictory purposes.[8]

POLITICS AND MARKETS: THE HIGH SCHOOL

The public high school in the United States bears the marks of the tensions that have characterized the society within which it developed, a society that is both democratic and capitalist.[9] On the one hand, it had its origins in the same political purposes that motivated the founders of the common school. The rapid growth of market capitalism in the first half of the nineteenth century stirred up a powerful current of possessive individualism, which Whig reformers saw as a substantial threat to the preservation of republican community and Protestant morality. A rise in the opportunity for the pursuit of private gain, and in the legitimacy of this pursuit, promised to undercut the civic virtue and public morality that formed the classic prerequisites for a successful republic. In an effort to respond to this threat without shutting off the wealth-creating capitalist engine, reformers created a variety of new institutions. The most comprehensive and durable of these was the common school, which was designed as a place that would draw together students from all social classes and imbue them with a shared vision of responsible citizenship and public service. The result would be to help re-create the republican community in the face of growing class divisions and self-interested commercial pursuits and thus help save political equality from the ravages of economic inequality.

The founders and early supporters of the high school saw it as a natural extension of the common school, serving the same political goals. After visiting one of these institutions, a state education official noted with satisfaction, "The course of instruction is in every way calculated to attach [students] to the institutions of our country, to fill their minds with a devotion to our republican government, and inspire them with a laudable ambition to become useful and eminent citizens of the community in which they live."[10]

At the same time that it served as a republican hedge against capitalist encroachments, the public high school also took on the characteristics of a market institution. One way it came to play a market role was by becoming established as an important gateway to social mobility — offering individuals the opportunity to compete for badges of merit (educational credentials) that offered a legitimate form of privileged access to desirable social positions.[11] Unlike the elementary school, the early high school was highly selective, unrepresentative, and consumer-sensitive. Very few students actually attended high school during the nineteenth century—as late as 1890, high school students still accounted for only 1.6 percent of all elementary and secondary enrollments—and only a small proportion of these succeeded in graduating.[12] Thus, while access to high school was formally open, the experience was anything but common.[13] Most families simply could not afford to lose the earnings of teenagers while they attended high school, and those who wanted to attend had to pass an examination in order to gain admission. As a result, the early high school had a clientele that was tiny and disproportionately upper middle class, and its market position—especially in the larger cities, where there was typically only one institution for the entire population—was extraordinarily strong.

In a market society, therefore, where social stratification was seen as the natural outcome of interpersonal competition, the most attractive thing about the early high school was not its promise of republican socialization but its offer of preferential social selection. And the secret of its ability to carry through on this offer was its very uncommonness, the fact that, unlike the common school, it carried a cachet born of market scarcity. Gradually the new institution became an integral part of the process by which its middle-class constituency socially and culturally formed itself.

But in a democratic society it proved politically impossible for officials to limit access to this valuable cultural commodity for very long. The market exclusiveness that made the high school attractive to its clientele contradicted the political inclusiveness that gave the common schools their legitimacy. The result was growing pressure to expand the opportunity to attend high school, which in the 1880s led to a strong surge in secondary enrollments that continued for the next fifty years. This development constituted a victory for the democratic political aims of the high school, but it posed a problem from the perspective of social mobility, for wider access threatened to dilute the exchange value of high school credentials for the institution's traditional middle-class clientele.

At this point, the high school began to assume a second and very different kind of market role, one that was based less on individual concerns for social mobility than on collective concerns for social efficiency. At the end of the nineteenth century, business leaders, politicians, and educators started to talk openly about the problem of how high schools could best serve the needs of the economy. They argued that the country's hopes for economic growth rested on the ability of schools to provide students with the differentiated skill training required by an increasingly specialized and stratified occupational structure.

Caught in the midst of these contradictory purposes — political equality, social mobility, and social efficiency — educators arranged a compromise solution for the high school by introducing curriculum tracks at the same time that they opened the doors to new students. Four tracks developed during the first two decades of the twentieth century, each leading to its own particular social outcome: academic (leading to college and the professions), commercial (leading to white-collar business positions), mechanical (leading to engineering), and industrial (leading to the factory). For a time it appeared that these tracks would be located within different schools, but the undemocratic implications of such a rigidly stratified system led eventually to the formation of that characteristically American institution, the comprehensive high school. The latter provided access to secondary education for everyone within a single school but also made possible a sharply stratified set of educational experiences under that one roof. The result was an institution that tried simultaneously to serve both political democracy and capitalist markets — allowing for inclusive enrollment, exclusive credentials (as the lower tracks drained off the flood of new students and thus protected the upper track from a potential devaluation of its credentials), and efficient allocation of personnel.[14]

For the rest of this century, the high school has maintained the compromise model evolved during the Progressive era. The results of this compromise are mixed, as suggested by the title of an article by David Cohen and Barbara Neufeld, "The Failure of High Schools and the Progress of Education."[15] The comprehensiveness and accessibility of the high school represent a major political victory, but one that is undermined by its highly undemocratic stratification of educational experiences and occupational outcomes. This stratified form of education helps protect the market value of academic high school credentials and thus the high school's differential usefulness for middle-class status attainment, but that value has been watered down by the rising tide of new students that filled the high school and then went on to fill the university as well.[16] The net effect of these contradictory pressures is to produce an institution in stasis, one that seems to be a failure at realizing any of its historic goals.

POLITICS AND MARKETS: THE COMMUNITY COLLEGE

The public junior college first appeared at the turn of the century, when the high school assumed its compromise structure. Shaped by the same contradictory impulses toward democratic equality and market differentiation that inspired that compromise, the new institution followed a developmental path that recapitulated many themes from the history of the high school. Like the Progressive-era high school, it sought both to promote inclusiveness and to protect exclusiveness, simultaneously providing for greater opportunity and greater stratification. Over the course of the twentieth century, the public junior college accumulated a series of four distinct social functions that derived from this underlying mix of purposes: the academic-transfer function, the vocational-terminal function, the general education function, and the community-adult education function. In the process, it developed a new composite identity — the community college — which embodied this confusing array of functions and left unresolved the long-standing struggle over the central aims of education in the United States.

These four functions are an expression of how the leaders of the public junior college have construed the evolving mixture of purposes that have characterized this institution.[17] I shall use these functions rather than my own analytical categories — the three educational goals — to organize the discussion that follows in order to make this discussion more compatible with the existing community college literature. Although the fit is by no means perfect, the general education and adult-community education functions largely serve the purposes of democratic equality, whereas academic-transfer serves social mobility and the vocational-terminal function serves social efficiency.

Academic-Transfer Function

The original impetus for the public junior college came from a series of midwestern university presidents who saw the need for such an institution to guard the gates of the university from a potential flood of students. As early as 1851, Henry P. Tappan (who was named president of the University of Michigan a year later) argued that if the United States were ever going to produce a true German-style university, it would have to purify itself by removing collegiate instruction to another location. He asserted that the contemporary American and English "college in distinction from a university is an elementary and preparatory school," whereas a full-fledged university should be devoted solely to research and the pursuit of advanced learning. "In Germany," he stated, "the Gymnasia are really the Colleges" and thus what U.S. higher education needed was its own version of the gymnasium to prepare students for the university and save the latter from this lowly duty.[18] In his 1869 inaugural address, the president of the University of Minnesota, William W. Folwell, picked up the same theme: "How immense the gain . . . if a youth could remain at the high school or academy, residing in his home, until he had reached a point, say, somewhere near the end of the sophomore year, there to go over all of those studies which as a boy he ought to study under tutors and governors! Then let the boy, grown up to be a man, emigrate to the university, there to enter upon the work of a man."[19]

It was not until the end of the century that anyone succeeded in creating this kind of intermediate educational institution. In 1892, President William Rainey Harper separated the four undergraduate years at the University of Chicago into two halves, first calling them the "academic college" and the "university college" and then four years later changing the names to "junior" and "senior" colleges.[20] In an address to the National Educational Association in 1900 he argued that junior colleges should be created in large numbers, both by converting many small colleges into two-year institutions and by extending high schools into six-year institutions. The benefits of such a change would be substantial, for "the money now wasted in doing the higher work superficially could be used to do the lower work more thoroughly," and "the student who was not really fitted by nature to take up the higher work could stop naturally and honorably at the end of the sophomore year."[21] At Harper's urging, the city of Joliet, Illinois, founded Joliet Junior College in 1901 as an extension of the local high school, making it probably the first independent public junior college (or at least the earliest that is still in existence).[22] Others followed suit — in Minnesota, Missouri, Kansas, Oklahoma, Texas, and California — so that by 1915 there were nineteen such institutions and by 1921 the number had risen to seventy.[23]

With the enthusiastic support of Stanford President David Starr Jordan and University of California Dean Alexis F. Lange, California quickly took the lead in the development of public junior colleges. In 1907 the state legislature authorized high schools to add two years of postgraduate instruction onto their normal four-year course and later granted permission for these extensions to be called junior colleges. Then in 1921 it authorized the establishment of independent junior college districts, and within five years the number of public junior colleges in the state had risen to thirty-one, with sixteen attached to high schools, six connected to state colleges, and nine with independent status.[24] By 1929, seventeen states had passed laws providing public support for junior colleges, and the number of such institutions nationally had grown to 178.[25]

In light of the history of U.S. secondary and higher education (and the political and market pressures that shaped this history), it is not surprising that the leaders of America's universities initiated the junior college movement and that they did so at the start of the twentieth century. For one thing, they wanted to buffer themselves from the glut of late nineteenth-century institutions that called themselves colleges. In 1880 the United States had the largest number of colleges per million population that it has ever had before or since, and at the same time it had more students attending college than were attending high school.[26] Under these unfavorable market conditions, most colleges found themselves competing with high schools for students. In such undistinguished company, the universities had a powerful incentive to promote a clearly differentiated hierarchy of schools, in which each level would screen students for the next higher level. Thus during the 1890s the National Education Association's Committee of Ten established guidelines for a college preparatory high school curriculum, and its Committee on College Entrance Requirements proposed a standard system for measuring high school credits (which evolved into the Carnegie unit).[27] As a result of these and other efforts by university presidents, a hierarchy did begin to take shape at the turn of the century — leading from grammar school to high school to college to graduate and professional school. The junior college was simply a further elaboration of this emerging pattern of structural differentiation within education in the United States, creating an additional level between the high school and the university.

In addition, universities were responding (perhaps a bit prematurely) to the sharp increase in high school enrollments that began in 1880 and seemed likely to continue indefinitely. If it proved politically impossible to bar open access to secondary education, how could higher education resist the pressure from a growing number of high school graduates seeking admission to the university? The junior college seemed to provide an answer. As the University of Chicago's James R. Angell wrote in a 1915 article, "Where . . . the press of undergraduate students is so great as seriously to embarrass the facilities of the institution (this is the case in many of the large state institutions as well as in some of those under private endowment), it is not unnatural that a welcoming hand should be held out to any movement which promises to lessen the number of these undergraduates." Later in the article he put the case more bluntly: "There is a good deal of evidence to indicate that anything which would serve to discourage some of our applicants for college entrance from actual attendance on the institution would be enormously in the interest of all concerned."[28] Berkeley's Lange reinforced this argument by asserting the pressing need for "the University to reduce its 'swollen fortune' in freshmen and sophomores by actively promoting their distribution among federated colleges, normal schools, and the six-year high schools that are to be and will be."[29]

This growth in demand for access to college began to materialize in the 1920s, bringing about two significant developments: individual colleges started to restrict the number of students admitted, and junior college enrollments began to increase sharply.[30] From the perspective of universities early in this century, therefore, the function of the junior college was to protect their market position by draining off excess demand. It could provide students with a general academic education, preparing the most worthy for pursuit of advanced study at the university while screening out "the student who was not really fitted by nature to take up the higher work." Thus the public junior college at its inception bore the marks of the same compromise between access and differentiation that characterized the birth of the comprehensive high school. Like the high school, the junior college satisfied the democratic demand for expanded educational opportunity while protecting the exchange value of elite educational credentials and promoting the efficient allocation of students into the job structure. Just as the high school funneled newcomers into the newly created lower-track curricula, the university sought to channel the lower-middle-class and skilled-working-class students who were beginning to graduate from high school into the newly created lower track in higher education, the junior college. The net result in both cases was fewer students in the upper track and thus preservation of the relative scarcity of the credentials offered by preparatory programs within the high school and by the advanced programs of study in the university.[31]

The public junior college therefore first appeared in significant numbers shortly after the comprehensive high school, and it emerged from the same contradictory impulses that led to the creation of the latter. The early promoters of the junior college saw it as a new level in the pyramid of U.S. education which was located between the high school and the university, providing an outlet for the graduates of the former and a buffer for the elite position of the latter. The dream of these founders was for the junior college to become institutionalized in this role so that the university could abandon its first two years entirely, producing a progression through the educational levels that would move students from elementary to junior high to senior high to junior college to university (in the form 6-3-3-2-2, or perhaps, in an upgraded high school variant, 6-4-4-2).[32] The ultimate failure of this dream is best understood in light of the additional functions that were loaded on the public junior college during the course of the twentieth century.

Vocational-Terminal Function

The same circumstances that brought about the creation of the public junior college as an academic-transfer institution quickly led proponents of the new college to add a second function — providing terminal vocational programs for those students who proved unfit for promotion to the university. In the absence of such programs, these educators asserted, students who did not transfer would be left with an education that prepared them for an eventuality that had not materialized. Thus the junior college needed to focus its attention on meeting the special needs of these terminal students. As a result, as one observer noted, "No topic received greater attention and more agreement among the community-junior college national spokesmen during the 1920s and 1930s than the importance of terminal education in the junior college."[33] Dean Lange took an early lead in advocating this role for the new school, and like later proponents he defined it as more important than the transfer role. In 1917 he declared: "The junior college cannot make preparation for the University its excuse for being. Its courses of instruction and training are to be culminal rather than basal. . . . The junior college will function adequately only if its first concern is with those who will go no farther, if it meets local needs efficiently, if it enables thousands and tens of thousands to round out their general education, if it turns an increasing number into vocations for which training has not hitherto been afforded by our school system."[34]

Once again the junior college mirrored the high school, for it was also in 1917 that concern about secondary vocational education reached a high point. The U.S. Congress passed the Smith-Hughes Act providing funds for high school vocational programs, and a year later the Commission on the Reorganization of Secondary Education announced that vocational training was one of the "cardinal principles" of high school education.[35] Junior college leaders, however, wanted vocational training within these institutions to provide preparation for higher-level positions than the vocational programs in high school. One speaker at the 1928 meeting of the American Association of Junior Colleges (AAJC) spelled out the special aims and characteristics of vocational training at junior colleges in terms of what he and other spokesmen liked to call "semi-professional" occupations:

> More than all . . . it is necessary to set up a series of courses which have been designated as terminal in character. Various phrases have been used to describe the content of these courses. One name with reference to them has been that these courses are semi-professional. It is certain that these courses must be above the level of routine and handicraft vocational courses that are given in high school. These students will undoubtedly enter vocations that have a great deal of routine work in them. This routine, however, will be above the manipulative level. Perhaps it can be said that the thing that will characterize the semi-professional courses will be that they will prepare students to live on the level of intellectual routine rather than manipulative routine. Junior engineers in architects' and engineers' offices will be examples. The nursing profession is another. People who enter these vocational fields will be the masters of certain definite bodies of technique and will be expected to use intelligence

of a rather high order in their work. They are distinctly below the highly professional specialization that takes place on the university level.[36]

Both the high school and the junior college in the 1920s and 1930s were heavily influenced by a discourse of social efficiency. While both promoted vocational programs in part as a way to provide students with expanded opportunity (appealing to aspirations for political equality and social mobility), they also dealt explicitly with the differential social outcomes that awaited students in the different tracks within each institution. Like the high school, the junior college was designed to prepare students in the academic tracks for positions in upper management and the professions via the university and to prepare students in the terminal-vocational tracks for less elevated positions in the occupational hierarchy. But while high school vocational programs were supposed to get students ready for skilled manual work, junior college vocational programs were supposed to get them ready for middle-level positions in which they would perform routine forms of white-collar work. In order to fill the latter positions with well-trained workers, the junior colleges would have to keep turning out a large number of graduates from its terminal programs.

But junior college students often had other ideas. A large majority of them saw the junior college as a convenient and inexpensive (often tuition-free) way to acquire two years of college credits and then transfer to a four-year institution. Apparently unswayed by the attractions of the semiprofessions, they dauntlessly pursued a bachelor's degree as the entree to the good life. David Levine provides a vivid account of the middle-class "culture of aspiration," which emerged between the two world wars and which re-formed this class around a model of socialization and status attainment that increasingly required a four-year college education.[37] Pursuing a B.A. became a part of what it meant to be middle class in America, and thus for working-class and middle-class students to abandon this pursuit by enrolling in a terminal program at a junior college was to give up the hope of upward mobility.[38] This situation left junior college leaders thoroughly distraught. Walter Crosby Eells, a Stanford professor who later became executive director of the AAJC, expressed alarm over the problem at the association's 1929 meeting: "It will be most unfortunate if the junior college becomes so successful as a popularizing agency that it makes all of its students plan on full university courses. Probably the proportion of those continuing should be nearer fifty than ninety per cent. This report of ninety per cent is a distinct danger signal ahead."[39]

During the 1920s and 1930s a noticeable gap emerged between the social efficiency aims of national junior college leaders and the social mobility orientation of the students, faculty, and administrators of the individual junior colleges, as the former pushed terminal education and the latter continued to focus on transfer programs. Surveys of junior colleges revealed that the proportion of total course offerings devoted to terminal courses grew only modestly in spite of all the pressure in this direction from the national leadership, rising from 17.5 percent in 1917 to 28.0 percent in 1921 and 33.0 percent in 1930 and then leveling off at 32.0 percent in 1947.[40] When Leonard Koos examined the catalogues of 23 public junior colleges in 1923, he found that 22 stressed college preparation in their statements of purpose, while only 12 even mentioned vocational training.[41] A similar review in 1930 found that the transfer function was emphasized more than the terminal function in two-thirds of the 343 catalogues examined.[42]

Both political and market pressures have made the local leadership of public junior colleges wary of pushing vocationalism too hard. As publicly supported organizations with voluntary attendance, these colleges have had to depend on the community for both funding and enrollments. The messages they have received from these sources have been mixed. Government and business have often promoted a social efficiency goal (which led the junior colleges to emphasize vocational training), while the consumer preferences of the local constituency have often stressed the goal of social opportunity (which led the colleges to emphasize transfer to the university). Thus in order to maintain political support and sustain enrollments, public junior colleges have been compelled to be quite sensitive to the continuing significance of these colleges as local mechanisms for achieving upward mobility, even if this has meant backing off on the training of semiprofessionals.[43]

General Education Function

The academic-transfer and vocational-terminal programs define the polarities of function that have characterized both the U.S. high school and the public junior college during the course of the twentieth century. Writers about the junior college have agreed on the nature of its bifurcated goals even though they disagree about the consequences of this split. Those who see these colleges as agents for reproducing social inequality argue that this combination of aims serves to draw students in with the false promise of upward mobility and then "cools them out" by blunting their aspirations and diverting them into vocational programs. From this point of view, transfer programs provide a cover of legitimacy for the college's real task, which is to channel working-class students back into working-class jobs.[44] Those who see community colleges as agents of meritocratic opportunity, however, argue that this combination of functions is essential in order to provide students with the possibility of acquiring the training necessary to perform in the widest possible range of occupational roles. From this point of view, a broad mix of courses provides the community college with a comprehensiveness of function that allows it to realize the promise claimed but never achieved by the early high school and early land grant college — to serve as an all-purpose "people's college."[45]

It is important to understand that these polar functions both serve market purposes. Programs in both tracks are seen as mechanisms for gaining preferential access to a good job; both define schooling as an adjunct to the occupational structure; and both represent a divergence from the political and moral aims that motivated the founders of the high school. The primary difference between the two is merely in the level of job for which one's educational credentials can be exchanged. And the tension that the pair of functions introduces into education is over the relatively narrow issue of which market goal should be stressed — individual mobility or social efficiency, creating opportunities or filling slots.

The other two functions for the public junior college that emerged in the twentieth century — general education and adult-community education — represent at least a partial break from the market-centered functions that defined the institution's core concerns during this period. Both suggest the possibility that this college might evolve away from its market role and acquire a more community-centered place for itself in the educational environment, potentially playing down the creation of human and cultural capital and playing up the production of social, political, and personal competencies.

A concern about "general education" has been prominent in the rhetoric of the public junior college throughout its history, but the term has carried two quite different meanings. Construed one way, it is an important adjunct to vocational education, which helps to round out the social efficiency of this form of training. The basic argument from this perspective is that vocational students need more than narrowly defined job skills in order to be effective workers and good citizens. In addition to vocational techniques, they need training in morality, civic responsibility, and cultural awareness. The discussion of this function by junior college leaders is strongly reminiscent of the arguments raised by industrialists in the 1840s who wrote to Horace Mann about the usefulness of common-school education in training factory workers. In their letters, these men stressed not job skills (which common schooling did not provide) but the salutary occupational effects of education more generally. As one of them put it, "I have found the best educated, to be the most profitable help." The reason for this occupational superiority, he asserted, was that "I have uniformly found the better educated as a class possessing a higher and better state of morals, more orderly and respectful in their deportment, and more ready to comply with the wholesome and necessary regulations of an establishment."[46]

Nicholas Ricciardi, California Commissioner of Vocational Education and later a junior college president, echoed these sentiments eighty-five years later. In 1927 he wrote about the need for general education as an adjunct to vocational training:

> Industry is realizing more and more clearly that the head and the hand function best when the heart is right; and character building makes the heart right.
>
> Industry wants well-trained workers of character. The chief concern of the schools is to train young people so that they may develop into efficient workers and citizens of character. Industry and the schools, therefore, should join hands to establish the kind of training program which will accomplish the ends which they have in common.[47]

In remarks before the 1940 AAJC convention he quoted approvingly from another vocational education advocate who made the point more graphically: "I can teach a person to become an efficient locksmith, but whether or not he becomes a socially useful citizen depends on what we give him besides the skill and technical knowledge required to make or repair locks; whether he goes out to repair a lock or to pick it will depend on his social understanding."[48]

The link between vocational and general education was indissoluble in the minds of leaders such as these. As one commentator put it, "Although community-junior college national spokesmen continued to make verbal distinctions between social-civic and vocational aspects of terminal education, they did not really think that there was any basic difference between training a student to be a good citizen and training him to be a good worker."[49]

Yet the junior college literature also contains another vision of general education that was unalloyed with vocationalism. This vision harks back to the broad concerns with civic virtue and moral education that were prominent in the common-school movement and which were part of an effort to protect the republic from markets rather than simply to train docile workers. Although the discussion of general education among junior college people did not become prominent until the 1930s and 1940s, this broad construction of the subject was visible from the beginning of the junior college movement. The transfer curriculum itself was seen as providing a general liberal arts education preparatory to the specialized studies a student would encounter in the university. James Angell concluded his essay on the junior college movement with the claim that the development of this institution should "disseminate in the commonwealth more widely than ever before the desire for sound learning whose perfect fruit is sanity of judgment and sobriety of citizenship."[50] Robert Hutchins developed this theme in his 1936 essays on the junior college, in which he argued that the primary purpose of this institution should be to provide a broad spectrum of the population with "a good general education" that was quite distinct from job preparation, while of course protecting the university from having to play this role.[51]

A number of prominent leaders of the junior college movement expressed strong support for the view that a junior college education should amount to more than narrow preparation for the university or the workplace. This view extended beyond the normal confines of an argument for the liberal arts over vocationalism, an argument that within the junior college was subsumed in the debate over transfer versus terminal programs. The rhetoric defined a much broader, more inclusive, and less traditional educational role for the junior college than as a purveyor of the humanities. For example, Walter Crosby Eells, AAJC executive director during the Second World War, stated the case this way in a 1941 book:

> Increasingly is there need for young people to be prepared better for civic responsibility, social understanding, home duties and responsibilities, law observance, and devotion to democracy. At a time when the democratic way of life and of government is on trial as never before, it is essential to have a well-educated and intelligent citizenry. Educated leadership is not sufficient. Educated followship is also essential. On the whole the university tends to select and educate young people of superior native ability and intelligence. In a democracy, however, the vote of the citizen of moderate or inferior native ability counts quite as much in the ballot box as the vote of the genius.[52]

The political arguments for general education in the public junior college attained a prominent place in the 1947 report by President Truman's Commission on Higher Education. This report made a strong case for the rapid expansion of the "community college," arguing that "the time has come to make education through the fourteenth grade available in the same way that high school education is now available."[53] A key element of the charge given to this expanding sector of higher education was to carry on the important work of spreading general education. In boldface type, the report put it this way, using rhetoric that sounds remarkably similar to that found in the Life Adjustment movement that was then the rage in U.S. high schools:

> Today's college graduate may have gained technical or professional training in one field of work or another, but is only incidentally, if at all, made ready for performing his duties as a man, a parent, and a citizen. Too often he is "educated" in that he has acquired competence in some particular occupation, yet falls short of that human wholeness and civic conscience which the cooperative activities of citizenship require. . . .
>
> The crucial task of higher education today, therefore, is to provide a unified

general education for American youth. Colleges must find the right relationship between specialized training on the one hand, aiming at a thousand different careers, and the transmission of a common cultural heritage toward a common citizenship on the other.[54]

Adult-Community Education Function

With a helpful boost from the Truman Commission, it became increasingly common during the 1950s to refer to public junior colleges as community colleges. The growth of the fourth function, adult and community education, served to reinforce this trend because this function cast the college in the role of an all-purpose institution devoted to service to the community. By 1960, all of the pieces of the contemporary community college were in place. This latest incarnation of the public junior college came to be defined as a publicly subsidized and locally controlled postsecondary educational institution with open admissions, low-cost tuition, and a bulging catalogue offering an extraordinary range of courses and other services pitched at every conceivable segment of the community. Compared to the other three functions, adult and community education is thoroughly heterogeneous. One defining characteristic of this function is that it represents a marked shift away from the transfer curriculum, because many of the new courses are not taken for degree credit. Many offerings are not even courses but take the form of college-sponsored community activities.

As was the case with general education, however, adult and community education at the community college displays a mixed relation to the market. On the one hand, many of these offerings are courses, seminars, workshops, and lectures aimed at providing continuing on-the-job vocational training for a wide variety of occupational groups. Whether it is a real estate agent seeking a cram course for a licensing exam, a computer worker requiring an introduction to the latest software, or an employee of a school for the deaf who needs training in sign language, the local community college is willing and able to provide what is needed. In general, courses in this category are offered for degree credit even if students who take them are frequently unconcerned about pursuing degrees.

On the other hand, many of these offerings are entirely disconnected from instrumental market concerns. Adults in the community may take a course in aerobic dance or color photography or European history or remedial English just because of personal interest or an urge for self-improvement and not with the idea of accumulating credits for a degree or cashing in on the educational experience to obtain a promotion. Like courses in continuing vocational education, these course may or may not carry college credit. Statistics on community college enrollments, including those cited elsewhere in this chapter, are normally limited to those students taking courses for degree credit. This plus the informal character of community education offerings makes it difficult to estimate enrollments in this area accurately, but these enrollments have certainly been booming. One source estimates that noncredit enrollments in community college amounted to about 4.0 million in 1980, while degree-credit enrollments totaled 4.3 million.[55]

While both traditional transfer and vocational community college students are on average older and attend part-time more often than other college students, adult and community education students are even more likely to demonstrate these characteristics. They are not using the college for the time-honored purpose of acquiring a degree in order to gain entry to a particular occupation. Instead they are using it as either a support institution for their present job or as a place to pursue personal enrichment and community activity. Both purposes tend to draw older people who already hold full-time jobs. This added adult and community education function, therefore, has radically increased both the size and the heterogeneity of the student body at the community college.

Again note the parallel to the high school, where adult and community education courses offered at night and on weekends have also become a big business in recent years, representing a natural outgrowth of the school's long-standing role as a broad institution serving community needs. Like the high school, the community college has come to assume a broad social-service role in the community. Thus during its relatively short history, the community college has quickly taken on four major functions — college preparation, vocational training, general education, and adult and community education — that have expressed the same mix of sociopolitical and market purposes that shaped the history of the old people's college, the American high school, during its much longer institutional existence. The end result is a complex comprehensive institution that has, like the high school, many of the characteristics of a huge shopping mall.[56] Like shoppers in a mall, community college students are given access to a wide range of educational commodities in a setting that combines elements of democracy and commerce. Just as the mall serves as both a community center (providing a public space for social interaction, recreation, information, and even political rallies) and a marketplace, the community college provides opportunities for both community enrichment and individual status attainment.

The Last College

The community college has in many ways recapitulated the history of the high school, but there is a limit to this parallel. The key difference is that the community college has never been able to achieve the thoroughgoing comprehensiveness attained by the high school. True, the educational purposes, course offerings, and student bodies of the two institutions are marked by a similar degree of heterogeneity.[57] But two factors have prevented the community college from taking on the full role of the comprehensive high school, and both have to do with the fact that attendance there is voluntary.

First, because the community college lacks the high school's legal sanction to compel students to take its classes, its student body does not represent the same cross section of the community. Second, unlike the high school, the community college has not succeeded in establishing for itself an exclusive rung on the educational ladder. There is little that the community college offers that cannot be acquired somewhere else. It provides access to the university, but students can always choose to bypass this step by entering a four-year institution of higher education directly from high school, and most of them do. Vocational training is available at the community colleges—and also in high schools, proprietary schools, county-level intermediate units, and on the job. General education and adult-community education are offered in a wide range of settings, including high schools, universities, community organizations, continuing education centers, places of employment, and commercial seminars.

The community college, lacking the high school's authority to treat nonattendance as truancy and also lacking its exclusive control over access to desirable educational products, does not benefit from the same legal and market pressures that compel high school students to attend. Without this compulsion, community college is more like a shopping mall than is the high school, for it must be particularly sensitive to shifting demand in the market—forced to find ways to attract a wide range of consumers who can always choose to go somewhere else or stay at home. The result is an unselective school that depends on student self-selection.[58] A pure creature of the market, the community college achieves comprehensiveness only to the extent that it succeeds in its entrepreneurial effort to attract as many different kinds of customers as possible. The early high school was also such a creature, but it evolved into an institution whose comprehensiveness was guaranteed and whose survival was assured.[59] The community college, like an aging shopping mall, must constantly hustle to keep from being outflanked and outclassed by the competition. In this freewheeling and uncertain environment, competitive failure could mean either a radically altered structure of students and programs or simple extinction.

Viewed from this perspective, the community college looks less like the new comprehensive high school than like the latest form of college. As Martin Trow has pointed out, U.S. colleges and universities are unique among the world's institutions of higher education in their vulnerability and responsiveness to the market.[60] The history of higher education in the United States is a story of entrepreneurial institutions that took advantage of every market opportunity and eagerly serviced every possible segment of consumer demand in order to ensure their own survival and enhance their standing in the status hierarchy.[61] In this sense, the community college has merely been following in a path of institutional mobility that was carved out of the wilderness by the first American colleges (spurred on by the personal mobility aspirations of the educational consumer) and then worn smooth by their many successors. The problems that the latest of the colleges encountered along the way have been the result of the institution's position at the end of a very long procession.

PROTECTED MARKETS AND INSTITUTIONAL MOBILITY

The pattern of expansion in U.S. higher education has always been to create a new form of college to deal with each new wave of college enrollments. First came a group of private colleges, many of them founded before the revolution, but with a rapid growth in numbers throughout the next century; then, in the nineteenth century, came a series of state universities; these were followed by a number of secondary public land grant colleges and universities in each state; early in the twentieth century, the growth industry in higher education was teachers colleges; and finally, in the 1960s, the community college took over that role.[62]

The new colleges in this educational succession have usually been at a competitive disadvantage. Older schools have held most of the strong cards. Relative to newcomers, the first college founded in a given market area had a loyal constituency, an established reputation, stable sources of public and private funding (including a solid endowment), credentials with a proven exchange value, a set of alumni occupying powerful positions, and a strong association with the social elite (who were most likely to attend college when no one else was). The result of these advantages is that the older colleges were more likely than the newer schools to have the edge in political and economic power, social reputation, ability to enhance status, faculty quality, student selectivity, student academic ability, and social class.[63] A recent reputational ranking of universities in the United States provides some insight into the impact of date of founding on college status.[64] The oldest universities dominate the list. Of the top twenty-five national universities, twenty-two are private institutions, including all of the top twenty. All were founded before 1900, while eighteen were founded before the end of the Civil War and nine were founded before 1800.[65]

The colleges that emerged in the later waves of expansion — land grant schools, teachers colleges, and community colleges—were forced to occupy the lower tiers of this stratified system of higher education. The colleges from the first two waves used their superior influence to protect themselves from the growing number of students pursuing postsecondary education by introducing new institutions at each spurt in enrollments. The problem they confronted was the same one that faced the early high school. The exchange value of a college's credentials is a function of their relative scarcity in the credentials market. Thus the demand for these credentials is likely to be highest—and the institution's prestige most elevated—when access is most restricted. For a school to provide its students with the competitive advantage they seek in the pursuit of social status, it must keep enrollment from expanding too rapidly. Yet from the point of view of democratic politics, such a policy has proven to be unacceptably elitist, threatening to undermine the school's legitimacy. Private colleges were partially buffered from this problem, but public colleges could not ignore it. Creating new forms of higher education instead of expanding the old ones was a way to meet the political demand for access to college while protecting the market position of existing institutions.[66]

At each stage of expansion, the new colleges and universities had a number of characteristics that distinguished them from their predecessors. First, of course, they were more accessible to the kind of students who never attended the older colleges. But in addition, beginning with the land grant college and continuing through to the community college, the expansion schools were generally assigned to play a more practical-vocational function than those that preceded them.[67] The new type of college, while drawing off increasing enrollments, was not supposed to provide direct competition with existing colleges for their traditional constituency. This meant not only creating new colleges but also making sure that they were functionally differentiated from the old ones. The resulting system of higher education would then be able to play a social efficiency role, allocating differentially trained graduates to positions in a stratified job structure.

The emergence of the land grant college provides the best early example of this process. The private and public colleges and universities that were founded before the Civil War tended to adopt a fairly traditional educational role. They provided a standard academic undergraduate education as a preparation for students who sought to enter the professions, a role that served the aspirations of their upper-middle-class constituents nicely. But the Morrill Act of 1862 mandated an explicitly practical and vocational purpose for the new land grant colleges, one that was justified by a mixture of human capital theory and democratic theory. The idea was that these colleges were good investments for the country because they would provide it with an enhanced set of agricultural and mechanical skills that would spur economic development and because they would simultaneously provide opportunities for higher education to a broader spectrum of the population. These purposes were spelled out clearly in the act, which required that the proceeds from each state's land grant should be used for "the endowment, support, and maintenance of at least one college where the leading object shall be, without excluding other scientific and classical studies, and including military tactics, to teach such branches of learning as are related to agriculture and the mechanic arts, in such manner as the legislatures of the States may respectively prescribe, in order to promote the liberal and practical education of the industrial classes in the several pursuits and professions in life."[68]

These land grant funds were used to endow existing state universities, to found such universities in states that had none, and to launch new secondary state colleges in states that already had a university. These schools generally reflected the concerns for practicality and accessibility embedded in the law, but this was most obvious in the case of the latter category. State universities (especially those that existed before the act) came to adopt an all-purpose curriculum stretching from liberal to practical education, from professional to vocational training, while the second-tier land grant schools tended to take a more narrowly "A and M" approach from the start. Initially this meant that private colleges and the liberal programs in older state universities remained comfortably buffered from the new students enrolling in the new lower track in higher education — the clearly differentiated practical programs and colleges.

What happened in the late nineteenth century, however, was a powerful trend within U.S. higher education toward adoption of the German university model, with its stress on graduate and professional education and on faculty research.[69] This university model provided a sharp contrast to the land grant model, which threatened to widen the gap between the two new tracks in higher education. While the former stressed research and advanced academic study, the latter emphasized teaching and vocational skill training. As was true in the differentiated high school curriculum that emerged at the same time, the upper track focused on providing students with a credential with a high exchange value, while the lower track aimed at providing them with an education distinctive for its use value.

In a society that is imbued with the values of democratic opportunity and upward mobility, it is hardly surprising that students and educators proved reluctant to settle for a lower-track college program when the upper track offered access to the most attractive social positions. As a result, land grant colleges and universities, urged on by the market pressure from ambitious students, embarked on a campaign of institutional mobility in pursuit of the new university ideal. This meant shifting the emphasis from practical-vocational to academic-professional education and from undergraduate instruction to graduate research. The change occurred unevenly and it took time, but the results were dramatic. By 1955, for example, most land grant schools had become full-fledged universities, enrolling 20 percent of all students in higher education but granting nearly 40 percent of all doctoral degrees.[70]

As land grant colleges climbed the hierarchy of higher education, the vocational education that had been central to their original mission fell increasingly into the hands of the expanding comprehensive high school and junior college. But by the turn of the century a new wave of colleges had emerged to meet another growing practical need, the production of schoolteachers. State teachers colleges, many of them outgrowths of old secondary-level normal schools, appeared in large numbers. Like the land grant schools, their initial mandate was to stick to a narrow vocational goal. But the state teachers college found itself subject to the same market pressures that faced its predecessor, as students began to demand that these schools provide an opportunity for a liberal education whose exchange value was higher in the status attainment market than a teaching certificate.[71] Gradually during the twentieth century these schools evolved into state liberal arts colleges, and by the 1970s most had been transformed into regional state universities.[72]

This brief look at the impact of market pressures on the development of higher education presents a picture of an institution at odds with itself. Older colleges have consistently sought to confine increases in college enrollment within new institutions that are defined by a narrowly practical mission. As agencies of social efficiency and stratified mobility opportunities, the latter were supposed to prepare the new students for lower-level social positions and thus protect the status of the former as the exclusive gateway to the better social positions. The lower-track colleges, however, resisted this assignment and actively modeled themselves after the upper-track institutions, seeking and achieving university status. One result was the rise of a plethora of multipurpose universities and a shift from vocationalism to liberal arts. Another result was the emergence of a new hierarchy of higher education based less on the practical-liberal distinction and more on the differentiated exchange value of university credentials. And the market advantages enjoyed by the institutions that were founded earliest tended to place them at the top of this structure, with each new wave of expansion institutions deployed at successively lower strata. In short, with colleges succumbing to political pressure for wider access and consumer pressure for a kind of credential that would enhance the chances for social mobility, the structuring principle of U.S. higher education has evolved from social efficiency to stratified credentialing.[73]

NONEXCLUSIVE MARKETS AND BLOCKED MOBILITY

Representing the last wave of college expansion, the community college at the end of twentieth century finds itself on the bottom rung of the status hierarchy in higher education. Like those that preceded it, this new college has been assigned a narrowly defined vocational mission. But as its predecessors discovered, consumer pressure has not favored the fulfillment of this mission. In a society where status is distributed to a significant degree based on the exchange value of educational credentials, a college offering a degree with use value (skill training) — a degree that provides access only to the less attractive forms of routine white-collar work — is at a severe competitive disadvantage. Such a college in fact serves to block student mobility chances. Historically the credentials market has provided a partial solution to this problem by allowing students to get a boost up the social ladder by riding on the back of an upwardly mobile college.

As the last in a long succession of colleges, however, the community college faces two problems that restrict its ability to follow the path of institutional mobility forged by its predecessors. One, as we have seen, is its failure to establish for itself an exclusive position in the educational progression leading from primary school to secondary school, college, and graduate school. Unable to capitalize on its ambiguous identity as both extended high school and junior college, the community college never succeeded in defining itself as the prime route for making the transition from high school to the university. Instead, it remains a lower-track alternative route.

The other problem is that it fell victim to the mobility experience of its predecessors, as legislators and business leaders refused to allow it to pursue the same path toward isomorphism with the university. Seeking to preserve the vocational mission of the community college within the socially efficient division of educational labor, public and private officials have generally been able to block its institutional mobility by denying it the right to award the bachelor's degree, thus freezing it in a permanently junior status within higher education.

As we have seen, the rhetoric of the leaders of the public junior college movement has long emphasized the institution's vocational function. By the time the early leaders of the movement — university presidents who were primarily interested in the screening function of the new college — gave way to the next generation in the 1920s, vocationalism had become the dominant motif in the speeches and literature emanating from the upper levels of the AAJC. This effort was frequently a frustrating one, for individual colleges persisted in offering programs that were primarily aimed at preparing students for transfer to the university. Student demand for this service, coupled with the market sensitivity of entrepreneurial junior college leaders, encouraged these schools to resist a full commitment to vocational principles.[74] One form of market pressure did push these local leaders into a partial involvement with vocationalism — the skill demands of local businesses encouraged the creation of a variety of specially tailored training programs — but these programs remained in the minority for a long time.

Efforts at the national and state level, however, were more successful in creating an ideological climate that favored a vocational role for the junior college and in establishing a permanently subordinate status for this institution that would freeze it in that role. The Carnegie Foundation played an important role in shaping the discourse on vocationalism, as Levine observes: "The 1932 Carnegie panel of educational experts . . . asserted that a public junior college that emphasized its university preparatory function rather than its terminal vocational function was undemocratic. The team recited the litany of complaints against ambitious local educational entrepreneurs and parents and students. It sharply criticized local districts for their slavish imitation of 'expensive, higher-type schools.' "[75]

The Truman Commission had a similar influence. Its 1947 report on higher education encouraged the expansion of the community college as an agent of both vocational and general education.[76] Thirteen years later the Eisenhower Commission proposed that the community college should take on half of all college enrollments and that it should see terminal vocational training as its primary function.[77] Then in 1970 another Carnegie report on higher education argued the case for preserving the junior status of the community college in order to maintain its vocational function:

> The Commission believes that public two-year community colleges should be actively discouraged by state planning and financial policies from becoming four-year institutions, as has happened in some cases. . . .
>
> There is . . . concern that, if two-year colleges become four-year colleges, they will place less emphasis on occupational programs and thus leave an unmet need in the local community.[78]

Two federal laws helped reinforce the vocational role of the community college. The Vocational Education Act of 1963 broke new ground by providing federal funding for vocational education at the postsecondary level, money that had previously been granted only to secondary schools. The money was specifically directed toward community colleges, and the Higher Education Act of 1972 explicitly "exclud[ed] any program to prepare individuals for employment in occupations . . . to be generally considered professional or which require a baccalaureate or advanced degree."[79] These laws formalized the status of the community college as the vocational track in U.S. higher education.

Two states also played a leading part in trying to fix the function and status of the community college. Early on, California set up a three-level system of higher education, ascending from community colleges through the California State University (CSU) campuses and culminating with the University of California (UC) system. The state's Master Plan, adopted in 1960, established a structure of differential access that granted high school graduates open access to community colleges but restricted admission to CSU to the top third of the class and limited admission to UC to the top eighth.[80] In 1948 New York established a stratified state university system in which community colleges would play the familiar role of absorbing the bulk of the projected increase in enrollments and would serve primarily a vocational-terminal function.[81] The state regents argued that the community college offered "distinctive services" and as a result, "existing two-year colleges should not be converted to four-year baccalaureate college status as an approach to the expansion of college programs in any region of the state."[82]

Over the opposition of these national leaders and state authorities, some junior colleges did succeed in making the transition from two-year to four-year status. Detroit Junior College, for example, which emerged as an extension of Detroit High School in 1917, became the four-year College of the City of Detroit in 1923 and evolved into Wayne State University ten years later.[83] One study found that between 1953 and 1964, seventy-two junior colleges became senior colleges. Only eleven of these, however, were public institutions; the rest were private or religiously affiliated. The latter two categories of colleges had increasing trouble competing with the rapidly expanding publicly supported schools, and they developed into or merged into four-year schools simply in order to survive. And because they were not subject to public authority, they were free to pursue institutional mobility despite opposition from public officials.[84] As one commentator sadly notes, such a change tends to shift the focus away from vocationalism: "When a junior college acquires senior college status, its perspective becomes narrower and emphasis shifts to the academic program as being of primary importance."[85]

Not only have community colleges for the most part retained their junior status, but they have also in recent years enjoyed a sudden increase in vocational enrollments. According to Pincus, the proportion of community college students receiving vocational degrees rose from 45 percent in 1970 to 71 percent in the 1980s.[86] Karabel reports that between 1970 and the mid-1980s, the proportion of community college students enrolled in vocational programs increased from one-third to two-thirds.[87] Meanwhile, the proportion that transferred with junior standing to a four-year college fell to less than 5 percent, and the transfers that did occur were more likely to be into the less prestigious strata of higher education, such as regional state universities.[88] This decline in transfer rate occurred despite a simultaneous increase in the average class rank of students entering community colleges. In 1970, half of the entering full-time students were in the top half of their high school classes, while in 1982 the proportion had risen to three-quarters, with 20 percent of the students coming from the top quarter.[89] One conclusion that can be drawn from these figures is that the efforts by social efficiency–minded leaders to keep the community college in its place have finally taken hold. Increasingly, students who are looking for a bachelor's degree are bypassing the community college and entering directly into a four-year program, which means that most of those who enter the community college are now already resigned to taking a position within the routine white-collar work of the semiprofessions.

Karabel argues that the impact of this situation on community college students is uniformly negative.[90] They find themselves locked into the lower track of higher education, which reduces their likelihood of ever receiving a B.A. and which puts them at a disadvantage in competition for jobs and pay (even when compared with persons with an equal number of years of education). A growing body of literature supports this view of the community college as an agent of social reproduction rather than a pathway to opportunity.[91] Dougherty has done a careful review of the evidence about the effect of community colleges on the status attainment prospects of their students who aspire to a bachelor's degree. He concludes that, even after controlling for a number of student characteristics, community college students are less likely to earn a B.A. and be hired for a high-level job than those who enroll directly in four-year schools because of a three-stage process of accelerated attrition. Community college students are more likely to drop out than four-year students in the first two years of college; they have more difficulty gaining admission to the junior class of a four-year college than does a student who is already enrolled in the latter; and they have a higher dropout rate in their junior and senior years than those who were admitted to a four-year school in the first place.[92]

Scholars have identified a number of factors that promote the attenuated educational attainment of community college students:

- a lack of deep involvement by students in community college life as a result of commuter status
- the lack of selectivity and the low prestige of the college
- an antiacademic student culture
- low faculty expectations for student performance
- the vocational orientation of community colleges and the downplaying of the transfer option, reinforced by counseling
- an institutional emphasis on achievement, cognitive skills, and norm-referenced objective tests (as opposed to the greater emphasis on nurturing, exploration, and criterion-referenced essay tests in four-year colleges)
- the difficulty of adjusting to a change in schools
- four-year schools' preference for their own lower-division students over transfers and the reduced opportunities for financial aid offered to the latter
- loss of credits in the process of transfer
- higher academic standards in the four-year college
- the cultural and psychological stresses that attend social mobility in general[93]

This evidence suggests that the community college, unlike any previous form of U.S. higher education, has been forced to carry out the land grant mission of vocational-terminal education. As the last new form of college in a long queue, the community college has not been allowed to imitate the university as its predecessors were but has been kept in a junior status, playing out a lower-track educational role. The consequences for its students have been to "cool them out," scaling down their aspirations for social mobility and fitting them into the less attractive and less rewarding positions in the lower middle range of the occupational structure. In spite of the powerful consumer demand for college credentials that will promote upward mobility, political and business leaders have insisted that the community college continue to act as an agent of social efficiency, thereby blocking these mobility prospects.[94]

An analysis of the historical development and current role of the community college in the United States appears to support the view expressed by such scholars as Karabel, Pincus, and Zwerling that, in spite of "false promises" to provide equal opportunity, the primary function of this institution is to promote the reproduction of social inequality. But the key issue is that the community college has largely failed to carry out its promises because, in characteristically American fashion, it has promised to produce two contradictory kinds of outcomes. On the one hand, it has presented itself as the most democratic of educational institutions, opening its doors to virtually every adult within commuting distance and offering to serve as the medium for fulfilling a wide range of social and political needs in the community. At the same time, it has presented itself as the ultimate market institution, providing training in a wide variety of job skills required by the local economy and offering to serve as the medium for fulfilling the personal aspirations of everyone who seeks to attain a higher position in the existing social structure.

The tension between the demands of democratic politics and capitalist markets is evident in all U.S. educational institutions, but in the case of the community college this tension seems particularly public. On a daily basis, Americans must construct their lives not "under circumstances chosen by themselves, but under circumstances . . . transmitted from the past," which include a political structure grounded in equality and a socioeconomic structure grounded in inequality.[95] In the course of trying to make their way in the midst of that historical inheritance, these actors form themselves into social classes, and the peculiar character of the community college is just one result of this class-formation process. Drawing on the discourse of democracy, the members of the less advantaged classes have sought to use the community college as a mechanism for making U.S. society more egalitarian; and because of the political power of this discourse, these efforts have taken hold within the new institution. But at the same time, the more privileged classes have sought to use the community college as a way to meet the needs of the existing economic structure; and these efforts, too, have taken root within it.

At the institutional level, the ideological goals that define the universe of the community college are a concern for political equality and a concern for social efficiency. In between them is a third goal, social mobility, which combines elements of both positions in a discourse that accepts the permanence of social inequality as long as everyone has an equal opportunity to attain a privileged position within it. This social mobility goal is politically charged but market based; it sees the community college as providing individuals with the position they have earned through educational achievement rather than the one they were assigned out of concern for social efficiency. The history of the community college suggests that the tension between politics and markets has played itself out in two rather different ways — as a broad-based struggle for institutional control between democratic and capitalist goals, and as a more narrowly defined struggle over the nature of its market-based goals between the demand for social mobility and the demand for social efficiency. The latter struggle has been the most visible, as policymakers have sought to impose vocationalism on the community college in the name of social efficiency while students have sought to use the school as a transfer point in the pursuit of upward mobility. The result is that the community college has not been terribly successful in accomplishing either its vocational or its transfer function.

Vocational training has been much in favor among community college leaders for most of this century, but students have shown a remarkable ability to contain their enthusiasm for these programs. Until the past decade, they have shown a consistent and strong preference for the transfer option, regarding the new form of college as an inexpensive, accessible, and convenient way to pursue an old goal — the attainment of higher social status through the acquisition of a bachelor's degree. Even the recent rise of vocational enrollments seems to reflect less a growing student demand for vocational skill training than the cumulative impact of a variety of social, political, cultural, educational, and market pressures that have made the community college a less credible and less attractive means of acquiring a B.A. The expansion of public colleges and their ascent to university status has made it easier and more attractive for students who seek a B.A. to enter directly into a four-year institution, especially given the extra problems that confront students trying to follow the transfer route. In addition, credential inflation in the 1980s reduced the value of this degree, leading to a leveling off of college enrollments and further reducing the incentive to transfer. The increase in vocational enrollments seems to be a result of a reduction in more attractive alternatives rather than a consequence of an increase in the return on vocational training.[96]

Although the failure of the vocational function occurred in spite of the best efforts of policymakers (public officials, businesspersons, and community college leaders), the failure of the transfer function was, as I have shown, in part the result of a deliberate campaign orchestrated by these same individuals. Over the years, most community college students enrolled in degree-credit programs have expressed an initial intent to transfer to a four-year college, but then an array of pressures have encouraged most of them to switch to a vocational program or drop out. As a result, the community college has not succeeded very well in either of its original approaches to preparing students for the job market. Students found that the college's offer of an entree into the semiprofessions was one that they could easily refuse and that the offer of transfer to the university was one that the college was both unwilling and increasingly unable to redeem.

This focus on the failure of the community college as a market institution, however, which is at the heart of the social reproduction critique, ignores an important lesson learned from the history of the high school. For the high school has also come under heavy fire in recent years because of its failure to provide students with either skill training or credentials that have sufficient credibility to grant these students privileged access to good jobs. As a market institution, the high school, too, is a failure. Yet, as Cohen and Neufeld have pointed out, the high school failed in the market role because of its great success in the political role.[97] Providing access to secondary education for the entire population within the walls of a single comprehensive school was a remarkable achievement for an institution that was founded in large part as an expression of democratic principles and a mechanism for promoting republican community. Although the institution was partially adapted to market goals by the introduction of educational stratification, this political accomplishment nonetheless had the effect of undermining much of the exclusiveness that had formed the basis for the high school's early market success. Open access reduced the exchange value of its educational credentials and left the high school in a position where it was no longer able to deliver on its promise to provide graduates with a competitive advantage in the pursuit of social status.

Historically, the community college has also embodied a complex mixture of goals. Like the high school, its inability to carry out either of its market functions effectively is understandable largely in light of its accessibility to the widest possible range of the population and its democratic effort to provide programs to meet every conceivable community need. These outcomes are a sign that the community college has achieved considerable success in meeting its political aims. From the perspective of marketability, however, these outcomes are a sign that the community college has been forced to adopt a loser's strategy. The way for a college to provide students with an edge in the race for status attainment is to give them credentials that have a high exchange value. And, as the history of higher education in the United States shows, this can be accomplished by a college that adopts the university model, emphasizes research, focuses on transmitting abstract academic knowledge, and restricts admissions. Because of its responsiveness to the goals of both democratic access and social efficiency, the community college has been unable to do any of these things. Instead, it has retained its junior status within higher education, emphasized teaching, focused on the transmission of practical-vocational knowledge, and left admissions wide open.

One solution to the problem of marketability, for each type of school, would be to adapt gracefully to the situation by abandoning both market roles as a lost cause. This would mean self-consciously assuming a role as an inclusive educational institution with a clear mandate to model democratic values and prepare students for participation in a democratic society. Such a change would require the community college to turn its back on both of its oldest and most prominent market functions, university access and vocational training, and instead emphasize the more recent and still subordinate functions of providing general education and community education. To concentrate on the latter would serve important social, political, and cultural needs in the community. This solution, however, would be much more difficult for the community college to pursue than for the high school for two reasons — its market position and its claim to legitimacy.

Because it lacks both an exclusive location in the graded structure of U.S. education and the political authority to require attendance, the community college is completely dependent on the voluntary enrollment of students. As a result of this relatively weak position in the market, it (more than the high school) has to be extremely sensitive to the shifting tides of consumer demand. In this society, where schooling is seen as a mechanism for getting a good job, the community college would be likely to lose the majority of its degree-credit enrollments if it disbanded its vocational and transfer programs. Students interested in obtaining vocational and bachelor's degrees in order to impress an employer would drop out, leaving the college with only those students who had an intrinsic interest in the courses they were taking. Such an exodus would lead to a radical downsizing and restructuring of the institution. Given the consumer and business pressures on the community college to continue playing its market role and also the college's organizational incentive to survive and grow, this shift in purposes seems unlikely.

The other problem with a democratic solution to the failure of the community college as a market institution is that it would threaten the college's legitimacy. A key part of the social significance of both the high school and the community college is that they keep alive a belief in social mobility and in meritocratic distribution of social rewards. To disband the transfer function and focus on vocational training would deny community college students the hope of getting ahead and freeze them in a lower educational track heading inevitably away from the more desirable social positions. The result would be to strip the college of its mantle of legitimacy as the locus of social opportunity, leaving it with the identity of a school for those who aren't worthy of advancement — and providing an ironic twist to the once proud title, "poor man's college." To abandon both the transfer and vocational functions would leave the college with a respectable (though smaller) role as a community service institution operating independently of the market. But this move would pose serious problems for the legitimacy of U.S. institutions more generally. If the most accessible and socially representative institution of higher education withdraws from the status attainment process, how are the lower classes in American society supposed to get the opportunity to demonstrate their merit and achieve success?

Like the high school, the community college seems to be caught in a bind that was constructed historically, as it sought to accomplish the contradictory aims of promoting political equality and market inequality within a single institution. Unable to achieve either of these goals very effectively, it is also unable to abandon either of them. Neither policymakers nor its own students seem willing to allow it to focus on the pursuit of a more coherent and internally consistent set of outcomes. Both have a stake in preserving its ambiguous identity even though the social, political, and fiscal costs of this effort are high. As a consequence, the community college may well keep muddling along in something like its current form, continuing to make grand promises and produce disappointing results.

9

The Lowly Status of Education Schools

Calls to reform teacher education are once again being voiced as part of a more general discussion of ways to improve public schooling in the United States. This is not a new phenomenon but a frequent occurrence in the history of U.S. education. In the past few years, however, there has been a remarkable outpouring of books and articles that criticize teacher education and present plans for reforming it.[1] In order to evaluate the kinds of diagnoses rendered and prescriptions offered by these critics, it is important to examine the history of American teacher education and how this history has led to the ailments for which reformers now seek a cure. But because there is already a number of good general accounts of this history, my aim in this chapter is to examine the historical roots of one particular problem that has long plagued teacher education in the United States: its lowly status.[2]

Over the years, teacher education has received little respect in U.S. educational and cultural life. University professors, educational leaders, teachers, and even teacher educators themselves have heaped scorn on the field. The titles of a few of the volumes in this ongoing literature of character assassination capture the disdain: Arthur Bestor's *Educational Wastelands* (1953), James Koerner's *The Miseducation of America's Teachers* (1963), and Rita Kramer's *Ed School Follies* (1991).

In this chapter I argue that the issue of status is central to the kinds of problems that teacher education presents to potential reformers in the 1990s. That is, in spite of what some critics have suggested, the lowly status of teacher education in the United States is not a simple reflection of the purportedly low quality of professional preparation that it offers. Rather than being a natural consequence of failure, I argue, this status is a primary cause of the kinds of failure that teacher education has experienced over the years. In particular, I will explore the way in which the status of teacher education has been shaped by the workings of the market.[3] Market forces have treated teacher education quite badly over the past 150 years, assigning it to a position of meager prestige and influence and forcing it to adopt practices that have frequently proved educationally counterproductive. In short, market pressures have in large part led to the low status of teacher education and have contributed significantly to its inability to carry out its functions effectively.[4]

One caveat is in order. Not only am I stressing status over role in my analysis of teacher education, but I am also focusing primarily on those aspects of this status that have been most affected by market pressures. As a result I largely bypass gender and class, both of which have exerted enormous downward pressure on the status of these programs. In the nineteenth century, teaching in the United States was transformed into a female occupation, which meant that teacher education came to occupy a subordinate status in relation to those programs that were preparing people for the high professions of medicine and law, both of which remained male domains. During the same period, teacher education came to attract a large number of working-class and lower-middle-class students, who saw it as a way to acquire a respectable middle-class job. In conjunction with the process of feminization, the influx of less genteel students into teaching served to further stigmatize teacher education in relation to those more elevated programs of study (both liberal and professional) pursued by students from the more privileged classes.

Given the power of class and gender in shaping the status of teacher education, why focus on the market factor? Two reasons. First, in recent years a sizable amount of scholarly attention has been directed at exploring the impact of class and gender on teacher education, but there has been less work focused on the impact of markets on education school status.[5] This is a theme, in short, that needs further development.

Second, by examining the market factor more closely, we can gain insight into some of the characteristics that distinguish U.S. teacher education from similar programs in other countries. Of the nations in the world with the highest degree of economic development, the United States is the most market-oriented and has been since the mid-nineteenth century. Nowhere else has the doctrine of laissez-faire attained such earnest and long-lasting acceptance. No other industrial power has so persistently protected private enterprise from public interference, so effectively fragmented the state and limited its power, and so prominently elevated the idea of market competition to a central ideological principle.

In such a market-centered society, it is not surprising that education, too, finds itself subject to a wide range of persistent market pressures. Consider the example of the high school. As I have argued elsewhere, the high school early on emerged as a valued commodity that gave some consumers the means to enhance or reinforce their social position.[6] As a result of this market pressure, high schools became stratified—across programs within individual schools and across different schools within a community—according to the exchange value of the credentials offered by each program or school. Martin Trow and others argue that higher education in the United States has been particularly sensitive to market forces, especially given the glut of colleges and universities, the lack of centralized state control over this sector, and the resulting dependency of these institutions on the consumer preferences of students.[7]

Given the market-saturated environment in which it arose, U.S. teacher education throughout its history has been subjected to a degree of market pressure well beyond that experienced by teacher education in other societies. Focusing on market effects can thus illuminate the special character of teacher education in the United States from a comparative perspective.

Images

Perhaps the most striking fact about much of the critical literature on teacher education is its scornful tone. There is a quality about some of this writing that suggests that teacher education is almost beneath contempt. In his exposé *The Miseducation of American Teachers,* James Koerner describes his subject in a language that underscores the lowly position of teacher education in the educational hierarchy. Faculty, students, curriculum—all come under his verbal lash. In the middle of a list of grievances, he issues the following indictments:

> (5) It is an indecorous thing to say and obviously offensive to most educationists, but it is the truth and it should be said: the inferior quality of the Education faculty is the fundamental limitation of the field, and will remain so, in my judgment for some time to come. . . . Until the question of the preparation and the intellectual qualifications of faculty members is faced head-on in Education, the prospects of basic reform are not bright.

(6) Likewise, the academic caliber of students in Education remains a problem, as it always has. . . . Education students still show up poorly on standardized tests and still impress members of the academic faculty as being among their less able students. . . .

(7) Course work in Education deserves its ill-repute. It is most often puerile, repetitious, dull, and ambiguous — incontestably. Two factors make it that way: the limitations of the instructor, and the limitations of the subject-matter that has been remorselessly fragmented, sub-divided, and inflated, and that in may cases was not adequate to its uninflated state. . . . The intellectual impoverishment of the course work remains a major characteristic of the field.[8]

People frequently complain about professional education in a wide range of fields other than teaching, but they don't generally adopt this same tone of scorn when they discuss the preparation of doctors and lawyers. There is something about the status of teacher education that makes it an easy target, a free-fire zone in the realm of higher education.[9] Sterling McMurrin, a former U.S. Commissioner of Education, notes this in his introduction to Koerner's book: "As is well known, for the past several years criticism of the professional education schools has been a favorite sport among the faculties of other professional schools and of the sciences and arts." Yet though he adopts a more judicious approach to the subject than does Koerner, McMurrin endorses the latter's central judgment: "While recognizing the outstanding work of both individuals and institutions in pointing new directions in teacher education, I must agree with Mr. Koerner that when one views the national scene as a whole the quality of our teacher education schools and colleges is a weak element in our educational complex, a weakness at the point where the most damage can be done — and where all too often it is done."[10]

Even when the tone of the critical voice softens and the gaze turns more sympathetic, many of the same themes continue to emerge. The underlying charge remains that teacher education as an enterprise suffers from a basic condition of inferiority. Judith Lanier, who wrote an influential review of "Research on Teacher Education," is certainly a sympathetic voice.[11] As the dean of an education school and president of the Holmes Group, she constructed this review as a platform from which to launch the group's effort to reform both teaching and teacher education. Yet her list of ailments requiring a remedy sounds similar in substance if not in tone to the list spelled out by Koerner. Like him, she finds teacher education cursed with an inferior status and finds the roots of this status in part in characteristics of its faculty, students, and curriculum.

On faculty: "There is an inverse relationship," she notes, "between professorial prestige and the intensity of involvement with the formal education of teachers." When one examines the characteristics of the professors themselves, the "research, in general, suggests that education professors differ from the academic counterparts in that they have less scholarly production and lower social class origins." Such faculty members demonstrate "conformist orientations and utilitarian views of knowledge," which helps "explain why teacher educators, as some researchers have observed, 'have difficulty in adjusting to and accepting the norms and expectations of academe.'" On students: "Here the research seems unequivocal. Those who teach teachers encounter a substantial number of learners with average and high scores on standardized measures of academic ability. But the overall group norm for teacher education students falls below the average for all college students due to the larger numbers of learners scoring in the lowest ranks on such measures." And on curriculum: "The research is unequivocal about the general, overall course work provided for teachers. It remains casual at best and affords a poorly conceived collage of courses across the spectrum of initial preparation and an assembly of disparate content fragments throughout continuing education. The formal offerings lack curricular articulation within and between initial and continuing teacher education, and depth of study is noticeably and consistently absent."[12]

Both sympathetic and unsympathetic observers agree that teacher education occupies an inferior status in the U.S. educational hierarchy. The open question, however, seems to be whether or not this lowly status is well deserved. For critics like Koerner, the answer is clear. Teacher education has a bad reputation because it has weak faculty, students, and courses. But for critics like Lanier, the issue is more complex. Yes, she notes, all these aspects of teacher education are indeed weak, but she seems to be of two minds about what this means. On the one hand, she sees these particular weaknesses themselves as the problem and argues for strengthening each of these areas as the key to improving the status of teacher education in the United States. This is at the core of the Holmes Group proposals in *Tomorrow's Teachers* for reforming education schools — promoting an academic research orientation among faculty, improving the academic quality of students, and producing a more extended, rigorous, and relevant program of study.

Yet on the other hand, Lanier also identifies factors for which education schools cannot be blamed that nonetheless depress their status. These factors include the gender and class character of education school faculty and students (female and lower middle class). They also include such factors as the lower prestige accorded to practical over theoretical knowledge, the marginal position accorded a vocational program like education within a university setting dominated by the liberal arts, and the impact that the sheer size of the teacher education enterprise has on its ability to make claims of academic exclusiveness and intellectual superiority. These last factors are directly traceable to the kind of market situation within which U.S. teacher education has found itself over the years.

A Short History of Market Influences on Teacher Education

Market pressures have affected teacher education in three different ways — by pushing the education school to become a teacher factory, by encouraging it to evolve into a people's college, and by elevating it to the university level.

THE TEACHER FACTORY: FILLING EMPTY CLASSROOMS

The biggest single problem facing U.S. school officials in the nineteenth and early twentieth centuries had nothing to do with curriculum or pedagogy. The persisting challenge was to find a way to build enough classrooms for all the students who required education and to fill these classrooms with teachers. The aim of the common-school movement, which swept out of New England and across the country in the years before the Civil War, was to have each community establish a publicly funded system of elementary schooling that would provide a common educational experience for all of the young people in that community. And in keeping with the American suspicion of centralized state power, the responsibility for paying for the new schools and hiring the new teachers that were required by this expansion fell primarily on local government.

By 1870, when the federal government began gathering data on schools, there were already 200,000 public school teachers in the United States, and the number doubled by 1900. At this point, when the supply of elementary schooling was finally beginning to catch up with demand, the sudden growth of high schools set off another dizzying spiral of educational expansion, which by 1930 once again doubled the size of the public school teaching force, bringing the total to almost 850,000.[13]

In the mid-nineteenth century, the insatiable demand for teachers — combined with the radical decentralization of control over schools and the absence of consistent standards for certification — meant that the emphasis was on finding warm bodies to fill classrooms rather than on preparing qualified professionals. The following examination of a teacher candidate in a New England town during the 1860s was not unusual:

CHAIRMAN: How old are you?

CANDIDATE: I was eighteen years old the twenty-seventh day of last May.

CHAIRMAN: Where did you last attend school?

CANDIDATE: At the Academy of S——.

CHAIRMAN: Do you think you can make our big youngsters mind?

CANDIDATE: Yes, I think I can.

CHAIRMAN: Well, I am satisfied. I guess you will do for our school. I will send over the certificate by the children tomorrow.[14]

As Michael Sedlak concludes in his review of teacher hiring in this period, "A general teacher shortage, combined with wildly fluctuating and inconsistent prerequisite qualifications, virtually assured any prospective teacher some sort of job, and secured someone for most communities needing a teacher."[15]

It was in the midst of this difficult period in the history of the market for teachers that the normal school appeared in the United States. By many accounts, the first public normal school opened in 1839 in Lexington, Massachusetts, under the leadership of Cyrus Peirce.[16] Looking back on this experience a dozen years later, Peirce spelled out the aims of his pathbreaking institution in a letter to Henry Barnard, sounding themes that defined the core concerns of the whole normal-school movement:

> I answer briefly, that it was my aim, and it would be my aim again, to make better teachers, and especially, better teachers for our common schools; so that those primary seminaries, on which so many depend for their education, might answer, in a higher degree, the end of their institution. Yes, to make better teachers; teachers who would understand, and do their business better; teachers who should know more of the nature of children, of youthful developments, more of the subject to be taught, and more of the true methods of teaching; who would teach more philosophically, more in harmony with the natural development of the young mind, with a truer regard to the order and connection in which the different branches of knowledge should be presented to it, and, of course, more successfully.[17]

This was a tall order indeed. And although "the formal history of American teacher education and professionalization is conventionally a story of one triumphal march," the reality was a story of rear-guard action by the stalwart normal-school advocates while the opposing hoard swept around them on both flanks.[18] By the time of the Civil War, there were only twelve state normal schools in existence in the entire country, so that in spite of the high ideals of these institutions, their actual impact was minimal at best.[19] Until late in the nineteenth century, the large majority of teachers entered into the classroom without benefit of a normal-school diploma. There was a wide range of ways for a prospective teacher to acquire training and obtain a job. Cities often set up their own normal schools to supply teachers to the local elementary schools. High schools frequently offered a short course in pedagogy toward the same end. At an even more rudimentary level, local school districts would provide a brief preparation in the grammar school so that a graduate could almost immediately return to his or her old classroom as the teacher. There was a widespread network of teacher institutes that offered training during the summer, both for prospective teachers and for teachers already on the job. But a large number of teachers were hired and kept on the job with no formal training and no qualifications at all except the ability to make the "large youngsters mind."

Consider the problems that this situation posed for the status of the normal school. In order for a form of professional education to attain a high status in the educational marketplace, it must meet two primary prerequisites: monopoly and selectivity. The current situation of law schools and medical schools serves as a case in point. Each has established itself as the only door through which a person can gain entry to the profession. And each has made it difficult to get through that door, by instituting restrictive admissions and rigorous programs of study. When Cyrus Peirce and Horace Mann and others established the first normal schools, they chose to ignore the market component and concentrate on developing a sound program of professional preparation for future teachers. But the professional schools they nurtured into life ran the risk of being irrelevant to the realities of the job market for teachers. Because no one had to attend a normal school in order to teach and because all the alternative modes of access to teaching were easier and less costly, the normal-school leaders found themselves standing on the sidelines, watching others do the real work of training and hiring teachers.

Normal-school leaders faced a choice between selectivity and monopoly. Their schools could remain elite institutions providing an idealized form of professional preparation for a small number of aspiring teachers — "teachers who would understand and do their business better" — and allow other routes to teaching to remain dominant. Or they could expand the system to meet the demand for teachers, eventually establishing a monopoly over access to the profession while risking the dilution of the normal-school ideal in the process. They chose expansion.

Between 1865 and 1890, the number of state normal schools grew from 15 to 103.[20] A key element of this expansion was the growing tendency of state governments to employ certification as a mechanism for restricting the pool of teacher candidates from which local districts could hire their faculty and to employ teacher education as a criterion for certification. As Sedlak observes, "By 1873, according to a leading analyst of this issue, policy deliberations were beginning to recognize credentials from normal schools as 'professional licenses,' and several states were relying on them as the basis for certification. By 1897, 28 states accepted normal-school diplomas, and by 1921 all but one state 'recognized graduation from normal schools and universities as evidence of qualification for certification.' By the World War I era, therefore, certification policies that bestowed licenses on the basis of credential acquisition had become the rule nationwide." The expansion of normal schools and their growing monopoly over access to teaching was accelerated "as graduates of professional programs assumed leadership roles in state departments of education."[21]

Once normal schools moved toward establishing a monopoly on access to teaching, they also took on the responsibility for meeting the full weight of the market's demand for teachers. The natural result was that teacher education came under intense pressure to produce large numbers of teachers as quickly and cheaply as possible. Two factors served to intensify this pressure. One was the feminization of the teaching force and the kind of career pattern that accompanied this shift. The standard pattern in the late nineteenth and early twentieth centuries was for young women to enter teaching for a half dozen years or so, beginning in their late teens and ending with marriage. The short tenure in the classroom for the average teacher meant that normal schools had to produce large numbers of graduates in order to keep replacing young teachers who were leaving the classroom. The other factor was a fiscal problem. If teacher training took on aspects of mass production, and if the product was not expected to last very long anyway, then the cost of producing each unit had to be kept down in order to sustain the operation. Under these circumstances, an intensive and prolonged process of professional education was difficult to justify to legislators and taxpayers.

The pressure for warm bodies to fill empty classrooms continued throughout the nineteenth and early twentieth centuries, and the impact on both the content and the status of teacher education was devastating. All three problem areas identified by the critics of teacher education — faculty, students, and curriculum — have their origins to a considerable degree in this pressure to meet the demand for teachers. The burgeoning normal-school system had to mass-produce faculty members to staff its own classrooms, without the luxury of being particularly selective about whom to admit or of being especially thorough in preparing these people. Meanwhile, the rapid expansion of normal schools in the late nineteenth century necessarily meant that these schools had to open their doors wide to admit the flood of candidates required to meet demand. The normal school became, as Jurgen Herbst points out, a true people's college, which offered a chance at advanced education to a wide range of the population that had previously been confined to a grammar school education.[22] And the curriculum felt the effects of this market pressure as well. The need to produce a large number of teachers quickly meant that normal schools could not enforce an extensive and rigorous professional education. These schools operated under the constant threat of being bypassed. If they made access to or completion of teacher education difficult, the number of graduates would decline and school districts would be forced to find other sources for teachers. One way or the other, the classrooms would be filled, and the normal-school leaders chose to fill them with their own graduates, whatever the cost.

The cost was high. A thinly educated faculty, academically weak students, and a foreshortened and unchallenging curriculum — all were consequences of the effort by normal schools to meet the continuing high level of demand for teachers. As a result, the normal school became a kind of teacher factory, mass-producing as many practitioners as the market required. But by pressing the normal school to choose quantity over quality, the market exerted an impact on the status of this institution as well as its content. Selectivity is a crucial component of the status of an educational institution. The current status hierarchy of U.S. higher education is closely related to the degree of difficulty that students experience in gaining access to credentials of individual colleges, which range from highly selective Ivy League–type schools at the high end of the scale to open-admissions community colleges at the low end. The normal school was the community college of the late nineteenth century, easily accessible and thus lacking in distinction. By choosing to meet the demand for teachers, this institution gave up any claim it might once have had for elite status. By becoming socially useful, it lost social respect. Much of the scorn that has been directed at teacher education over the years can be traced to the simple fact that it has earnestly sought to provide all of the teachers that were asked of it.[23]

THE PEOPLE'S COLLEGE: MEETING CONSUMER DEMAND

As we have seen, one market influence on U.S. teacher education came from employers, as school districts demanded a large number of teachers, and normal schools chose to supply this demand despite the negative impact on both the content and the status of teacher education. But another market influence came from educational consumers, as students demanded a particular kind of educational product, and normal schools chose to give it to them. The first imposed a social efficiency function on these schools, requiring them to subordinate concerns about institutional status and effective professional education to the pressing social need for teachers.[24] However, the second market influence imposed a social mobility function on normal schools, requiring them to provide the kind of educational choices that would best serve the needs of students who were competing for desirable social positions.

The reverence for individual freedom of choice — construed both as political choice and consumer choice — has deep roots in U.S. cultural history. Louis Hartz, in his classic essay *The Liberal Tradition in America,* defined the issue this way: "Here, then, is the master assumption of American political thought, the assumption from which all of the American attitudes discussed in this essay flow: the reality of atomistic social freedom. It is instinctive to the American mind, as in a sense the concept of the polis was instinctive to Platonic Athens or the concept of the church to the mind of the middle ages."[25] This assumption is at the heart of the market as a social institution. In a market system, consumers exercise individual freedom of choice by expressing their personal desires, and entrepreneurs prosper by more efficiently meeting these desires. As Trow has put it so succinctly, in the United States "the market preceded society," with the result that the consumer has long been king.[26]

This central characteristic of American social life has been a powerful force contributing to the distinctiveness of U.S. educational institutions, which have been shaped by consumerism to a far greater extent than educational institutions elsewhere in the world. According to Trow,

> We in the United States, surely the most populist society in the world, accept a larger role [than do Europeans] for the influence of consumer preference on cultural forms — even in the provision of what and how subjects are taught in colleges and universities. Europeans try to reduce the influence of consumer preference in a number of ways. Most importantly, they try to insulate their financing of institutions of higher education from student fees. By contrast, in the United States, enrollment-driven budgets in all but a few institutions, both public and private, ensure that most institutions are extremely sensitive to student preferences.[27]

In a setting where the educational consumer is highly influential, educational leaders are compelled to respond in a thoroughly entrepreneurial fashion if they wish to thrive or even survive. If they fail to meet consumer demand, students will vote with their feet by enrolling elsewhere in a school that is all too eager to give them what they want.

This was the situation facing normal-school leaders in the second half of the nineteenth century.[28] First, although teacher education gradually attained a monopoly over access to the teacher workforce through increasingly restrictive certification requirements, this was a long time in coming. Second, a glut of post–grammar school educational institutions were competing for the student's tuition dollars. In 1880, for example, there were more than sixteen colleges and universities for every million in the population, the highest ratio ever in U.S. educational history.[29] The normal schools had to find a way to make their programs attractive to prospective consumers, and this meant listening very closely to the educational preferences being expressed by students.

What students were saying was clear. They didn't want to be trapped in a single-purpose school that provided them with a narrow vocational education and then channeled them into a single occupational slot. Instead they wanted an advanced educational setting that would, in the classic American fashion, provide them with the maximum choice of programs and with access to the widest array of attractive occupational possibilities. In short, they wanted to pursue social mobility and wanted educational institutions to facilitate this pursuit. But this was not a vision that fit comfortably with the alternative visions of the normal school that were also in place. The founders of normal schools saw them as places for instilling sound professional skills; school districts saw them as one among several sources for warm bodies to fill empty classrooms; and students saw them as one among several places where they could acquire the credentials that would enhance their future status. The possibilities for conflict over the purposes of these schools were great, leaving them subject to an array of competing pressures.

In spite of efforts to put normal schools into the service of teacher professionalization or social efficiency, social mobility quickly emerged as a central function through the medium of students exercising their own consumer choices. And this form of pressure was there from the very beginning. Cyrus Peirce ran into the problem shortly after he opened his pathbreaking normal school in Lexington. According to Herbst, "Peirce's frustrations increased as time went on. He was particularly chagrined to find that some of his students did not even want to become teachers, and others did not have the necessary ability."[30]

When Herbst examined the records of Wisconsin's first state normal school in Platteville, he found that, between its founding in 1866 and 1880, "on the average no more than 45 percent of all attending students were enrolled in the normal classes."[31] Bowing to this demand for a broader and less vocationally oriented educational experience, normal schools began to offer increasing numbers of liberal arts courses, and

> many students, especially those who lived near the colleges, came for those courses rather than the teacher training curriculum that formed the original mission of such institutions. Other students used the normal school as a "junior college," completing its program as a step toward enrollment at a state university. To ensure that students who entered the normal departments would actually teach, Illinois Normal not only required that they pledge their

intent to teach for three years after graduation; students also had to report their employment, whatever it was, to the state superintendent of public instruction. Signing a pledge to teach and signing a contract with a school district were two different matters. Records at Illinois indicate that only 30 percent of the alumni during the 1860s spent any time in teaching.[32]

For many American families who otherwise would never have considered pursuing advanced education, normal schools provided an opportunity to gain social advantages that previously had been restricted to the more privileged members of society, who could afford to send their children away to college. In the eyes of these families, the normal school became more than a place for training teachers; it became a kind of people's college. Herbst puts it this way: "Normal schools, rather than the land grant universities, were the pioneers of higher education for the people. Almost everywhere the state universities and agricultural and mechanical colleges were developed at a central location or state capital, whereas the normal schools were scattered to the small country towns across the prairies."[33] These schools "took higher education to where the people lived and worked."[34]

Although some normal schools tried to remain focused on their original professional mission, most gradually yielded to the pressure to broaden their vocational curriculum in order to meet the persistent demand for general academic education and social opportunity. The lure of expanding enrollments was difficult for them to resist, especially in the tuition-driven educational economy in which they had to operate. In addition, shifting in the direction of servicing the community rather than simply training teachers also gained them the support of legislators, who found that promoting people's colleges was good politics.

What effect did this consumer pressure have on normal schools? Essentially, it served to undermine, marginalize, and diffuse the goal of teacher professionalization that had led to the creation of these schools in the first place, as well as the professionally oriented curriculum that had accompanied this goal. Normal schools were evolving from single-purpose vocational schools into general-purpose schools of advanced educational opportunity, within which teacher education was just one program, and not necessarily the most popular or prestigious one at that. One result was a growing confusion about the identity of these schools: were they teacher training schools or people's colleges? Another result was a watering-down of the professional curriculum. It was difficult for normal schools to maintain a rigorous and focused program of teacher preparation when many, often most, of the students wanted something different and when even prospective teachers intended to move on to business and professional careers after a short stint in the classroom.[35] This problem of curriculum diffusion was exacerbated by social efficiency pressures, which prodded normal schools to turn out graduates in large numbers in order to meet the demand for teachers who could fill new slots in expanding school systems and to provide a steady stream of replacements for teachers whose average tenure in the classroom tended to be brief.

Under these circumstances, normal schools were under considerable market pressure to make teacher education as undemanding as possible. In their twin roles as teacher factories and people's colleges, these schools were compelled to make the teacher preparation program easy, so students would be encouraged to sign up for it rather than other potentially more attractive but more difficult alternatives; flexible, so they could fit it into a larger set of studies that would grant them opportunities outside of teaching; and inexpensive, so that the state could afford to produce teachers at a unit cost commensurate with their brief shelf life in the classroom, and so that students would consider the program a worthwhile investment, even given their modest commitment to a career in teaching.[36]

All in all, the impact of the market on U.S. teacher education has hardly been elevating. The pressure from both the job market and the credentials market, from both employers and consumers, has tended to marginalize, minimize, and trivialize the process of educating future teachers.

FROM NORMAL SCHOOL TO UNIVERSITY: EFFECTS ON STATUS

Between the 1890s and the 1970s, market factors propelled the normal school through a process of institutional evolution that eventually transformed it into a general-purpose university. The consequences of this change for the status of teacher education were both profound and profoundly mixed. To put it simply, the institutional status of the normal school rose dramatically during this period while the status of teacher education within the institution declined just as dramatically.

The outlines of this evolutionary development are clear. Normal schools experienced a remarkably linear process of institutional mobility. In the words of William Johnson, "the history of twentieth-century teacher training can be seen as a series of institutional displacements, with normal schools becoming state teachers colleges, then multipurpose liberal arts colleges, and now, in many instances, regional state universities."[37] But as Altenbaugh and Underwood note, "normal schools actually began this transition well before the turn of the century." As they expanded their academic course offerings and broadened their appeal, normal schools "began to raise admission standards, requiring high school diplomas, and to extend the program of study." During most of the nineteenth century, normal schools had been operating at the same level as high schools, taking in grammar school graduates and sending them out with something like a high school diploma. But by 1900 these schools were beginning to look more like junior colleges, and "after 1920, two- and three-year normal schools evolved to four-year teachers colleges." One indicator of the rapid pace of this change is that between 1920 and 1933 the number of state and city normal schools fell from 170 to 66 and the number of state teachers colleges rose from 46 to 146. "By 1940, the term normal school had become obsolete. . . . State teachers' colleges likewise experienced a short life, since by the 1960s they had begun to evolve into multipurpose state colleges or state universities, which granted liberal arts and other degrees as well as education degrees."[38] At the same time that normal schools were turning into universities, existing universities were incorporating at least an attenuated form of teacher education within their own arrays of program offerings.

Market factors propelled this remarkable process of institutional mobility, whose final outcome was to move teacher education from its own niche at the lower fringe of U.S. higher education and lodge it firmly within the confines of the university.[39] Later the fiscal cost and social inefficiency of the transformation became clear. But this elevation of the status and function of the normal school took place primarily because of the overwhelming demand for it that developed from all sides. It seemed to benefit everyone concerned. Through the mechanism of the expanding and rising normal school, citizens received access to higher education far beyond what was available through state universities and land grant schools. Legislators won a politically popular program on which voters were eager to spend tax dollars. For students, the upward movement meant that they could gain the advantages of both a normal-school education (accessibility, low cost, and teacher certification) and a college education (bachelor's degree, institutional prestige, and access to a wide range of white-collar jobs beyond teaching). For teachers, the change meant a symbolic elevation, as a college diploma came to represent the minimum educational requirement for entry into the occupation. Teacher educators found themselves evolving from trade school instructors into college professors, a heady increase in occupational status. And universities found in teacher education a lucrative cash cow that attracted large numbers of students, as well as a politically beneficial demonstration to the state legislature of the practical benefits of a university education.[40]

Compare this market perspective on the evolution of the normal school with the traditional view of this transformation that has been espoused by the educational establishment. Merle Borrowman captures the essence of this view: "The formal history of American teacher education and professionalization is conventionally a story of one triumphal march from Samuel R. Hall's Concord, Vt., normal school in 1823 to the modern National Education Association and the great graduate schools of education. This version of history is misleading."[41] What is misleading about it is the assumption that the institutional elevation of teacher education represents progress, that is, a steady and ineluctable improvement in the quality of teacher education and (consequently) of teaching. In fact, the elevation of the status of the normal school and the incorporation of teacher education within the university have less to do with the quality of the professional education of teachers than with the quantity of consumer demand for higher education and the market conditions that encouraged educational institutions to meet that demand. Thus the content of teacher education was less important to this process than its institutional form, and preparing people effectively to carry out the role of a teacher was less important than simply providing them with the status of a college graduate.

The transformation of the status and locus of teacher education had wide-ranging effects. It reduced the social efficiency of these programs, undermined their ability to provide professional preparation, stratified the way in which they were delivered, and marginalized them within their home institutions.

First, the elevation of normal schools and their transformation into general-purpose universities signaled the subordination of the original social efficiency goal of the normal school to the social mobility goal that came to dominate U.S. higher education more generally. While providing enhanced educational and social opportunities for a wide array of Americans who otherwise would not have had them, this change introduced a radical degree of social inefficiency into the task of preparing teachers. Providing individuals with open access to higher education through an expanded and broadened system of teachers colleges may be very attractive to the individuals who benefit from it and may be justifiable politically as an effort to democratize the delivery of education, but it is hardly an efficient investment of social resources. This educational expansion was based not on the social need for skills that could be provided only through a college education but rather on the individual desire for improved personal status. And it did nothing to meet the need for qualified teachers to staff the nation's classrooms. The normal schools that were created to meet the latter need were thus subverted by the market, transformed into institutions of general education in response to pressing consumer demand. In short, teacher education ended up subsidizing individual ambition and social opportunity at the expense of preparing teachers.

Second, this reorientation of the normal school away from social efficiency and toward social mobility had the effect of undermining professional education. Originally, these schools were seen by their founders and by many of the students attending them as places that focused on providing a practical education in the knowledge and skills required to be an effective teacher. That is, their function was to provide an education with considerable use value. This function changed, however, when consumers asserted their strong preference for an institution that would provide them with educational credentials carrying substantial exchange value. This inevitably shifted the focus within the schools from the content to the form of education, because students increasingly attended them less for the usable knowledge they could acquire there than for the social advantage they could gain by attending there.

In this manner, the transformation of the normal school was a key step in the commodification of U.S. higher education during the twentieth century, as status attainment shouldered aside learning as the central aim of students and as colleges and universities quickly adapted themselves to this changing consumer demand.[42] In this commodified setting, the kind of practical learning represented by teacher education lost appeal because students were driven more by concerns about the marketability of education than by concerns about its applicability. From the consumer's perspective, who cared what you learned in college as long as your diploma gave you access to a good job? Under these circumstances, the former normal schools that became state colleges and universities had no market incentive to sustain a rigorous program of professional teacher preparation. As a result, even sympathetic observers have often found these programs feeble and undemanding.[43] The market-centered environment of higher education in the United States has provided little incentive to make them otherwise.

Third, the evolution of the normal school also tended to reinforce the stratification of the various functions of professional education. In a market setting, where entrepreneurial educators needed to be concerned about maintaining the exchange value of their educational credentials, there was a strong incentive to focus an institution's attentions on those parts of the educational task that would bring the greatest prestige and influence. As Herbst (1989a) has pointed out in some detail, this meant turning one's back as much as possible on the low-status task of preparing elementary teachers and catering to the more prestigious parts of the education market. Even the early normal-school leaders in Massachusetts tried to adopt this strategy: "The educators . . . tended to assign the preparation of elementary teachers to short-term city training schools. Most of the educators preferred to use their state normal schools for the training of secondary school teachers and administrators as well as educational specialists."[44]

By the early twentieth century, however, the structure of teacher education had become considerably more complex and more stratified, with the result that the various professional preparation functions were allocated across a wider span of institutions. Normal schools, as the lowest rung in the ladder of teacher education, were responsible for the education of elementary teachers, the group no one else wanted. Colleges and universities dominated the market for preparing secondary teachers. And the new graduate schools of education at leading universities took on increasing responsibility for the preparation of school administrators and nonteaching educational professionals.[45] But when normal schools evolved into general-purpose colleges and universities, the distinction between the two lower rungs of the ladder became blurred. The preparation of both elementary and secondary teachers became the responsibility of four-year institutions in general, with the primary distinction being that former teachers colleges drew a larger share of teacher candidates of all types.

This led to a fourth effect of the elevation of the normal school. The incorporation of teacher education within the university meant that the tendency to stratify teacher education functions now became an internal matter defining relations between university departments. Teacher education came to occupy a marginal status in the academic hierarchy of the university — often, as Goodlad has noted, even within the universities that were once teachers colleges.[46] One reason for this marginality is that teacher education programs concentrate on providing students with usable knowledge about teaching. In the commodified setting of U.S. education, usable knowledge is low-status knowledge. The more removed knowledge is from ordinary concerns and the more closely associated it is with high culture, the more prestige it carries with it. Just as the low-track English class in high school focuses on reading job applications while the high-track class focuses on Elizabethan poetry, teacher education at the university is seen as following the low road of practical instruction while the arts and sciences departments pursue the high road of more esoteric knowledge.[47]

Another reason for the marginal status of teacher education in its new home in the university was that it was designed to prepare students for a marginal profession. Medical schools and law schools both provide intensely practical education to their students, but this does not harm the high standing of these schools because of the elevated status of those professions. The high exchange value of a medical or law degree — measured by the high status of the positions to which these degrees provide access — means that no one considers these programs "vocational" in the pejorative sense that is applied to programs in auto repair and hairdressing or, at a somewhat higher status, in nursing or teacher education. In part, then, the status of teacher education in the university has been inseparable from the status of teaching in American society.

Teacher educators therefore have come to be doubly stigmatized within the university, because of their association with low-status practical knowledge and because of their association with an occupation seen as a semiprofession.

This combination leaves them at the lowest tier of the academic hierarchy. As Lanier and Little note, "It is common knowledge that professors in the arts and sciences risk a loss of academic respect, including promotion and tenure, if they assume clear interest in or responsibility for teacher education. Professors holding academic rank in education units are in even greater jeopardy of losing the respect of their academic counterparts in the university, because their close proximity makes association with teacher education more possible. And, finally, those education professors who actually supervise prospective or practicing teachers in elementary and secondary schools are indeed at the bottom of the stratification ladder."[48]

Changing Conditions

I have identified two broad types of market influence that have shaped the history of teacher education in the United States. One imposed a social efficiency function on teacher education and the other imposed a social mobility function. Pressure for the social efficiency agenda came from educational providers (school districts and the states): teacher education should provide an adequate supply of teachers at a reasonable cost. Pressure for the social mobility agenda came from educational consumers: the original teacher education institution (the normal school) should transform itself into a form of educational commodity that was more useful in the attainment of higher social status (the general-purpose university). Both of these forms of market pressure have tended to depress the status of teacher education. Both have also tended to marginalize, diffuse, and undercut the quality of professional preparation which these programs have offered.

A key question is to define to what extent this legacy is still exerting a lingering impact on U.S. teacher education in the 1990s. Have things changed substantially, or are many of the same market factors still exerting pressure on these programs?

SOCIAL EFFICIENCY

Many of the factors that promoted the original social efficiency pressures on teacher education in the nineteenth and early twentieth centuries have indeed changed. There is no longer a chronic teacher shortage. The rapid growth in enrollments that drove so much of the demand for teachers has been replaced by a more stable demographic framework. Also, although turnover remains relatively high and commitment to the job relatively low, teaching is no longer the temporary pursuit that it once was. Since World War II, teaching has turned into a career that women and, with growing frequency, men have pursued all the way to retirement. In large part this is because of the gains in pay, job security, and fringe benefits that teacher unions achieved during this period.

In spite of these changes, however, social efficiency pressures on teacher education still exist, albeit in reduced intensity and altered form. In 1993 there were 2.8 million elementary and secondary teachers in the United States, and replacing those who quit or retire calls for about 20 percent of the new group of college graduates every year.[49] Teacher education, as always, is under pressure to meet this continuing demand. It holds a stronger monopoly over access to teaching than it did during the normal-school era, a condition that intensifies the pressure to produce the numbers required every year even if the demand for teachers is not growing as fast as it did in the past century. And reinforcing this pressure is an old threat that has returned in recent years, the threat that teacher education will be bypassed in the hiring of teachers. A number of state legislatures have enacted or proposed plans for "alternative certification" of teachers based on work experience or academic major, without benefit of traditional teacher education. Market rhetoric has supported these plans as ways of restoring choice and opportunity to a teacher job market too long constrained by the education school monopoly. Reinforcing this trend is the move toward mobilizing market forces in K–12 education through such mechanisms as schools of choice and charter schools, which would free schools to hire teachers without the usual restrictions imposed by certification rules. The message seems to be that if teacher education fails to become more efficient in cranking out teachers, the state or the market will find other ways to fill classroom vacancies.

Fiscal pressure on state universities has also intensified in the past few years as state appropriations have leveled off or even declined, leaving universities more dependent than ever on enrollments and tuition as a source of revenue. Under these circumstances, universities are unlikely to do anything to undercut the traditional profitability of teacher education programs, with their high enrollments and low costs. The result is a familiar pattern: teacher education is being asked to produce a large number of teachers as efficiently and inexpensively as possible or else these teachers will be hired from another source. There is little in this market situation to encourage teacher education to move away from its historic pattern of maintaining programs that are easy, flexible, and cheap.

SOCIAL MOBILITY

Teacher education is no longer asked to serve as the conduit for Americans' social aspirations. There is now a large number of people's colleges — including one thousand community colleges and a wide array of nonselective four-year colleges and universities (the latter drawn largely from the ranks of former normal schools) — through which people can gain a chance at social mobility. But consumer pressure on the normal school and the teachers college to provide students with marketable credentials that can be exchanged for a good job has had the long-term effect of locating teacher education within an institution, the university, where it is looked upon with disdain. In the stratified world of contemporary higher education in the United States, teacher education occupies an anomalous position. It is the low-status option for students in the high-status institution; it offers a practical education in a decidedly academic setting; and it sells itself as a provider of occupational use value in a market that prices educational products on the basis of exchange value.

In this commodified educational world that consumer demand helped create, teacher education finds itself thoroughly marginalized. The preparation of teachers is no longer under its control but is spread across the various colleges within the university, where it is shaped by a number of people who view the whole enterprise with suspicion. As a result, its purposes are diffused and teacher educators find themselves marginalized even within the teacher education program. It is not surprising, then, to find that there is little incentive within the university to enhance the quality, tighten the focus, heighten the field-experience component, or raise the standards of teacher education.

Two Proposals for Reform

All of this discussion about the impact of market forces on the status and content of U.S. teacher education over the years leads back to the problem of how to reform these programs. Reform proposals necessarily start with the state of teacher education today, a state that has been shaped historically in considerable part by the kind of market pressures that I have outlined. The historical legacy of teacher education affects reformers in two related ways. It defines the kinds of problems within these programs that require reform solutions; and it defines the structural factors and continuing influences that are likely to have an impact on the success or failure of any particular effort to reform these problems.

I would like to focus on two recent proposals for reforming teacher education in the United States, one developed by the Holmes Group in *Tomorrow's Teachers* and the other developed by Geraldine Joncich Clifford and James W. Guthrie in *Ed School: A Brief for Professional Education.*[50] Other reform proposals have come to the fore in the past few years, but these two best fit the analytical approach I have taken.[51] Both of them identify the low status of teacher education as a critical problem that affects its ability to carry out its functions effectively and that therefore needs to be resolved. Both of them see professionalization as a key component of any solution to this problem. But they take very different approaches to the task of accomplishing this professionalization, with the Holmes Group advocating a strategy that would tie teacher education more closely to the university and Clifford and Guthrie advocating a strategy that would ally the programs more closely with the teaching profession.[52] In light of the similar goals put forward in these proposals and the different strategies suggested for achieving these goals, the two proposals lend themselves to evaluation in tandem. And given the way that both plans respond to and at the same time suggest remedies for the status difficulties of teacher education, this comparative evaluation depends on a firm understanding of the legacy of the market influences that have affected this status. Therefore the evaluation provides a convenient test for the usefulness of my analysis here.

TOMORROW'S TEACHERS

Early in its report, the Holmes Group zeroes in on the status problem that has plagued teacher education over the years, connecting it to the status problem that has also affected teaching: "Unhappily, teaching and teacher education have a long history of mutual impairment. Teacher education long has been intellectually weak; this further eroded the prestige of an already poorly esteemed profession, and it encouraged many inadequately prepared people to enter teaching. But teaching long has been an underpaid and overworked occupation, making it difficult for universities to recruit good students to teacher education or to take it as seriously as they have taken education for more prestigious professions." Acknowledging that "the legendary problems of teacher education in America have been lamented since the turn of the century," the group charges that the solutions commonly proposed for these problems have not worked in large part because of "a failure to appreciate the extent to which teacher education has evolved as a creature of teaching." If mutual impairment is the ailment, then mutual improvement is the remedy. As a result, as Judith Lanier puts it in the preface to the report, the Holmes Group "is organized around the twin goals of the reform of teacher education and the reform of the teaching profession," where the latter refers to "nothing less than the transformation of teaching from an occupation into a genuine profession."[53]

To professionalize teaching calls for significant changes in the structure of teacher roles and rewards within schools. But institutions like the members of the Holmes Group at the time of the report — approximately one hundred education schools at top universities — have little control over these areas, which lie within the province of local school boards. As a result, the report's authors concentrate their attention on the ways that these institutions can draw on their strengths as research-oriented, university-based education schools to promote the professionalization agenda: "The work that we propose is therefore distinctively the province of the university: study, research, and teaching. What is new in our proposals is the idea that these distinctive academic resources be focused on the problems of teacher education, and that the universities make the solution of these problems a top priority."[54]

What education schools can do is create a program of professional education modeled after programs used as preparation for such professions as medicine and law: "The established professions have, over time, developed a body of specialized knowledge, codified and transmitted through professional education and clinical practice. Their claim to professional status rests on this. For the occupation of teaching, a defensible claim for such special knowledge has emerged only recently. Efforts to reform the preparation of teachers and the profession of teaching must begin, therefore, with the serious work of articulating the knowledge base of the profession and developing the means by which it can be imparted." Fortunately, as noted earlier in the report, "Within the last twenty years, . . . the science of education promised by Dewey, Thorndike, and others at the turn of the century, has become more tangible."[55]

In sum, the logic of the argument in *Tomorrow's Teachers* is this: Teacher education has a poor reputation in part because it is intellectually weak and in part because teaching itself has a low status. The elevation of teacher education requires the professionalization of teaching. From the vantage point of the university, where education schools reside, the most potent and accessible way to promote the latter goal is to restructure teacher education around a research-based core of professional knowledge. This is a strategy that capitalizes on the historical contingencies that brought teacher education up from the lowly normal school and into the university. Teacher educators are university professors who (can or do) carry out scientific research on teaching in the classic university manner. So why not shore up the intellectual weakness of teacher education (its lowbrow practicality, its atheoretical character) with some of this high-status, academically validated knowledge? In effect this means calling on teacher educators to outdo the university at its own game, carrying out academically credible research on teaching and then passing this knowledge on to prospective teachers. The high exchange value of this form of knowledge will then be transferred to both teacher educators and teachers, elevating both to a higher status. This is a pure market-based strategy, which draws on the aura of the university to advance the cause of both groups.

There are two major problems with this strategy, which cast doubt on its effectiveness as a mechanism for enhancing the status of either teachers or teacher educators. First, there is little reason to think that the kind of enhanced professional education proposed by the Holmes Group would bring about a significant improvement in the status of teachers. This would be the case only if use-value were the key to occupational status: then, indeed, one's prestige would depend on what one knows. In the market for occupational status, however, exchange value matters most. Medicine and law are high-status professions not because they have rigorous programs of professional education; rather, they have highly selective professional education programs because they are enormously rewarding professions and therefore draw many more candidates than can be accommodated.

Raising the credential requirements for a subordinate occupation group raises the cost of entry, but it does nothing to raise the power, prestige, or salary of the occupation itself. Nursing has been trying this strategy in recent years, moving toward the point where every registered nurse will be required to hold a bachelor's degree. But this will do nothing to change the way in which nurses remain subordinate to doctors; at best, it will serve to draw a firmer boundary between registered nurses and licensed practical nurses, protecting the former against downward mobility rather than promoting professional advancement.[56] If professional education were the critical factor, then pharmacists would be members of an elevated profession. They pursue advanced study of pharmacology in order to carry out a job that often requires them to do little more than transfer pills from one bottle to another. By pursuing a strategy of increased educational requirements, teaching and nursing likewise may run the risk of overcredentialing people for a job that is not changing to meet the new levels of professional preparation.

In fact, as I have argued in Chapter 6, the Holmes Group strategy in *Tomorrow's Teachers* is perhaps designed to enhance the professional status of the teacher educator more than that of the teacher. The effort to install academic research at the center of the professional curriculum serves to displace the clinical knowledge of the practitioner and establish the teacher educator rather than the teacher as the prime authority on correct professional practice. This strategy may actually improve the position of the teacher educator at the expense of the teacher. In addition, it is designed to shore up the status of teacher educators within the university, by highlighting their credentials as academic researchers and knowledge producers. But that leads to a second problem with this strategy: there is little reason to think that this effort to emulate the other professors in the university will in fact yield teacher educators the kind of respect they desire. This point is at the heart of Clifford and Guthrie's analysis in *Ed School,* and it forms the basis for their recommendation for reforming teacher education.

Clifford and Guthrie begin their book with a quotation from a president of Harvard, who, as far back as 1865, had the same idea as the authors of *Tomorrow's Teachers*. He felt, as they do, that by investing teacher education with the full prestige of the university, teaching could be elevated to a true profession. In his words, "The establishment of a Normal School in a University, and of a special course for Bachelor of Arts in a Normal School, would be steps calculated to raise the standard of excellence required of teachers, and would lift towards its proper dignity the high profession of teaching."[57] But the authors sharply disagree with this conclusion and announce that the main point of their book is to argue that the approach suggested by this university president 130 years ago has been tried and has been proven a failure:

> This book is about those "normal schools in the university" in the United States: about their origins, historical evolution, continuing problems, and future prospects. Our thesis is that schools of education, particularly those located on the campuses of prestigious research universities, have become ensnared improvidently in the academic and political cultures of their institutions and have neglected their professional allegiances. They are like marginal men, aliens in their own worlds. They have seldom succeeded in satisfying the scholarly norms of their campus letters and science colleagues, and they are simultaneously estranged from their practicing professional peers. The more forcefully they have rowed toward the shores of scholarly research, the more distant they have become from the public schools they are duty bound to serve. Conversely, systematic efforts at addressing the applied problems of public schools have placed schools of education at risk on their own campuses.[58]

As we have seen, it was not the benevolent feelings of university presidents toward the profession of teaching that brought the normal school into the university but rather the intense pressure from educational consumers seeking advanced degrees. But once teacher education became lodged in this elevated setting, according to Clifford and Guthrie, teacher educators began to suffer from "the American disease of 'status anxiety,'" compelling them to cast about for ways to establish their own professional credentials within this new academic setting. Unfortunately, these methods did not succeed. "One presumed route to higher regard was to encourage abandonment of the classroom. . . . Another well-worn path that brought them far short of their destination was to be as academic as possible. The usual and unexpected reward was repudiation by other academics on the grounds that such work could only rarely be as worthy as the same work done in disciplinary departments."[59]

Two key points emerge from Clifford and Guthrie's analysis that are relevant to our discussion of *Tomorrow's Teachers* and of the larger issue of the role of markets in shaping teacher education. First, concerns by teacher educators about their own professional status — not the professionalization of teaching — inspired them to launch full-force into the task of constructing a body of academic research about education. Therefore the "science of teaching," which the first Holmes Group report sees as the basis for teacher professionalization, actually emerged as a side effect of the effort by education professors to professionalize themselves in ways that were more in tune with academic norms than teacher practice.[60]

Second, these efforts failed miserably. "Being as academic as possible" — by engaging in funded research, employing scientific methodology, writing strictly for an academic audience, producing mountains of refereed journal articles — could not erase the stigma of the normal school from the brow of the education professor. The status of teacher educators was fixed by factors outside their control. As latecomers to the major university faculties, they were fated to play a continuing game of status catch-up. With most of their numbers concentrated in the new regional universities that recently evolved from teachers colleges, they were tied to the low standing of these institutions in the established academic hierarchy. They were unavoidably linked to the practical knowledge and vocational orientation of a teacher preparation program in a setting that looked down on these things. And they were also inextricably tied to the low status of teaching.

For these reasons, Clifford and Guthrie argue, the best strategy for improving teacher education is for education schools to abandon their futile pursuit of academic status and focus attention on serving the profession of teaching. This calls for an abrupt about-face (in direct contradiction to the central thrust of *Tomorrow's Teachers*), with education schools being asked to turn their backs on the university and embrace the schools:

> Schools of education must take the profession of education, not academia, as their main point of reference. It is not sufficient to say that the greatest strength of schools of education is that they are the only places available to look at fundamental issues from a variety of disciplinary perspectives. They have been doing so for more than a half a century without appreciable effect on professional practice. It is time for many institutions to shift gears. . . .
>
> Their prime orientation should be to educate practitioners, and education faculty must be made more cognizant of the technical or experiential culture of schooling for that to happen. To require less is to continue to frustrate both research and training activities. We think it sound policy that faculty appointments in education redress the imbalance that exists on many graduate school faculties by including substantial professional criteria in the guidelines and processes of faculty appraisal. This appraisal should cover both appointment and promotion decisions.[61]

Although Clifford and Guthrie provide a cogent critique of the university-based strategy for reforming teacher education proposed by the Holmes Group, their profession-based strategy poses its own problems. The key problem relates again to the issue of status. It seems wholly unrealistic and even counterproductive to ask teacher education to turn its back on the high-status setting it has come at last to occupy, however uncomfortably, and throw itself into the arms of an occupation whose status is markedly lower. Even though teacher educators are not accorded high status within the university, holding the position of university professor carries with it a wide range of external status benefits. Whereas education professors do not add much to the aura of the university (as their arts and sciences colleagues are quick to point out), they enjoy the illumination of its glow. By contrast, as the authors of *Tomorrow's Teachers* so accurately point out, the status of teaching tends to exert a downward pull on the public standing of teacher education. This downward pull is the factor that Clifford and Guthrie ignore in *Ed School*, in the process undercutting the potential effectiveness of their effort to reform teacher education.[62]

My point, then, is a simple one: market pressures have played a significant role in shaping the distinctive history of teacher education in the United States, and they have left it with a disabling legacy. Education schools have been, and continue to be, torn between competing concerns about social efficiency and social mobility. They continue to occupy a status at the lower end of the educational hierarchy, which has both undermined their ability to carry on sound programs of professional preparation and interfered with efforts to strengthen these programs. Those who would like to reform teacher education will have to tangle with this legacy if they are serious about making change. The alternative is to keep repeating the old cycle of attacking teacher education for its inferiority and thereby reinforcing its lowly status.

10

Schooling Consumers and Consuming the School

In U.S. schools the relentless urge to get ahead has undermined the opportunity to get an education. The preceding chapters have shown some of the ways that the private pursuit of personal advantage has reshaped the structure of public schooling. Market pressures have elevated private interests over the public interest in education, with the result that schooling has come to serve the competitive needs of the most ambitious and culturally advantaged educational consumers (for a leg up on the opposition) more than the substantive needs of society as a whole (for capable citizenship and competent workmanship). Consumer demand for credentials — and the economic leverage they bring — has compelled the educational system to assume a highly stratified form. The system has become better at creating invidious distinctions among students than at providing them with the political and social capacities required for a healthy society. In such a system, educational placement — in the right school, the right college, the right program — is more important than educational performance, and learning to work the system well is more important than learning to do the curriculum well. This is a system, in short, that puts a premium on the acquisition of educational credentials over the mastery of educational content.

The Nature of the Problem

Under these circumstances, it is hardly surprising that so many observers find that American students are remarkably disengaged from the educational process.[1] In a recent book Laurence Steinberg identifies student disengagement as the central problem facing education in the United States. Drawing on a study of twenty thousand high school students, he concludes: "An extremely high proportion of American high school students do not take school, or their studies, seriously."[2] The root of the problem, he says, is in the kind of rewards that schools have available to them to motivate academic effort:

> Most of the time, what keeps students going in school is not intrinsic motivation—motivation derived from the process of learning itself—but extrinsic motivation—motivation that comes from the real or perceived consequences associated with success or failure, whether these consequences are immediate (in the form of grades, the reactions of parents, or the responses of friends) or delayed (in the form of anticipated impact in other educational settings or in the adult world of work)....
>
> Over the course of their educational careers, students are increasingly exposed to extrinsic rewards for schoolwork.[3]

What Steinberg is saying, in effect, is that the key determinant of student engagement in schooling is the exchange value of education rather than its use-value, because the primary goal of pursuing an education has become the acquisition of educational credentials—symbolic goods, such as grades, credits, and degrees—rather than the acquisition of useful skills and knowledge. In an argument that is similar to the one I make in this book, Steinberg shows that students adapt themselves to this situation in a manner that is quite rational in light of the incentives and disincentives built into the system, but that undermines the process of acquiring an education:

> Do students believe in the benefits of schooling? Yes and no. Students believe in the benefits associated with getting a diploma or a degree, but they are skeptical about the benefits associated with either learning or doing well in class. In other words, students ... correctly believe that college graduates stand a better chance of getting good jobs than high school graduates, who, in turn, stand a better chance of occupational success than dropouts. At the same time, however, they do not associate later success either with *doing well* in school (in terms of their grades or the evaluations of their teachers) or with *learning* what schools have to teach. In students' eyes, then, what matters is only whether one graduates—not how well one does or what one learns along the way.
>
> If this is the prevailing belief among contemporary students—and our study suggests that it is—it is easy to understand why so many students coast through school without devoting much energy to their schoolwork....

> Within a belief system in which all that counts is graduation — in which earning good grades is seen as equivalent to earning mediocre ones, or worse yet, in which learning something from school is seen as unimportant — students choose the path of least resistance.[4]

Up to this point, Steinberg's argument is parallel to my own. The conclusions he draws from this analysis, however, are quite different. As a psychologist, he ultimately chooses to portray student disengagement from learning as an attitude problem, and the solutions he proposes are aimed at changing that attitude. His basic strategy for reform is to raise the cost of academic failure. Students have been able to coast along at school without exerting serious effort to learn because a failure to learn brings few significant consequences; with a minimum amount of work and a modest amount of learning, they can still pass their courses and graduate. But we can raise the cost of academic failure at home, he says, by encouraging parents to become more engaged in their children's schooling and to put increased pressure on students to take their schoolwork seriously. We can also raise the cost of academic failure in the workplace, he argues — by establishing high academic standards for promotion and graduation, enforcing them with a system of examinations, and giving them economic teeth by means of standardized transcripts that employers can use to select the most academically accomplished applicants for jobs.

As a sociologist, however, I have taken a different approach in trying to explain the dysfunctional characteristics of schooling identified by Steinberg. I have focused less on the attitudes and behaviors of the actors who populate U.S. education than on the systemic factors that have shaped these attitudes and behaviors. From the latter perspective, I have argued that many of the central problems facing education in the United States — student disengagement, for one, but also such issues as social inefficiency and persistent social inequality — are in considerable part the result of market pressures on the educational system. Each chapter of this book is a study in educational consumerism and credentialism, which shows how the market perspective has come to dominate our view of education. By redefining education as a commodity whose acquisition can help individuals get ahead of the pack, market pressures have led to the reconstruction of the educational system in the service of a private pursuit of individual advantage. This reconstruction around the goal of social mobility is far from complete, and it has been hotly contested over the years by supporters of competing educational goals, who argue for an educational system that serves to promote social efficiency and/or democratic equality. But as I have tried to show, in one context after another the influence of this private perspective on U.S. education has been profound.

What we have seen is a portrait of a public educational system that increasingly has been put in the service of private purposes. This analysis suggests that the primary problem with education in the United States is not unmotivated students, uncaring parents, and undemanding standards (as Steinberg would have it) but something more fundamental — our unwillingness as a society to defend the public interest in education against the encroachments of individual consumers who seek to exploit the system for private benefit. The market forces that so powerfully shape the nation's economic and social life — encouraging the individual pursuit of competitive advantage — have been working to turn education, too, into a form of private property, thereby making credentials the object rather than the byproduct of educational achievement.

As a result, the problems of personal attitude and motivation that so concern Steinberg are best understood in light of the incentives facing actors within an increasingly market-centered educational system. By working the system in order to gain the greatest individual benefit for the smallest investment of time and effort, students are only behaving like savvy consumers, who naturally want to obtain the most valuable commodity at the cheapest price. The core problem is not with student attitudes, which under the circumstances are quite understandable, but with the market-based incentives that shape these attitudes within U.S. education. What is irrational is not the behavior of educational consumers but the emerging structure of the educational system. There is, in fact, nothing rational about such a system — which promotes personal advantage at public expense; which goes out of its way to create and preserve educational distinctions that undercut real educational accomplishment; and which produces more graduates than employers need or taxpayers can afford.

The Historical Roots of the Problem

A central theme of this book has been to explain how it is that education in the United States came to assume its current form as a system that is both highly sensitive to consumer demand and highly focused on the acquisition of educational credentials. A useful way to explore this theme in greater depth is to examine a case study of one of the most dramatic and consequential events in the history of schooling in this country: the extraordinarily rapid expansion of higher education in the late nineteenth and early twentieth centuries. This case also provides a chance to consider more systematically the validity of credentialism as a theory of educational development.

In *Degrees of Control,* David Brown tackles an important question that has long puzzled scholars who wanted to understand the central role that education plays in American society: why did the United States experience such extraordinary growth, compared with other Western countries, in higher education at such an early point in time? Whereas in most societies higher education has long been seen as a privilege that is granted to a relatively small proportion of the population, in this country it has increasingly come to be seen as a right of the ordinary citizen. And this rapid increase in accessibility is not only a recent phenomenon. As Brown notes, between 1870 and 1930 the proportion of college-age persons who attended institutions of higher education rose from 1.7 percent to 13.0 percent.[5] This change occurred long before the proliferation of regional state universities and community colleges made it possible at the end of the twentieth century for the majority of youth in the United States to enroll in some form of higher education.

The range of possible answers to this question is considerable, and each alternative reflects its own distinctive image of the nature of U.S. political and social life. For example, perhaps the rapid growth in the opportunity for higher education was an expression of egalitarian politics and a confirmation of the American Dream; perhaps it was a political diversion, providing ideological cover for persistent inequality; or perhaps it was merely an accident, an unintended consequence of a struggle for something altogether different. Brown explains the spectacular growth and peculiar structure of U.S. higher education in light of the role of college credentials in American life.

Traditional explanations do not hold up very well under scrutiny. Structural-functionalist theory argues that an expanding economy created a powerful demand for advanced technical skills (human capital), which only a rapid expansion of higher education could fill. But Brown notes that during this expansion most students pursued programs not in vocational-technical curricula but in liberal arts, which meant that the forms of knowledge they were acquiring were remote from the economically productive skills supposedly demanded by employers. Social reproduction theory treats the university as a mechanism that emerged to protect the privilege of the upper middle class behind a wall of cultural capital, during a time (with the decline of proprietorship) when it became increasingly difficult for economic capital alone to provide such protection. But while this theory points to a central outcome of college expansion, it fails to explain the historical contingencies and agencies that actually produced this outcome. In fact, both of these theories are essentially functionalist in approach, portraying higher education as arising automatically to fill a social need — within the economy, in the first case, and within the class system, in the second.

Credentialist theory, however, helps explain the socially reproductive effect of expanding higher education without denying agency. It conceives of higher-education diplomas as a kind of cultural currency that becomes attractive to status groups seeking an advantage in the competition for social positions, and therefore it sees the expansion of higher education as a response to consumer demand rather than functional necessity. Upper classes tend to benefit disproportionately from this educational development, not because of an institutional correspondence principle that preordains such an outcome but because they are socially and culturally better equipped to gain access to and succeed within the educational market.

This credentialist theory of educational growth is the one that Brown finds most compelling as the basis for his own interpretation. When he plunges into a close examination of U.S. higher education, however, he finds that the standard formulation of this theory — as spelled out by Randall Collins — often does not match the historical evidence.[6] Collins does not examine the nature of labor market recruitment, which is critical for credentialist theory because the pursuit of college credentials makes sense only if employers are rewarding degree holders with desirable jobs. Like Collins, Brown shows that between 1800 and 1880 the number of colleges in the United States grew dramatically, but Brown observes that enrollments at individual colleges were quite modest. He argues that this binge of institution creation was driven by a combination of religious and market forces but not (contrary to Collins) by the pursuit of credentials. There simply is no good evidence that a college degree was much in demand by employers during this period. Instead, a great deal of the growth in the number of colleges was the result of the desire by religious and ethnic groups to create their own settings for producing clergy and transmitting culture. Brown argues that an additional spur to this growth came from markedly less elevated sources — local boosterism and land speculation — as development-oriented towns sought to establish colleges as a mechanism for attracting land buyers and new residents.

Brown's version of credentialist theory identifies a few central factors that are required in order to facilitate a credential-driven expansion of higher education, and by 1880 several of these were already in place. One such factor is substantial wealth. Higher education is expensive, and expanding it for reasons of individual status attainment rather than societal necessity is a wasteful use of a nation's resources that is feasible only for a very wealthy country. The United States was already a very wealthy country in the late nineteenth century. A second factor is a broad institutional base. At this point, the United States had the largest number of colleges per million residents in the country's history, before or since. Because most colleges had small enrollments, there was great potential for growth within an already existing institutional framework. This potential was reinforced by a third factor, decentralized control. Colleges were governed by local boards rather than central state authorities and depended for funding on student tuition more than state appropriations.

This encouraged entrepreneurial behavior by college leaders, especially in the intensively competitive market environment they faced.

But three other factors that are essential for rapid credential-based growth in higher education were still missing in 1880. First, colleges were not going to be able to attract large numbers of new students — who were after all unlikely to be motivated solely by the love of learning — unless they could offer these students both a pleasant social experience and a practical educational experience, neither of which was the norm at colleges for most of the nineteenth century. Second, colleges could not function as credentialing institutions until they had a monopoly over a particular form of credentials, but in 1880 they were still competing directly with high schools for the same students. Finally, their credentials were not going to have any value on the market unless employers began to demonstrate a distinct preference for hiring college graduates, and such a preference was still not obvious at this stage.

According to Brown, a major shift in each of these factors occurred in the 1880s. The trigger for this change was a significant oversupply of institutions relative to existing demand. In this life-or-death situation, colleges desperately sought to increase the pool of potential students. It is no coincidence that this period marked the rapid diffusion of efforts to improve the quality of social life on campuses (from the promotion of athletics to the proliferation of fraternities) and also the shift toward a curriculum with a stronger claim of practicality (emphasizing modern languages and science over Latin and Greek). At the same time, colleges sought to guarantee a flow of students from feeder institutions, which required them to establish a hierarchical relation with high schools. The end of the century was the period in which colleges began requiring completion of a high school course as a prerequisite for college admission instead of the traditional entrance examination. This system provided high schools with a stable outlet for its graduates and colleges with a predictable flow of reasonably well-prepared students. None of this would have been possible, however, if the college degree had not acquired a significant exchange value in the labor market. Without this, there would have been only social reasons for attending college, and high schools would have had little incentive to submit to college mandates.

The issue of employer preference has posed a significant, perhaps fatal, problem for credentialist theory, which has asked the reader to accept two apparently contradictory assertions about credentials. First, the theory claims that a college degree has exchange value but not necessarily use-value; that is, it is attractive to the consumer because it can be cashed in on a good job more or less independently of any learning that was acquired along the way. Second, this exchange value depends on the willingness of employers to hire applicants based on credentials alone, without direct knowledge of what these applicants know or what they can do. But this raises a serious question about the rationality of the employer in this process. After all, why would an employer, who presumably cares about the productivity of future employees, hire people based solely on a college's certification of competence in the absence of any evidence of that competence?

Brown notes that work became gradually more rationalized in the late nineteenth century, and thus large-scale bureaucracies were developed to administer this work within both private corporations and public agencies. One result was the creation of a rapidly growing occupational sector for managerial employees who could function effectively within such a rationalized organizational structure. College graduates seemed to fit the bill for this kind of work. They emerged from the top level of the newly developed hierarchy of educational institutions and therefore seemed like natural candidates for management work in the upper levels of the new administrative hierarchy, which was based not on proprietorship or political office but on apparent skill. And what kinds of skills were called for in this line of work? What the new managerial employees needed was not so much the technical skills posited by human capital theory, he argues, but a general capacity to work effectively in a verbally and cognitively structured organizational environment, as well as a capacity to feel comfortable about assuming positions of authority over other people.

These were things that the emerging American college could and did provide. The increasingly corporate social structure of student life on college campuses provided good socialization for bureaucratic work, and the process of gaining access to and graduation from college provided students with an institutionalized confirmation of their social superiority and qualifications for leadership. Note that these capacities were substantive consequences of having attended college, but they were not learned as part of the college's formal curriculum. That is, the characteristics that qualified college graduates for future bureaucratic employment were a side effect of their pursuit of a college education. In this sense, then, the college credential had a substantive meaning for employers that justified them in using it as a criterion for employment, less for the human capital that college provided than for the social capital that college conferred on graduates. Therefore this credential, Brown argues, served an important role in the labor market by reducing the uncertainty that plagued the process of bureaucratic hiring. After all, how else was an employer to gain some assurance that a candidate could do this kind of work? A college degree offered a claim to competence, which had enough substance behind it to be credible even if this substance was largely unrelated to the content of the college curriculum.

By the 1890s all the pieces were in place for a rapid expansion of college enrollments, strongly driven by credentialist pressures. Employers had reason to give preference to college graduates when hiring for management positions. As a result, middle-class families had an increasing incentive to provide their children with privileged access to an advantaged social position by sending them to college. For the students themselves, this extrinsic reward for attending college was reinforced by the intrinsic benefits accruing from an attractive social life on campus. All of this created a strong demand for expanding college enrollments, and the preexisting institutional conditions in higher education made it possible for colleges to respond aggressively to this demand. A thousand independent institutions of higher education, accustomed to playing entrepreneurial roles in a competitive educational market, were eager to capitalize on the surge of interest in attending college and to adapt themselves to the preferences of these new tuition-paying consumers. The result was a powerful and unrelenting surge of expansion in college enrollments that continued for the next century. As we have seen, this same pattern of consumer-driven credential-seeking expansion also characterized the history of the high school, normal school, and junior college.

The Consequences

The urge to get ahead has transformed the basic function of U.S. education from public service to private service, and this transformation has brought significant consequences for the people who attend, work in, pay for, and in various ways depend on American schools.

One major problem is that focusing on selling credentials to consumers is astonishingly inefficient. Education is the largest single public investment made by most modern societies, and this investment is justified on the grounds that it provides a critically important contribution to the collective welfare. The public value of education is usually calculated as some combination of two types of benefits, the preparation of capable citizens (the political benefit) and the training of productive workers (the economic benefit). However the argument I have advanced in this book suggests that these public benefits are not necessarily being met and that the primary beneficiaries are in fact private individuals. From this perspective, higher education (and the educational system more generally) exists largely as a mechanism for providing individuals with a cultural commodity that will give them a competitive advantage in the pursuit of social position. In short, education becomes little but a vast public subsidy for private ambition.

The practical effect of this subsidy is the production of a glut of graduates.

The difficulty posed by this outcome is not that the population becomes over-educated (such a state is difficult to imagine) but that it becomes overcredentialed, as people pursue diplomas less for the knowledge they are thereby acquiring than for the access that the diplomas themselves will provide. The result is a spiral of credential inflation, for as each level of education in turn gradually floods with a crowd of ambitious consumers, individuals have to keep seeking ever higher levels of credentials in order to move a step ahead of the pack. In such a system nobody wins. Consumers have to spend increasing amounts of time and money to gain additional credentials because the swelling number of credential holders keeps lowering the value of credentials at any given level. Taxpayers find an increasing share of scarce fiscal resources going to support an educational chase with little public benefit. Employers keep raising the entry-level education requirements for particular jobs (as the average education level of applicants rises), but they still find that they have to provide extensive training before employees can carry out their work productively. At all levels, this is an enormously wasteful system, one that is increasingly draining for rich countries like the United States and positively impoverishing for less developed countries that imitate the U.S. educational model.

A second major problem is that credentialism undercuts learning. In both college and high school, students are all too well aware that their mission is to do whatever it takes to acquire a diploma, which they can cash in on what really matters — a good job. This assumption has the effect of reifying the formal markers of academic progress — grades, credits, and degrees — and encouraging students to focus their attention on accumulating these badges of merit for the exchange value they offer. That strategy means directing attention away from the substance of education, reducing student motivation to learn the knowledge and skills that constitute the core of the educational curriculum. Under such conditions, it is quite rational, even if educationally destructive, for students to seek to acquire their badges of merit at a minimum academic cost, to gain the highest grade with the minimum amount of learning. This perspective is almost perfectly captured by a common student question, one that sends chills down the back of the learning-centered teacher but that makes perfect sense for the credential-oriented student: "Is this going to be on the test?"[7] We have credentialism to thank for the aversion to learning that, to a great extent, lies at the heart of our educational system. This aversion is further exacerbated by the problem of credential inflation, which continually undercuts the exchange value of a given level of credentials and therefore reinforces the consumer's sense that these credentials are not worth a substantial investment of time and effort.

A third problem posed by consumer-driven credentialism is the way it reinforces social inequality under the guise of expanding educational opportunity. The opportunity is real enough, as far as it goes, for the connection between social class and education is neither as direct nor as automatic as social reproduction theory suggests. Market forces mediate between the class position of students and their access to and success within the educational system. That is, there is a general competition for admission to institutions of higher education and for levels of achievement within these institutions. Class advantage is no guarantee of success in this competition because such factors as individual ability, motivation, and luck all play a part in determining the result. Market forces also mediate between educational attainment (the acquisition of credentials) and social attainment (the acquisition of a social position). Some college degrees are worth more in the credentials market than others, and they provide privileged access to higher-level positions independent of the class origins of the credential holder.

In both of these market competitions, however, one for acquiring the credential and the other for cashing it in, higher class position provides a significant competitive edge. The economic, cultural, and social capital that comes with higher class standing gives the bearer an advantage in getting into college, in doing well at college, and in translating college credentials into desirable social outcomes. The market-based competition that characterizes the acquisition and disposition of educational credentials gives the process a meritocratic set of possibilities, but the influence of class on this competition gives it a socially reproductive set of probabilities as well. The danger is that, as a result, a credential-driven system of education can provide meritocratic cover for socially reproductive outcomes. In the single-minded pursuit of educational credentials, both student consumers and the society that supports them can lose sight of an all-too-predictable pattern of outcomes that is masked by the headlong rush for the academic gold.

The Downside of Upward Mobility

In spite of all the evidence and analysis that fills the pages of this book, however, my argument may appear puzzlingly wrong-headed to many readers. After all, here I am attacking the American system of education for what is generally recognized as its most praiseworthy attribute — its emphasis on providing all members of society with open access to educational opportunities. Whereas other school systems around the world give greater emphasis to social efficiency (providing workers with the necessary job skills) and/or democratic equality (providing citizens with the necessary social and political skills), the U.S. system stresses social mobility. In practice, this means a system that is organized primarily around the goal of providing individuals with the educational chance to get ahead socially.

Americans and non-Americans alike see great benefit arising from such a system. Unlike a system devoted to social efficiency concerns, the U.S. system seeks to maximize student options and minimize the educational barriers to the exercise of these options. And unlike a system devoted to democratic equality concerns, the U.S. system seeks to maximize the variety of possible educational experiences and outcomes. The result is a structure of education that is widely admired and frequently imitated.

The secret of the consumer appeal and organizational success of the American educational model lies in its responsiveness to the market. In contrast with most systems of education around the world, control of the U.S. system is radically decentralized. Governance of educational institutions at all levels tends to be local, rather than concentrated in the hands of an educational ministry, and finances depend heavily on student enrollment (either directly, through tuition dollars, or indirectly through per capita appropriations). Such a system is remarkably flexible, adapting quickly to local market conditions and changes in consumer demand, and it is also remarkably differentiated, as particular institutions and individual school systems come to occupy specialized niches in the highly competitive educational arena. Constructed from the ground up rather than the top down and responding to consumer pressure rather than central planning, this system comes to offer the broadest range of educational programs in the most structurally diverse array of institutional settings that are made accessible to the most heterogeneous collection of students. In short, the system maximizes individual choice, structural variety, and public access.

In these ways — choice, variety, and access — the U.S. model of education is understandably the pride of most Americans and the envy of many foreign observers. My aim in this book is not to denigrate the accomplishments of this model; as I pointed out in Chapter 1, a number of the most progressive characteristics of American education have their roots in the social mobility perspective, especially in the areas where it has overlapped with the democratic equality perspective. Instead, the aim is to point out the unintended consequences of this consumer-based model, consequences that have been devastating for both school and society.

My point is simply this: by constructing a system of education so heavily around the goal of promoting individual social mobility, we have placed public education in service to private interests. The result, as we have seen, is to undercut other goals for education that serve the interests of the public as a whole, such as the production of competent citizens and productive workers.

Social mobility, I conclude, needs to be balanced by democratic equality and social efficiency, or else we will continue to reproduce an educational system that is mired in consumerism and credentialism. Too often this system, in its eagerness to provide individual consumers with the credentials they demand, undercuts learning, overproduces credentials, and reinforces social advantage. Ironically, an educational system dedicated to promoting upward mobility frequently interferes not only with getting an education but also with getting ahead. The system, it seems, is all too effective at allowing individuals to gain a social advantage by climbing the educational ladder, and the result is a structure of selection and attrition that promotes opportunity for some by preserving disadvantage for others.

Notes

1. Public Schools for Private Advantage

This chapter was previously published as "Public Goods, Private Goods: The American Struggle over Educational Goals" in *American Educational Research Journal* 34 (Spring 1997). An earlier version was presented at the 1996 meeting of the American Educational Research Association in New York; I am grateful to John Rury for his thoughtful and detailed comments as a critic at that meeting and to Kathleen Murphey and Norton Grubb for their helpful comments in response to that session. I am also grateful to three anonymous reviewers who provided me with extraordinarily constructive and empathetic guidance in making revisions. In addition, I want to thank David Cohen and Cleo Cherryholmes for their comments on a very early version of this essay. Finally, I am indebted to my students in the College of Education at Michigan State University, with whom I have talked about these issues for years.

1. Berliner and Biddle (1995) have written a cogent defense of public schools against a number of accusations, drawing on a wide array of evidence to support this defense. In a similar vein, Gerald Bracey (1995) publishes annual reports in which he exposes the misinformation that underlies much of public education's bad press.

2. A classic effort to summarize what research says about U.S. education is the booklet *What Works: Research about Teaching and Learning,* published by the U.S. Department of Education in 1986.

3. See Curti (1959).

4. A large number of scholars have seen this tension as central in understanding the history of U.S. education. For example, see Hogan (1985), Katznelson and Weir (1985),

Curti (1959), Cohen and Neufeld (1981), Cohen (1984), Reese (1986), and Carnoy and Levin (1985).

5. In my earlier thinking on this issue (Labaree [1988]), I defined these educational goals simply as "democratic politics" and "capitalist markets." I am grateful to David Hogan (personal communication) for pointing out to me that the latter goal consists of two distinct and frequently contradictory market purposes, which I have chosen to identify as social mobility and social efficiency.

6. Many scholars have written about the conflicting purposes embedded within U.S. education, although they have defined and categorized these purposes in a variety of ways that differ from my own approach. In addition to the sources cited in note 4, examples include: Tyack and Cuban (1995), Goodlad (1979, 1984), Boyer (1983, 1987), Fullan (1991, 1993), Paris (1995), Aronowitz and Giroux (1985), Apple (1982), Kozol (1991), Gutmann (1987), de Lone (1979), Cusick (1992), and Connell et al. (1982).

7. The three goals that serve as the focus for this chapter do not encompass all of the goals that Americans have for their schools. There are a number of such additional purposes. Among other things, we ask schools to deliver medical and psychological services, to act as baby-sitters for children and warehouses for surplus adolescent workers, to promote esthetic awareness and physical conditioning, to serve as community centers and a municipal symbol, to foster personal empowerment and healthy social development, and to pursue many other goals as well. I choose to focus on the three goals spelled out here because these goals are particularly important in defining the way in which we talk about and act toward our schools. That is, they are more socially salient and more politically resonant than other educational goals. The reason for this, as I have suggested, is that these goals arise from the basic contradiction between political equality and social inequality that lies at the heart of the American experience.

8. For strong statements of this vision of education, see Gutmann (1987), Barber (1992), Hirsch (1987), Welter (1962), and Meier (1995).

9. Kaestle (1983), Cremin (1980).

10. Meyer et al. (1979).

11. Mann (1848/1957, p. 92).

12. Kaestle (1983), Cremin (1980), Labaree (1988).

13. National Commission on Excellence (1983, p. 7).

14. Gutmann (1987, p. xi), Hirsch (1987).

15. Turner (1960).

16. National Education Goals Panel (1995, p. 11).

17. Mann (1848/1957, pp. 85–87).

18. Katz (1978, 1987), Katznelson and Weir (1985), Labaree (1988).

19. Katznelson and Weir (1985).

20. Labaree (1984a; 1988); also see Chapter 2.

21. Cohen and Neufeld (1981).

22. See Chapter 8.

23. Cohen and Neufeld (1981).

24. See Giddens (1984).

25. Lazerson and Grubb (1974).

26. Cole (1996).

27. National Center for Education Statistics (1995, table 132).

28. Lynd and Lynd (1929, p. 194).

29. National Commission on Excellence (1983, p. 5)

30. National Educational Goals Panel (1995, p. 11).

31. See National Center for Education Statistics (1995, table 33).

32. Oakes (1985).

33. Olson (1971).

34. This is not to say that everyone receives the same benefit. The social efficiency benefit of education is collective, in that everyone receives some payoff from increased productivity and economic growth, but those whom the educational system sorts out early and assigns to the lower social positions benefit markedly less than those who emerge later and end up in higher level positions. In short, social efficiency offers a "trickle down" version of education as a public good.

35. Hirschman (1970).

36. Neoclassical economics argues that the pursuit of individual ambition produces collective benefits to society through the "guiding hand" of the market. From this perspective, there is nothing socially dysfunctional about treating education as a private good for personal gain. My argument in this chapter, however, is that the educational and social consequences of this self-interested approach to education are in fact often (but not always) negative.

37. Green (1980, p. 25).

38. Collins (1979), Boudon (1974).

39. Hogan (1987).

40. Brown (1995), Collins (1979), Labaree (1988), Hogan (1987).

41. Collins (1979, p. 183).

42. Kingston and Lewis (1990), Cookson and Persell (1985), Levine (1986).

43. Kozol (1991), Rubin (1972).

44. Klitgaard (1985).

45. Fox (1993), Griffin and Alexander (1978).

46. Quoted in Eng and Heller (1996).

47. A classic example is the University of Chicago, which decided in the 1980s that it might lose appeal with consumers if it failed to charge as much as its competitors from the Ivy League. As a result, it nearly quadrupled annual tuition between 1980 and 1995, pushing charges to $27,000 (Eng and Heller [1996]).

48. Rosenbaum (1976), Oakes (1985), Griffin and Alexander (1978).

49. Wells and Serna (1996), Cusick (1992).

50. Bourdieu (1986).

51. Oakes (1985), Wells and Serna (1996), Rubin (1972, 1976).

52. Thurow (1977).

53. Spence (1974).

54. Berg (1971).

55. Collins (1979). I am racing quickly through complex territory here, in the process brushing past a number of significant distinctions. Credentialing theory (Collins [1979], Berg [1971]), signaling theory (Spence [1974]), and labor queue theory (Thurow [1977]) all take somewhat different positions on the question of how employers use credentials in

the hiring process. (See Grubb [1993] for a review of this literature.) For my purposes, however, the key point is that for all these scholars the exchange value of educational credentials is not a simple reflection of their human capital content.

56. Becker (1964), Schultz (1961).

57. Collins (1979), Dore (1976), Freeman (1976), Rumberger (1981), Shelley (1992).

58. Steinberg (1996), Sedlak et al. (1986), Powell et al. (1985), Cusick (1983).

59. I use the word *political* in two senses in this chapter. In one sense, as used here, I argue that democratic equality is the most political of the goals because of its focus on mobilizing education to serve the needs of democracy. From this perspective, the other two goals in contrast focus on mobilizing education to meet the needs of the market. But in another sense, I argue that all three goals are elements of the politics of education because they all represent political positions about the role that schools should play. From this perspective, social efficiency promotes the politics of human capital, and social mobility promotes the politics of pluralism (that is, the competition among interest groups over relative shares of political power). I am grateful to an anonymous reviewer for help in sorting out this distinction.

60. Hogan (1987, 1989, 1990c, 1992b), Labaree (1988). Also see Chapter 2.

61. Parsons (1959), Dreeben (1968).

62. Eckert (1989), Connell et al. (1982), MacLeod (1995), Oakes (1985).

63. Bowles and Gintis (1976), Carnoy and Levin (1985).

64. "Normalizing judgment": Foucault (1977).

65. This brief historical sketch draws on work that is elaborated elsewhere: Labaree (1988, 1996) and Hogan (1987, 1990, 1992).

66. Tyack and Cuban (1995).

67. Tyack (1974).

68. Tyack and Cuban (1995) make a strong case for thinking about education change as, at one level, regular swings of policy talk and reform initiatives and, at another level, underlying trends that are more evolutionary than cyclical in nature.

69. Turner (1960).

70. Brown (1995), Trow (1988), Collins (1979). See Chapter 8.

71. Hogan (1989, 1990, 1992), Cohen and Neufeld (1981). See Chapter 9.

72. See Chapter 8.

73. I am grateful to Jay Featherstone and Steve Raudenbush for pointing out to me the powerful political role played by a progressive coalition based on both social mobility and democratic equality goals.

74. Hurn (1985, pp. 135–136).

75. Grubb and Lazerson (1982, p. 52).

76. Clark (1960).

77. Oakes (1985), Church and Sedlak (1976), Lazerson and Grubb (1974), Katznelson and Weir (1985).

78. Dougherty (1994), Brint and Karabel (1989). See Chapters 8 and 9.

79. Turner (1960). U.S. education fits this contest mobility model rather than what James Rosenbaum (1986) called a "tournament mobility" model. The former offers multiple reentry possibilities, while the latter shuts down these possibilities by forcing the student, at each decision point, either to advance to the next level or leave the tournament altogether.

80. Kerckhoff (1993), Oakes (1985), Wells and Serna (1996).

81. I am grateful to a particularly generous anonymous reviewer for showing me how to define concisely the differences in the educational consequences of these two goals.

82. Macpherson (1962).

83. Collins (1979).

84. Katznelson and Weir (1985), Beyer (1994).

85. One telling sign of this change was the move to end the practice of adjusting academic grades in line with a student's conduct. Harvard College and the Central High School of Philadelphia, to cite two examples, both eliminated this practice around 1860 (Labaree [1988], Smallwood [1935]). Henceforth grades, the primary currency of reward within schools, would be pure measures of academic achievement, and conduct would be seen as a simple matter of controlling student behavior for the convenience of school operations.

86. Sedlak et al. (1986, p. 183).

87. Steinberg (1996).

88. The classic essay on the subject is Marx's "The Fetishism of Commodities and the Secret Thereof" in the first volume of *Capital* (Marx [1867/1967]).

89. Goldman and Tickamyer (1984).

90. Different report writers have focused on different causes. The Carnegie Task Force on Teaching (1986), Goodlad (1990, 1994), and the Holmes Group (1986, 1995) pointed to the structure of teaching and the quality of teacher education. The National Commission on Excellence in Education (1983) blamed curriculum, as did a wide range of subject-matter groups issuing proposals for national standards (for example, National Center for History in the Schools [1994], American Association for the Advancement of Science [1990]). A diverse group ranging from Sarason (1990) and Chubb and Moe (1990) to Goodlad (1984) and Boyer (1983) placed particular blame on the organization of schooling. Still others argued that the achievement deficiencies themselves were incorrect or overstated (Berliner and Biddle [1995], Bracey [1995]).

91. For more on this subject, see Steinberg (1996), Sedlak et al. (1986), Powell et al. (1985), Cusick (1983), Labaree (1988), and Meyer and Rowan (1983).

92. Boudon (1974).

93. Sedlak et al. (1986), Powell et al. (1985).

94. Sedlak et al. (1986, p. 182).

95. Labaree (1988); also see Chapter 8.

96. Boudon (1974).

97. Collins (1979), Boudon (1979).

98. Carnoy and Levin (1985).

99. There is modest but growing literature developing different components of what might become a theory of educational credentialing. Boudon (1974) and Collins (1979) explain the basic logic of a credentialist view of education. Dore (1976), Freeman (1976), Rumberger (1981), and Oxenham (1984) examine the scope of the problem credentialism poses and its economic consequences. Grubb and Lazerson (1982) explore the issue of how treating education like a private good affects education, particularly the way it undercuts the motivation for consumers to support the education of "other people's children." Brown (1995) reinforces Collins by showing how the expansion of higher education in the United States occurred primarily in response to consumer demand for

credentials rather than economic demand for useful skills. My own work explores the role of consumer demand and credentialism in shaping the history of high schools, colleges, and teachers colleges (Labaree [1988, 1990, 1995, 1996]), while Hogan's focuses on the effect of the credentials market on school organization, curriculum, and educational stratification (Hogan [1987, 1990, 1992]). Becker et al. (1968) and Richardson et al. (1983) consider the impact of consumerism on student academic behavior in college; Steinberg (1996), Sedlak et al. (1986), and Powell et al. (1985) do the same for elementary and secondary schooling. Thurow's (1977) theory of the labor queue, Berg's (1971) work on business employment practices, and the related economic literature on job signaling (Spence [1973, 1974]) identify the function of credentials as tickets of access and signals of employability whose value is independent of what is actually learned in school.

2. *The Social Meaning of Student Promotion and Retention*

I am grateful to David Hogan for the many stimulating discussions that we have had about issues of markets, merit, and credentials, and I am grateful to Norman Newberg for first prompting me to explore the promotion question many years ago.

1. Labaree (1984a).

2. The federal government has never collected such data, and neither have most states; Shepard and Smith (1989b).

3. Tyack and Cuban (1995, p. 90).

4. Board of Public Education (Philadelphia) (1908–1945).

5. Vinovskis, Angus, and Mirel (1995, p. 190).

6. Shepard and Smith (1989b, pp. 6–7).

7. Alexander, Entwisle, and Dauber (1994, table 1.1).

8. Shepard and Smith (1989b, pp. 7–8).

9. Jackson (1975), Selden (1982), Southwest Educational Development Laboratory (1981).

10. Reiter (1973), Thompson (1980), Haddad (1979), Holmes and Matthews (1984), Holmes (1989).

11. Holmes (1989, pp. 27–28).

12. Shepard and Smith (1989a).

13. House (1989, p. 204).

14. Alexander, Entwisle, and Dauber (1994, pp. 12, 214).

15. Anyone interested in pursuing this topic should examine the books by Alexander and colleagues and by Shepard and Smith; also see the brief commentary on the retention literature by Gary Natriello (1996).

16. Meyer and Rowan (1977, 1983). The designation *ritual classification* is from Meyer and Rowan (1983). For a close analysis of the usefulness of Meyer and Rowan's thesis for an understanding of the history of educational organization, see Hogan (1990c).

17. Quotations from, respectively, Weick (1976) and Meyer and Rowan (1983, p. 71).

18. Meyer and Rowan (1983, pp. 72, 83).

19. Meyer and Rowan (1983, p. 84).

20. Meyer and Rowan (1983, p. 77).

21. House (1989, p. 208).

22. The historical discussion that follows in the next three sections draws heavily on three papers. One, by Maris Vinovskis, David Angus, and Jeffrey Mirel (1995), lays out the basic pattern of historical development of graded schooling in the United States and also defines the shifting pattern of promotion practices within this graded structure. The other two, by David Hogan (1987, 1990a), provide a powerful interpretation of these events in light of meritocratic ideology and stratified credentialing. I strongly recommend that readers examine Hogan's interpretations of these and related events (see Hogan [1987, 1989, 1990a, 1990b, 1992a, 1992b, and 1992c]).

23. Hamilton (1987), Vinovskis, Angus, and Mirel (1995).

24. Hogan (1987, p. 25); quotations from, respectively, Mann (1848/1957, p. 92) and Dunlap (1851, p. 15).

25. For more on the republican origins of the common-school system, see Kaestle (1983), Cremin (1980), Labaree (1988), and Hogan (1987, 1990a).

26. Hogan (1987), Labaree (1988).

27. Samuel Breck, quoted in Hogan (1987, pp. 22–23).

28. See Chapter 1 for a detailed discussion of these three educational goals. A broader sense of education for social efficiency, based on the production of socially useful human capital, was not strongly evident at this point but emerged at the end of the nineteenth century.

29. See Hogan's (1992b) discussion of the origins of the classroom system and the graded structure of schooling.

30. Tyack and Cuban (1995).

31. Metz (1990).

32. For example, as Mary Metz (1990) argues, the schools that most aggressively assert their compliance with the "real school" script are precisely those that are most at variance with it — for example, inner-city schools whose standards for academic achievement are well below average.

33. Hogan (1987, p. 25).

34. Hamilton (1987), Labaree (1984a).

35. Vinovskis, Angus, and Mirel (1995).

36. Kaestle (1973), Hogan (1989, 1990a, 1992b).

37. Vinovskis, Angus, and Mirel (1995, p. 178).

38. Katz (1968), Hogan (1990b).

39. Hogan (1990b).

40. Labaree (1988).

41. Vinovskis, Angus, and Mirel (1995, p. 179).

42. This discussion of the meaning of a high school diploma for the middle class draws heavily on my earlier work on the subject (Labaree [1988]) and also on the analysis of David Hogan (1987, 1992a).

43. Labaree (1988), Hogan (1992a).

44. Labaree (1988), Hogan (1987).

45. Hogan (1987).

46. Pennsylvania Department of Public Instruction (1922, pt. 2, p. 188).

47. Ayres (1908, pp. 96–97).

48. Thorndike (1908).

49. Quoted in Vinovskis, Angus, and Mirel (1995, p. 181).

50. Ayres (1908, p. 199).

51. Hamilton (1989, p. 6) defines this change as a shift from "batch processing" in the earlier structure to a system of processing according to "individual differences" in the structure that evolved at the turn of the century.

52. This analysis of the benefits offered by the new system of graded schooling for middle-class consumers draws heavily on David Hogan's interpretation of this subject (Hogan [1987]) and on my own work (Labaree [1988]).

53. Hogan (1987) calls the earlier unified and merit-based system "contest mobility," drawing on Turner's (1960) phrase, and he calls the later system "stratified credentialing."

54. Vinovskis, Angus, and Mirel (1995).

55. National Commission on Excellence (1983, p. 30).

56. National Education Goals Panel (1995, p. 11).

57. Gerstner quoted in Toch (1996); Clinton (1996).

58. Hurt (1996).

59. Dao (1996).

60. See Chapter 1 for further discussion of this issue.

61. Hogan (1992a, p. 192), citing Howe (1988) and Murphy and Welch (1989).

62. Collins (1979).

63. Thurow (1977, p. 333), quoted in Hogan (1992a, p. 192).

64. Shelley (1992, pp. 13–14).

65. Shelley (1992, p. 17).

66. The strategies cited appear to have strong public support. In a March 1996 poll by *U.S. News and World Report* (U.S. News School Standards Poll [1996]), 75 percent of respondents supported higher academic standards in schools and 87 percent favored requiring an academic examination to qualify for graduation from high school.

The continuing rise in rates of high school graduation and college attendance during the 1990s only serves to reinforce consumer demand for enhanced forms of academic distinction, because such academic attainments as a high school diploma and a college transcript are becoming increasingly commonplace.

67. This is a very rough estimate based on the data presented by Shepard and Smith (1989b, p. 7); there are no reliable national data on nonpromotion.

68. Shepard and Smith (1989b, pp. 6–7).

69. "Real school": Metz (1990).

70. Oakes (1985).

71. Hogan (1987) refers to the system's capacity for fostering success among those in the upper tracks as a form of sponsored mobility, in contrast with the contest mobility that characterized the earlier system. These terms come from Turner (1960). The notion of success as a self-fulfilling prophecy for middle-class students is from Rist (1970).

72. Meyer and Rowan (1983).

3. Raising Standards in the American High School

This chapter is a revised version of a paper published as "Academic Excellence in a U.S. High School" in *Social Problems* 31, 558–567. Copyright © 1984 by the Society for the

Study of Social Problems; reprinted by permission. It is based on research that was supported in part by the National Institute of Education (grant 9–0173; Michael Katz, principal investigator). I am grateful to Michael Katz and David Hogan for their comments on an early version of this paper.

1. Major reports from this period that sounded the theme of excellence include: Adler (1982), Boyer (1983), Coleman et al. (1982), Goodlad (1984), National Commission on Excellence (1983), Sizer (1984), Task Force on Education (1983), Twentieth Century Fund (1983).

2. National Commission on Excellence (1983, p. 5).

3. National Commission on Excellence (1983, p. 8).

4. National Center for Education Statistics (1995, table 124).

5. National Center for Education Statistics (1995, tables 3 and 178).

6. Berliner and Biddle (1995, p. 21).

7. National Commission on Excellence (1983, p. 8), Husen (1983).

8. Berliner and Biddle (1995, p. 54).

9. National Commission on Excellence (1983, pp. 18–19).

10. Angus and Mirel (1995, table 12.1).

11. National Commission on Excellence (1983, pp. 19–21).

12. See Chapter 2.

13. Angus and Mirel (1995, table 12.1).

14. National Center for Education Statistics (1995, table 132).

15. Nonpromotion rates: Alexander et al. (1994, table 1.1).

16. Bracey (1995, p. 153).

17. Sedlak et al. (1986), Powell et al. (1985), Labaree (1988).

18. Krug (1964, 1972).

19. Counts (1969), Katz (1968), Perlmann (1988), Troen (1975), Ueda (1987), Reese (1995), Vinovskis (1995).

20. Labaree (1988).

21. Board of Public Education (1871, p. 29).

22. Quotation from National Commission on Excellence (1983, p. 18).

23. Labaree (1988, chapter 6).

24. Board of Public Education (1880).

25. Katz and Davey (1978).

26. Labaree (1988, table 3.2).

27. Labaree (1983, table 1.1).

28. Labaree (1983, tables 3.11 and 4.13, p. 307).

29. Labaree (1983, table 3.5).

30. Labaree (1988, p. 54).

31. Labaree (1988, tables 3.6–3.8).

32. Board of Public Education (1880).

33. Dunlap (1851, pp. 15–16), emphasis in original.

34. Edmonds (1902, pp. 319–349), Labaree (1988, chapter 5).

35. Bache (1859, p. 7).

36. National Center for Educational Statistics (1995, table 148).

37. Coleman and Hoffer (1987), Salganik and Karweit (1982).

38. MacLeod (1995), Ogbu (1974).

39. Coleman et al. (1982), Coleman and Hoffer (1987), Bryk et al. (1993).

40. Gamoran (1996); *Sociology of Education* 55:2/3 (1982), Special issue on Coleman, Hoffer, and Kilgore's report "Public and private schools."

41. National Commission on Excellence (1983, p. 22).

42. U.S. Bureau of the Census (1993, table 243).

43. Labaree (1988, chapter 5).

44. Board of Public Education (1880).

45. See Chapter 7 for more on this subject.

46. National Center for Education Statistics (1995, table 98), National Education Goals Panel (1995, vol. 1, p. 45).

47. See Dorn (1996) and Kett (1995) for more historical background on the rise of dropping out as a social problem.

48. Cohen and Neufeld (1981).

49. National Commission on Excellence (1983, p. 12).

4. The Middle Class and the High School

This chapter is a substantially revised version of a paper that was previously published as "Curriculum, Credentials, and the Middle Class: A Case Study of Nineteenth-Century High School" in *Sociology of Education* 59 (January 1986), 42–57. An earlier version was presented at the 1984 meeting of the American Sociological Association in Washington, D.C. The research for this chapter was supported in part by the National Institute of Education (grant 9–0173; Michael Katz, principal investigator). I want to thank David Hogan for contributing many of the ideas that appear here.

1. The functional and meritocratic perspective has its roots in the work of Emile Durkheim (1933). Central writings in this vein include Davis and Moore (1945), Becker (1975), and Parsons (1959). The social reproduction perspective has its roots in the work of Karl Marx (1867/1967). Prime examples of writing in this vein include Bowles and Gintis (1976), Bourdieu and Passeron (1977), and Apple (1979).

2. The analysis that follows draws heavily on my book about Central High School (Labaree [1988]), especially chapter 6.

3. Whereas meritocratic theory draws on Durkheim and reproduction theory draws on Marx, this market-based perspective on the relation between school and society draws inspiration from the work of Max Weber (1968). Major examples of writings in this vein include Collins (1979), Berg (1971), Sedlak et al. (1986), and Hogan (1987).

4. Central's leaders, who were well aware of the school's social importance, kept a complete record of its activities for posterity, and these records serve as the basis for this analysis. They include a set of published annual reports written by various principals (Philadelphia Board of Public Education [1840–1915]), a complete set of detailed faculty-meeting minutes from 1840 to the present, three published histories (Cliff [1888], Edmonds [1902], Cornog [1952]), and the records of all students who ever attended the school. I drew a sample of about two thousand students from the latter source, choosing those who entered in federal census years from 1840 to 1920. When possible, these school records were linked to the students' family records from census manuscripts (U.S. Bureau of the Census [1850–1900]). This discussion draws heavily on the more complete analysis in Labaree (1988).

5. Board of Public Education (1843, p. 65). The school's principals were known as presidents during the nineteenth and early twentieth centuries.

6. Labaree (1986, table 1).

7. Labaree (1986, table 1).

8. Dunlap (1851, p. 16), emphasis in original.

9. Labaree (1986, table 2). Class membership was ascertained from the occupational titles indicated on school records and census manuscripts. The proprietary middle class consists of self-employed individuals, including proprietors, master artisans, and professionals; the employed middle class consists of white-collar employees; the skilled working class consists of skilled workers who were not self-employed; the unskilled working class consists of semiskilled and unskilled workers. Persons whose occupational title was missing or unclassifiable are included in the "missing and other" category.

10. Labaree (1986, table 3).

11. MCA is a form of multiple regression analysis that permits the use of categorical (as opposed to continuous) independent variables. It is useful here for showing that the powerful impact of grades and the weak impact of social class on chances for graduation do not change when considered in combination with each other and with a variety of other possible causes; see Labaree (1988, tables 3.6, 3.7, and 3.8). One statistical note about this analysis: the use of a binary dependent variable (graduated, did not graduate) violates the assumption of homoscedasticity that is required for regression analysis. Although some have argued that regression should not be used in such cases (e.g., Kousser, Cox, and Galenson [1982]), I feel that its use is justified here. First, as Bohrnstedt and Carter (1971) have argued, regression is a remarkably robust procedure even when its assumptions (except for measurement error) are violated. Second, the primary effects of heteroscedasticity are an increase in the variance of the regression estimates and bias in the tests of significance. But because I use MCA primarily to establish gross differences between variables (via the betas) rather than fine differences in graduation rates, and because I base no conclusions on the significance tests, these effects pose no problem for the analysis. Third, graduation is the best available variable for measuring educational attainment. The number of terms a student has been enrolled in school confounds achievement (promotion) with failure (repeating a grade). The highest grade level achieved would provide a multilevel measure of achievement, but it is not available for most years. Finally, students' educational attainment was more dichotomous than continuous: students either dropped out in the first two years or they graduated. When I performed the same MCAs with the other two dependent variables, the relative importance of all the key factors remained the same.

12. Labaree (1986, table 6).

13. Rothman (1971), Scull (1977), Trattner (1979), Ryan (1981), Johnson (1978), Gusfield (1963), and Kaestle (1983).

14. Kaestle (1983), Tyack and Hansot (1982).

15. Quotation from Board of Public Education (1853, p. 125).

16. Board of Public Education (1850, p. 118).

17. Connell et al. (1983, p. 42).

18. Harvard College took a similar step ten years later, ranking students by grades alone (Rudolph [1962, p. 348]).

19. Board of Public Education (1859, p. 133).

20. Labaree (1988, chapter 4).

21. This was especially true between Central High School and its local rival, the University of Pennsylvania. During this period, the average age of admission was 16 at Penn and 14.5 at Central. Because there was a wide range of ages at each school, there was considerable overlap (Burke [1982, p. 116]).

22. Collins (1979, pp. 119–121).

23. Johnson (1978).

24. Ryan (1981, p. 152).

25. Labaree (1986, table 7).

26. Bledstein (1976).

27. Kett (1977, p. 154).

28. Veysey (1965).

29. Labaree (1986, table 1).

30. Labaree (1986, table 8). For a thorough examination of the market-driven transformation of curriculum and the structure of credentialing in Philadelphia at the turn of the century, see the work of David Hogan (1987; also 1990c, 1992a).

5. The Carnegie Cult of Social Efficiency

This chapter is a revised version of an essay previously published as "A Kinder and Gentler Report: Turning Points and the Carnegie Tradition" in *Journal of Education Policy* 5 (1990), 249–264. Reprinted by permission of Taylor and Francis. A version of the essay was presented at the annual meeting of the History of Education Society in Atlanta in 1991. I am grateful to Barry Franklin for suggesting the idea of writing about this report, and I am grateful to Cleo Cherryholmes, Eliot Singer, and Lauren Young for their helpful comments on an early draft. The title of this chapter plays off the title of Raymond Callaghan's influential book *Education and the Cult of Efficiency* (1962), which examined the prominence of scientific management and social efficiency in the reform efforts of educational administrators during the early part of the twentieth century.

1. Task Force on Education of Young Adolescents (1989).

2. See, for example, Bowles and Gintis (1976), Karier (1978), and Spring (1989).

3. Task Force on Teaching as a Profession (1986).

4. I treat the Foundation and the Corporation as essentially interchangeable here. This seems reasonable, given the perpetual dependency of the Foundation on the Corporation for money and the continuing willingness of the Corporation to support the Foundation's educational initiatives. From 1955 to 1979, the two organizations even shared a president.

5. Pifer (1984, pp. 107–108).

6. Lagemann (1983).

7. Pifer (1984, p. 114).

8. Lagemann (1987, p. 220).

9. This brief historical review of the nature of Carnegie educational philanthropies draws heavily on Ellen Condliffe Lagemann's perceptive histories of the Carnegie Foundation for the Advancement of Teaching (1983) and the Carnegie Corporation (1987, 1989), the only full-length scholarly assessments of the subject. Other sources on the

Foundation include Howard Savage's official history of its first half century (1953) and Alan Pifer's reflections on the first seventy-five years (1979). Additional sources include Abraham Flexner's biography of Henry S. Pritchett (1943) and Pifer's review of Corporation activities in the 1950s and 1960s (1984). Finally, I have looked selectively at annual reports of both organizations and at books and reports they have commissioned. Given my aims for this chapter, I did not delve systematically into the primary sources on Carnegie activities, sources that Lagemann examined extensively. As a historical sociologist rather than a historian, my main interest in this exploration is to focus on the process by which social efficiency concerns have shaped U.S. education, using Carnegie reports as cases in point.

    10. Lagemann (1983, pp. 21–22).

    11. Quoted in Lagemann (1983, p. 32).

    12. Church and Sedlak (1976).

    13. Looking back on these events seven decades later, President Alan Pifer complained about the emergence of a "powerful mythology" that, through the creation of the Carnegie unit, the Foundation had taken on the role of a "standardizing agency." Yet he then proudly pointed out "the tremendously important role that the free pension program played in helping to define American higher education. . . . The changes made by a number of institutions to qualify for the pension influenced other institutions of their states and regions and produced a general upgrading of higher education and also of secondary education as high schools sought to meet the new entrance standards" (Pifer [1979, pp. 16–17]).

When the Foundation discovered that the pension program was outstripping its limited resources, it established in 1918 a self-perpetuating and contributory agency for carrying on this function, the Teachers Insurance Annuity Association (TIAA), which has helped provide a sound financial base for the expansion of American higher education in the twentieth century.

    14. Brint and Karabel (1989, p. 47).

    15. Brint and Karabel (1989, pp. 51–52). For a discussion of the historical origins of the current pattern of stratification in higher education, see Chapter 8.

    16. Carnegie Commission on Higher Education (1973).

    17. Carnegie Commission on Higher Education (1973, p. 30). In an earlier report, the commission had asserted "that public two-year community colleges should be actively discouraged by state planning and financial policies from becoming four-year institutions." The reason? "Concern that, if two-year colleges become four-year colleges, they will place less emphasis on occupational programs and thus leave an unmet need in the local community" (Carnegie Commission on Higher Education [1970, pp. 15–16]).

    18. Quoted in Carnegie Commission on Higher Education (1973, p. 30).

    19. Pifer (1979, p. 33).

    20. McDonald (1973, p. 33).

    21. Lagemann (1989, pp. 253–263).

    22. Lagemann (1983), Savage (1953).

    23. Pifer (1984).

    24. Conant (1959, p. 49).

    25. Task Force on Teaching (1986, p. 2).

26. "Science of education": Holmes Group (1986, p. 52).

27. The antibureaucratic impulse thrives despite the fact that there is a serious question about just how effective school bureaucracies are in controlling the way teachers teach. See, for example, Bidwell (1965), Lortie (1975), and Meyer and Rowan (1983).

28. Cherryholmes (1987, p. 504).

29. Bradley (1994).

30. Task Force on Education (1989, p. 12).

31. Task Force on Education (1989, pp. 27–29).

32. Task Force on Education (1989, p. 15).

33. Task Force on Education (1989, p. 58).

34. Task Force on Education (1980, pp. 49–50).

35. Task Force on Education (1989, p. 50).

36. Task Force on Education (1989, pp. 50–52).

37. Nielsen (1972, p. 42).

38. Pifer (1984, p. 202).

39. Silberman (1970), Jencks et al. (1972).

40. Lagemann (1983, p. 192). The change is striking if one compares the more recent panels with the Commission on Higher Education, whose "members were, with one exception, either industrialists or highly placed college administrators. All were white, there was only one woman, and only one person was younger than 45. When they looked at each other across the table, each commission member saw a reflection of himself" (Wolfe [1971, p. 20]).

41. Meier (1995).

42. Pifer (1984, pp. 227–228).

43. Myrdal (1944), Keniston (1977), de Lone (1979).

44. Cohen and Neufeld (1981, p. 82).

6. Rethinking the Movement to Professionalize Teaching

This chapter is a revised version of an essay that was previously published as "Power, Knowledge, and the Science of Teaching: A Genealogy of Teacher Professionalization" in *Harvard Educational Review,* 62 (2), 123–154. Copyright © 1992 by the President and Fellows of Harvard College. All rights reserved. Reprinted by permission. I am grateful to the following colleagues for their comments on earlier drafts of this paper: Andrew Abbott, Barbara Beatty, Cleo Cherryholmes, Christopher Clark, David Cohen, Mark Conley, Philip Cusick, Stephen Esquith, Jay Featherstone, Susan Florio-Ruane, David Hogan, Diane Holt-Reynolds, Timothy Lensmire, Susan Melnick, Mary Metz, Stephen Raudenbush, Laura Roehler, Brian Rowan, Michael Sedlak, and Bruce VanSledright. In 1990, I presented an early version of this paper in a colloquium at the Michigan State University College of Education and at the annual meeting of the American Sociological Association in Washington, D.C.; in 1991, I presented a later version of the paper at the University of Western Ontario and the University of Wisconsin.

1. The group was named after Henry W. Holmes, dean of the Harvard Graduate School of Education during the 1920s, who argued that "the training of teachers is a highly significant part of the making of the nation" (Holmes Group [1986, p. 24]).

2. Task Force on Teaching (1986, p. 2).

3. The present pattern of medical education emerged early in the twentieth century, propelled in part by the famous Flexner report (1910), which, like *A Nation Prepared* and *Tomorrow's Teachers,* was supported by Carnegie funding (see Chapter 5).

4. The Carnegie and Holmes efforts have been closely coordinated from the beginning. The only education school dean on the Carnegie panel, Judith Lanier from Michigan State University, was also the organizer and later president of the Holmes Group. As these reform efforts gathered momentum, they reached out from their original bases (educational policymakers and teacher educators, respectively) and increasingly began to draw from the same network of national-level leaders in education, teacher education, government, business, labor, and foundations.

5. Two scholars in particular, Gary Sykes and Lee Shulman, have written about these patterns as part of an effort to establish the historical basis for the Carnegie and Holmes Group proposals (Shulman [1986], Shulman and Sykes [1986], Sykes [1986, 1987, 1990]).

6. Abbott (1988, p. 8).

7. For example, Parsons (1939/1954).

8. Abbott (1988).

9. For a more extended discussion of many of these points see Lortie (1975), Cohen (1988), Freidson (1986, pp. 223–225), Sykes (1986, 1990), Labaree (1996b), Holmes Group (1986), Carnegie Task Force on Teaching (1986).

10. Sykes (1986).

11. Sykes (1990).

12. After issuing three reports over ten years — *Tomorrow's Teachers* (1986), *Tomorrow's Schools* (1990), and *Tomorrow's Schools of Education* (1995) — the Holmes Group membership in 1996 voted to reconstitute itself as the Holmes Partnership, focusing on professional development partnerships between colleges of education and schools (Bradley [1996]).

13. Task Force on Teaching (1986, p. 21).

14. For functionalist sociology approaches, see Carr-Saunders and Wilson (1933), Parsons (1939/1954).

15. Densmore (1987), Noble (1977).

16. Foucault (1965, 1977).

17. Collins (1979), Larson (1977).

18. Sykes (1986, 1990).

19. Rooted in the work of Friedrich Nietzsche and elaborated in the last quarter century by Michel Foucault, genealogy is "a form of history which can account for the constitution of knowledges, discourses, domains of objects, etc., without having to make reference to a subject which is either transcendental in relation to the field of events or runs in its empty sameness throughout the course of history" (Foucault [1980, p. 117]).

That is, "it rejects the metahistorical deployment of ideal significations and indefinite teleologies. It opposes itself to the search for 'origins' " (Foucault [1984, p. 77]). Refusing to explain a historical event by means of constructs abstracted from historical context, genealogy seeks to establish the lines of descent that led to the event. The genealogist also resists the tendency to search for the "timeless and essential secret" behind things and thus uncovers "the secret that they have no essence or that their essence was fabricated in a piecemeal fashion from alien forms" (Foucault [1984, p. 78]). As one interpreter put it, in the end one must learn to treat each historical "element" as something that "is made up of components belonging to antecedent elements" (Noujain [1987, p. 167]). Doing genealogy, then, means identifying the preexisting components that constitute the historical event under consideration.

20. Elie Noujain points out that one of the advantages of this approach is that with it, "value judgments [can] be directly embedded in the genealogic narrative" (1987, p. 172). That is, "genealogy makes it possible to show that what might be today passed off as acceptable and good might, equally by today's standards, turn out to possess an objectionable 'ancestry' " (p. 169).

21. See Chapter 1.

22. National Commission on Excellence (1983), Task Force on Education for Economic Growth (1983), Twentieth Century Fund (1983).

23. Passow (1989).

24. Task Force on Teaching (1986, p. 21), Holmes Group (1990).

25. Elmore and McLaughlin (1988, p. v).

26. Lortie (1969, 1975), Tyack (1974).

27. Task Force on the Education of Young Adolescents (1989), Elmore et al. (1990), Sizer (1985).

28. Holmes Group (1986, p. 4).

29. Chubb and Moe (1990).

30. Task Force on Teaching (1986, p. 67).

31. Shulman and Sykes (1986).

32. Feiman-Nemser and Floden (1986), Lortie (1973), Patrick, Griswold, and Roberson (1985), Strober and Tyack (1980), Weiler (1988).

33. Sedlak (1989), Sedlak and Schlossman (1986).

34. Carnegie Task Force on Teaching (1986, pp. 26–31), Holmes Group (1986, pp. 331–336).

35. Weiler (1988).

36. Greene (1988), Grumet (1988), Kristeva (1988).

37. See Susan Laird (1988) for a useful look at alternative ways of thinking about the femaleness of teaching.

38. "Pumpkins and firewood": Holmes Group (1986, p. 8); Sedlak (1989), Elsbree (1939).

39. Elsbree (1939).

40. Sykes (1990, p. 70).

41. See Randall Collins (1979) for a full-length discussion of the growing problem of credential inflation in the competition for social status.

42. Larson (1977).

43. Holmes Group (1986; quotations from, respectively, pp. 63, 50, 51–52).

44. Holmes Group (1986, p. 6). For the purposes of this chapter, I am defining teacher educators quite narrowly — that is, as the faculty members in colleges of education who teach teacher candidates. This excludes from consideration the rest of the undergraduate university faculty, who also share in the education of teachers by providing instruction in general education and in subject-matter majors. Only about a quarter of an elementary

teacher's education occurs at the hands of the education school faculty; for high school teachers the proportion is even smaller. But I am choosing to focus on the education school faculty because it is they, and not the liberal arts faculty, who are pushing for the professionalization of teaching, and it is they who have the greatest stake in the outcome of this effort.

45. Lanier and Little (1986, p. 531).

46. Guba and Clark (1978), cited by Lanier and Little (1986, p. 531).

47. Holmes Group (1986, p. 91); emphasis in the original has been removed.

48. A more detailed account of the historical weakness of teacher educators within the U.S. university can be found in Chapter 9.

49. Lanier and Little (1986).

50. It should be noted that a small number of teachers continue to receive preparation at four-year colleges, where the faculty are more inclined to see themselves as educators rather than teacher educators and to eschew university status and the research orientation that accompanies it.

51. Tom (1984), Liston and Zeichner (1991).

52. Callaghan (1962), Tyack and Hansot (1982).

53. Powell (1976).

54. Cuban (1984).

55. Gage (1963), Travers (1973), Wittrock (1986).

56. Holmes Group (1986, pp. 29–30).

57. Lortie (1975).

58. Lanier and Little (1986), Cohen (1988).

59. Cohen (1987).

60. Britzman (1986).

61. I draw on Toulmin (1990) here because he provides a recent, sweeping, and accessible critique of formal rationality in modern thought. For other critiques, see Rorty (1979, 1989), Cherryholmes (1988), and Foucault (1977, 1980, 1984).

62. Toulmin (1990, pp. 30–35).

63. Weber (1968).

64. Tom (1984). I am grateful to Stephen Raudenbush and David Cohen for pointing out to me some of the earlier efforts at establishing a science of teaching.

65. Dewey (1929, pp. 30, 19).

66. Gage (1963).

67. Gage (1963, preface).

68. Travers (1973).

69. This development helped spur a phenomenal growth within AERA generally. At its annual meeting in 1965, only eighty sessions were offered; in 1990 there were one thousand. In 1965, the organization had six divisions and no special-interest groups; in 1990, it had eleven divisions and ninety-eight special-interest groups (AERA [1990, p. 9]).

70. Gage (1989), Gage and Needels (1989), Gage (1978), Gage and Berliner (1989).

71. Shulman (1986).

72. See Cherryholmes (1988), for a convincing analysis and critique of the scientific paradigm in educational research. His arguments have exerted a strong impact on my view of the field.

73. Gage (1978).
74. Shulman (1986, p. 21).
75. Kuhn (1970).
76. I refer to this paradigm as "scientistic" rather than scientific because of the way it reifies science into a method for establishing abstract and timeless truth. By contrast, a practitioner of mere science is content to make claims that are more limited and tentative.
77. Shulman (1986, pp. 29, 31).
78. Lindblom (1990).
79. "Disciplinary power": Foucault (1977).
80. Holmes Group (1990), Labaree (1992b).
81. In a strange turn of events, the leadership of the Holmes Group in 1995 issued a third report, *Tomorrow's Schools of Education,* which disavowed much of the main argument laid out in *Tomorrow's Teachers.* In particular, the report denounced elite education schools for their predilection toward academic research and their disdain for schools, and it demanded that these institutions subordinate their research and teaching efforts to concerns arising from the classroom practice of teachers. Disenchantment with the tone and content of the report among Holmes Group members contributed to the restructuring of the organization and its eventual mutation into the Holmes Partnership. For a discussion of this turnaround and its implications, see Labaree (1995), Labaree and Pallas (1996), Murray (1996), and Bradley (1996).
82. I am grateful to Stephen Raudenbush for pointing out how to define the analytical significance of these two factors.
83. Toulmin (1990).
84. Lortie (1969), Meyer and Rowan (1978).
85. Holmes Group (1986, pp. 28–31).
86. Cherryholmes (1987, p. 504).
87. Labaree (1992b).
88. Beyer and Zeichner (1987), Giroux and McLaren (1987).
89. Sykes (1990), Gutmann (1987).

7. *Career Ladders and the Early Schoolteacher*

This chapter is a revised version of an essay previously published as "Career Ladders and the Early Public High School Teacher: A Study in Inequality and Opportunity," in Donald R. Warren (ed.), *American Teachers: Histories of a Profession at Work.* Reprinted by permission of Macmillan Reference USA, a Division of Simon and Schuster. Copyright © 1989 by American Educational Research Association. An early version of this essay was presented at the 1988 meeting of the American Educational Research Association in New Orleans, and a later version was presented at the 1989 meeting of the History of Education Society in Toronto. I am grateful to the following colleagues for their comments and suggestions on an earlier version of this chapter: Bill Reese, James Fraser, Donald Warren, Cleo Cherryholmes, Michael Sedlak, and Michael Apple.

1. For example, Lortie (1975).
2. Holmes Group (1986), Task Force on Education (1986).
3. Holmes Group (1986, p. 36).

4. To study career ladders, one must examine a series of individual career histories and look for the patterns within them. The major sources I used to uncover these career histories of high school teachers included their own published memoirs, correspondence, and diaries and biographical sketches provided by colleagues, children, and former students. These kinds of sources pose some obvious difficulties. They strongly favor the most successful high school teachers, for these are the ones who were most likely to publish their memoirs and to be remembered by others in print. For the most part, the subjects I found made education a career. Yet Thorndike (1909) found that the modal high school teacher in 1907 had only three years of experience; most people, especially the women, passed through the occupation quickly. The voice of these more typical short-timers is missing from this study. For a study of career ladders, however, it is precisely the careerists who should be the objects of analysis, for we need to look at the ones who climbed the ladder, rather than those who stepped off after the first rung.

5. U.S. Bureau of Education (1894, tables 1 and 19).

6. Sketches are derived from Bradford (1932), Hanus (1937), Ingram (1954), and Fuller (1977), respectively.

7. This book is written as a memoir, not a historical record, and as a result there are very few dates in it. Some can be inferred, but for the most part the passage of time is recorded in a thoroughly impressionistic fashion.

8. Ingram (1954, p. 271).

9. Ingram (1954, p. 284).

10. Ingram (1954, p. 289).

11. Fuller (1977, p. 451).

12. Fuller (1977, p. 463).

13. Fuller (1977, pp. 469–470).

14. Fuller (1977, p. 471).

15. One answer to this problem was for rural areas to create consolidated high schools. But the issue of consolidation created conflict within rural communities over whether to build such a high school (which would be accredited and graded and blessed with a substantial faculty and an appropriate facility) or to keep the small, unaccredited high schools that were more accessible locally. Localism tended to win out because, in the absence of good transportation, the residents of the town where the consolidated school was located tended to benefit from it much more than did the surrounding farmers. See, for example, Balyeat (1959/1960).

16. Coffman (1911).

17. Labaree (1989a, table 6.1).

18. The figures are for 1880; Tyack and Strober (1981).

19. Thorndike (1909, pp. 13–14).

20. Labaree (1989a, table 6.2).

21. Cotton (1904).

22. Given the ease with which a school district could assign a grammar school teacher part-time to teach a few "advanced" courses to a small number of students, then call this a high school operation, data on the exact number of high schools were difficult to obtain and varied according to the compiler's definition of what it took to be considered the equivalent of such a school.

23. Labaree (1989a, table 6.3).

24. Average salaries ranged from $520 to $1,100; the latter was at Indianapolis Short-ridge High School, founded in 1853.

25. Labaree (1989a, table 6.4).

26. Johnson (1943).

27. Labaree (1989a, table 6.4).

28. Thorndike (1909, p. 41).

29. Thorndike (1909, pp. 16–17).

30. Metcalf (1892).

31. Labaree (1989a, table 6.5).

32. Labaree (1989a, table 6.6).

33. Edmonds (1902, pp. 319–349), Labaree (1983, table 2.2).

34. Ferriss (1922, p. 105). He also found that the median salary for teachers was only $1,222 (p. 108).

35. Ferriss (1925, pp. 2, 13).

36. Rufi (1926, p. 63).

37. Pannell (1933, pp. 33, 36, 39).

38. Rufi (1926, p. 50).

39. In 1890, only 9 out of 59 high schools in Connecticut were located in separate buildings; in Illinois, only 38 out of 258 were thus differentiated (Sizer [1964, pp. 39–40]).

40. Sources, respectively, are Magill (1907), Swett (1969), Thomas (1914), Lord (1954), Reese (1929), Johnson (1943), Beaumont (1957), Boss (1954), Taylor (1961), and Rasey (1953). Dates and locations are difficult to determine from this last impressionistic account.

41. Rasey (1953, pp. 137, 139).

42. Coffman (1911, pp. 38–39), Thorndike (1909, pp. 13–14).

43. National Education Association (1905, pp. 16, 106–114). The average figures are for communities larger than eight thousand.

44. Labaree (1989a, tables 6.7 and 6.8).

45. Cotton (1904, p. 194), Ferriss (1925, p. 2).

46. Ferriss (1925, pp. 16, 18–19).

47. In a collection of biographical sketches of Michigan educators in 1900 one can find a sizable number of female high school principals listed, but they almost always worked in the smallest communities (Caro, Vassar, Blissfield, Allegan, Constantine, Norway, and so on), and six retained major teaching responsibilities (Educators of Michigan [1900]).

48. Swett (1969).

49. Stuart (1949).

50. Gildart and Lord (1957).

51. Coffman's analysis would seem to contradict the importance of education to occupational mobility. He argues that for teachers in general in 1909 "there is no uniform tendency or relation existing between salary and education." But he notes that it is the first four years of school after the elementary level (the high school years) that have little career impact. He found, however, that the "correlation between salary and education becomes increasingly marked with each succeeding year after the fourth year." It is precisely this more advanced level of education that those teachers sought who aspired to

positions in the high school and beyond (Coffman [1911, p. 45]). Thorndike (1909, p. 41) found a strong relation between the education and pay of high school teachers.

52. John Rury (1986) has argued this point for teachers in general at the turn of the century, analyzing teachers listed in the 1900 census public-use sample.

53. Nightingale (1896).

54. These averages are at best rough estimates. Some superintendents reported an average pay, but others simply reported two or three pay levels without indicating how many teachers earned each amount. In the latter case, I simply computed the average between the high and low figures, although this probably biases the result upward.

55. Strober and Langford (1986) found that in the largely urban school systems where schools were formalized (graded, with a longer school year and more credentials required for teaching), the proportion of female teachers was higher, and so was the pay differential between men and women.

56. Nightingale (1896, p. 92).

57. National Education Association (1905, pp. 16, 106–114).

58. Nightingale (1896, pp. 89–90).

59. Strober and Best (1979).

60. Powell (1976).

61. Urban (1982).

62. Redcay (1935, pp. 57, 63).

63. Bullock (1967, table 4).

64. This discussion of meritocratic ideology and career advancement owes a considerable amount to a book by David Tyack and Elisabeth Hansot (1982).

65. Especially for men in the mid-nineteenth century, this entrepreneurship frequently took the form of establishing proprietary schools. It was a common practice for men to gain experience and a following through teaching in the public schools, then cash in by going private. For example, Anson D. P. Van Buren (1889), after teaching in a variety of public schools, took over the proprietary Battle Creek (Michigan) High School in 1849. Then, a year later, at the urging of local authorities, he merged his school into the public Battle Creek Union School and took over as head. But in 1851 he set up his own select high school in town.

66. For an elaboration of this point in relation to one prominent example of such a school, the Central High School of Philadelphia, see Labaree (1988, chapter 4).

8. The Rise of the Community College

This chapter is a revised version of an essay published as "From Comprehensive High School to Community College: Politics, Markets, and the Evolution of Educational Opportunity," in Ronald G. Corwin (ed.), *Research on Sociology of Education and Socialization* (9 [1990], 203–240). Reprinted with permission of the publisher, JAI Press, Inc., Greenwich, Connecticut, and London. An early version of this essay was presented at the 1989 meeting of the American Educational Research Association in San Francisco. I would like to thank the following colleagues for their helpful comments on an earlier draft of this paper: David Cohen, Michael Sedlak, Robert Church, Cleo Cherryholmes, and Eliot Singer. I owe a special debt to David Hogan for his stimulating insights and fruitful suggestions, which had a substantial impact on the way I came to understand the argument I am making here.

1. U.S. Bureau of the Census (1975, series H424), Collins (1979, table 1.1).

2. In this chapter, I use the terms *public junior college* and *community college* interchangeably. The former is the original name given to this institution at the start of the twentieth century, while the latter is the name that came to be applied to it after the Second World War.

3. National Center for Education Statistics (1987, table 102).

4. U.S. Bureau of the Census (1987, table 233).

5. The historians of higher education have largely tended to ignore the public junior college, restricting themselves to a brief discussion or a few passing references. For example, see Brubacher and Rudy (1968, pp. 258–267), Rudolph (1962, pp. 351, 443, 463, 476, and 487), and Veysey (1965, p. 338). Until recently, the closest to a good book-length critical evaluation of junior college history was an interesting monograph by Goodwin (1973) on the history of junior college ideology (available only as an ERIC document). After I drafted this essay in 1989, two major works dealing with the history of the community college appeared in print. Brint and Karabel's 1989 book combines a perceptive general history of the community college with a case study of the institution's recent development in Massachusetts, focusing in particular on the factors that shifted the focus of these colleges from transfer to terminal programs, thereby bringing about what they call "the diverted dream." Dougherty's book (1994) provides an insightful analysis of the evolution of this "contradictory college," portraying college leaders as actors seeking to position their institutions advantageously in a difficult political and social environment. The arguments in both of these books are generally compatible with the arguments I develop in this chapter.

Other useful but less analytically enlightening general sources include Diener's collection of historical documents (1986), Brick's uncritical history of the American Association of Junior Colleges (1963), and Palinchak's unfocused and chaotically organized account of the "evolution of the community college" (1973). The most widespread and accessible historical information, however, is buried within books or articles intended as general overviews of the junior college as an institution. In this category, only a few authors attempt a serious historical analysis: Karabel (1972) provides a good brief review of the history of vocational-terminal education in junior colleges; Zwerling (1976) offers an interesting though less rigorous evaluation of the same subject; Levine (1986) includes an excellent chapter on the junior college between world wars; and Dougherty (1988) gives an informative account of the process of community college expansion.

The rest of these historical fragments appear in works whose primary purpose is to promote the community college movement. Examples include Thornton (1960), Fields (1962), Cohen and Brawer (1982), Bogue (1950), Yarrington (1969), and Eells (1931, 1941). As avid boosters, these authors use history to legitimize the institution and mobilize support for its future expansion. They have contributed to a large uncritical literature on community colleges, now enshrined in its own ERIC database and dominated by the movement's leaders. Such men as Doak S. Campbell, Walter C. Eells, Jesse P. Bogue, Edmund J. Gleazer (all at one time executive directors of the American Association of Junior Colleges), and Arthur M. Cohen (head of the ERIC Clearinghouse for Junior

Colleges) have produced the books on the junior college that are most often cited in the literature and most often carried on library shelves. In short, the junior college is a subject that still needs serious scholarly historical attention.

6. Hutchins (1936a, p. 454).

7. The first comprehensive survey of U.S. high schools revealed that these schools contained twice as many elementary students as they had high school students (U.S. Bureau of Education [1893–1894, tables 1 and 19]).

8. The discussion of the historical development of the U.S. public high school in this section is drawn from Labaree (1988). That account, in turn, owes a heavy debt to Cohen and Neufeld (1981), Kaestle (1983), and Krug (1964).

9. This account of conflicting goals draws heavily on the analysis in Chapter 1.

10. Board of Public Education (Philadelphia) (1842–1843, p. 56).

11. I am grateful to David Hogan for helping me reconceptualize the market role of the high school and community college by suggesting that this role has consisted of two distinct components — social mobility and social efficiency.

12. National Center for Education Statistics (1987, calculated from table 28).

13. Cohen (1984).

14. Hogan (1990c) makes a similar argument. He notes that after the turn of the century a compromise between "majoritarian" and "meritocratic" pressures produced the comprehensive high school, with its distinctive structure of "stratified credentialing."

15. Cohen and Neufeld (1981).

16. The best basic analyses of problems of supply and demand in the market for educational credentials (and of the inherent tendency toward inflation in the value of these credentials) are Boudon (1974), Collins (1979), and Thurow (1977).

17. Among writers on the subject (who, as I discussed in an earlier note, are primarily drawn from the ranks of community college leaders), there is universal agreement about the importance of the academic-transfer and vocational-terminal functions. They generally recognize the other two functions, general education and community-adult education, as well, and see the latter as arising after the first two. Depending on the source, however, these new functions may be identified by different labels, combined into a single category, or separated into three or more identifiable functions. For example, Goodwin (1973) notes the rise of citizenship and general education goals after the Second World War; Palinchak (1973) describes this change as a shift toward community service; Tillery and Deegan (1985) describe the third function as part of the "community college" phase and the fourth as part of the "comprehensive community college" phase; Cross (1985) calls the general education goal an "integrated" focus and defines two additional functions, "comprehensive" and "remedial;" and Cohen and Brawer (1982) see a total of five functions, which they call "collegiate," "career," "general," "community," and "compensatory."

18. Tappan (1851/1986, p. 26).

19. Quoted in Thornton (1960, p. 46).

20. Thornton (1960, p. 46).

21. Harper (1900/1986, pp. 57–58).

22. Palinchak (1973, p. 27), Zwerling (1976, p. 47).

23. Brick (1963, table 1).

24. Palinchak (1973, p. 79, Tyler (1969, p. 158).

25. Levine (1986, p. 175), Brick (1963, table 1).

26. Collins (1979, table 5.2), National Center for Education Statistics (1987, tables 28 and 100).

27. Krug (1964).

28. Angell (1915, pp. 292, 294).

29. Quoted in Thornton (1960, p. 48).

30. Levine (1986), Wechsler (1977).

31. The public junior college promoted tracking in another sense as well. Not only was it institutionally defined as the lower track of higher education, but it also contained within it two curricular tracks that paralleled the high school — academic-transfer and vocational-terminal.

32. Palinchak (1973, pp. 43–45), Brick (1963, pp. 79–87).

33. Goodwin (1973, pp. 140–141).

34. Quoted in Thornton (1960, p. 51).

35. Krug (1964).

36. Quoted in Goodwin (1973, p. 157). The AAJC has since been renamed the American Association of Community and Junior Colleges.

37. Levine (1986).

38. Karabel (1972) has characterized this tension between students and junior college leaders over vocational education as a form of "submerged class conflict."

39. Quoted in Goodwin (1973, p. 106).

40. Thornton (1960, p. 51).

41. Koos (1924, 1, table V).

42. Levine (1986, p. 178).

43. Levine (1986, pp. 180–181).

44. Karabel (1972, 1986), Pincus (1980, 1986), Zwerling (1976).

45. Palinchak (1973), Cohen and Brawer (1982), Diekhoff (1950), President's Commission on Higher Education (1947).

46. Mann (1842, pp. 93, 94).

47. Quoted in Goodwin (1973, p. 121).

48. Quoted in Goodwin (1973, p. 122).

49. Goodwin (1973, p. 142).

50. Angell (1915, p. 302).

51. Hutchins (1936a, 1936b, p. 602).

52. Quoted in Goodwin (1973, p. 110).

53. President's Commission on Higher Education (1947, 1, p. 37).

54. President's Commission on Higher Education (1947, 1, pp. 48–49).

55. Cohen and Brawer (1982, p. 259).

56. Powell, Farrar, and Cohen (1985).

57. Obviously, the community college displays considerably more age variation.

58. Clark (1960).

59. It is possible to overstate this difference. High schools can compel attendance only to a certain age, and they cannot compel motivated compliance on the part of those who do attend. Thus in order to function effectively, the high school, too, must seek to please the educational consumer.

60. Trow (1988).

61. See Brown (1995) for a thorough examination of the role of consumerism in shaping the expansion of U.S. higher education.

62. These waves of expansion are not as neatly defined as this abbreviated categorization might suggest. In many states the previously existing state university became the land grant school, while in others the land grant formed the basis for founding a state university. The land grant stage identified here is intended to represent the increase in enrollments and shift in purpose that affected higher education as a consequence of the land grant phenomenon.

63. Notable exceptions to this pattern, including such instantly successful latecomers as the University of Chicago and Stanford University, can be explained as the result of extraordinary financial backing and local market conditions.

64. National Universities (1996).

65. *Information Please Almanac* (1995, pp. 865–890); *World Almanac* (1987, pp. 234–250).

66. This pattern of growth kept the supply of higher education and the demand for it in relative balance until the 1920s and 1930s, when elite schools began restricting admissions.

67. Steven Zwerling (1976, p. 61) identifies this tendency as an example of what he calls "Zwerling's Law: As the rate of enrollment-increase in any educational system becomes geometric, a second vocational education track emerges."

68. Quoted in Eddy (1957, p. 33).

69. Veysey (1965), Rudolph (1962).

70. Zwerling (1976, p. 56).

71. Herbst (1989), Levine (1986).

72. See Chapter 9 for a more detailed discussion of the evolution of the teachers college.

73. Hogan (1987).

74. Dougherty (1988) provides a discussion of the entrepreneurial character of community college administrators.

75. Levine (1986, p. 182).

76. President's Commission on Higher Education (1947).

77. Zwerling (1976, p. 63).

78. Carnegie Commission on Higher Education (1970, pp. 15–16).

79. Quoted in Karabel (1972, p. 545).

80. Zwerling (1976, pp. 68–69).

81. Martorana (1969), Zwerling (1976, p. 71).

82. Quoted in Palinchak (1973, pp. 96–97).

83. Hanawalt (1968).

84. Palinchak (1973, pp. 94–95).

85. Palinchak (1973, p. 95).

86. Pincus (1986).

87. Karabel (1986).

88. There is a problem in estimating transfer rates because of a question about what constitutes the appropriate population to use as a base for such an estimate. Palmer (1986) reports on one California study, which shows that the transfer rate is 3 percent for

all community college students; 17 percent for full-time, college-age students; 59 percent for first-time, full-time, college-age students; and 71 percent for first-time, full-time, college-age students who stated an initial intent to transfer.

89. Bernstein (1986).

90. Karabel (1986).

91. Prominent examples drawn from this literature include Karabel (1972, 1974, 1986), Pincus (1980), Zwerling (1976), Grubb (1984), Grubb and Lazerson (1975), and a collection of essays edited by Zwerling (1986).

92. Dougherty (1987) likens these successive rounds of elimination to the process of "tournament mobility" that Rosenbaum (1976) found in high schools.

93. The best recent review of the research about factors affecting the attrition of community is found in Dougherty (1987), from which most of these factors were drawn. Other sources used include Bernstein (1986) and London (1986).

94. See Dougherty (1994) and Brint and Karabel (1989) for a more thorough discussion of the factors pressing the community college to adopt vocationalism as its primary function.

95. Quotation from Marx (1869/1963, p. 15).

96. Bernstein (1986), Pincus (1986).

97. Cohen and Neufeld (1981).

9. The Lowly Status of Education Schools

This chapter is a revised version of an essay that was previously published as "The Lowly Status of Teacher Education in the U.S.: The Impact of Markets and the Implications for Reform," in Nobuo K. Shimihara and Ivan Z. Holowinsky (eds.), *Teacher Education in Industrialized Nations* (New York: Garland, 1995), pp. 41–85. Reprinted by permission. I first explored ideas about the relation between markets and teacher education in a lecture delivered at the conference on Continuity and Change in Teacher Education, University of Western Ontario, 1991, and in an article for *Phi Delta Kappan* (1994). An early version of this essay was presented at the Rutgers International Seminar on Education in 1994. I am grateful to William Firestone for his helpful comments at that seminar. I am particularly grateful to Andrew Gitlin for his insights about many of the issues raised in this chapter that emerged during our intensive collaboration on a paper about the early history of teacher education; that paper was presented at the 1994 meeting of the American Educational Research Association in New Orleans.

1. See, for example, Holmes Group (1986, 1995), Clifford and Guthrie (1988), Goodlad (1990, 1994), Gideonse (1992), Popkewitz (1987), Liston and Zeichner (1991), Ginsburg (1988), Kramer (1991).

2. On the history of teacher education in the United States see Borrowman (1956), Herbst (1989a), Goodlad, Soder, and Sirotnik (1990). Articles: Borrowman (1971), Urban (1990), Warren (1985), Johnson (1987), Clifford (1986), Herbst (1980, 1989b), Clifford and Guthrie (1988), Johnson (1989), Herbst (1989b), Ginsburg (1988), Liston and Zeichner (1991), Tom (1984), Goodlad (1990).

3. For the purposes of this chapter, I define a market as a social arena in which individual or organizational actors competitively pursue private gain through the ex-

change of commodities (the buying and selling of goods and services). The value of these commodities, and thus the degree of benefit enjoyed by producers and consumers, is established by the relation between supply and demand rather than by any intrinsic qualities in the goods or services themselves.

4. For a more comprehensive and more sociological analysis of the factors shaping the lowly status of education schools, see Labaree (1996).

5. On the impact of class and gender see Ginsburg (1988), Popkewitz (1987), Lanier and Little (1986), and Clifford and Guthrie (1988). Warren (1985) and Urban (1990) both touch suggestively on one part of the market issue, dealing with the recurring scarcity of teachers, but do not have the space to develop this point. Only Herbst (1989a) has developed an extended analysis of the market pressure that educational consumers exerted on normal schools and the impact that this pressure had on the evolution of these schools into general-purpose colleges. Eisenmann (1990) provides an interesting case study of this form of market pressure in Pennsylvania. Altenbaugh and Underwood (1990) capture some key elements of this issue in their review of the evolution of the normal school.

6. Labaree (1988).

7. Trow (1988) and, for example, Collins (1979) and Brown (1995).

8. Koerner (1963, pp. 17–18).

9. Warren (1985, p. 5) lists a whole series of colorful slanders on teacher education issued during the 1980s:

> One report announces that "never before in the nation's history has the caliber of those entering the teaching profession been as low as it is today." . . . Colorado Governor Richard Lamm comments, "List the ten most somnolent courses in a university, and nine of them will be teacher courses." That remark pales in quotability next to Gary Sykes' characterization of teacher preparation as "higher education's dirty little secret." H. Ross Perot, the Texas industrialist credited with the recent passage of that state's school reform bill, likens teacher education to a fire drill. . . . The hyperbole borders on silliness, but it gives historians something to chew on.

10. Koerner (1963, p. xii).

11. Lanier and Little (1986).

12. Lanier and Little (1986, pp. 530, 531, 535 [quoting Ducharme and Agne (1982, p. 33)], 540, 549).

13. Warren (1985, p. 7), Sedlak and Schlossman (1986, table 11).

14. Quoted in Sedlak (1989, p. 261).

15. Sedlak (1989, p. 262).

16. Some assign this honor to Samuel Hall, who founded a normal school in 1823 in Concord, Vermont (Borrowman [1971]).

17. Quoted in Borrowman (1965, p. 65).

18. Quotation from Borrowman (1971, p. 71).

19. Elsbree (1939, p. 152).

20. Borrowman (1956, p. 70).

21. Sedlak (1989, p. 266); the "leading analyst" cited is Cook (1927, p. 3).

22. Herbst (1989a).

23. None of this should be taken to mean that the normal school failed to provide anyone with an adequate professional education. As I have suggested in Chapter 7, a small number of women and men in the nineteenth century acquired an educational preparation at the normal school that served them very well in their later careers. See Thornburg (1995) for a discussion of the benefits of a normal-school education.

24. See Chapter 1.

25. Hartz (1955, p. 62).

26. Trow (1988, p. 17).

27. Trow (1988, p. 17).

28. As Brown (1995) has shown, this situation faced all institutions of higher education in the United States in the late nineteenth century.

29. Collins (1979, p. 119).

30. Herbst (1989b, p. 219).

31. Herbst (1989a, p. 129).

32. Altenbaugh and Underwood (1990, p. 164).

33. Herbst (1980, p. 227); quoted in Altenbaugh and Underwood (1990, p. 143).

34. Herbst (1989a, p. 6).

35. Herbst (1989a, p. 135).

36. In spite of all these pressures, however, the normal school provided a significant boost to the job prospects of a small number of its students — mostly women — who ended up pursuing extended careers in education. These alumnae looked back on their normal-school experience with fondness and gratitude. (See Chapter 7.)

37. Johnson (1989, p. 243); quoted in Altenbaugh and Underwood (1990, p. 149).

38. Altenbaugh and Underwood (1990, pp. 149, 150).

39. For a fascinating case study of the role that the market played in the evolution of normal schools in Pennsylvania, see Eisenmann (1990).

40. See Labaree (1996) for a discussion of the many constituencies that benefited from the evolution of the normal school and that continue to benefit from the role played by the university-based education school.

41. Borrowman (1971, pp. 71–72).

42. For close examination of the causes and effects of commodification on education in the United States and the impact of the social mobility goal on educational institutions, see Labaree (1988), Collins (1979), Goldman and Tickamyer (1984), and Green (1980).

43. Lanier and Little (1986), Goodlad (1990).

44. Herbst (1989a, p. 4).

45. Powell (1980).

46. Goodlad (1990).

47. For a perceptive analysis of the tension between the academic and the vocational within university-based schools of education, see Clifford and Guthrie (1988, chapter 3).

48. Lanier and Little (1986, p. 530).

49. National Center for Education Statistics (1992, table 4), Clifford and Guthrie (1988, p. 21).

50. Holmes Group (1986), Clifford and Guthrie (1988).

51. One high-visibility proposal for the reform of teacher education in recent years was

put forward by John Goodlad in *Teachers for Our Nation's Schools* (1990) and two supporting volumes (Goodlad, Soder, and Sirotnik [1990a, 1990b]). On the issues that divide *Tomorrow's Teachers* and *Ed School,* Goodlad tends to take a middle road. As a result, it is less useful for this discussion than the other two, which provide a clear set of alternatives that can be addressed through the kind of market analysis I have developed.

52. To further confuse matters, the Holmes Group issued another report in 1995 *(Tomorrow's Schools of Education),* in which it effectively renounced the university-based reform strategy defined in *Tomorrow's Teachers* and embraced a school-based and teacher-oriented approach that closely resembles the argument laid out in *Ed School.* See my analysis of this dramatic turnaround (Labaree [1995b]). In spite of this reversal of positions, the Holmes Group's first report remains an important and influential statement about how to resolve teacher education's status problem by drawing on the resources of the university.

53. Holmes Group (1986, pp. 6, 25–26, ix).

54. Holmes Group (1986, p. 20).

55. Holmes Group (1986, pp. 62–63, 52).

56. Witz (1992) provides a discussion of the various defensive strategies adopted by semiprofessional occupations seeking to close off competition from below.

57. Thomas Hill, quoted in Clifford and Guthrie (1988, p. 3).

58. Clifford and Guthrie (1988, p. 3).

59. Clifford and Guthrie (1988, p. 325).

60. See Chapter 6.

61. Clifford and Guthrie (1988, pp. 349–350).

62. Why is the status of teaching relatively low in the United States? First, with 2.8 million teachers on the job at any one time, teaching is a mass occupation and as such cannot credibly claim to be an elite profession. And with more than two hundred thousand new recruits called for every year, teacher education is never going to be an exclusive form of professional preparation. Second, teacher salaries are dependent on the public purse, and because voters have the opportunity to express their preferences about school funding through frequent millage elections, there is an effective ceiling on what members in this occupation can make. Under these circumstances, it is unlikely that teachers in the United States will ever be able to earn an income that puts then substantially above the level of the average taxpayer. Third, public school teachers suffer from the negative image of public employment that characterizes this market-oriented society. Market ideology in the United States labels private-sector workers as productive and public employees as drones. The high professions have played into this ideology effectively by identifying themselves as small-scale entrepreneurs operating under the fee-for-service model. Teachers cannot make this same claim. Fourth, in the public eye, there is nothing mysterious about teaching that might justify high status and elevated pay. Everyone has seen it up close as a student, and the subject matter that teachers purvey seems commonsensical to most adults who have already acquired this learning. The esoteric knowledge and private language of law and medicine are missing from teaching. Fifth, teaching is seen as women's work, and this nudges its status downward in the direction of nursing and social work, in contrast to the male-dominated high professions.

10. Schooling Consumers and Consuming the School

A portion of this chapter was previously published as the foreword to David K. Brown, *Degrees of Control: A Sociology of Educational Expansion and Occupational Credentialism* (New York: Teachers College Press), pp. ix–xvi. Copyright © 1995 by Teachers College, Columbia University. All rights reserved. Reprinted by permission of the publisher.

1. For example, see Goodlad (1984), Powell et al. (1985), and Sedlak et al. (1986).

2. Steinberg (1996, p. 18). This book summarizes the results of a large-scale study carried out by Steinberg, Bradford Brown, and Sanford Dornbusch.

3. Steinberg (1996, pp. 72–73).

4. Steinberg (1996, p. 75).

5. Brown (1995, table 1.1); Brown defines "college age" as eighteen to twenty-one years old.

6. Collins (1979).

7. Sedlak et al. (1986, p. 182).

References

Abbott, Andrew. 1988. *The system of professions*. Chicago: University of Chicago Press.

Adler, Mortimer. 1982. *The paideia proposal: An educational manifesto*. New York: Macmillan.

Alexander, Karl A., Doris R. Entwisle, and Susan L. Dauber. 1994. *On the success of failure: A reassessment of the effects of retention in the primary grades*. New York: Cambridge University Press.

Altenbaugh, Richard J., and Kathleen Underwood. 1990. The evolution of normal schools. In John I. Goodlad, Roger Soder, and Kenneth A. Sirotnik (eds.), *Places where teachers are taught* (pp. 136–186). San Francisco: Jossey-Bass.

American Association for the Advancement of Science. 1990. *Science for all Americans: Project 2061*. New York: Oxford University Press.

American Educational Research Association. 1990. Annual meeting program. Washington, D.C.: AERA.

Angell, James R. 1915. The junior-college movement in high schools. *School Review* 23, 289–302.

Angus, David, and Jeffrey Mirel. 1995. Rhetoric and reality: The high school curriculum. In Diane Ravitch and Maris A. Vinovskis (eds.), *Learning from the past: What history teaches us about school reform* (pp. 295–328). Baltimore: Johns Hopkins University Press.

Apple, Michael W. 1979. *Ideology and curriculum*. Boston: Routledge.

———. 1982. *Education and power*. Boston: Routledge.

Aronowitz, Stanley, and Henry A. Giroux. 1985. *Education under siege*. South Hadley, Mass.: Bergin and Garvey.

Ayres, Leonard. 1908. *Laggards in our schools.* New York: Russell Sage Foundation.

Bache, Alexander Dallas. 1959. Address before the alumni association of Central High School (February 10). Philadelphia: Alumni Association.

Balyeat, Frank A. 1959/1960. County high schools in Oklahoma. *Chronicles of Oklahoma* 37, 196–210.

Barber, Benjamin. 1992. *An aristocracy of everyone: The politics of education and the future of America.* New York: Ballantine.

Beaumont, Nellie. 1957. Emma Lott, 1867–1937. *Michigan History Magazine* 41, 335–363.

Becker, Gary S. 1964. *Human capital: A theoretical and empirical analysis with special reference to education.* New York: Columbia University Press.

———. 1975. *Human capital* (2d ed.). New York: National Bureau of Economic Research.

Becker, Howard S., Blanche Geer, and Everett C. Hughes. 1968. *Making the grade: The academic side of college life.* New York: Wiley.

Berg, Ivar. 1971. *Education and jobs: The great training robbery.* Boston: Beacon.

Berliner, David C., and Bruce J. Biddle. 1995. *The manufactured crisis: Myths, fraud, and the attack on America's public schools.* Reading, Mass.: Addison-Wesley.

Bernstein, Allison. 1986. The devaluation of transfer: Current explanations and possible causes. In Steven Zwerling (ed.), *The community college and its critics* (pp. 31–40). San Francisco: Jossey-Bass.

Bestor, Arthur. 1953. *Educational wastelands: The retreat from learning in our public schools.* Urbana: University of Illinois Press.

Beyer, L. E. 1994. The aims of schooling: Marketization, democracy, and the public good. *Educational Foundations* 8, 43–58.

Beyer, Landon E., and Kenneth Zeichner. 1987. Teacher education in cultural context: Beyond reproduction. In Thomas Popkewitz (ed.), *Critical studies in teacher education* (pp. 298–334). Philadelphia: Falmer.

Bidwell, Charles. 1965. The school as a formal organization. In James March (ed.), *Handbook of organization* (pp. 972–1022). Chicago: Rand McNally.

Bledstein, Burton. 1976. *The culture of professionalism: The middle class and the development of higher education in America.* New York: Norton.

Board of Public Education [Philadelphia]. 1819–1945. Annual reports.

Bogue, Jesse P. 1950. *The community college.* New York: McGraw-Hill.

Bohrnstedt, George W., and T. Michael Carter. 1971. Robustness in regression analysis. In H. L. Costner (ed.), *Sociological methods* (pp. 118–146). San Francisco: Jossey-Bass.

Borrowman, Merle L. 1953. *The liberal and technical in teacher education: A historical survey of American thought.* New York: Teachers College Press.

——— (ed.). 1965. *Teacher education in America: A documentary history.* New York: Teachers College Press.

———. 1971. Teachers, education of: History. In L. C. Deighton (ed.), *Encyclopedia of education,* vol. 9 (pp. 71–79). New York: Macmillan.

Boss, Agnes Houghton. 1954. Grace Annie Hill, 1874–1944. *Michigan History Magazine* 38, 153–156.

Boudon, Raymond. 1974. *Education, opportunity, and social inequality: Changing prospects in western society*. New York: Wiley.

Bourdieu, Pierre. 1986. The forms of capital. In J. G. Richardson (ed.), *Handbook of theory and research for the sociology of education* (pp. 241–258). New York: Greenwood.

Bourdieu, Pierre, and Jean-Claude Passeron. 1977. *Reproduction: In education, society, and culture*. Beverly Hills, Calif.: Sage Publications.

Bowles, Samuel, and Herbert Gintis. 1976. *Schooling in capitalist America*. New York: Basic.

———. 1986. *Democracy and capitalism: Property, community, and the contradictions of modern social thought*. New York: Basic.

Boyer, Ernest. 1983. *High school: A report on secondary education in America*. New York: Harper and Row.

———. 1987. *College: The undergraduate experience in America*. New York: Harper and Row.

Bracey, Gerald W. 1995. The fifth Bracey report on the condition of public education. *Phi Delta Kappan 77*, 149–160.

Bradford, Mary D. 1932. *Memoirs of Mary D. Bradford: Autobiography and historical reminiscences of education in Wisconsin, through progressive service from rural school to city superintendent*. Evansville, Wis.: Antes.

Bradley, Ann. 1996. Holmes Group expands scope in reform push: Ed school network seeks school links. *Education Week*, February 7.

Brick, Michael. 1963. *Forum and focus for the junior college movement: The American Association of Junior Colleges*. New York: Teachers College Press.

Brint, Steven, and Jerome Karabel. 1989. *The diverted dream: Community colleges and the promise of educational opportunity in America, 1900–1985*. New York: Oxford University Press.

Britzman, Deborah P. 1986. Cultural myths in the making of a teacher. *Harvard Educational Review 56*, 442–456.

Brown, David K. 1995. *Degrees of control: A sociology of educational expansion and occupational credentialism*. New York: Teachers College Press.

Brubacher, John S., and Willis Rudy. 1968. *Higher education in transition: A history of American colleges and universities, 1636–1968* (rev. ed.). New York: Harper.

Bryk, Anthony S., Valerie E. Lee, and Peter B. Holland. 1993. *Catholic schools and the common good*. Cambridge: Harvard University Press.

Bullock, Henry A. 1967. *A history of Negro education in the South: From 1619 to the present*. Cambridge: Harvard University Press.

Burke, Colin B. 1982. *American collegiate populations: A test of the traditional view*. New York: New York University Press.

Callaghan, Raymond E. 1962. *Education and the cult of efficiency: A study of the social forces that have shaped the administration of the public schools*. Chicago: University of Chicago Press.

Carnegie Commission on Higher Education. 1968. *Quality and equality*. New York: McGraw-Hill.

———. 1970. *The open-door colleges: Policies for community colleges*. New York: McGraw-Hill.

———. 1973. *Priorities for action.* New York: McGraw-Hill.

Carnoy, Martin, and Henry M. Levin. 1985. *Schooling and work in the democratic state.* Stanford: Stanford University Press.

Carr-Saunders, A. P., and P. A. Wilson. 1933. *The professions.* Oxford: Oxford University Press.

Cherryholmes, Cleo H. 1987. The political project of Tomorrow's Teachers. *Social Education* 51, 501–505.

———. 1988. *Power and criticism: Poststructural investigations in education.* New York: Teachers College Press.

Chubb, John E., and Terry M. Moe. 1990. *Politics, markets, and America's schools.* Washington, D.C.: Brookings Institution.

Church, Robert, and Michael Sedlak. 1976. *Education in the United States.* New York: Free Press.

Clark, Burton R. 1960. *The open door college.* New York: McGraw-Hill.

Cliff, George H. 1888. The Central High School of Philadelphia: An historical sketch. In *The semi-centennial celebration of the Central High School of Philadelphia.* Philadelphia: Semi-Centennial Committee.

Clifford, Geraldine Joncich. 1986. The formative years of schools of education in America: A five-institution analysis. *American Journal of Education* 94, 427–446.

Clifford, Geraldine Joncich, and James W. Guthrie. 1988. *Ed school: A brief for professional education.* Chicago: University of Chicago Press.

Clinton, Bill. 1996. Remarks by the president at the National Governors Association Education Summit (March 27). White House press release.

Coffman, Lotus D. 1911. *The social composition of the teaching population.* Columbia University Contributions to Education, no. 41. New York: Teachers College Press.

Cohen, Arthur M., and Florence B. Brawer. 1982. *The American community college.* San Francisco: Jossey-Bass.

Cohen, David K. 1984. The American common school: A divided vision. *Education and Urban Society* 16, 253–261.

———. 1987. Educational technology, policy, and practice. *Educational Evaluation and Policy Analysis* 9, 153–170.

———. 1988. Teaching practice: Plus ça change. In Philip W. Jackson (ed.), *Contributing to educational change: Perspectives on research and practice* (pp. 27–84). Berkeley, Calif.: McCutchan.

Cohen, David K., and Barbara Neufeld. 1981. The failure of high schools and the progress of education. *Daedelus* 110, 69–89.

Cole, Kenneth. 1996. The price of learning: Engler puts adult ed on '97 endangered list. *Detroit News,* June 4.

Coleman, James S., and Thomas Hoffer. 1987. *Public and private high schools: The impact of communities.* New York: Basic.

Coleman, James S., Thomas Hoffer, and Sally Kilgore. 1982. *High school achievement: Public, Catholic, and private schools compared.* New York: Basic.

Collins, Randall. 1979. *The credential society: An historical sociology of education and stratification.* New York: Academic.

Conant, James B. 1959. *The American high school today.* New York: McGraw-Hill.

————. 1961. *Slums and suburbs.* New York: McGraw-Hill.

Connell, Robert W., et al. 1982. *Making the difference: Schools, families, and social division.* Boston: Allen and Unwin.

Cook, K. M. 1927. State laws and regulations governing teachers' certificates. Bulletin no. 19. Washington, D.C.: Bureau of Education.

Cookson, Peter W., Jr., and Caroline H. Persell. 1985. *Preparing for power: America's elite boarding schools.* New York: Basic.

Cornog, William H. 1952. *School of the republic, 1893–1943.* Philadelphia: Associated Alumni of Central High School.

Cotton, Fassett A. 1904. *Education in Indiana: An outline in the growth of the common school system.* Indianapolis: Superintendent of Public Instruction.

Counts, George S. 1969. *The selective character of American secondary education.* New York: Arno.

Cremin, Lawrence. 1980. *American education: The national experience, 1783–1876.* New York: Harper and Row.

Cross, K. Patricia. 1985. Determining missions and priorities for the fifth generation. In William L. Deegan et al. (eds.), *Renewing the American community college* (pp. 34–50). San Francisco: Jossey-Bass.

Cuban, Larry. 1984. *How teachers taught.* New York: Longman.

Curti, Merle. 1959. *The social ideas of American educators* (rev. ed.). Totowa, N.J.: Littlefield, Adams.

Cusick, Philip A. 1983. *The egalitarian ideal and the American high school: Studies of three schools.* New York: Longman.

————. 1992. *The educational system: Its nature and logic.* New York: McGraw-Hill.

Dao, James. 1996. Regents to insist on passing board's test for diploma. *New York Times,* April 24.

Davis, Kingsley, and Wilbert E. Moore. 1945. Some principles of stratification. *American Sociological Review* 10, 242–249.

de Lone, Richard H. 1979. *Small futures: Children, inequality, and the limits of liberal reform.* New York: Harcourt Brace Jovanovich.

Densmore, Kathleen. 1987. Professionalism, proletarianization and teacher work. In Thomas Popkewitz (ed.), *Critical studies in teacher education* (pp. 130–160). Philadelphia: Falmer.

Dewey, John. 1929. *The sources of a science of education.* New York: Liveright.

Diekhoff, John S. 1950. *Democracy's college: Higher education in the local community.* New York: Harper.

Diener, Thomas. 1986. *Growth of an American invention: A documentary history of the junior and community college movement.* New York: Greenwood.

Dore, Ronald. 1976. *The diploma disease: Education, qualification, and development.* London: Allen and Unwin.

Dorn, Sherman. 1996. *Creating the dropout: An institutional and social history of school failure.* New York: Greenwood.

Dougherty, Kevin. 1987. The effects of community colleges: Aid or hindrance to socio-economic attainment. *Sociology of Education* 60, 86–103.

——. 1988. The politics of community college expansion: Beyond the functionalist and class-reproduction explanations. *American Journal of Education* 96, 351–393.

——. 1994. *The contradictory college: The conflicting origins, impacts, and futures of the community college*. Albany: State University of New York Press.

Dreeben, Robert. 1968. *On what is learned in school*. Reading, Mass.: Addison-Wesley.

Ducharme, Edward R., and Russell M. Agne. 1982. The educational professoriate: A research-based perspective. *Journal of Teacher Education* 33 (6), 30–36.

Dunlap, Thomas. 1851. Introductory address of the commencement of Central High School (February 12). Philadelphia: Board of Controllers.

Durkheim, Emile. 1933. *The division of labor in society*. New York: Free Press.

Eckert, Penelope. 1989. *Jocks and burnouts: Social categories and identity in the high school*. New York: Teachers College Press.

Eddy, Edward D. 1957. *Colleges for our land and time: The land-grant idea in American education*. New York: Harper.

Edmonds, Franklin S. 1902. *History of the Central High School of Philadelphia*. Philadelphia: Lippincott.

Educators of Michigan: Biographical. 1900. Chicago: J. H. Beers.

Eells, Walter C. 1931. *The junior college*. Boston: Houghton-Mifflin.

——. 1941. *Present status of junior college terminal education*. Washington, D.C.: American Association of Junior Colleges.

Eisenmann, Linda. 1990. The influence of bureaucracy and markets: Teacher education in Pennsylvania. In John I. Goodlad, Roger Soder, and Kenneth A. Sirotnik (eds.), *Places where teachers are taught* (pp. 287–329). San Francisco: Jossey-Bass.

Elmore, Richard F., and Milbrey W. McLaughlin. 1988. *Steady work*. Santa Monica, Calif.: RAND.

Elmore, Richard F., et al. 1990. *Restructuring schools: The next generation of educational reform*. San Francisco: Jossey-Bass.

Elsbree, Willard S. 1939. *The American teacher: Evolution of a profession in a democracy*. New York: American Book.

Eng, Lily, and Karen Heller. 1996. College costs will rise higher as lure of prestige persists. *Philadelphia Inquirer*, April 4.

Feiman-Nemser, Sharon, and Robert E. Floden. 1986. The culture of teaching. In Merlin C. Wittrock, *Handbook of research on teaching* (3d ed., pp. 505–526). New York: Macmillan.

Ferriss, Emery N. 1922. *The rural high school: Rural school survey of New York State*. Philadelphia: William F. Fell.

——. 1925. *The rural high school: Its organization and curriculum*. U.S. Bureau of Education bulletin no. 10. Washington, D.C.: Government Printing Office.

Fields, Ralph R. 1962. *The community college movement*. New York: McGraw-Hill.

Flexner, Abraham. 1910/1960. *Medical education in the United States and Canada*. Bulletin no. 4. New York: Carnegie Foundation for the Advancement of Teaching.

——. 1943. *Henry S. Pritchett: A biography*. New York: Columbia University Press.

Foucault, Michel. 1965. *Madness and civilization*. New York: Vintage.

——. 1977. *Discipline and punish: The birth of the prison*. Trans. A. Sheridan. New York: Pantheon.

——. 1980. *The Foucault reader*. Ed. Paul Rabinow. New York: Pantheon.

——. 1984. *Power/knowledge.* Ed. Colin Gordon. New York: Pantheon.

Fox, Marc. 1993. Is it a good investment to attend an elite private college? *Economics of Education Review* 12, 137–151.

Freeman, Richard B. 1976. *The over-educated American.* New York: Academic.

Freidson, Eliot. 1986. *Professional powers.* Chicago: University of Chicago Press.

Fullan, Michael G. 1991. *The new meaning of educational change* (2d ed.). New York: Teachers College Press.

——. 1993. *Change forces: Probing the depths of educational reform.* Bristol, Pa.: Falmer.

Fuller, Rosalie Trail (ed.). 1977. A Nebraska high school teacher in the 1890s: The letters of Sadie B. Smith. *Nebraska History* 58, 447–474.

Gage, Nathaniel L. (ed.). 1963. *Handbook of research on teaching.* Chicago: Rand McNally.

——. 1978. *The scientific basis of the art of teaching.* New York: Teachers College Press.

——. 1989. The paradigm wars and their aftermath. *Educational Researcher* 18 (7), 4–10.

Gage, Nathaniel L., and David C. Berliner. 1989. Nurturing the critical, practical, and artistic thinking of teachers. *Phi Delta Kappan* 71 (3), 212–214.

Gage, Nathaniel L., and M. C. Needels. 1989. Process-product research on teaching: A review of the criticisms. *Elementary School Journal* 89, 253–300.

Gamoran, Adam. 1996. Review of *Catholic Schools and the Common Good* [Bryk, Lee, and Holland (1993)]. *Teachers College Record* 97, 483–486.

Giddens, Anthony. 1984. *The constitution of society.* Berkeley: University of California Press.

Gideonse, Henrik D. (ed.). 1992. *Teacher education policy: Narratives, stories, and cases.* Albany: State University of New York Press.

Gildart, Mabel, and Mary A. Lord. 1957. A. Fern Persons. *Michigan History Magazine* 41, 471–476.

Ginsburg, Mark B. 1988. *Contradictions in teacher education and society: A critical analysis.* New York: Falmer.

Giroux, Henry, and Peter McLaren. 1987. Teacher education as a counter public sphere: Notes towards a redefinition. In Thomas Popkewitz (ed.), *Critical studies in teacher education* (pp. 266–297). Philadelphia: Falmer.

Goldman, Robert, and Ann Tickamyer. 1984. Status attainment and the commodity form: Stratification in historical perspective. *American Sociological Review* 49, 196–209.

Goodlad, John I. 1979. *What schools are for.* Bloomington, Ind.: Phi Delta Kappa Educational Foundation.

——. 1984. *A place called school: Prospects for the future.* New York: McGraw-Hill.

——. 1990. *Teachers for our nation's schools.* San Francisco: Jossey-Bass.

——. 1994. *Educational renewal: Better teachers, better schools.* San Francisco: Jossey-Bass.

Goodlad, John I., Roger Soder, and Kenneth A. Sirotnik (eds.). 1990a. *Places where teachers are taught.* San Francisco: Jossey-Bass.

—— (eds.). 1990b. *The moral dimensions of teaching.* San Francisco: Jossey-Bass.

Goodwin, Gregory L. 1973. A social panacea: A history of the community-junior college ideology. ERIC document ED 093–427.

Green, Thomas F., with David P. Ericson and Robert M. Seidman. 1980. *Predicting the behavior of the educational system.* Syracuse: Syracuse University Press.

Greene, M. 1988. *The dialectic of freedom.* New York: Teachers College Press.

Griffin, Larry J., and Karl L. Alexander. 1978. Schooling and socioeconomic attainments: High school and college influences. *American Journal of Sociology* 84, 319–347.

Grubb, W. Norton. 1984. The bandwagon once more: Vocational preparation for high-tech occupations. *Harvard Educational Review* 54, 429–451.

———. 1993. Further tests of screening on education and observed ability. *Economics of Education Review* 12, 125–136.

Grubb, W. Norton, and Marvin Lazerson. 1975. Rally round the workplace: Continuities and fallacies in career education. *Harvard Educational Review* 45, 452–474.

———. 1982. *Broken promises: How Americans fail their children.* Chicago: University of Chicago Press, 1982.

Grumet, Madeline R. 1988. *Bitter milk.* Amherst: University of Massachusetts Press.

Guba, E. G., and D. L. Clark. 1978. Levels of R and D productivity in schools of education. *Educational Researcher* 7 (5), 3–9.

Gusfield, Joseph R. 1963. *Symbolic crusade.* Urbana: University of Illinois Press.

Gutmann, Amy. 1987. *Democratic education.* Princeton: Princeton University Press.

Haddad, Wadi D. 1979. Educational and economic effects of promotion and repetition practices. World Bank staff working paper no. 319. Washington, D.C.: World Bank.

Hamilton, David. 1989. *Towards a theory of schooling.* New York: Falmer.

Hanawalt, Leslie L. 1968. *A place of light: The history of Wayne State University.* Detroit: Wayne State University.

Hanus, Paul H. 1937. *Adventuring in education.* Cambridge: Harvard University Press.

Harper, William Rainey. 1900/1986. Changes affecting the small college which may be expected and which are to be desired. In Thomas Diener (ed.), *Growth of an American invention: A documentary history of the junior and community college movement* (pp. 53–59). New York: Greenwood.

Hartz, Louis. 1955. *The liberal tradition in America.* New York: Harcourt, Brace and World.

Herbst, Jurgen. 1980. Nineteenth-century normal schools in the United States: A fresh look. *History of Education* 9, 219–227.

———. 1989a. *And sadly teach: Teacher education and professionalization in American culture.* Madison: University of Wisconsin Press.

———. 1989b. Teacher preparation in the nineteenth century: Institutions and purposes. In Donald Warren (ed.), *American teachers: Histories of a profession at work* (pp. 213–236). New York: Macmillan.

Hirsch, E. D., Jr. 1987. *Cultural literacy: What every American needs to know.* New York: Vintage.

Hirschman, Albert O. 1970. *Exit, voice, and loyalty.* Cambridge: Harvard University Press.

Hogan, David. 1985. *Class and reform: School and society in Chicago, 1880–1930.* Philadelphia: University of Pennsylvania Press.

———. 1987. From contest mobility to stratified credentialing: Merit and graded schooling in Philadelphia, 1836–1920. *History of Education Review* 16, 21–42.

———. 1989. The market revolution and disciplinary power: Joseph Lancaster and the psychology of the early classroom system. *History of Education Quarterly* 29, 381–417.

———. 1990a. Moral authority and the antinomies of moral theory: Francis Wayland and nineteenth century moral education. *Educational Theory* 40, 95–119.

———. 1990b. Modes of discipline: Affective individualism and pedagogical reform in New England, 1800–1850. *American Journal of Education* 99, 1–56.

———. 1990c. The organization of schooling and organizational theory: The classroom system in public education in Philadelphia, 1818–1918. In Ronald G. Corwin (ed.), *Research in Sociology of Education and Socialization* 9, 241–294. Greenwich, Conn.: JAI.

———. 1992a. " . . . the silent compulsions of economic relations": Markets and the demand for education. *Educational Policy* 6, 180–205.

———. 1992b. Examinations, merit, and morals: The market revolution and disciplinary power in Philadelphia's public schools, 1838–1868. *Historical Studies in Education* 4, 31–78.

Holmes, C. Thomas. 1989. Grade level retention effects: A meta-analysis of research studies. In Lorrie A. Shepard and Mary Lee Smith (eds.), *Flunking grades: Research and policies on retention* (pp. 16–33). New York: Falmer.

Holmes, C. Thomas, and K. M. Matthews. 1984. The effects of nonpromotion on elementary and junior high school pupils: A meta-analysis. *Review of Educational Research* 54, 225–236.

Holmes Group. 1986. *Tomorrow's teachers.* East Lansing, Mich.: Holmes Group.

———. 1990. *Tomorrow's schools.* East Lansing, Mich.: Holmes Group.

———. 1995. *Tomorrow's schools of education.* East Lansing, Mich.: Holmes Group.

House, Ernest R. 1989. Policy implications of retention research. In Lorrie A. Shepard and Mary Lee Smith (eds.), *Flunking grades: Research and policies on retention* (pp. 202–213). New York: Falmer, 1989.

Howe, W. 1988. Do education and demographics affect unemployment rates? *Monthly Labor Review* 111, 1

Hurn, Christopher J. 1985. *The limits and possibilities of schooling: An introduction to the sociology of education* (2d ed.). Boston: Allyn and Bacon.

Hurt, Charles. 1996. In Detroit: School board revises goals to include "exit skills" requirement. *Detroit News,* April 5.

Husen, Thorsten. 1983. Are standards in the U.S. schools really lagging behind those in other countries? *Phi Delta Kappan* 66, 455–461.

Hutchins, Robert Maynard. 1936a. The confusion in higher education. *Harper's* 173, 449–458.

———. 1936b. What is a general education? *Harper's* 173, 602–609.

Illitch, Ivan. 1971. *Deschooling Society.* New York: Harper.

Information Please Almanac, Atlas, and Yearbook, 1996. 1995. Boston: Houghton Mifflin.

Ingram, Margaret Fogelsong. 1954. *Toward an education.* New York: Comet.

Jackson, Gregg. 1975. The research evidence on the effects of grade retention. *Review of Educational Research* 45, 613–635.

Jencks, Christopher, and David Riesman. 1968. *The academic revolution.* Chicago: University of Chicago Press.

Jencks, Christopher, et al. 1972. *Inequality: A reassessment of the effect of family and schooling in America.* New York: Basic.

Johnson, Henry. 1943. *The other side of Main Street: A history teacher from Sauk Centre.* New York: Columbia University Press.

Johnson, Paul E. 1978. *A shopkeeper's millennium.* New York: Hill and Wang.

Johnson, William R. 1987. Empowering practitioners: Holmes, Carnegie, and the lessons of history. *History of Education Quarterly* 27, 221–240.

——. 1989. Teachers and teacher training in the twentieth century. In Donald Warren (ed.), *American teachers: Histories of a profession at work* (pp. 237–256). New York: Macmillan.

Kaestle, Carl F. (ed.). 1973. *Joseph Lancaster and the monitorial school movement: A documentary history.* New York: Teachers College Press.

——. 1983. *Pillars of the republic: Common school and American society, 1780–1860.* New York: Hill and Wang.

Karabel, Jerome. 1972. Community colleges and social stratification: Submerged class conflict in American higher education. *Harvard Educational Review* 42, 521–562.

——. 1974. Protecting the portals: Class and the community college. *Social Policy* 5, 12–18.

——. 1986. Community colleges and social stratification in the 1980s. In L. Steven Zwerling (ed.), *The community college and its critics* (pp. 13–30). San Francisco: Jossey-Bass.

Karier, Clarence. 1978. Testing for order and control in the corporate liberal state. In Clarence Karier, Paul Violas, and Joel Spring, *Roots of crisis.* Chicago: Rand McNally.

Katz, Michael B. 1968. *The irony of early school reform: Educational innovation in mid–nineteenth century Massachusetts.* Boston: Beacon.

——. 1978. Origins of the institutional state. *Marxist Perspectives* 1, 6–23.

——. 1987. *Reconstructing American education.* Cambridge: Harvard University Press.

Katz, Michael B., and Davey, Ian. 1978. School attendance and early industrialization in a Canadian city. *History of Education Quarterly* 18, 271–293.

Katznelson, Ira, and Margaret Weir. 1985. *Schooling for all: Class, race, and the decline of the democratic ideal.* New York: Basic.

Keniston, Kenneth. 1977. *All our children.* New York: Harcourt Brace Jovanovich.

Kerckhoff, Alan C. 1993. *Diverging pathways: Social structure and career deflections.* New York: Cambridge University Press.

Kett, Joseph F. 1977. *Rites of passage.* New York: Basic.

——. 1995. School leaving: Dead end or detour? In Diane Ravitch and Maris A. Vinovskis (eds.), *Learning from the past: What history teaches us about school reform* (pp. 265–294). Baltimore: Johns Hopkins University Press.

Kingston, Paul W., and Lionel S. Lewis (eds.). 1990. *The high-status track: Studies of elite schools and stratification.* Albany: State University of New York Press.

Klitgaard, Robert. 1985. *Choosing elites: Selecting the "best and the brightest" at top universities and elsewhere.* New York: Basic.

Koerner, James D. 1963. *The miseducation of America's teachers.* Boston: Houghton Mifflin.

Koos, Leonard V. 1924. *The junior college.* Minneapolis: University of Minnesota Press.

Kousser, J. Morgan, Gary W. Cox, and David W. Galenson 1982. Log-linear analysis of contingency tables: An introduction for historians with an application to Thernstrom on the "floating proletariat." *Historical Methods* 15, 152–169.

Kozol, Jonathan. 1991. *Savage inequalities: Children in America's schools.* New York: Crown.

Kramer, Rita. 1991. *Ed school follies: The miseducation of America's teachers.* New York: Free Press.

Kristeva, Julia. 1988. *The Kristeva reader.* Ed. T. Moi. New York: Columbia University Press.

Krug, Edward A. 1964. *The shaping of the American high school, 1880–1920.* Madison: University of Wisconsin Press.

———. 1972. *The shaping of the American high school, 1920–1941.* Madison: University of Wisconsin Press.

Kuhn, Thomas S. 1970. *The structure of scientific revolutions* (2d ed.). Chicago: University of Chicago Press.

Labaree, David F. 1983. The people's college: A sociological analysis of the Central High School of Philadelphia, 1838–1920. Ph.D. diss., University of Pennsylvania.

———. 1984a. Setting the standard: Alternative policies for student promotion. *Harvard Educational Review* 54, 67–87.

———. 1984b. Academic excellence in an early U.S. high school. *Social Problems* 31 (5), 558–567.

———. 1986. Curriculum, credentials, and the middle class: A case study of a nineteenth century high school. *Sociology of Education* 59 (1), 42–57.

———. 1987. Politics, markets, and the compromised curriculum. *Harvard Educational Review* 57 (4), 483–494.

———. 1988. *The making of an American high school: The credentials market and the Central High School of Philadelphia, 1838–1920.* New Haven: Yale University Press.

———. 1989a. Career ladders and the early public high school teacher: A study of inequality and opportunity. In Donald Warren (ed.), *American teachers: Histories of a profession at work* (pp. 157–189). New York: Macmillan.

———. 1989b. The American high school has failed its missions. *MSU Alumni Magazine* 7 (Fall), 15–17.

———. 1990a. A kinder and gentler report: Turning points and the Carnegie tradition. *Journal of Education Policy* 5, 249–264.

———. 1990b. From comprehensive high school to community college: Politics, markets, and the evolution of educational opportunity. In Ronald G. Corwin (ed.), *Research on the Sociology of Education and Socialization* 9, 203–240. Greenwich, Conn.: JAI.

———. 1992a. Power, knowledge, and the rationalization of teaching: A genealogy of the movement to professionalize teaching. *Harvard Educational Review* 62, 123–154.

———. 1992b. Doing good, doing science: The Holmes Group reports and the rhetorics of educational reform. *Teachers College Record* 93 (4), 628–640.

———. 1994. An unlovely legacy: The disabling impact of the market on American teacher education. *Phi Delta Kappan* 75 (8), 591–595.

———. 1995a. The lowly status of teacher education in the U.S.: The impact of markets and the implications for reform. In Nobuo K. Shimahara and Ivan Z. Holowinsky (eds.), *Teacher education in industrialized nations* (pp. 41–85). New York: Garland.

———. 1995b. A disabling vision: Rhetoric and reality in *Tomorrow's schools of education* [Holmes Group (1995)]. *Teachers College Record* 97 (2), 166–205.

———. 1995c. Foreword to David K. Brown, *Degrees of control: A sociology of educational expansion and occupational credentialism* (pp. ix–xvi). New York: Teachers College Press.

———. 1996. The trouble with ed schools. *Educational Foundations* 14 (4), 1–19.

———. 1997. Public goods, private goods: The American struggle over educational goals. *American Educational Research Journal* 34 (1), in press.

Labaree, David F., and Aaron M. Pallas. 1996. Dire straits: The narrow vision of the Holmes Group. *Educational Researcher* 25 (5), 25–28.

Lagemann, Ellen Condliffe. 1983. *Private power for the public good.* Middletown, Conn.: Wesleyan University Press.

———. 1987. The politics of knowledge: The Carnegie Corporation and the formulation of public policy. *History of Education Quarterly* 27, 205–220.

———. 1989. *The politics of knowledge: The Carnegie Corporation, philanthropy, and public policy.* Middletown, Conn.: Wesleyan University Press.

Laird, Susan. 1988. Reforming "women's true profession": A case for "feminist pedagogy" in teacher education? *Harvard Educational Review* 58, 449–463.

Lanier, Judith E., and Judith W. Little. 1986. Research on teacher education. In Merlin C. Wittrock (ed.), *Handbook of research on teaching* (3d ed., pp. 527–569). New York: Macmillan.

Larson, Magali S. 1977. *The rise of professionalism.* Berkeley: University of California Press.

Lazerson, Marvin, and W. Norton Grubb. 1974. *American education and vocationalism: A documentary history, 1870–1970.* New York: Teachers College Press.

Levine, David O. 1986. *The American college and the culture of aspiration, 1915–1940.* Ithaca, N.Y.: Cornell University Press.

Lindblom, Charles E. 1990. *Inquiry and change: The troubled attempt to understand and shape society.* New Haven: Yale University Press.

Liston, Daniel P., and Kenneth M. Zeichner. 1991. *Teacher education and the social conditions of schooling.* New York: Routledge.

London, Howard B. 1986. Strangers to our shores. In L. Steven Zwerling (ed.), *The community college and its critics* (pp. 91–100). San Francisco: Jossey-Bass.

Lord, Mary A. 1954. Julia Anne King. *Michigan History Magazine* 38, 306–312.

Lortie, Dan C. 1969. The balance of control and autonomy in elementary school teaching. In Amitai Etzioni (ed.), *The semi-professions and their organization* (pp. 1–53). New York: Free Press.

———. 1973. Observations on teaching as work. In R. M. W. Travers (ed.), *Handbook of research on teaching* (2d ed., pp. 474–497). Chicago: Rand McNally.

———. 1975. *Schoolteacher.* Chicago: University of Chicago Press.

Lynd, Robert S., and Helen M. Lynd. 1929. *Middletown: A study in modern American culture.* New York: Harcourt, Brace and World.

MacLeod, Jay. 1995. *Ain't no makin' it: Leveled aspirations in a low-income neighborhood.* Boulder, Colo.: Westview.

Macpherson, C. B. 1962. *The political theory of possessive individualism.* Oxford: Clarendon.

Magill, Edward Hicks. 1907. *Sixty-five years in the life of a teacher, 1841–1906.* Boston: Houghton Mifflin.

Mann, Horace. 1842. Secretary's report to the board of education of Massachusetts. Boston: Board of Education.

———. 1848/1957. Twelfth annual report. In Lawrence A. Cremin (ed.), *The republic and the school: Horace Mann on the education of free men* (pp. 79–112). New York: Teachers College Press.

Martorana, S. V. 1969. Progress and plans in the empire state. In Roger Yarrington (ed.), *Junior colleges: 50 states/50 years* (pp. 169–179). Washington, D.C.: American Association of Junior Colleges.

Marx, Karl. 1867/1967. *Capital.* New York: International Publishers.

———. 1869/1963. *The eighteenth Brumaire of Louis Bonaparte.* New York: International Publishers.

McDonald, Donald. 1973. A six million dollar misunderstanding. *The Center Magazine* 6 (5), 32–52.

Meier, Deborah. 1995. *The power of their ideas: Lessons from a small school in Harlem.* Boston: Beacon.

Metcalf, Richard Alston. 1892. *A history of Princeton High School.* Princeton, Ill.: Princeton High School.

Metz, Mary. 1990. The real school. In Douglas E. Mitchell and Margaret Goetz (eds.), *Education politics for the new century* (pp. 75–91). New York: Falmer.

Meyer, John W., and Brian Rowan. 1977. Institutionalized organizations. *American Journal of Sociology* 83, 340–363.

———. 1983. The structure of educational organizations. In John W. Meyer and William R. Scott (eds.), *Organizational environments: Ritual and rationality* (pp. 71–97). Beverly Hills, Calif.: Sage.

Meyer, John W., et al. 1979. Public education as nation-building in America: Enrollments and bureaucratization in the American states, 1870–1930. *American Journal of Education* 85, 591–613.

Murphy, K., and F. Welch. 1989. Wage premiums for college graduates: Recent growth and possible explanations. *Educational Researcher* 19 (3), 24–26.

Murray, Frank B. 1996. The narrow and broad readings of *Tomorrow's schools of education* [Holmes Group (1995)]. *Educational Researcher* 25(5), 28–31.

Myrdal, Gunnar. 1944. *An American dilemma.* New York: Harper.

National Center for Educational Statistics. 1987. *Digest of education statistics, 1987.* Washington, D.C.: Government Printing Office.

———. 1992. *Digest of Educational Statistics, 1992.* Washington, D.C.: Government Printing Office.

———. 1995. *Digest of Education Statistics, 1995*. Washington, D.C.: Government Printing Office.

National Center for History in the Schools. 1994. *National standards for United States history: Exploring the American experience*. Los Angeles: National Center for History in the Schools.

National Commission on Excellence in Education. 1983. *A nation at risk: The imperative for educational reform*. Washington, D.C.: U.S. Department of Education.

National Education Association. 1905. Report of the committee on salaries tenure and pensions of public school teachers in the United States. Winona, Minn.: National Education Association.

National Education Goals Panel. 1995. The national education goals report [Core Report]. Washington, D.C.: U.S. Government Printing Office.

National Universities. 1996. *U.S. News* online: The 1997 college rankings.

Natriello, Gary. 1996. For the record: Scholarship and practice, the case of research on retention. *Teachers College Record* 97, 357–361.

Nielsen, W. 1972. *The big foundations*. New York: Columbia University Press.

Nightingale, A. P. 1986. Ratio of men to women in the high schools of the United States. *School Review* 4, 86–98.

Noble, David F. 1977. *America by design*. New York: Knopf.

Noujain, Elie G. 1987. History as genealogy: An exploration of Foucault's approach to history. In A. Griffiths (ed.), *Contemporary French philosophy* (pp. 157–174). New York: Cambridge University Press.

Oakes, Jeannie. 1985. *Keeping track: How schools structure inequality*. New Haven: Yale University Press.

Ogbu, John U. 1974. *The next generation*. New York: Academic.

Olson, Mancur. 1971. *The logic of collective action: Public goods and the theory of groups*. Cambridge: Harvard University Press.

Oxenham, J. (ed.). 1984. *Education versus qualifications?* London: Allen and Unwin.

Palinchak, Robert. 1973. *The evolution of the community college*. Metuchen, N.J.: Scarecrow.

Palmer, Jim. 1986. Sources of information: The social role of the community college. In L. Steven Zwerling (ed.), *The community college and its critics* (pp. 101–114). San Francisco: Jossey-Bass.

Pannell, Henry C. 1933. *The preparation and work of Alabama high school teachers*. Columbia University Contributions to Education no. 551. New York: Teachers College Press.

Paris, David C. 1995. *Ideology and educational reform: Themes and theories in public education*. Boulder, Colo.: Westview.

Parsons, Talcott. 1939/1954. The professions and the social structure. In *Essays in sociological theory* (rev. ed., pp. 34–49). New York: Free Press.

———. 1959. The school as a social system: Some of its functions in American society. In *Social structure and personality* (pp. 129–154). New York: Free Press.

Passow, A. Harry. 1989. Present and future directions in school reform. In Thomas J. Sergiovanni and John H. Moore (eds.), *Schooling for tomorrow: Directing reforms to issues that count* (pp. 13–39). Boston: Allyn and Bacon.

Patrick, A., R. L. Griswold, and C. A. V. Roberson. 1985. Domestic ideology and the teaching profession. *Issues in Education* 3 (2), 139–157.

Pennsylvania State Department of Public Instruction. 1922. Report of the survey of the public schools of Philadelphia, pt. 2. Philadelphia: Public Education and Child Labor Association.

Perlmann, Joel. 1988. *Ethnic differences: Schooling and social structure among the Irish, Italians, Jews, and Blacks in an American city, 1880–1935.* New York: Cambridge University Press.

Pifer, Alan. 1979. A foundation's story: The first seventy-five years of the Carnegie Foundation for the Advancement of Teaching. In the Seventy-fourth annual report of the Carnegie Foundation for the Advancement of Teaching, 1978–1979 (pp. 11–40).

———. 1984. *Philanthropy in an age of transition.* New York: Carnegie Corporation.

Pincus, Fred L. 1980. The false promises of community colleges: Class conflict and vocational education. *Harvard Educational Review* 50, 332–361.

———. 1986. Vocational education: More false promises. In L. Steven Zwerling (ed.), *The community college and its critics* (pp. 41–52). San Francisco: Jossey-Bass.

Popkewitz, Thomas S. (ed.). 1987. *Critical studies in teacher education: Its folklore, theory and practice.* New York: Falmer.

Powell, Arthur G. 1976. University schools of education in the twentieth century. *Peabody Journal of Education* 54, 3–20.

———. 1980. *The uncertain profession: Harvard and the search for educational authority.* Cambridge: Harvard University Press.

Powell, Arthur G., Eleanor Farrar, and David K. Cohen. 1985. *The shopping mall high school: Winners and losers in the educational marketplace.* Boston: Houghton Mifflin.

President's Commission on Higher Education. 1947. *Higher education for American democracy.* Washington, D.C.: Government Printing Office.

Rasey, Marie J. 1953. *It takes time: An autobiography of the teaching profession.* New York: Harper.

Redcay, Edward E. 1935. *County training schools and public secondary education for Negroes in the South.* Washington, D.C.: John F. Slater Fund.

Reese, Lizette Woodworth. 1929. *A Victorian village.* New York: Farrar and Rinehart.

Reese, William J. 1986. *Power and the promise of school reform: Grass-roots movements during the progressive era.* Boston: Routledge.

———. 1995. *The origins of the American high school.* New Haven: Yale University Press.

Reiter, Robert G. 1973. *The promotion/retention dilemma: What the research tells us.* Office of Research and Evaluation report no. 7416. Philadelphia: School District of Philadelphia.

Richardson, R. C., Jr., E. C. Fisk, and M. A. Okun. 1983. *Literacy in the open-access college.* San Francisco: Jossey-Bass.

Rist, Ray C. 1970. Student social class and teacher expectations: The self-fulfilling prophecy in ghetto education. *Harvard Educational Review* 40, 411–451.

Rorty, Richard. 1979. *Philosophy and the mirror of nature.* Princeton: Princeton University Press.

———. 1989. *Contingency, irony, and solidarity.* New York: Cambridge University Press.

Rosenbaum, James E. 1976. *Making inequality: The hidden curriculum of high school tracking.* New York: Wiley.

———. 1978. The structure of opportunity in school. *Social Forces* 57, 236–256.

———. 1986. Institutional career structures and the social construction of ability. In John G. Richardson (ed.), *Handbook of theory and research for the sociology of education* (pp. 139–172). New York: Greenwood.

Rothman, David J. 1971. *The discovery of the asylum: Social order and disorder in the new republic.* Boston: Little, Brown.

Rubin, Lillian B. 1972. *Busing and backlash: White against white in an urban school district.* Berkeley: University of California Press.

———. 1976. *Worlds of pain: Life in the working-class family.* New York: Basic.

Rudolph, Frederick. 1962. *The American college and university: A history.* New York: Vintage.

Rufi, John. 1926. *The small high school.* Columbia University Contributions to Education no. 236. New York: Teachers College Press.

Rumberger, Russell W. 1981. *Overeducation in the U.S. labor market.* New York: Praeger.

Rury, John L. 1986. Gender, salaries, and career: American teachers, 1900- 1910. *Issues in Education* 4, 215–235.

Ryan, Mary P. 1981. *Cradle of the middle class: The family in Oneida County, New York, 1790–1865.* New York: Cambridge University Press.

Salganik, Laura H., and Nancy Karweit. 1982. Voluntarism and governance in education. *Sociology of Education* 55, 152–161.

Sarason, Seymour. 1990. *The predictable failure of educational reform: Can we change course before it's too late?* San Francisco: Jossey-Bass.

Savage, Howard J. 1953. *Fruit of an impulse: Forty-five years of the Carnegie Corporation, 1905–1950.* New York: Harcourt, Brace.

Schultz, Theodore W. 1961. Investment in human capital. *American Economic Review* 51, 1–17.

Scull, Andrew T. 1977. *Decarceration.* Englewood Cliffs, N.J.: Prentice-Hall.

Sedlak, Michael W. 1989. Let us go and buy a schoolmaster. In Donald Warren (ed.), *American teachers: Histories of a profession at work* (pp. 257–290). New York: Macmillan.

Sedlak, Michael W., and Steven Schlossman. 1986. *Who will teach?* Santa Monica, Calif.: RAND.

Sedlak, Michael W., et al. 1986. *Selling students short: Classroom bargains and academic reform in the American high school.* New York: Teachers College Press.

Selden, Steven. 1982. Promotion policy. In Harold E. Mitzel III (ed.), *Encyclopedia of Educational Research* (pp. 1467–1474). New York: Free Press.

Shelley, Kristina J. 1992. The future jobs of college graduates. *Monthly Labor Review,* July, pp. 13–19.

Shepard, Lorrie A., and Mary Lee Smith (eds.). 1989a. *Flunking grades: Research and policies on retention.* New York: Falmer.

———. 1989b. Introduction and overview. In Lorrie A. Shepard and Mary Lee Smith (eds.), *Flunking grades: Research and policies on retention* (pp. 1–15). New York: Falmer.

Shulman, Lee S. 1986. Paradigms and research programs in the study of teaching: A contemporary perspective. In Merlin C. Wittrock (ed.), *Handbook of research on teaching* (3d ed., pp. 3–36). New York: Macmillan.

Shulman, Lee S., and Gary Sykes. 1986. A national board for teaching? In search of a bold standard. Unpublished paper prepared for the Carnegie Task Force on Teaching as a Profession.

Silberman, Charles. 1970. *Crisis in the classroom.* New York: Random House.

Sizer, Theodore R. 1964. *Secondary schools at the turn of the century.* New Haven: Yale University Press.

———. 1984. *Horace's compromise: The dilemma of the American high school.* Boston: Houghton Mifflin.

Smallwood, M. L. 1935. *An historical study of examinations and grading systems in early American universities.* Cambridge: Harvard University Press.

Southwest Educational Development Laboratory. 1981. The literature on social promotion versus retention. Unpublished paper.

Spence, A. Michael. 1973. Job market signaling. *Quarterly Journal of Economics* 87, 355–374.

———. 1974. *Market signaling: Informational transfer in hiring and related screening procedure.* Cambridge: Harvard University Press.

Spring, Joel. 1989. *The sorting machine revisited.* New York: Longman.

Steinberg, Laurence. 1996. *Beyond the classroom: Why school reform has failed and what parents need to do.* New York: Simon and Schuster.

Strober, Myra H., and Laura Best. 1979. The female/male salary differential in public schools: Some lessons from San Francisco, 1879. *Economic Inquiry* 17, 218–236.

Strober, Myra H., and Audrey Gordon Langford. 1986. The feminization of public school teaching: Cross-sectional analysis, 1850–1880. *Signs* 11, 212–235.

Strober, Myra H., and David B. Tyack. 1980. Why do women teach and men manage? *Signs* 3, 494–503.

Stuart, Jesse. 1949. *The thread that runs so true.* New York: Scribners.

Swett, John. 1969. *Public education in California.* New York: Arno.

Sykes, Gary. 1986. The social consequences of standard-setting in the professions. Unpublished paper prepared for the Carnegie Task Force on Teaching as a Profession.

———. 1987. Reckoning with the spectre. *Educational Researcher* 16 (6), 19.

———. 1990. Fostering teacher professionalism in schools. In Richard Elmore et al., *Restructuring schools: The next generation of educational reform* (pp. 59–96). San Francisco: Jossey-Bass.

Tappan, Henry. 1851/1986. University education. In Thomas Diener (ed.), *Growth of an American invention: A documentary history of the junior and community college movement* (pp. 23–28). New York: Greenwood.

Task Force on Education for Economic Growth. 1983. *Action for excellence: A comprehensive plan to improve our nation's schools.* Denver, Colo.: Education Commission of the States.

Task Force on Education of Young Adolescents. 1989. *Turning points: Preparing American youth for the 21st century.* Washington, D.C.: Carnegie Council on Adolescent Development.

Task Force on Teaching as a Profession. 1986. *A nation prepared: Teachers for the 21st century.* New York: Carnegie Forum on Education and the Economy.

Taylor, Inez. 1961. I am a teacher. *Michigan History Magazine* 45, 263–276.

Thomas, Charles Swain. 1914. *A memorial to Samuel Thurber: Teacher and scholar, 1837–1913.* Boston: New England Association of Teachers of English.

Thompson, Sidney. 1980. *Grade Retention and Promotion.* Burlingame: Association of California School Administrators, 1980.

Thornburg, Laura Docter. 1995. Between the common school and the college: Michigan State Normal School, 1849–1899. Paper presented at the annual meeting of the History of Education Society, Minneapolis.

Thorndike, Edward L. 1906. *Principles of teaching, based on psychology.* New York: Seiler.

———. 1907. *The elimination of pupils from school.* Bureau of Education bulletin 4. Washington, D.C.: Government Printing Office.

———. 1909. *The teaching staff of secondary schools.* Bureau of Education bulletin 4. Washington, D.C.: Government Printing Office.

Thornton, James W., Jr. 1960. *The community junior college.* New York: Wiley.

Thurow, Lester. C. 1977. Education and economic equality. In J. Karabel and A. H. Halsey (eds.), *Power and ideology in education* (pp. 325–335). New York: Oxford University Press.

Tillery, Dale, and William L. Deegan. 1985. The evolution of two-year colleges through four generations. In William L. Deegan et al. (eds.), *Renewing the American community college* (pp. 3–33). San Francisco: Jossey-Bass.

Toch, Thomas. 1996. The case for tough standards. *U.S. News and World Report,* April 1.

Tom, Alan R. 1984. *Teaching as a moral craft.* New York: Longman.

Toulmin, Stephen. 1990. *Cosmopolis: The hidden agenda of modernity.* New York: Free Press.

Trattner, Walter L. 1979. *From poor law to welfare state* (2d ed.). New York: Free Press.

Travers, R. M. W. (ed.). 1973. *Handbook of research on teaching* (2d ed.). Chicago: Rand McNally.

Troen, Selwyn K. 1975. *The public and the schools: Shaping the St. Louis system, 1838–1920.* Columbia: University of Missouri Press.

Trow, Martin. 1988. American higher education: Past, present, and future. *Educational Researcher* 17 (3), 13–23.

Turner, Ralph. 1960. Sponsored and contest mobility and the school system. *American Sociological Review* 25, 855–867.

Twentieth Century Fund. 1983. *Report of the Twentieth Century Fund task force on federal elementary and secondary policy.* New York: Twentieth Century Fund.

Tyack, David. 1974. *The one best system.* Cambridge: Harvard University Press.

Tyack, David, and Larry Cuban. 1995. *Tinkering toward utopia: Reflections on a century of public school reform.* Cambridge: Harvard University Press.

Tyack, David, and Elisabeth Hansot. 1982. *Managers of virtue.* New York: Basic.

Tyack, David B., and Myra H. Strober. 1981. Jobs and gender: A history of the structuring of educational employment by sex. In Patricia Schmuck, W. W. Charters Jr., and

Richard O. Carlson (eds.), *Educational policy and management: Sex differentials* (pp. 131–152). New York: Academic.

Tyler, Henry T. 1969. Full partners in California's higher education. In Roger Yarrington (ed.), *Junior colleges: 50 states/50 years* (pp. 158–168). Washington, D.C.: American Association of Junior Colleges.

Ueda, Reed. 1987. *Avenues to adulthood: The origins of the high school and social mobility in an American suburb.* New York: Cambridge University Press.

U.S. Bureau of the Census. 1840–1920. *Population schedules, Philadelphia County.* Washington, D.C.: National Archives.

———. 1975. *Historical statistics of the United States, colonial times to 1970.* Washington, D.C.: Government Printing Office.

———. 1987. *Statistical abstract of the United States, 1988.* Washington, D.C.: Government Printing Office.

U.S. Bureau of Education. 1894. Statistical review of secondary education. *Report of the Commissioner of Education 1893–1894* (pp. 33–95). Washington, D.C.: Government Printing Office.

U.S. Department of Education. 1986. *What works: Research about teaching and learning.* Washington, D.C.: U.S. Department of Education.

U.S. News Standards Poll. 1996. Most Americans say that school standards should be higher than they currently are, a new U.S. News poll reports. *U.S. News and World Report,* March 23.

Urban, Wayne J. 1982. *Why teachers organized.* Detroit: Wayne State University Press.

———. 1990. Historical studies of teacher education. In W. R. Houston (ed.), *Handbook of research on teacher education* (pp. 59–82). New York: Macmillan.

Van Buren, Anson D. P. 1889. The log schoolhouse era in Michigan. *Michigan Pioneer and Historical Society Historical Collections* 14, 283–403.

Veysey, Laurence R. 1965. *The emergence of the American university.* Chicago: University of Chicago Press.

Vinovskis, Maris A. 1995. *Education, society, and economic opportunity: A historical perspective on persistent issues.* New Haven: Yale University Press.

Vinovskis, Maris A., David Angus, and Jeffrey Mirel. 1995. Historical development of age stratification in schooling. In Maris A. Vinovskis, *Education, society, and economic opportunity: A historical perspective on persistent issues* (pp. 171–193). New Haven: Yale University Press.

Warren, Donald. 1985. Learning from experience: History and teacher education. *Educational Researcher* 14 (10), 5–12.

——— (ed.). 1989. *American teachers: Histories of a profession at work.* New York: Macmillan.

Weber, Max. 1968. *Economy and society.* Berkeley: University of California Press.

Weick, Karl. 1976. Educational organizations as loosely coupled systems. *Administrative Science Quarterly* 21, 1–19.

Weiler, Kathleen. 1988. *Women teaching for change.* South Hadley, Mass.: Bergin and Garvey.

Wells, Amy S., and Irene Serna. 1996. The politics of culture: Understanding local political resistance to detracking in racially mixed schools. *Harvard Educational Review* 66, 93–118.

Welter, Rush. 1962. *Popular education and democratic thought in America.* New York: Columbia University Press.

Wittrock, M. (ed.). 1986. *Handbook of research on teaching* (3d ed.). New York: Macmillan.

Witz, Ann. 1992. *Professions and patriarchy.* New York: Routledge.

Wolfe, Alan. 1971. Reform without reform: The Carnegie Commission on Higher Education. *Social Policy* 2 (May–June), 18–27.

World Almanac and Book of Facts, 1988. 1987. New York: World Almanac.

Yarrington, Roger (ed.). 1969. *Junior colleges: 50 states/50 years.* Washington, D.C.: American Association of Junior Colleges.

Zwerling, L. Steven. 1976. *Second best: The crisis of the community college.* New York: McGraw-Hill.

Index